CROWNED for Purpose

ANOINTED FOR PROMISE

Yahweh's Divine Plan for Vigilance, Strength & Purpose in the Latter Days!

Mya Chavis Enterprise™

Intrigue, Attract, Inspire

Mya A Chavis

Written by Mya A Chavis

Mya Chavis Enterprise LLC

www.myachavis.com

TABLE OF CONTENTS

Crowned for Purpose

Chronicles 2 23:11

DEDICATION

"I Dedicate this devotional to the blessed "Holy Trio" *The Father* who cradled me in His incubator of Love, protected, covered and favored me when I felt like letting go. *The Son* who bared my sins (which are many) and ransomed me; paying a debt I could never afford to pay, so that I may live again and not be robbed of my eternal inheritance. *The Holy Spirit* who leads me on a plain path of righteousness for salvation's sake, even when I didn't want to follow. I'm staying in His will. His will be done, on earth, as it is in heaven! Whatever the world does, Yahweh, I am available to you!

Mya A Chavis

"For I reckon that the sufferings of this present time are not worthy to be compared with the glory which shall be revealed in us".
Romans 8:18-23

Behold I'm Coming Quickly

Romans 8: 18-23

BIBLICAL CAUTIONING

"Blessed is the man who remains steadfast under various trials, for when he has stood the test of time, he will receive the crown of life, which God has promised to those who love him". "I have fought the good fight, I have finished the race, I have kept the faith. Henceforth there is laid up for me the crown of righteousness, which the Lord, the righteous judge, will award to me on that day, and not only to me but also to all who have loved his appearing." "In that day the Lord of hosts will be a crown of glory, and a diadem of beauty, to the remnant of his people". I have said these things to you, that in me you may have peace. *In the world you will have tribulation.* But take heart; I have overcome the world." "Behold, I am coming quickly, and My reward is with Me, to give to every one according to his works".

James 1:12, 2 Timothy 4:8, Isaiah 28:5
John 16:33, Revelation 22:12

Crowned for Purpose

Revelation 22:12

INTRODUCTION

In the latter days of a dark world where fiery trials, spiritual warfare, and painful tribulations of life, sets-out and seeks to stop Gods purpose, pain often obscures or distracts the believers "divine-kingdom-assignment" perfectly orchestrated by Yahweh. Faith is constantly being tested in a carnal habitat of this *"mysterious spiritual experience"* we call life. *Crowned for Purpose: Anointed for Promise* is a heartfelt exploration of finding God's will in the midst of life's storms, reminding readers that every trial refines them for a greater calling. It underscores the truth that God's sovereignty, faithfulness, and promises are unshakable, even when the path seems unclear. Through scriptural insights and personal reflections, this literature encourages believers to embrace their divine purpose, stand firm in their anointing, and walk boldly into the promises of God. This devotional invites believers to step into the fullness of their God-ordained destiny, in spite of dark forces that may attempt to stop Gods Plan, guiding them through the divine process of preparation, anointing, and ultimate victory through the appointed, anointed promises of Yahweh. Through reflective biblical insights, relatable examples, and actionable principles, we will uncover the eternal significance of our kingdom calling and the crowns that awaits us beyond this temporary mere existence; crowns of life, righteousness, rejoicing and glory. More than just shallow encouragement or prosperity gospel, this book is a war-cry to embrace full surrender, spiritual refinement, and unwavering

perseverance, outlaying a path to spiritual maturity, kingdom growth and rapture readiness. Each page equips believers to rise above the temporary and fix their eyes on the eternal, where every trial is redeemed, every sacrifice rewarded, and every purpose fulfilled in Christ. My dedication to delivering the un-altered, emphatical Word of our God Yahweh, is invariable and sincere. Delivering the truth of God's Word, it is imperative that biblical accuracy paves the way to the ultimate goal of winning souls to Christ. As we uncover purpose in the pain, and refinement in the fiery trials of life, we must stand firm, fix and unmovable, refusing to conform; with the eternal hope of always <u>abounding in the Kingdom Work</u> assigned by our creator Yahweh, while we are here on earth and while we have time. Together we will uncover and tackle complex biblical topics, deep theological truths, and prophetic insights, all intricately crafted together to form a timeless, unfiltered piece of kingdom-literature,

specifically designed to glorify God and point others to His promises of "<u>Truth</u> and <u>Deliverance</u>". This devotional is sure to touch lives, transform hearts, and bring lost souls into the Kingdom of God with much expectancy. We boldly explore under a microscope, the Good, Bad and the Ugly of Gods "unchanging-truth". Therefore, I caution that this study is "specially designed" for those who want to know the TRUTH of God's word, unfiltered and uncut with no sugar on top. Through this study we gain a clearer understanding of our God-given purpose and how it aligns with our daily walk with Jesus Christ the King! God's word provides comfort and strength when facing tumultuous challenges of life. We intricately explore how God uses trials to refine and prepare His people for His divine will and ultimate plan of salvation. In these last and evil days, we must remain awake, focused and steadfast on kingdom eternal rewards rather than temporary, perishing earthly pursuits, realigning priorities to reflect Jesus Christ Prophetic Warnings, Gods Commandments and Kingdom values. God's Word never returns void (Isaiah 55:11). Giving all and complete glory to our God Yahweh, may the fruit of this labor bring glory to the King of kings and Lord of lords, and may the seeds sown through these words yield an eternal harvest. _When you walk in your unfiltered divine purpose the light of Christ shines through your work and designed purpose, through the anointed promises of Yahweh truly your living is not in-vain._ Let's get into it.

What is a Christian? A Christian is a person of whom Jesus Christ Dwelleth! (Colossians 1:27), It is Christ within us, the full circulation of the Holy Spirit working and moving on the inside of our being (Romans 8:9). It is the Hope of an "Eternal-Glory" that leads us to salvation from the throne room of heaven, through Jesus Christ, the Son of God, in the acceptable presence of Abba, God, our father (Romans 8:15-16). It means, that you have a personal relationship with the Lord Jesus Christ, not just a mere "once a week acquaintance"! It is a life altering "**transformational-spiritual-encounter**" that has taken place in your life, the flesh now crucified, (Romans 10:9-10) you have willfully, and joyfully received and accepted Jesus Christ, not only as Lord, but also as Savior; knowing and understanding that His will for our lives is perfect and acceptable (Romans 12:2). A Christian, though **_not perfect_**, is anchored in the solid rock of "kingdom foundation", a mystery higher than us, surrendering all unto Him who is able to lead us from every temptation and direct us into a blessed life of eternity, Indeed! Thats, what a Christian is!

THE <u>CRADLE</u>, <u>CROSS</u>, <u>COFFIN</u> AND THE <u>CROWN</u>

The Cradle

Virgin Birth (Jesus as the son of God in the Flesh)

➢ Scripture: (Isaiah 7:14) prophesies that a virgin will conceive and give birth to a son, and (Matthew 1:23) confirms this fulfillment in Jesus Christ.

➢ Jesus was born of the virgin Mary, fulfilling the prophecies about the Messiah. His birth was miraculous and showed God's intervention in the human world. John 1:14 describes this as "the Word became flesh and dwelt among us."

Jesus entered the world in poverty, humility and innocence, highlighting God's plan for redemption from the very beginning. As Christians, this reminds us of the divine purpose that begins in humble beginnings.

The Cross

Trial, Conviction, and Crucifixion
(Persecuted for Innocence)

➢ Scripture: (Isaiah 53:3-7) describes the suffering of the "Suffering Servant," which Jesus fulfilled through His rejection and unjust trial (Matthew 27:11-26).

➢ Persecution and Sacrifice; Jesus endured false accusations, was sentenced to death without cause (Luke 23:4, John 19:4), and bore the sins of humanity. His ultimate act of love was expressed on the cross where He said, "It is finished" (John 19:30).

Jesus' suffering was central to God's redemptive plan. As Christians, our purpose also involves carrying our crosses, enduring hardship, persecution, and rejection, as seen in (Luke 9:23) "Take up your cross daily".

The Coffin (Grave)

Burial and Resurrection (Victorious over Death)

➤ Scripture: After His death, Jesus was buried in a borrowed tomb (Matthew 27:59-60), fulfilling (Isaiah 53:9). His resurrection on the third day, as He foretold (Matthew 16:21), is key to the Christian faith.

➤ Victory Over Death; (1 Corinthians 15:3-4) emphasizes how Jesus died, was buried, and rose again as the foundation of our belief. The grave could not hold Him. He defeated sin and death, giving believers hope of eternal life.

Christians, too, are called to die to sin and live a resurrected life in Christ, as (Romans 6:4-5) teaches. Our purpose involves walking in the newness of life, empowered by His victory over the grave.

The Crown

Ascension, Reign, and Second Coming (Christ the King)

➤ Scripture: (Acts 1:9-11) narrates Jesus' ascension into heaven, where He sits at the right hand of God (Mark 16:19). (Revelation 19:11-16) describes His return as the triumphant King and Commander and Chief of the heavenly kingdom armies.

➤ The Crown of Glory; Jesus will return not as a suffering servant but as the King of Kings and Lord of Lords, ruling in power and glory. His reign will establish a new heaven and new earth (Revelation 21:1-4)

As ambassadors of Christ (2 Corinthians 5:20), we are called to prepare for His return by living a life worthy of our heavenly calling, spreading the Gospel, and exemplifying His kingdom on earth.

The journey of every believer mirrors the path of Christ, encompassing the <u>cradle</u>, the <u>cross</u>, the <u>coffin</u>, and ultimately, the <u>crown</u>. The cradle represents the humility and divine purpose of Jesus' divine, miraculous birth, emphasizing God's plan to redeem humanity through humble beginnings (Isaiah 7:14; Matthew 1:23). The cross highlights the trials and ultimate sacrifice of Jesus, who bore our sins and exemplified endurance and obedience to God's will, even in persecution (Isaiah 53:3-7; Luke 9:23). The coffin represents death, persecution and resurrection, reminding believers that victory over sin and death is possible through Jesus Christ sacrifice at the cross. We are called to walk in the newness of life (Romans 6:4-5). *Finally, the crown represents the glorious reign of Jesus as the King of Kings, a promise of eternal life for those who endure and remain faithful (Revelation 19:11-16). This progression calls believers to live purposefully, reflecting Christ's journey as they prepare to receive the Crown of Life.*

A Synopsis of "Crowned for Purpose: Anointed for Promise!

This devotional is a comprehensive spiritual guide/study of scripture, designed to walk believers through various dimensions of the Christian journey, walking with Yahweh, providing encouragement, insight, warning and direction. The title itself, *Crowned for Purpose, Anointed for Promise*, emphasizes the core central message: every believer is not only called to pursue God, along with His purpose, but also are entrusted with *divine assignments*, *enduring hardships*, and *preparing for eternal rewards*. The "spiritually radical" transformative journey through trials, self-emptying, perseverance, purpose, and spiritual readiness, using Scriptural Biblical Evidence as both anchor and inspiration. It encourages believers to embrace their identity as ambassadors for Christ, secure the crowns of life, walk in the anointing of Gods Promise, and live with the eternal perspective that defines true faith.

Who Is This Devotional For?

This devotional is for followers of Christ, Looking to strengthen their belief", understand God's purpose for trials, and remain steadfast in their spiritual walk with Yahweh; on their way to their permanent home, which reigns for eternity with Christ. It speaks directly to those who feel the weight of life's hardships and need assurance that these fiery trials are not in vain rather are at the nucleus of Gods ordained purpose. Whether a new believer or a seasoned disciple, this devotional offers insight, warning, encouragement, guidance, and scriptural support to help readers gain kingdom understanding while pressing forward in these "last and evil days". _Crowned For Purpose_ cuts to the chase of the **good**, **bad** and **ugly** prophetic apocalyptic events of the latter days of Christ return. It especially resonates with those yearning to align their lives with God's promises, His purposes while preparing for Jesus Christ's return, emphasizing vigilance, faithfulness, self-emptying and spiritual transformation.

What Does this Devotional Examine?

The devotional is structured around key themes that encompass a Christ-centered-life, including spiritual growth, perseverance, divine purpose in suffering, vigilance against the enemy's deception, and preparation for eternal rewards. Through these "key-areas-of-study", it guides believers in their roles as ambassadors for Christ and helps them understand the deeper significance of spiritual crowns. Each section presents specific scriptural lessons, blending personal reflection with biblical truth to encourage readers in their pursuit of God.

> ➤ **Manifold Refinement of Grace**
> This section emphasizes that fiery trials are not necessarily, always, hell-formatted-obstacles but rather opportunities to experience Gods spiritual manifold-refinement through grace. Mans' extremities has always been Gods opportunity to show up and show out a miracle through his multifaceted

"manifold-grace". Metaphorically as refining of pure-gold and precious-silver, Scriptures such as *(Job 23:10)* and *(Malachi 3:3)* show how God uses the difficulties of pain, trials and tribulations to purify, strengthen believers by fortifying a sincere-pure-faith that shines with perseverance, authenticity and much resilience *(James 1:2-4)*. Readers are enlightened to realize the hardships God allows as acts of grace, transforming them into Christ-like reflections.

➤ **Purpose in Suffering**

Rather than viewing suffering as a pointless affliction of punishment or an irreversible smite of Gods wrath, this section explores how God works through pain to fulfill His plans of expanding, upholding and defending the heavenly tenancy of His Kingdon both on heaven and on earth. The story of Joseph in *(Genesis 50:20)* and the reminder from *(Romans 8:28)* that "God works all things for the good of those who love Him and keep his commandments", offers rich insight into how difficulties, pain and suffering molds' believers and aligns them with divine purpose. Naomi's journey in *Ruth* further demonstrates that even grief can become a testimony of God's provision and faithfulness.

➤ **Perseverance and the Crown**

Faithful endurance leads to eternal rewards, symbolized by crowns in Scripture. This section draws from verses such as *(James 1:12)* and *(Revelation 2:10)*, highlighting the connection between trials and eternal life. Believers are reminded that the trials they face today will ultimately be the victories they celebrate tomorrow, if they remain steadfast, the earthly hard place will ultimately result in praise and honor when Christ returns *(1 Peter 1:6-7)*.

➤ **The Devil's Deceptive Strategy to Steal Your Crown**

This devotional warns readers about the enemy's schemes to derail their spiritual progress, downplay the sovereign significance of Jesus Christ. Rob you of your inheritance and steal your Holy Crown of Life. Verses like *(John 10:10)* and *(Ephesians 6:11)* emphasize the need for vigilance and spiritual armor to resist deception. Believers are encouraged to stay alert, knowing that the enemy seeks to destroy their faith and steal the rewards God has promised them.

➤ **Ambassadors of Reconciliation**

This section calls believers to embrace their identity as ambassadors for Christ, spreading the message of reconciliation to the world *(2 Corinthians 5:18-20)*. It encourages readers to let their light shine through ministry, spreading the gospel of Christ, glorifying God and reflecting His love to others *(Matthew 5:14-16)*.

➤ **Christ's Sovereign Ministry of Reconciliation**

The emphasis here is on Christ's atoning work as the foundation for reconciliation. Through *(Romans 5:10)* and *(Colossians 1:20)*, readers are reminded of the vital cruciality to be reconciled to Christ. Their mission as ambassadors reignites from His priceless sacrifice at the cross; His shed blood at calvaries cross as an *acceptable* atonement of sin. His life, death and resurrection empowers' kingdom builders to extend the message of grace, repentance, reconciliation, and Christ great commission to the world.

➤ **Crowned with Purpose: Anointed for God's Eternal Promise**

This section examines the significance of spiritual crowns (earthly and heavenly) as symbols of Yahweh's divine promises. It draws from *(1 Corinthians 9:24-25)* and *(2 Timothy 4:8)*, inspiring believers to pursue these crowns through faithful living. Certain crowns represent rewards for perseverance, righteousness, and faithfulness to God's call, while others showcase punishment for wickedness and unrepentance.

➢ **Rapture Readiness**

Vigilance and Spiritual-Preparedness are key themes here, underscoring the importance of being prepared for Christ's return and ultimately eternity. Drawing on the parable of the ten virgins *(Matthew 25:1-13)*, this devotional stresses the need for believers to keep their "kingdom lamps" filled with "kingdom oil", symbolizing a life rooted in faith and purity, perseverance and obedience.

➢ **Vitality of Your Kingdom-Lamp Being Filled with Kingdom-Oil**

This segment emphasizes that spiritual preparedness of Christ return should be an everyday, ongoing self-assignment. The rapture according to biblical prophecy could happen at any time and at any moment. Jesus Christ is not dead, rather away preparing a heavenly home for his redeemed. As with a Galilean wedding ceremony, the only one who knew the time in which the Bride-Groom would return to collect his bride, was the Father, yet it was the obligation of the bride to be on the lookout, ready and pre-paired for the bridegroom. Having your kingdom lamp filled with kingdom oil on the day of His return is crucial to you reigning with Christ eternally and you collecting your heavenly inheritance. Don't let the demon-of-distraction distract you from your call or purpose. Verses like *(Matthew 24:44)* and *(Romans 13:11)* urges believers to stay awake spiritually, knowing that the time of Christ's return is closer than ever.

➢ **Eternal Life: Eternal gain, Death for His Sheep**

Death for God's faithful, triumph as overcomers is not as an end, but as a glorious transition into eternal life with Christ. In *(Philippians 1:21)*, Paul declares, "To live is Christ, and to die is gain," encouraging believers to face death without fear. This devotional helps its readers develop an eternal spiritual perspective, viewing life and death through the lens of God's promises.

> **Yahweh's Sovereign Decree: His Final Word**
> This section focuses on the unchanging nature of God's promise and purpose. If Yahweh declared it, I accept it and that settles it. He is an Omnipotent, Sovereign God, all authority throughout the ages bow in subjection to Him. He is incapable of lying as He watches over His word to perform it. Scriptures such as (*Isaiah 46:10*) and (*Hebrews 6:17-18*) remind readers that God's decrees are eternal and trustworthy. Believers are called to anchor their faith in His promises, knowing that His purposes will prevail.

> **Salt of the Earth: Pilgrims in a Foreign Land**
> In this final section, believers as Christ Ambassadors are encouraged to embrace their role as "salt" in a conforming world, distant and sometimes-distracted, yet they should remain mindful and aware that their true home is with Christ (*Hebrews 11:13*). This insightful devotional challenges followers of God, to live purposefully, making a difference while keeping their eyes fixed on their heavenly citizenship.

When & Why Does This Devotional Matter?

Crowned for Purpose connects with Gods redeemed at a critical time, offering hope and guidance to a broken world filled with a lot of hellish-distractions, uncertainty, doubt, hurt and pain, witchcraft and the rise of upfront "in-yo-face" satanism. Its message is urgent to end time survival, especially given the spiritual challenges of modern life, where distractions, trials, and temptations threaten to weaken, deter, or destroy faith as the great falling away is at hand. The spiritual-hot-topics of perseverance, readiness, vigilance and spiritual determination will resonate with Christians who are navigating personal hardships or seeking deeper spiritual purpose during this temporary earthly voyage. This work equips believers to stay the course, reminding them that the journey of faith is one of

both hardship-struggles and reward. It highlights a timely call to appropriately prepare for Christ's return, secure within one's own heart the knowledge that God's promises are assured.

What Will Readers Gain Through This Devotional?

Readers who explore this devotional will be enlightened, cultivated and transformed in their understanding of suffering, pain-yoked-in-purpose, and spiritual readiness. They will develop a renewed sense of identity as ambassadors for Christ, empowered to live a Christ-Centered-Life, with eternal perspective and purpose. They will also be equipped to recognize the enemy's strategies and resist them with the shield of faith and the sword of the spirit. Ultimately, this devotional will inspire believers and babes in Christ, to chase Yahweh with fervor, knowing that every trial, every step of perseverance, and every act of faith brings them closer to the crowns God has prepared for them in eternity. They will become bold, purposeful, and spiritually ready; anchored in the promises of God through the edified purpose of our existence we prepare ourselves to reign with Him forever.

Romans 8:28 reveals that God orchestrates all things both joys and challenges, for the good of those who love Him and are called according to His purpose. This verse highlights the certainty that every believer's life has meaning and purpose, aligning with God's divine plan. While His sheep may receive an "earthly crown of purpose," which signifies a life lived intentionally for God, even non-believers have a role in His larger redemptive plan. God's purpose is all-encompassing, and every person is invited to discover the ultimate fulfillment found in living for Him and ultimately, embracing Christ through death, as reflected in (Philippians 1:21): *"For to me, to live is Christ, and to die is gain."*

The crown of purpose in a believer's life isn't merely about personal achievements but about advancing God's kingdom by becoming a living witness to His love and truth. (Ephesians 2:10) reminds us,

"For we are His workmanship, created in Christ Jesus for good works, which God prepared beforehand, that we should walk in them." This means that each person, whether they realize it or not, has been given a specific role in God's design. Believers are called to repent, forgive and walk in obedience, knowing that even their struggles serve a purpose that glorifies God and strengthens their faith. Meanwhile, non-believers also find meaning in life through the opportunity to respond to the gospel, fulfilling the purpose for which they were created; to know God and reflect His glory.

Ultimately, God's purpose for our existence extends beyond earthly life into eternity. In (John 12:24), *Jesus teaches, "Unless a grain of wheat falls into the earth and dies, it remains alone; but if it dies, it bears much fruit."* This reflects the reality that both life and death serve God's perfect divine purposes. For believers, dying for Christ is not a loss but the culmination of a life well-lived for Him that leads to an eternal reward, a transition into eternal glory. Even those who come to Christ later in life demonstrate how God's purposes are fulfilled in every stage of life. Whether in living or in dying, all people, believers and non-believers alike, are drawn into the larger story of God's love, grace, and redemption.

In (2 Peter 1:3-4), *"As His divine power has given to us all things that pertain to life and godliness, through the knowledge of Him who called us by glory and virtue, by which have been given to us exceedingly great and precious promises, that through these you may be partakers of the divine nature, having escaped the corruption that is in the world through lust."* Peter emphasizes that God's divine power has granted believers everything they need to live a life pleasing to Him. This power is not limited by human weaknesses or circumstances but flows from God's infinite wisdom, strength and sufficiency. It equips believers for both spiritual growth and practical godliness, kingdom preparedness ensuring they have the resources to pursue a Christ-centered-life. Through the Holy Spirit, believers are empowered to develop virtues such as faith, love, and self-control, enabling them to navigate life's challenges with grace and

righteousness. Nothing is lacking for those who seek God. His power is fully available to meet every spiritual and practical need.

Peter further emphasizes the significant role of God's promises in shaping and ordaining the believer's life. These promises serve as assurances of God's faithfulness and the future hope He offers. Through them, believers become participants in the divine nature, meaning they share in God's grace, mercy, love, and wisdom. This transformative process allows believers to reflect God's character more deeply as they grow in faith. The promises of salvation, eternal life, and the indwelling of the Holy Spirit offer not only hope but also the motivation to persevere in faith, even amidst trials.

Moreover, God's promises enable followers of Christ to escape the corruption that is present in the world due to sinful desires. The world is stained by sin, perversion, rebellion, hatred, greed, selfishness, lust, and carnal worldly influence but those who embrace God's promises freely live above the curse and find freedom from such influences. As believers internalize God's truth, accept His laws and follow His commandments, they are set apart from the decay and destruction that sin brings. This divine empowerment allows them to live counter-culturally not be conformed to this world but renewed, walking in love, wisdom, compassion, forgiveness, repentance, insight, purity and purpose. In doing so, they experience the abundant life that Jesus promised, rooted in God's power and His faithfulness to fulfill every word He has spoken in Biblical Prophecy.

All for the glory of Jesus Christ! There's nothing better than walking boldly in the purpose He's given us! You were BUILT for this, living for His kingdom here on earth and preparing to reign with Him in eternity. We must, even in the final hour of Christ return, keep pressing on, chasing Yahweh, and shining that kingdom-light deposited within us, because the world needs what God has placed in you! We move in victory! We walk in purpose! Every step, every trial, every triumph, it's ALL working together for His plan, No better way than Gods' perfect way, let's get into it.

Behold I'm Coming Quickly

2 Corinthians 5:20

AMBASSADOR OF RECONCILIATION

RESTORING HEARTS TO GOD'S KINGDOM!

Restoring hearts to God is a transformative process that goes beyond outward actions, focusing on humility, inner repentance and renewal. True restoration begins when believers turn to God with humility and genuine repentance, as emphasized in (Joel 2:12-13). It requires acknowledging brokenness and seeking God's mercy, not merely through rituals but with deep remorse. This inward transformation is essential for aligning with God's will and experiencing His grace and compassion.

Scripture teaches that God initiates this restoration by replacing hardened hearts with new ones, that are tender and responsive to His Spirit (Ezekiel 36:26). A restored heart trusts God fully (Proverbs 3:5-6) and treasures His presence above all earthly pursuits (Matthew 6:21). It also reflects undivided devotion, as only the pure in heart can truly experience intimacy with God (Matthew 5:8). Restoration shapes not only individual faith but also fosters community revival, uniting believers in obedience to God's Word and His mission.

Ultimately, heart restoration is a lifelong journey of spiritual growth and alignment with God's purposes. Believers are called to love God wholeheartedly (Matthew 22:37), relying on His strength in every challenge (Psalm 73:26). Through the ongoing work of repentance and renewal (Psalm 51:10-12), believers remain rooted in faith, allowing God to shape their desires, actions, and priorities. In this way, <u>restoring hearts to God becomes the foundation for a genuine</u> <u>relationship with Him and the power to fulfill His mission of</u> <u>reconciliation in the world.</u>

The Cruciality of Restoring Hearts to God

Restoring the heart to God is essential for spiritual transformation and alignment with His Holy-Will. Scripture emphasizes that the heart is the center of one's relationship with God, influencing obedience, worship, and reconciliation. Below are key insights summarizing the importance of heart restoration:

> ➤ **Restoration Starts with Repentance**
>
>   Genuine restoration begins when believers turn to God with humility and repentance, as seen in Joel 2:12-13. This involves an inner transformation, acknowledging brokenness and seeking God's mercy, beyond mere religious acts.
>
> ➤ **God Gives a New Heart (Ezekiel 36:26)**
>
>   Restoration is a divine act, where God replaces a hardened heart with one that is tender and responsive to His Spirit. This new heart enables believers to walk in obedience, fostering both personal renewal and communal revival.
>
> ➤ **Trusting God Fully (Proverbs 3:5-6)**
>
>   A restored heart is marked by unwavering trust in God, even beyond human reasoning. Complete dependence on His wisdom allows believers to experience His guidance, provision, and protection.
>
> ➤ **Purity of Heart Enables Intimacy with God (Matthew 5:8)**
>
>   Purity of heart means having undivided devotion to God, free from hypocrisy and selfish motives. Such purity is essential for experiencing God's presence and understanding His ways.

> ➤ **God Values the Heart Over Appearances (1 Samuel 16:7)**
> God looks beyond outward appearances and focuses on the condition of the heart. A restored heart aligns with His priorities, shaping believers into vessels of authenticity and faithfulness.

> ➤ **Transformation through God's Word (Hebrews 4:12)**
> God's Word penetrates and reveals the heart's true intentions. Embracing, accepting and discerning the Word is critical for spiritual growth, as restoration requires ongoing reflection and alignment with God's truth.

> ➤ **The Heart's Treasure Reveals Priorities (Matthew 6:21)**
> A restored heart treasures God's Kingdom above earthly pursuits. When the heart is aligned with God, it leads to a life of surrender and obedience.

> ➤ **Loving God with All the Heart (Matthew 22:37)**
> The ultimate expression of a restored heart is wholehearted love for God. This love drives every thought, desire, and action, reflecting total devotion to Him.

> ➤ **God Weighs the Heart (Proverbs 21:2)**
> Spiritual health is measured by the sincerity and alignment of the heart with God's will. Restoration is essential for living authentically in faith and obedience.

> ➤ **God's Strength Sustains the Heart (Psalm 73:26)**
> A restored heart relies on God's strength rather than human resilience, allowing believers to persevere through trials and challenges with confidence in His power.

> ➤ **Ongoing Purification of the Heart (Psalm 51:10-12)**
> Heart restoration is not a one-time event but a continual process. Through repentance and renewal, believers remain aligned with God's holiness and purpose.

The restoration of the heart is crucial for living as ambassadors of Christ. It enables believers to love God wholeheartedly, walk in obedience, and participate in His mission of reconciliation. A restored heart reflects God's priorities, treasures His Kingdom, and finds strength in His presence, resulting in a life that brings glory to Him.

Restoring hearts to Yahweh is a reconstructive process that goes beyond outward actions, focusing on inner repentance and renewal. True restoration begins when believers turn to God with humility and genuine repentance, as emphasized in (Joel 2:12-13), *"Now, therefore," says the Lord, "Turn to Me with all your heart, With fasting, with weeping, and with mourning." So, rend your heart, and not your garments; Return to the Lord your God, For He is gracious and merciful, Slow to anger, and of great kindness; And He relents from doing harm."* It requires acknowledging brokenness and seeking God's mercy, not merely through "traditional-rituals" but with deep repentance. This inward transformation is essential for aligning with God's will and experiencing His grace and compassion.

Scripture teaches that God initiates this restoration by replacing hardened hearts with new ones that are tender and responsive to His Spirit (Ezekiel 36:26). A restored heart trusts God fully (Proverbs 3:5-6) and treasures His presence above all earthly pursuits (Matthew 6:21). It also reflects undivided devotion, as only the pure in heart can truly experience intimacy with God (Matthew 5:8). Restoration shapes not only individual faith but also fosters community revival, uniting believers in obedience to God's Word and His mission.

Ultimately, heart restoration is a lifelong journey of spiritual growth and alignment with God's purposes. Believers are called to love God wholeheartedly (Matthew 22:37), relying on His strength in every challenge (Psalm 73:26). Through the ongoing work of repentance and renewal (Psalm 51:10-12), believers remain rooted in faith, allowing God to shape their desires, actions, and priorities. In this way, restoring hearts to God becomes the foundation for a genuine relationship with Him and the power to fulfill His mission of reconciliation in a broken world.

A Fully Surrendered Heart and True Intimate Relationships

A fully surrendered heart to God parallels the dynamics of a deep, intimate personal relationship, where authenticity, trust, and commitment are essential. Just as a relationship between two people cannot flourish without heartfelt sincerity, God desires our hearts as the foundation of our connection with Him. A relationship devoid of the heart becomes empty; lacking trust, honesty, and real intimacy. Similarly, God, who calls us to be His ambassadors and ministers of reconciliation, asks for our complete surrender because only a heart fully yielded to Him can reflect His love and purpose to the world.

In human relationships, surrendering emotionally means being vulnerable, open, and willing to give ourselves fully. This mirrors the spiritual surrender God seeks, trusting Him completely, even when we don't understand His ways (Proverbs 3:5-6). Just as withholding part of ourselves in a relationship creates distance, withholding our hearts from God blocks the intimacy He offers. God, who already owns everything, doesn't ask for material things but longs for our hearts, the very core of our being. When we surrender to Him, we align our desires with His, fostering a genuine connection that fuels our mission to love others and reconcile them to God.

Ultimately, surrendering our hearts to God is an act of love and trust. It allows Him to shape our character, guide our paths, and empower us to live with purpose. Just as human relationships thrive when both parties are fully invested, our relationship with God deepens when we give Him all of ourselves; our fears, hopes, weaknesses, and strengths. In doing so, we become vessels of His grace, embodying His message of reconciliation with authenticity and love. The greatest thing we can surrender to a sovereign God is not what we have, but who we are; our hearts, willingly offered as a response to His boundless love.

A fully surrendered heart is exactly what God is calling us to in these last days. There's no room for half-hearted faith or divided affections.

He's looking for hearts that are all in! Now more than ever, He's raising up ambassadors who will love boldly, serve faithfully, and reconcile others to Him with pure devotion.

When we surrender everything, our fears, plans, weaknesses, and even our strengths we position ourselves to experience the fullness of His power. It's in that surrender where _we find freedom, purpose, and intimacy with Him._ Just as Jesus said, "He who loses his life for My sake will find it" (Matthew 10:39). Surrendering isn't losing its gaining everything in Christ.

These times demand warriors with surrendered hearts, those who hear His voice, trust His guidance, and move in His Spirit. Surrender isn't just a single act but a lifestyle, a continual "yes" to God. With every surrender, His strength fills the gaps and His light shines brighter through us. We are His vessels, and it's through our yielded hearts that He reconciles a broken world back to Himself. Now is the time to lay it all down and let Him work through us, until His Kingdom comes in its fullness!

What does it mean that The love of Christ compels us (2 Corinthians 5:14)?

Second Corinthians 5:14 says, _"For Christ's love compels us, because we are convinced that one died for all, and therefore all died."_ Through this scriptural passage, the Apostle Paul speaks of his "internal inspiration" for his chosen ministry. When the apostle Paul wrote, _"The love of Christ compels us,"_ he was re-counting the powerful, Spirit-filled motivation that should drive{followers of Christ to share the gospel [with enthusiasm], in ways that persuade people to commit their lives to Jesus. The love of Christ compelled Paul as a chosen vessel of God to share the "goodness of the Gospel of Jesus Christ". The phrase the _love of Christ_ could be interpreted in two ways: Christ's love for people, or the apostles' love for Christ. Either provides encouragement to spread the gospel to remote corners and distant

territories in the face of opposition. The great love of Christ was such that "Christ died for all" people (2 Corinthians 5:14). Paul's love for Christ was such that he was willing to die to self (see Galatians 2:20).When we possess this compelling, Spirit-driven enthusiasm and inspiration of Christ's love, we are fervent in seeing the lost reconciled with God. We willfully go to the lost, rather than letting them come to us. We are willing to make ourselves "a slave to everyone, to win as many souls to God as possible" (1 Corinthians 9:19); we "become all things to all people so that by all possible means [we] might save some" (verse 22). The love of Christ compels us to love the lost enough to share the good news of salvation with them.

What does it mean to be an Ambassador for Christ!

To be an Ambassador for Christ means to epitomize Jesus Christ and His message to others in the world. The concept derived from (2 Corinthians 5:20), where the Apostle Paul emphasized "*We are therefore Christ's ambassadors, as though God were making His appeal through us.*" An ambassador is someone who represents and acts on behalf of another, particularly in a spiritual context, conveying the message and authority of Jesus Christ the Messiah (2 Corinthians 5:20). Ambassadors are charged with promoting reconciliation to Christ as well as His ministry of reconciliation and sharing the gospel, serving as intermediaries between God and his followers. The biblical role of an Ambassador encompasses the idea of reconciliation along with the responsibility that comes with it. Christ Ambassadors are not only expected to represent God's message but also to endure trials and hardships with grace, demonstrating a steadfast faith that reflects Christ's own endurance during His ministry.

We Are Called to Serve as Christ's Ambassadors. Christians of every era are called to be Christ's ambassadors. We are ambassadors for Christ, since God is making his appeal through us; we entreat you on behalf of Christ, be reconciled to God. (2 Corinthians 5:20) An ambassador is someone authorized to act on behalf of a higher authority; they serve as a representative of the kingdom. Jesus' words in (Acts 1:8) paints a vivid picture of being an ambassador of Christ. *"But you shall receive power when the Holy Spirit has come upon you; and you shall be witnesses to Me in Jerusalem, and in all Judea and Samaria, and to the end of the earth"*. Jesus does not send his followers to go witnessing, but to be his witnesses. (See Colossians 4:5-6)Be wise in the way you act toward outsiders; make the most of every opportunity. Let

your conversation be always full of grace, seasoned with salt, so that you may know how to answer everyone. "(2 Corinthians 5 18) All this is from God, who through Christ reconciled us to himself and gave us the ministry of reconciliation; (2 Corinthians 5 19) *that is, in Christ God was reconciling the world to himself, not counting their trespasses against them, and entrusting to us the message of reconciliation. (2 Corinthians 5 20) Therefore, we are ambassadors for Christ, God making his appeal through us. We implore you on behalf of Christ, be reconciled to God.* We are therefore Christ's ambassadors, as though God were making his appeal through us." This verse emphasizes the role of believers not only as representatives of Christ but also as vessels through which God's message of reconciliation is communicated.

Representation of God's Kingdom

According to Gods Holy scripture, an ambassador serves as a representative of God's kingdom on Earth. This role emphasizes the importance of living in a manner that reflects the values, principles, and teachings of the Christian faith. Ambassadors of Christ are called to embody the characteristics of their sovereign Commander and Chief, Jesus Christ, <u>demonstrating love, grace, compassion and truth in their interactions with others</u>. This representation is not merely about words but also about actions that align with the divine mission of restoring

the lost, of whom satan's eyes has darkened, back to Gods love and his unfailing grace. Another significant aspect of being an ambassador in the Bible is *the call to reconciliation*. Ambassadors are tasked with bridging gaps between God and the lost sheep of Christ kingdom, reconciliation with God and others, proclaiming the gospel of salvation to the lost. This involves sharing the message of salvation and encouraging others to seek a relationship with God. The role emphasizes the importance of forgiveness, healing, and restoring broken relationships, both with God and among individuals. Such kingdom responsibilities include

➤ Reconciliation with God and Others (*2 Corinthians 5:18-20*)
➤ Proclaiming the Gospel of Salvation (*Romans 1:16*)
➤ Living Examples of Christ's Love & Righteousness (*John 13:34-35*)
➤ Advocating for God's Kingdom Values (*Matthew 6:33*)
➤ Encouraging Repentance and Obedience to God (*Acts 3:19*)
➤ Living as Peacemakers and Unity Builders (*Matthew 5:9*)
➤ Suffering and Persevering for the Sake of Christ (*2 Timothy 3:12*)
➤ Representing Christ's Authority and Power (*Luke 10:19*)
➤ Being a Bridge Between God and Lost Souls (1 Timothy 2:5-6 & Jude 1:23)

Ambassadors also serve as witnesses to the world, showcasing the transformative power of faith. Their lives are meant to be a testimony of the hope and redemption found in a relationship with God. This witness is not limited to verbal proclamation but extends to living out one's faith authentically, thereby inspiring others to explore and embrace the teachings of Christianity. Through their example, ambassadors illuminate the path to spiritual truth and encourage others to seek a deeper understanding of God's love. Embrace every opportunity to serve brothers and sisters in the Kingdom of God, *Spread the Gospel of Jesus Christ*, *Fulfill the Great Commission*, *Win a Soul to Yahweh*, *Bear Witness of the Goodness of God*, *Bear Fruit as Jesus did*, and let love be your driving force of being Gods representative knowing those looking for Christ out to find Him in you. Surround yourself with a supportive community that encourages your growth and holds you accountable. Always remembering this journey although adventurous is temporal , We as Pilgrims are temporarily passing through to our Permanent home, please see the following!

Scriptural Encouragements for Ambassadors

➤ *(Ephesians 6:19-20: 19) and also for me, that words may be given to me in opening my mouth boldly to proclaim the mystery of the gospel, for which I am an ambassador in chains, that I may declare it boldly, as I ought to speak.*

➤ *(Isaiah 18:1-2) Ah, land of whirring wings that is beyond the rivers of Cush, which sends ambassadors by the sea, in vessels of papyrus on the waters. Go, you swift messengers, to a nation tall and smooth, to a people feared near and far, a nation mighty and conquering, whose land the rivers divide.*

➤ *(Philippians 3:20-21: 20) But our citizenship is in heaven, and from it we await a Savior, the Lord Jesus Christ, who will transform our lowly body to be like his glorious body, by the power that enables him even to subject all things to himself.*

➤ *(Matthew 28:18-20: 18)And Jesus came and said to them, "All authority in heaven and on earth has been given to me. Go therefore and make disciples of all nations, baptizing them in the name of the Father and of the Son and of the Holy Spirit, teaching them to observe all that I have commanded you. And behold, I am with you always, to the end of the age.*

➤ *(Romans 10:14-15: 14) How then will they call on him in whom they have not believed? And how are they to believe in him of whom they have never heard? And how are they to hear without someone preaching? And how are they to preach unless they are sent? As it is written, "How beautiful are the feet of those who preach the good news!"*

The Ambassador's Identity in Christ

To emphasize the ambassador's true, authentic identity in Christ, we must thoroughly examine the significant transformation that takes place <u>when God's chosen believers recognize their spiritual authority, identity, position, and inheritance in Christ</u>. This "kingdom identity" is not merely a title but an intangible reality grounded in biblical truth, shaping the ambassador's boldness, purpose, and unwavering commitment to God's Kingdom.

Understanding the Ambassador's Identity in Christ

An ambassador's identity in Christ is rooted in being born again as a "new creation" (2 Corinthians 5:17). This new identity involves a self-emptying, inner renewal, and a spiritual rebirth, where the old self marked by sin, doubt, and confusion is replaced by a new nature that reflects the righteousness of Christ. As co-heirs with Christ (Romans 8:17), ambassadors are adopted into God's family, having received the full rights of sonship to the Kingdom of God. This means they are not merely representatives of God's Kingdom but active participants in its inheritance and authority. This identity is anchored in God's Word, empowered by the Holy Spirit, and affirmed through an intimate relationship with Jesus Christ. It shapes their perspective, directs their actions, and fuels their mission as ministers of reconciliation.

True Ambassadors in Christ Have No Identity Crises

Clarity of Purpose: True ambassadors of Christ undeniably understand their purpose in the Kingdom: to glorify God, represent Christ faithfully and authentically, and reconcile the lost to Him. This leaves no room for identity confusion, as they are driven by the assignment and mandate given by Christ (Matthew 28:18-20).

Confidence in God's Sovereignty: Ambassadors in Christ have a deep-seated confidence that comes from understanding they serve the Sovereign King of all creation. They are fully aware of their royal position in the Kingdom, making them fearless in the face of opposition, persecution, or worldly pressures. Their boldness flows from the knowledge that God's authority backs their mission, making them warriors, not worriers.

Overcomers by Perseverance: Perseverance is central to an ambassador's identity. These believers recognize that the trials and pains they face are not gauges of defeat or punishment but are part of the refining process that produces spiritual maturity, endurance, and strength (Romans 5:3-5). Their identity is not shaken by hardships; rather, it is fortified through persevering pain, as they keep their eyes fixed on the eternal heavenly inheritance promised by God.

Unshakable in Heavenly Inheritance: The assurance of their inheritance in God's Kingdom gives ambassadors the unwavering certainty that their labor is not in vain (1 Corinthians 15:58). They know they are destined to reign with Christ, and that wisdom fuels their resolve and protects them from being robbed of their reward by the enemy's deceit or worldly distractions.

No Cowardice or Conformity: True ambassadors for Christ are without cowardice because they understand that fear is not from God but from the devil, who seeks to intimidate and paralyze believers (2 Timothy 1:7). As co-heirs with Christ, they have been given a spirit of power, love, and a sound mind. This boldness enables them to stand firm in their convictions, resisting the pressures of conformity to the world's values (Romans 12:2).

Light in Darkness: Ambassadors do not allow the darkness of the world to diminish the light God has placed within them (Matthew 5:14-16). Their identity as the light of the world compels them to shine brightly, <u>even in hostile or morally decaying environments</u>. Their light is not self-generated but comes from abiding in Christ, which empowers them to stand against the darkness with courage and clarity.

Sealed by the Holy Spirit: True ambassadors in Christ are sealed by the Holy Spirit (Ephesians 1:13-14), a mark of their eternal identity. This seal not only guarantees their inheritance but also serves as a constant reminder that they belong to God, ensuring that their sense of identity is rooted in divine truth, not shifting cultural narratives or worldly definitions of success.

Why True Ambassadors Are Without Identity Crises

Rooted and Grounded in Christ's Love: The love of Christ is the foundation of their identity (Romans 8:38-39). This love is inseparable, unconditional, and eternal. It affirms their worth, purpose, and mission, leaving no space for identity confusion or insecurity.

Strengthened by the Word of God: Ambassadors immerse themselves in Scripture, which serves as their weaponry in spiritual warfare, providing not just knowledge but wisdom, assurance, and clarity about who they are in Christ Jesus (Hebrews 4:12). Scripture becomes the unbreakable anchor of their identity, equipping them to withstand the devil's lies, deceptions, and attempts to rob them of their confidence and hope.

Empowered by the Holy Spirit: True ambassadors do not operate in their own strength but are empowered by the Holy Spirit (Acts 1:8). This divine empowerment not only enables them to fulfill their mission but also reinforces their identity as God's chosen vessels, ordained for good works and mighty acts in the Kingdom.

Focused on the Eternal Prize: Ambassadors keep their focus on the eternal prize (Philippians 3:14). This singular focus makes them resistant to distractions, temptations, or doubts about their identity. They are driven by the goal of hearing, "Well done, good and faithful servant" (Matthew 25:23), a goal that secures their sense of worth and purpose.

Declaratively, true ambassadors of Christ have no identity crises because their identity is solidified in their understanding of who they are in the Kingdom of God. They are co-heirs with Christ, warriors of light, and fearless representatives of His will on earth. They know that perseverance is the pathway to greater strength, and they do not allow the devil to rob them of their heavenly inheritance. Their identity, rooted in Christ and His sovereign calling, is marked by courage, clarity, and commitment. They stand as lights in the darkness, not conforming to this world but transforming it through the reconciling power of the Gospel.

The Urgency of God Raising Up Ambassadors of Christ

The urgency of God raising up ambassadors of Christ to restore lost souls before Jesus' return is of **critical mass proportion** for both Christ's army and the Church in these last days. As Christ's return draws nearer, the ministry of reconciliation becomes not just important but critical for the fulfillment of God's redemptive plan. Let's break it down into key details as to why it is essential.

✓ Fulfilling the Great Commission in Urgency (Matthew 28:18-20)

The Great Commission is Christ's mandate to His followers, commanding them to "go and make disciples of all nations." This is the nucleus of the end-time mission, directly involving the restoration of lost souls to God through Jesus Christ. As the world grows darker and spiritual confusion increases, the urgency of this mission intensifies. Ambassadors of Christ are called to act with the compassion of Christ, swiftly and boldly, knowing that time is short and that souls hang in the balance. The Great Commission is not just about numerical growth but eternal restoration, as God desires "all people to be saved and to come to a knowledge of the truth" (1 Timothy 2:4). This makes the work of reconciliation a matter of eternal consequence, and it cannot be delayed.

✓ The Imminence of Christ's Return (Matthew 24:14)

Jesus Himself taught that the Gospel of the Kingdom must be preached to all nations before the end comes (Matthew 24:14). This means that reconciliation is directly linked to the fulfillment of prophecy, making the role of ambassadors pivotal in preparing the world for Christ's return. The imminence of Jesus' return serves as a divine catalyst for God's people to rise up and urgently proclaim the message of reconciliation. Ambassadors are God's appointed agents to ensure that the lost, broken, and backslidden, have the opportunity to hear the Gospel and be restored before the window of opportunity closes. This sense of urgency is not born out of fear but out of love for souls and a deep awareness of the eternal stakes. True ambassadors understand that Jesus' return is not only imminent but will come like a thief in the night (1 Thessalonians 5:2), reinforcing the necessity to be ready and help others be ready.

✓ God's Desire for Restoration, Not Judgment (2 Peter 3:9)

God's heart is not for judgment but for repentance and restoration. He is patient, not wanting anyone to perish to hell, but everyone to come to repentance (2 Peter 3:9). This shows God's deep compassion and love, which must also be the driving force of His ambassadors. In the face of increasing rebellion and sin, God is raising up ambassadors to be instruments of His kingdom grace, offering a final opportunity for reconciliation before judgment comes. Ambassadors must embody God's mercy, emphasizing that there is still time to repent and be reconciled through Christ. This divine urgency is part of God's end-time strategy, ensuring that as many souls as possible can experience His love and grace before the return of Christ ushers in His righteous judgment.

✓ The Need for Ambassadors to Stand Against Deception (2 Corinthians 11:13-15)

In the last days, deception will be rampant, with false prophets, teachings, and distractions attempting to lead many astray (Matthew 24:24). Ambassadors of Christ must rise with clarity and authority, countering these lies with the truth of the Gospel. Ambassadors must not only reconcile souls but also protect them from deception, guiding them into a genuine relationship with Christ, free from false doctrines or compromise. The critical nature of this mission is underscored by the fact that deception is one of the devil's greatest tools to delay, diminish, or derail reconciliation. True ambassadors must have keen discernment, grounded in God's Word and led by the Holy Spirit, to expose lies and illuminate truth.

✓ The Power of the Holy Spirit in Raising End-Time Ambassadors (Acts 1:8)

God is not only raising up ambassadors but empowering them with the Holy Spirit for the last push of reconciliation before Jesus' return. The Spirit gives them boldness, wisdom, and supernatural ability to reach the lost, even in the most challenging circumstances. Ambassadors filled with the Holy Spirit will have divine guidance on where to go, what to say, and how to minister effectively. The Spirit's presence ensures that their work is not in vain but fruitful, breaking down spiritual barriers that hinder reconciliation. This empowerment is a fulfillment of Joel's prophecy that God would pour out His Spirit in the last days (Joel 2:28). It signifies a spiritual urgency that drives ambassadors to reach the lost with compassion and power.

✓ The Reality of Final Judgment and Eternal Separation from God (Revelation 20:11-15)

The reality of final judgment and eternal separation from God makes the role of ambassadors crucial. Reconciliation is not just about improving lives but about saving souls from permanent-eternal death. Ambassadors must communicate the gravity of eternity

clearly, emphasizing that reconciliation with God through Christ is the only way to escape the coming wrath and be part of God's eternal Kingdom (John 3:36). Their message must be both hopeful and urgent, revealing the reality of heaven and hell and compelling people to choose Christ before it's too late. Ambassadors are like fluorescent lights illuminating in worldly darkness (see Matthew 5:14-16). In the increasing darkness of the last days, God's ambassadors are to shine brightly, serving as visible witnesses of His love, blessed assurance, grace, and power. They must stand firm in their identity, fully aware that they carry the light of Christ within them. This is a call to courage; ambassadors cannot afford to be silent or passive. They must actively and visibly demonstrate the reconciling love of God, drawing the lost back to Him with unwavering commitment.

✓ The Critical Role of Ambassadors Before Jesus' Return

- ➤ The necessity for ambassadors of Christ to rise up and restore lost souls before Jesus' return cannot be overstated. They are the frontline of God's end-time mission, preparing the way for Christ by bringing as many as possible into reconciliation with God through Jesus.
- ➤ This mission is urgent, divinely mandated, and eternally significant. God's ambassadors must recognize that they are not only messengers but also warriors, intercessors, and deliverers of hope in a dark world on the brink of Christ's second coming.
- ➤ As co-heirs with Christ, ambassadors bear the responsibility and privilege of being God's representatives, ensuring that the lost are given every opportunity to be restored to Him before time runs out.

Ambassadors in Christ are not just participating in a ministry, they are fulfilling prophecy, hastening Christ's return by reconciling the lost souls to God. This is why their role is critical, urgent, and deeply blessed, and it's all part of God's glorious plan for the end-time harvest.

Obedient to Gods Command

As ministers of reconciliation, we must first be obedient to Christ's command, fully committed to making Him known in every corner of the earth. The Great Commission is not optional but an essential duty of every ambassador of Christ. In (Matthew 5:13), Jesus calls His followers the *"salt of the earth,"* a metaphor that emphasizes the preserving and purifying qualities of believers in the world. Salt, as a preservative, prevents decay; similarly, as ministers of reconciliation, we are called to preserve righteousness in a world plagued by sin and brokenness. Our role as ambassadors involves:

> ➤ **Influence and Impact:** We are to exert a positive, godly influence, representing the transforming power of Christ's reconciliation wherever we go.
> ➤ **Preservation of Truth:** We maintain and promote the truths of God's Word, bringing light and hope to those living in spiritual darkness.
> ➤ **Restoring Flavor:** The lost, broken, and backslidden are meant to find hope and meaning in Christ through us. We are to reflect His love and mercy, creating an appetite for God in others.

If the salt loses its flavor, it becomes ineffective. As ambassadors, we must ensure our faith remains vibrant and aligned with Christ's teachings so that we can be effective vessels of reconciliation.

Abiding in Christ (John 15:2-16:33)

John 15:2-16:33 outlines the importance of abiding in Christ to bear lasting fruit. This passage is fundamental to understanding how we, as ministers of reconciliation, can fulfill our mission.

> ➤ **Abiding for Fruitfulness:** Jesus emphasizes that we must "abide in Him" to bear fruit. Abiding means having a close, personal relationship with Christ, rooted in prayer, obedience, and dependence on the Holy Spirit. Without this

intimate connection, our efforts to reconcile others to God become ineffective, as we cannot bear the fruits of love, patience, and compassion on our own.

➤ **Cultivated for Effectiveness:** Just as a vine is pruned to increase fruitfulness, God allows us to go through seasons of refining so that we can better serve His Kingdom. As ambassadors, we should welcome God's pruning, understanding that it enhances our capacity to fulfill our role as reconcilers.

➤ **Overcoming the World:** In John 16:33, Jesus assures us, "In this world, you will have trouble. But take heart! I have overcome the world." This promise provides the courage we need to continue the work of reconciliation despite opposition, hardship, or rejection.

Christ's Ambassadors Reflecting Him

Those who are seeking Christ should be able to find Him in us. As ambassadors, our lives must consistently reflect the character of Jesus Christ, His love, humility, and commitment to God's will. This requires daily surrender to Christ, allowing the Holy Spirit to work in and through us. The reconciliation we offer is not merely a call to repentance but a demonstration of God's love in practical, tangible ways. We are to be living testimonies, showcasing the transformative power of God's grace.

The ultimate goal of reconciliation is the restoration of broken relationships, both between individuals and God, and among individuals themselves. Christ's atoning work on the cross makes this possible, breaking down barriers of sin and hostility. As ambassadors, we must work to heal divisions, promoting the purposes and promises of Gods Holy Word and forgiveness according to God's divine will.

As ministers of reconciliation, it is our duty to represent Christ, proclaim His Gospel, and restore the broken, lost, and backslidden to God. By living out the Great Commission, being the salt of the earth, and abiding in Christ, we fulfill our sacred calling to bring the light of Jesus into a dark and hurting world. Those who seek Christ should see Him clearly in us, for we are His ambassadors, entrusted with the powerful message of reconciliation that transforms lives and glorifies God.

The Significance of 2 Corinthians 5:12-20: *__Be Reconciled to God__*. The passage from 2 Corinthians 5:12-20 is rich in meaning, focusing on the inspiration for ministry, the transformative power of Christ's love, reconciliation, and the believer's role as an ambassador for Christ. Here's a breakdown of its significance:

Paul's Defense of His Ministry (Verses 12-13)

➢ Paul's sincerity and devotion, In verses 12-13, Paul clarifies that his defense is not for self-promotion but to offer the Corinthians a reason to be proud of his ministry.

➢ He emphasizes that he serves with a pure heart, devoted to God, even if it appears foolish to some. This reflects the authentic nature of God's servants, who are driven by devotion to God rather than human approval. They live for a cause, not an applause.

Compelled by Christ's Love (Verse 14)

➢ Paul explains that it is the love of Christ that compels him to minister tirelessly.

➢ The word "compels" suggests a strong driving force, indicating that believers are moved by Christ's sacrificial love, which serves as the core motivation behind all their actions and mission.

➢ This love is grounded in the understanding of Christ's sacrifice, as Jesus died for all, leading believers to live not for themselves but for Him who gave His life for them.

A New Creation in Christ (Verse 17)

➤ This verse emphasizes the transformational aspect of faith in Christ: "If anyone is in Christ, the new creation has come: The old has gone, the new is here!"

➤ This signifies a complete renewal of the believer's identity, mindset, and purpose. It underscores that salvation is not merely about personal change but about becoming a new person in the Kingdom of God, empowered by the Holy Spirit.

➤ The concept of a "new creation" affirms that believers have a new nature, reflecting Christ's righteousness and mission.

The Ministry of Reconciliation (Verses 18-19)

➤ These verses highlight that God reconciled us to Himself through Christ, and now He entrusts believers with the ministry of reconciliation.

➤ Reconciliation here is about restoring a broken relationship between God and the lost, made possible through Christ's atoning work on the cross.

➤ This passage also reinforces the idea that believers are co-workers with God, carrying forward the message of reconciliation, not by their own merit but by God's grace and empowerment.

Ambassadors for Christ (Verse 20)

➤ Believers are described as ambassadors for Christ, representing His interests on earth. The term "ambassador" signifies a high-ranking representative sent on behalf of a sovereign God.

➤ This role involves pleading with others to accept God's offer of reconciliation, not just as a duty but with urgency and genuine care.

➤ The verse emphasizes that God is making His appeal through believers, reflecting the privilege and responsibility of sharing the Gospel message.

➤ Ambassadors are called to be faithful messengers, speaking the truth with integrity and demonstrating God's love in action.

Significance of 2 Corinthians 5:12-20

1. **Love as the Driving Force:** *The passage reveals that Christ's love is the core motivation for ministry, guiding believers to serve tirelessly.*

2. **Transformation and Reconciliation:** *It emphasizes the believer's new nature and mission, highlighting their role in reconciling others to God.*

3. **Urgency of the Gospel:** *The passage stresses the urgency of the Gospel message, as ambassadors are called to share it with love and urgency.*

2 Corinthians 5:12-20 is significant for its focus on the believer's identity and mission. It calls Christians to be driven by Christ's love, live out their new nature, and actively fulfill their role as ambassadors of the Kingdom, promoting reconciliation in a world still estranged from God.

The Gospel of Reconciliation (Romans 10:15-17)

Romans 10:15-17 emphasizes the critical role of proclaiming the Good News; "How beautiful are the feet of those who bring good news!" The essence of our work as ministers of reconciliation is to spread the Gospel so that faith may arise in those who hear. It is through hearing the message of Christ that faith is birthed, leading people to believe, repent, and be reconciled to God. This passage highlights two vital aspects of our role.

1. **Proclaimers of Truth:** We are called to boldly preach the message of Christ's redemption so that others can hear, believe, and be saved.
2. **Faith Comes by Hearing:** The lost cannot be reconciled to God without hearing the message of Christ's love and sacrifice. Our mission as ambassadors is to make that message accessible and clear, bearing witness to God's mercy and grace.

The Great Commission (Matthew 28:18-20)

Jesus' words in (Matthew 28:18-20) provide the foundation for our mission as ambassadors; "Go therefore and make disciples of all nations." This command underscores the urgency and universality of the Gospel message. The Great Commission entails.

Go: As ambassadors, we are called to take the initiative to actively go to the lost, broken, and backslidden, rather than waiting for them to come to us.

Make Disciples: We are not merely to spread information but to make disciples baptizing and teaching others to follow Christ, grow in faith, and become ministers of reconciliation themselves.

All Nations: Our mission is global in scope. The Gospel's power to reconcile transcends cultural, racial, and national boundaries, reflecting the inclusive nature of Christ's love.

What is the "Ministry of Reconciliation" in 2 Corinthians 5:18?

The ministry of reconciliation is the ministry of reconciling the lost to God. You can have a restored relationship with God through Jesus Christ. The ministry of reconciliation in (2 Corinthians 5:18) refers to the task believers have been given to do and declare, so that those who have falling out of God's grace may have a restored relationship with Yahweh through Jesus Christ our "Promised Messiah". The ministry of reconciliation involves the proclamation of the gospel and its assurance that forgiveness of sin is available in Christ. Sin prevents us from having a relationship with God, this verse states, *"All this is from God, who reconciled us to himself through Christ and gave us the ministry of reconciliation."*

The ministry of reconciliation involves the proclamation of the gospel and its sound assurance that forgiveness of sin is available in Christ. Sin prevents us from having a relationship with God, but Jesus' perfect sacrifice on the cross made an acceptable atonement for sin (Hebrews 2:17) and brought harmony to mankind's relationship with Him. Jesus reconciled us to God. Now we ought to reconcile someone else to our God by proclamation that people can repent of their sin and be right with God again through the atonement of Sin through Jesus Christ redemption (Romans 5:10; Colossians 1:20–21).

We need reconciliation with God because our relationship with Him was broken through sin. God is holy and righteous, and our sin separates us from Him (Isaiah 59:2). Sin made us His enemies (Romans 5:10). On the cross, Jesus ransomed us through His love as he took our sins upon Himself, satisfying God's justice. Jesus' death made it possible for us to have peace with God, as (2 Corinthians 5:19) says, "God was reconciling the world to himself in Christ, not counting people's sins against them." Now we can be called God's "friends" (John 15:15) and Jesus' "brothers and sisters" (Hebrews 2:11). Those who have been justified through faith (Romans 5:1) by Jesus' blood (Romans 5:9) no longer have their sins counted against them. They are reconciled with God.

God has given believers the ministry of reconciliation, God uses his sheep to tell the world that they can be reconciled to God through Christ. In this way, we become "Christ's ambassadors, as though God were making his appeal through us" (2 Corinthians 5:20). Verse 19 describes this ministry of reconciliation as *"**proclaiming-the-message-of-reconciliation**."* The message we are to share with the world is this: *"Be reconciled to God"* (verse 20). By way of compassion, we are to communicate with others the wonderful opportunity they

have to be made right with God through Jesus. We implore them to believe in Christ. those who are reconciled to God through Christ, now have access to redemption of sin through the atonement of Jesus Christ "God made him who had no sin to be sin for us, so that in him we might become the righteousness of God" (verse 21).

This ministry of reconciliation is imperative to the kingdom of God. Yahweh is "making his appeal through us" (2 Corinthians 5:20). The ministry we've been given to turn hearts toward God, it is urgent and it is vital—it's truly a matter of life and death. Jesus paid the price for our reconciliation because God loves us (John 3:16), so we must share this message of reconciliation in love, and our lives need to reflect our message (Ephesians 4:1). Jesus is the One who saves, and the Holy Spirit is the One who convicts the world of guilt in regard to sin and righteousness and judgment (John 16:8), yet we have been given the privilege of being ambassadors for Christ.

Every believer plays a vital part in this ministry of reconciliation. One plants; one waters, and God brings growth (1 Corinthians 3:7). As we proclaim the gospel, we act as *"restorers of the breach"*, and God blesses such (Matthew 5:9). We tell and live out His message of reconciliation, lives are changed, and God gets the glory.

Jesus became what we were, so we could become what He was, the righteousness of God. Jesus has taken the sin of the world onto Himself. Justice has been accomplished. The debt for sin has been paid. God in His wisdom, has made a way to righteously justify us so that we can be free and without shame in relationship with Him. Jesus has given His righteousness as a gift for those who receive it by faith. Nothing could be better news! Righteousness draws all the blessings of God into your life. The ministry of reconciliation is proclaiming this news.

walkwiththewise.org describes such as this…

- ➤ The righteousness of faith (Romans 4:13, 9:30, and 10:6),
- ➤ The righteousness of God in Him (2 Corinthians 5:21)

- The righteousness of God without the Law (Romans 3:21)
- Christ Jesus being made righteousness unto us (1 Corinthians 1:30)
- Christ as righteousness to everyone who believes (Romans 10:4)
- Everlasting righteousness (Daniel 9:24)
- The LORD our righteousness (Jeremiah 23:6)
- The gift of righteousness (Romans 5:17)
- The robe of righteousness (Isaiah 61:10)
- Being found in Him (Philippians 3:9)

What does it mean that all things have become new (2 Corinthians 5:17)?

"If anyone is in Christ, he is a new creation; old things have passed away; behold, all things have become new" (2 Corinthians 5:17, NKJV).

When a person encounters Jesus Christ and surrenders to Him as Lord and Savior, that individual is now "in Christ," joined to Jesus in His death and resurrection: "We were therefore buried with him through baptism into death, just as Christ was raised from the dead through the glory of the Father, we too may live a new life" (Romans 6:4). We become a whole new creation in Jesus Christ (Galatians 6:15). Our "former way of life," or "old self," which was "corrupted by its deceitful desires" (Ephesians 4:22), was "one way," the "new self" in Christ, "created to be like God in true righteousness and holiness" (Ephesians 4:24), is "completely different." Scripture says that, when Mary Magdalene encountered Jesus, He cast seven demons out of her (Luke 8:1–3). After being set free, Mary was forever changed into a devoted follower of Christ.

All things have become new illustrates the beginning of our transformation, our inward renewal and regeneration that will culminate in the fullness of our salvation to be experienced in eternity. Jesus Christ death and resurrection ushered in a foretaste of

an entirely new world still to come: "But in keeping with his promise we are looking forward to a new heaven and a new earth, where righteousness dwells" (2 Peter 3:13). Eventually, everything in creation will be made new (Romans 8:19–20, Isaiah 65:17–25).

Through *inner-spiritual-renovation* from the Holy Spirit, believers grow into the image of Christ "with ever-increasing glory" (2 Corinthians 3:18). God promises to give us a new, undivided heart, removing our "heart of stone" and replacing it with a "heart of flesh" (Ezekiel 11:19; 36:26). "And I will put my Spirit in you and move you to follow my decrees and be careful to keep my laws" (Ezekiel 36:27). The changes begin in the heart but then spill out to our behavior (Romans 12:2). Paul explained that these changes don't happen through our own force of will and self-effort (Philippians 3:4–9) but through living by faith in Christ; "*My old self has been crucified with Christ. It is no longer I who live, but Christ lives in me. So I live in this earthly body by trusting in the Son of God, who loved me and gave himself for me*" (Galatians 2:20). For believers, all things have become new in us and in our relationships with other people. The inner workings of Christ Love compels' us. We now look at unbelievers with compassion, seeing them as Christ saw them "like sheep without a shepherd" or as lost sinners in need of a Savior (Matthew 9:36). No matter how different they may be, we recognize fellow Christians as part of one united body, the new creation: "*There is neither Jew nor Gentile, neither slave nor free, nor is there male and female, for you are all one in Christ Jesus*" (Galatians 3:28; see also Romans 12:5).

All things have become new through our union with Christ, and we no longer live for ourselves (2 Corinthians 5:15). To the new creation in Christ, Jesus said, "*A new command I give you: Love one another. As I have loved you, so you must love one another. By this everyone will know that you are my disciples, if you love one another*" (John 13:34–35). Instead of living to please ourselves, we now live to please Christ, serve Him (2 Corinthians 5:9; 1 Thessalonians 4:1), and look out for the interests of others (Philippians 2:3–4; Galatians 6:2). Our new self-hates the sin that still has a hold on us. The difference is that the new creation is no longer a slave to sin, as we formerly were. We are now freed from sin and it no longer has power over us (Romans 6:6-7). Now we are empowered by and for righteousness. We now have the choice to "let sin reign" or to count ourselves "dead to sin but alive to God in Christ Jesus" (Romans 6:11-12). Best of all, now we have the power to choose the latter. Paul tells us that all believers have died with Christ and no longer live for themselves. Our lives are no longer worldly; they are now spiritual. Our "death" is that of the old sin nature which was nailed to the cross with Christ. It was buried with Him, and just as He was raised up by the Father, so are we raised up to "walk in newness of life" (Romans 6:4).

The Ambassadors Identity in Christ

When believers recognize their spiritual authority, position, and inheritance in Christ they suffer no identity crises in the kingdom. This identity is not merely a title but a reality grounded in biblical truth, shaping the ambassador's authoritative boldness, purpose, and unwavering commitment to God's Kingdom. An ambassador's identity in Christ is rooted in being born again as a new creation (2 Corinthians 5:17). This new identity involves a spiritual rebirth, where the old self marked by sin, doubt, and confusion is replaced by a new nature that reflects the righteousness of Christ. As co-heirs with Christ (Romans 8:17), ambassadors are adopted into God's family, having received the full rights of sonship. This means they are not merely representatives of God's Kingdom but active participants in its inheritance and authority. This identity is anchored in God's Word, empowered by the Holy Spirit, and affirmed through an intimate relationship with Jesus. It shapes their perspective, directs their actions, and fuels their mission as ministers of reconciliation. True Ambassadors of Christ have NO identity-crises of self. True ambassadors for Christ understand their clear purpose in the kingdom, to glorify God, represent Christ faithfully, and reconcile

the lost to Him. This clarity leaves no room for identity confusion, as they are driven by the mission and mandate given by Jesus Christ (Matthew 28:18-20). Ambassadors in Christ have a deep-seated confidence that comes from knowing they serve the Sovereign King of the universe. They are fully aware of their royal position in the Kingdom, making them fearless in the face of opposition, persecution, or worldly pressures. Their boldness flows from the

knowledge that God's authority backs their mission, making them victors, and not victims. Perseverance is central to an ambassador's identity. These believers recognize that the trials and pains they face are not indicators of defeat but are part of the refining process that produces spiritual maturity, endurance, and strength (Romans 5:3-5). Their identity is not shaken by hardships; rather, it is fortified through perseverance, as they keep their eyes fixed on the heavenly inheritance promised by God. The assurance of their inheritance in God's Kingdom gives ambassadors the unwavering certainty that their labor is not in vain (1 Corinthians 15:58). They know they are destined to reign with Christ, an understanding that fuels their resolve and protects them from being robbed of their reward by the enemy's deceit or worldly distractions. No cowardice nor conformity, true ambassadors for Christ are without cowardice because they understand that fear is not from God but from the devil, who seeks to intimidate and paralyze believers (2 Timothy 1:7). As co-heirs with Christ, they have been given a spirit of power, love, and a sound mind. This boldness enables them to stand firm in their convictions, resisting the pressures of conformity to the world's values (Romans 12:2). Ambassadors do not allow the darkness of the world to diminish the light God has placed within them (Matthew 5:14-16). Their identity as the light of the world compels them to shine brightly, even in hostile or morally-immoral or disruptive surroundings. Their light is not self-generated but comes from abiding in Christ, which empowers them to stand against the darkness with courage and clarity. True ambassadors in Christ are sealed by the Holy Spirit (Ephesians 1:13-14), a mark of their eternal identity. This seal not only guarantees their inheritance but also serves as a constant reminder that they belong to God, ensuring that their sense of identity is rooted in divine truth, not shifting cultural narratives or worldly definitions of success.

Why True Ambassadors Are Without Identity Crises

Grounded in Christ's love; the love of Christ is the foundation of an Ambassadors identity (Romans 8:38-39). This love is inseparable, unconditional, and eternal. It affirms their worth, purpose, and mission, leaving no space for identity confusion or insecurity. Ambassadors immerse themselves in God's Word, which provides not just knowledge but wisdom, assurance, and clarity about who they are in Christ (Hebrews 4:12). Scripture becomes the anchor of their identity, equipping them to withstand the devil's lies, deceptions, and attempts to rob them of their confidence and hope. True ambassadors do not operate in their own strength but are empowered by the Holy Spirit (Acts 1:8). This divine empowerment not only enables them to fulfill their mission but also reinforces their identity as God's chosen vessels, ordained for good works and mighty acts in the Kingdom. Ambassadors keep their focus on the eternal prize (Philippians 3:14). This singular focus makes them resistant to distractions, temptations, or doubts about their identity. They are driven by the goal of hearing, "Well done, good and faithful servant" (Matthew 25:23), a goal that secures their sense of worth and purpose.

In Short, true ambassadors of Christ have no identity crises because their identity is solidified in their understanding of who they are in the Kingdom of God. They are co-heirs with Christ, warriors of light,

and fearless representatives of His will on earth. They know that perseverance is the pathway to greater strength, and they do not allow the devil to rob them of their heavenly inheritance. <u>Their identity, rooted in Christ and His sovereign calling, is marked by courage, clarity, and commitment. They stand as lights in the darkness, not conforming to this world but transforming it through the reconciling power of the Gospel.</u>

Ambassadors of Reconciliation: Representing Christ Kingdom and Restoring "Religious-Brokenness"

As ambassadors of reconciliation, Christians are called to restore the broken relationship between God and the broken, backslidden and lost. This divine mission is a central part of God's redemptive plan, realized through Jesus Christ. In (2 Corinthians 5:18-20), Paul reminds believers that they are Christ's ambassadors, tasked with the ministry of reconciliation. This mission is further emphasized in passages like (Romans 10:15-17, Matthew 28:18-20, Matthew 5:13, and John 15:2-16:33), where the authority, nature, and responsibility of being an ambassador for Christ are explored.

We examine believers as representatives of God's Kingdom, charged with the duty of reconciling the lost, broken, and backslidden to God. It highlights how Christians are called not only to restore through the Word of God, faith and actions but also to live in a way that reflects the gospel message and Christ's love.

Through this explorative reflection, we will explore how the call to be an ambassador for Christ is essential to the ministry of reconciliation. An ambassador serves as an official representative sent by a sovereign authority to another land, reflecting the will and policies of their home government. In the same way, Christians, as ambassadors for Christ, are entrusted with the responsibility of making God's appeal to the nations, *"Be reconciled to God"* (2 Corinthians 5:20). This ministry of reconciliation is not merely a suggestion but a mission that God has entrusted to believers through the work of Jesus Christ.

In (Romans 10:15-17), Paul stresses the importance of proclaiming the gospel, "*How beautiful are the feet of those who bring good news!*" This highlights that the mission of spreading the gospel, announcing that people can be reconciled to God through Christ, is a sacred responsibility. Faith, as Paul explains, comes from hearing the message of Christ, and therefore, believers are compelled to go into the world, spreading the message of reconciliation through their words and actions.

Reconciliation necessarily involves change. In Christian reconciliation, God does not change. He remains perfect. But He changes us. As a result, our relationship with Him changes. The means God used to reconcile us to Himself was His own Son, Jesus Christ; "All this is from God, who reconciled us to himself through Christ and gave us the ministry of reconciliation; that God was reconciling the world to himself in Christ, not counting men's sins against them" (2 Corinthians 5:18–19). In fact, it was "while we were God's enemies [that] we were reconciled to him through the death of his Son" (Romans 5:10). Jesus' death makes all the difference. When Christ died, He was "making peace through his blood, shed on the cross" (Colossians 1:20).

The fact that we needed reconciliation means that our relationship with God was broken. And the fact that God is holy means that we were the ones to blame. Our sin alienated us from Him. Jesus Christ's death on the cross is the basis of our forgiveness and justification. By grace through faith in His Son Jesus Christ, God thoroughly remakes us into the image of Christ. God and man are brought together: the formerly dead in sin are raised to new life. "We are no longer enemies, ungodly, sinners, or powerless. Instead, the love of God has been poured out in our hearts through the Holy Spirit whom he has given to us (Romans 5:5). Woodruff W Baker's said "*It is a change in the total state of our lives*".

Many trust that the Bible in and of its self represents the story of Christian reconciliation. We started off in the Garden of Eden as friends of God, unashamed and living in fellowship with God and each other. But then sin entered the world, and all our relationships were broken. We became enemies of God, seeking our own ways and living in open hostility to Him. The whole of Scripture, then, is a record of God's reconciling us to Himself. We ran away, and He pursued us. We were scattered as sheep, and He sent the Good Shepherd. We hid in darkness, and He sent the True Light. We were dying in a self-made drought, and He sent the Living Water. The grace and goodness of God are on full display in Christian reconciliation. *"You were his enemies, separated from him by your evil thoughts and actions. Yet now he has reconciled you to himself through the death of Christ in his physical body. As a result, he has brought you into his own presence, and you are holy and blameless as you stand before him without a single fault"* (Colossians 1:21–22). As those who have been reconciled to God, we have been given "the ministry of reconciliation" (2 Corinthians 5:18). We have been entrusted with "the message of reconciliation" (verse 19). We now take the gospel to a dying world, saying, "We implore you on behalf of Christ, be reconciled to God" (verse 20, ESV). Jesus' perfect sacrifice on the cross has made atonement for sin (Hebrews 2:17). By His death, He brought harmony to our relationship with God. We plead with the unsaved to have faith in Christ and know the joys of Christian reconciliation.

The Great Commission found in Matthew 28:18-20 affirms the believer's duty as an ambassador for reconciliation. **Jesus commands His followers to** *"Go and make disciples of all nations, baptizing them in the name of the Father, and of the Son, and of the Holy Spirit."* This commission is not limited to preaching but includes teaching others to obey everything Jesus commanded. In this sense, ambassadors for Christ are not only bearers of the message of reconciliation but also educators who help others grow in faith and maintain their relationship with God. This mission is carried out under Christ's authority. He declares, "*All authority in heaven and on earth has been given to me*," meaning that believers operate under the authority of the risen Christ, empowered by the Holy Spirit to spread the good news of reconciliation. This divine authority provides believers with confidence and assurance that Christ is with them always, "*to the very end of the age*" (Matthew 28:20).

In Matthew 5:13, Jesus tells His followers, "*You are the salt of the earth.*" This parable underscores the influence that believers have in society. As ambassadors for Christ, Christians are called to be agents of change, preserving righteousness and biblical truth. Salt enhances flavor and preserves food; similarly, believers are tasked with living in a way that reflects the love and grace of Christ, drawing others toward reconciliation with God. However, if salt loses its flavor, it becomes ineffective. In the same way, believers who fail to live in accordance with the gospel diminish their effectiveness as ambassadors for Christ. Therefore, their actions and words must continually point others toward God's offer of reconciliation. To be the "salt of the earth" is to live in such a way that those around them are influenced and drawn closer to Christ through their witness.

In John 15:2-16:33, Jesus speaks about the importance of spiritual growth and remaining in Him as the source of life. He uses the analogy of the vine and branches, stating that those who remain in Him will bear much fruit, while those who do not remain in Him can do nothing (John 15:5). As ambassadors for Christ, believers are expected to bear fruit on earth, fruits of righteousness, love, and reconciliation. The grace and love they receive from Christ flow through them to others, making their lives a testimony of God's transformative power. In (John 15:15), Jesus calls His followers "friends," highlighting the intimate relationship they have with Him.

This relationship forms the foundation for their mission as ambassadors. Because they have experienced reconciliation with God through Christ, they are uniquely positioned to invite others into that same relationship. Yet, Jesus also warns that the world will oppose those who represent Him. Nevertheless, He promises peace and victory: "*In this world, you will have trouble. But take heart! I have overcome the world*" (John 16:33).

Remaining connected to Christ ensures that believers can faithfully fulfill their mission, even in the face of adversity. The Holy Spirit empowers and guides them, enabling them to share the message of reconciliation with boldness, love, and conviction.

The ministry of reconciliation is not merely about sharing words but also about living a life that reflects God's grace. 2 Corinthians 5:19-20 states that God has chosen believers to make His appeal through them; "We are therefore Christ's ambassadors, as though God were making His appeal through us." This means that those searching for Christ should be able to find Him in the lives of His ambassadors. Christians must live out attitudes of forgiveness, humility, and compassion—qualities that reflect Christ's character. Just as Christ forgave us, we are called to extend that same grace to the lost, broken, and backslidden. The message of reconciliation involves not only proclaiming the gospel but also restoring relationships within the church and in the broader community. In doing so, believers embody the heart of God, who desires that all people come to repentance and be reconciled to Him (2 Peter 3:9).

The ministry of reconciliation is a weighty responsibility, as (2 Corinthians 5:21) explains. Through Christ, who became sin for us, believers have become "the righteousness of God." This exchanges our sin for Christ's righteousness, reveals the depth of God's love and underscores the urgency of sharing this message with the world. As ambassadors, Christians carry a life-changing message, those who receive Christ will have eternal life, while those who reject Him remain separated from God.

Each believer plays a vital role in this ministry. Some plant seeds of faith, while others water, but God is the one who makes things grow (1 Corinthians 3:7). While the Holy Spirit convicts' hearts, God invites believers to participate in His redemptive work. This partnership is not only a privilege but a significant responsibility, as believers are entrusted with the most important message in the world: "*Be reconciled to God*" (2 Corinthians 5:20).

Being an ambassador for Christ is an extraordinary calling. It is a life of service, influence, and dependence on Christ, where ambassadors are entrusted with the ministry of reconciliation. Through the authority given by Jesus, believers are commissioned to proclaim the good news, making disciples of all nations and teaching them to follow Him. As the salt of the earth, believers are called to live lives that reflect the transforming power of the gospel, influencing those around them toward reconciliation with God.

As followers of Christ, remaining connected to Him, the true vine, allows believers to bear fruit that glorifies God. Though challenges and opposition will come, the Holy Spirit strengthens and enables believers to persevere, making their lives a witness to the world of God's love and grace. The ministry of reconciliation is urgent, and every believer must take seriously their role in sharing this message. As God's ambassadors, believers stand as representatives of His Kingdom, imploring the world to be reconciled to God through Christ. In doing so, they join in God's redemptive work, bringing hope and restoration to a broken world.

We **Are** Called to Serve as Christ's Ambassadors

An Ambassador for Christ, according to biblical principles, is a representative of Jesus Christ on earth who is called to live, speak, and act in a way that reflects Christ's nature, mission, and message. This role is grounded in the understanding that believers are entrusted with the ministry of reconciliation, sharing God's offer of peace, forgiveness, and eternal life through Jesus.

Messenger of Reconciliation (2 Corinthians 5:18-20)

➢ Ambassadors for Christ are entrusted with the Gospel, which is the message of reconciliation between God and humanity through Jesus Christ.

➢ They have the responsibility to plead on Christ's behalf, urging others to be reconciled to God by accepting His grace and forgiveness.

Living Testimonies of Christ (Galatians 2:20)

➢ Ambassadors are called to embody Christ's teachings and character in every aspect of life.

➢ This means living as transformed individuals, having died to self and now living with Christ at the center, reflecting His love, humility, compassion, and righteousness.

Representatives of God's Kingdom (Philippians 3:20)

➢ Ambassadors understand that their permanent citizenship is in heaven, not on earth.

They represent the values, principles, and culture of the Kingdom of God, making their actions and words consistent with Christ's will, rather than the world's standards.

Empowered by the Holy Spirit (Acts 1:8)

➢ They rely on the guidance, wisdom, and boldness of the Holy Spirit to carry out their duties effectively.

➢ The Holy Spirit provides the power to witness boldly, overcome challenges, and discern God's will in different situations.

Servants of God's Will (Romans 12:1-2)

➢ Ambassadors for Christ prioritize God's will over their own desires, offering their lives as living sacrifices and refusing to conform to worldly patterns.

➢ They are transformed by the renewing of their minds, allowing them to discern and align with God's perfect will in their mission.

Engaged in Spiritual Warfare (Ephesians 6:10-20)

➢ They recognize that being an ambassador involves spiritual conflict, standing firm against the schemes of the enemy while clothed in the full armor of God.

➢ Prayer, righteousness, truth, faith, and the Word of God are essential weapons in their service.

Bound by Love (1 John 4:7-8)

➢ Above all, an ambassador's message and conduct must be rooted in God's love.

➢ Their mission is carried out not just in words, but also in genuine acts of love, compassion, and grace, mirroring Christ's love for the lost and sick.

In essence, an Ambassador for Christ is a faithful disciple sent to represent Christ's interests, promote His teachings, and bring others to reconciliation with God. They embody a life of integrity, dedication, and unwavering allegiance to Christ, even in a world that often rejects the values of God's Kingdom. They willingly restore hearts to God knowing their reward awaits in heaven.

Crowned for Purpose

1 Timothy 2:5-6

ENDURING HARDSHIP

Asoldier's combat may be tiresome, fierce, and unrelenting at times. Soldiers of Christ are warriors on the frontlines of faith constantly in these perilous last days, not with military weaponry like machine guns and grenades but with unwavering faith as their "unbreakable anchor" and "unyielding force." _Their battle is far more than a clash of flesh and blood; it's a high-stakes confrontation against false prophecy and teachers who pervert the gospel through syncretism and watered-down prosperity doctrines, polluting the purity of God's original Word, laws, and commandments_. They defend against spiritual forces and dark powers pressing in on every side, standing up for victims even when the Church may not. They are unashamed of the Gospel of Jesus Christ. Some have been jailed, beaten, persecuted, and even martyred for God's gospel and for Christ's sake. Nonetheless, they persevere with one kingdom mission in mind.

Each soldier is armed with the armor of God, the breastplate of righteousness, shining with a commitment to uprightness; the helmet of salvation, crowning their minds with the assurance of Christ's victory; and the sword of the Spirit, sharper than any two-edged blade, cutting through lies, doubt, and the enemy's schemes. Together, they press forward, bound by a call to fight not just for themselves but for the faith of those beside them and the glory of the One who leads them.

The combat is grueling; attacks come from every side; fiery darts of fear, whispers of inadequacy, attempts to weaken their resolve. Yet these kingdom-soldiers, warring on the frontlines of faith, though battered, do not stand alone see (Joshua 1:9). They draw strength from their King, are gifted confidence by their God, and receive timely aid from the Holy Spirit, whose voice echoes over the roar of battle, saying, "Take heart; I have overcome the world (John 16:33)." Victory is certain, yet the path demands courage, endurance, and unwavering trust. (Romans 13:4) This is no ordinary combat; it's a relentless, purposeful clash for the crown, for salvation, for God's will, and ultimately for the Kingdom itself (Psalm 144:1).

In a world where spiritual darkness grows deeper, the call to be a soldier of Christ is one of deep courage and resilience. This is no ordinary fight; it's a battle for souls, for the truth, and for the Kingdom. The Christian soldier's resolve is rooted in a faith that does not waver, facing down forces seen and unseen. With a heavenly mandate to uphold the gospel in its purity, they stand as guards on the frontlines—not with earthly weapons, but with the unbreakable armor of God(Ephesians 6:11-17). Each day, they march forward, knowing the cost and yet willing to sacrifice all for the One who has already won the ultimate victory.

"Thou therefore, my son, be strong in the grace that is in Christ Jesus. And the things that thou hast heard of me among many witnesses, the same commit thou to faithful men, who shall be able to teach others also. *Thou therefore endure hardness, as a good soldier of Jesus Christ. No man that warreth entangleth himself with the affairs of this life; that he may please him who hath chosen him to be a soldier. And if a man also strive for masteries, yet is he not crowned, except he strive lawfully*". (2 Timothy 2 1-5)

2 Timothy 2 ,presents a powerful analogy, of the "crown" as the ultimate eternal reward for those who strive lawfully, endure with confidence, and remain loyal through various types of afflictions. These exemplify the qualities that a committed soldier enlisted in Christ Army must have. The "crown" represents the highest recompence for those who persevere, and stay devoted soldiers in God's enlistment of kingdom servicemen or women. This "Soldier's Crown" represents the honor, achievement and recognition and success in the face of opposition. It is rewarded to kingdom-believers who faithfully and earnestly fulfill and have upheld God's highly appointed "Spiritually-Armed-Kingdom-Mission". The characteristics highlighted in 2 Timothy 2 are essential for a "Soldier of Christ" and serve as a model for Christian discipleship and ministry. Here's why each characteristic is vital for a soldier in Christ's Kingdom.

Endurance: Paul emphasizes endurance, saying, "endure hardship as a good soldier of Jesus Christ" (2 Timothy 2:3). This trait is vital because a Christian soldier will inevitably face challenges, opposition, and spiritual warfare. Endurance builds spiritual resilience, allowing a believer to remain steadfast in faith and continue serving God's mission, regardless of personal cost. This resilience reflects Christ's own endurance in suffering and serves as a testimony to God's strength in times of weakness.

Obedience and Lawful Striving: Paul's mention of "striving lawfully" (2 Timothy 2:5) underscores obedience to God's commandments and principles. Just as soldiers follow military regulations, a Christian soldier adheres to God's Word. This obedience demonstrates reverence for God's authority, establishes a foundation for righteous living, and aligns the believer's actions with God's will. Lawful striving is about more than moral adherence; it's about committing to the spiritual "guidelines" that cultivate integrity, humility, and submission to God.

Focus and Loyalty: Paul's analogy suggests that soldiers avoid entanglement in "civilian affairs" (2 Timothy 2:4). This reflects a focused, undistracted devotion to God's kingdom, resisting worldly temptations and distractions. A loyal soldier is steadfast in their mission, dedicated to pleasing Christ, their "commander." This loyalty ensures that one's priorities remain on eternal matters, leading

to a life that bears spiritual fruit. It represents a heart fully committed to the Kingdom of God, unwavering even amidst the pulls of the secular world.

Discipline: Implicit in the analogy of both the soldier and the athlete is a sense of self-discipline. Discipline is essential for personal growth, self-control, and diligence in one's walk with God. It enables a believer to train themselves spiritually, study God's Word, engage in prayer, and foster a lifestyle that honors Christ. Discipline epitomizes the consistency and accountability needed for growth in Christ and for leading others by example.

Courage and Sacrifice: Paul's authoritative call to endure hardship and stand against opposition. These traits are necessary for facing spiritual battles, spreading the Gospel, and maintaining faith under persecution. Just as earthly soldiers lay down their lives for their country, a soldier of Christ is called to take up their cross (Matthew 16:24), sometimes sacrificing comfort, relationships, or even personal safety for the sake of Christ.

These characteristics reflect not only commitment but the heart and values necessary for advancing God's kingdom. A "Soldier of Christ" who embodies these traits honors God and ultimately gains the crown of righteousness, prepared for those who persevere in faith (2 Timothy 4, 10)*"You therefore, my child, be strong in the grace that is in Christ Jesus. And the things that you have heard me say among many witnesses, entrust these to faithful men who will be qualified to teach others as well. Join me in suffering, like a good soldier of Christ Jesus. A soldier refrains from entangling himself in civilian affairs, in order to please the one who enlisted him"*. Likewise, a competitor does not receive the crown unless he competes according to the rules. The hardworking farmer should be the first to partake of the crops. Consider what I am saying, for the Lord will give you insight into all things......"the word of God cannot be chained (2 Timothy 2: 9-10)! *For this reason, I endure all things for the sake of the elect, so that they too may obtain the salvation that is in Christ Jesus, with eternal glory.* This is a trustworthy scripture exemplifying that *if we died with Him, we will also live with Him; if we endure, we will also reign with Him; if we deny Him, He will also deny us; if we are faithless, He remains faithful, for He cannot deny Himself"(Hebrews 12 3-12)*

Enduring hardship and standing against demonic opposition are foundational in the life of a "Soldier of Christ," capturing the strength and resolve required for a Kingdom-focused life.

Here's a closer look

Embracing the Call to Perseverance: Endurance is one of the defining qualities that Paul attributes to a faithful soldier of Christ. Here's why it's vital.

Jesus exemplified endurance in the face of suffering. He endured the cross, scorned shame, and faced humanity's rejection (Hebrews 12:2). Enduring hardship allows believers to mirror Christ's willingness to suffer for God's glory, embracing the trials that shape spiritual maturity.

Spiritual Refinement: Hardships refine faith like fire refines gold. James 1:2-4 says that trials produce patience, and patience matures believers, completing their faith. In a soldier's life, endurance is a means of spiritual purification, bringing out a refined, resilient faith that relies on God's strength over human ability.

Building Resilience for Kingdom Work: Trials prepare Christians to withstand future battles, reinforcing spiritual resilience. Just as earthly soldiers face rigorous training to strengthen them physically and mentally, God allows hardships to strengthen believers spiritually, shaping their faith into a sturdy foundation for advancing the Kingdom.

Recognizing and Resisting the Enemy: As soldiers of Christ, believers must also contend with spiritual warfare, which requires understanding the nature of demonic opposition and standing firm against it.

Awareness of the Enemy's Tactics: Paul reminds us in Ephesians 6:12 that we wrestle not against flesh and blood, but against principalities, powers, and

spiritual forces of evil. Recognizing that the Christian battle is not against people but spiritual influences, shifts' the focus, preparing believers to respond with spiritual, not worldly weapons. Awareness of demonic tactics, such as deception, temptation, and discouragement, helps believers remain vigilant and rooted in God's truth.

Equipped with the Armor of God: In Ephesians 6:13-17, Paul instructs believers to "put on the full armor of God" to withstand evil. This armor includes the belt of truth, breastplate of righteousness, shield of faith, helmet of salvation, and the sword of the Spirit (God's Word). Each piece equips believers to stand firm and resist demonic schemes, grounding them in God's promises and protection. The Word of God is the primary weapon for countering spiritual deception and declaring truth amid lies.

Relying on God's Strength through Prayer: Prayer is an essential tool for standing firm. Paul emphasizes in Ephesians 6:18 the importance of praying "in the Spirit on all occasions." This is where a believer's strength is renewed, as they petition for God's guidance and protection. Prayer connects the soldier directly with God's power, bringing divine reinforcement against opposition.

Courage to Stand Firm: Like a soldier in battle, courage is needed to stand against the relentless attacks of the enemy. This courage stems from faith in Christ's victory over evil (Colossians 2:15).

Believers can face opposition without fear, knowing Christ has already disarmed the powers of darkness. Courage is not about the absence of fear but about choosing to trust God's strength amid spiritual battles.

- ➤ **Seeing Hardships and Opposition as Part of the Mission:** For a "Soldier of Christ," enduring hardship and resisting opposition are not random, isolated events but are integral to the kingdom-mission.
- ➤ **Bearing Fruit Through Adversity:** Trials and opposition often open doors for believers to witness to others through their resilience and unwavering faith. Paul, for instance, faced imprisonments and sufferings that seemed to hinder his

ministry, yet he saw them as opportunities to advance the Gospel (Philippians 1:12-14). A Kingdom mindset embraces adversity as a chance to bear fruit, bringing God glory through faithfulness.

➢ **Rewards for Endurance:** The Bible promises a crown of life for those who remain steadfast under trial (James 1:12). This crown is not just a reward but a symbol of victory, a testament to enduring faith and loyalty to God. For soldiers of Christ, enduring opposition is not in vain; it builds an eternal reward and honors the call to faithfulness.

➢ **Victory Assured in Christ:** Lastly, the soldier's confidence rests in Christ's ultimate victory. Romans 8:37 reminds believers that they are "more than conquerors" through Christ. Facing hardship and spiritual opposition with confidence in Christ's victory empowers believers to stand strong. This perspective shifts the battle from one of personal struggle to one of Kingdom purpose, where every challenge contributes to a greater, divine victory.

In essence, a soldier of Christ is called to endure with courage, resist with spiritual discernment, and fight with a Kingdom-focused heart. Every hardship and every encounter with opposition becomes an opportunity to manifest Christ's strength, glorify God, and bring forth the Kingdom's power in a world often at odds with it. This endurance shapes a soldier not only for this life but for eternal reward, securing a crown that reflects their dedication and faithfulness in the face of every trial.

Faith Under Fire : Enduring the "**Mental-Spiritual-Battle**"

Soldiers of Christ often face immense mental, physical, and emotional challenges, often magnified by their dedication to Kingdom work. The experiences of figures like Daniel, Paul, Peter, Joseph, John the Baptist, and Jesus Christ offer exceptional insights into how each dimension, mental, physical, and emotional, plays a role in shaping their faith, endurance, and testimony.

Mental Toll

The mental burden of serving God faithfully often includes fear, uncertainty, loneliness, and sustained pressure to remain steadfast against threats or opposition.

1. **Daniel:** As a captive in Babylon, Daniel faced the constant mental pressure of living in a foreign pagan culture hostile to his faith. Threatened by the fiery furnace and lion's den for his refusal to compromise his beliefs, Daniel remained mentally fortified through constant prayer and faith in God's sovereignty (Daniel 6). His resilience reflects the mental fortitude required to navigate environments that challenge faith and personal values.

2. **Paul:** Imprisoned numerous times, Paul wrestled with intense mental strain. In prison, he grappled with isolation, rejection, and the risk of martyrdom, yet he remained mentally strong, focusing on God's promises and encouraging believers from within his cell (Philippians 1:12-14). Paul's writings often reveal a mind centered on Christ, keeping him resilient in the face of daunting circumstances.

3. **Jesus Christ:** Jesus experienced immense mental pressure, especially in Gethsemane, where He anticipated the suffering, He was about to endure. His prayer, "Not my will, but Yours be done" (Luke 22:42), reflects the intense mental surrender required to embrace God's plan, despite the agony it brought. His mental endurance was founded on submission to God's will, showing that mental strength for a soldier of Christ often involves complete trust in God's plan.

Physical Toll

The physical hardships faced by God's faithful soldier can be severe, including imprisonment, torture, exhaustion, and even death. These physical trials test the limits of endurance, revealing reliance on God's strength.

1. **Paul and Peter:** Both apostles endured frequent imprisonment, beatings, and deprivation. Paul lists his physical sufferings in 2 Corinthians 11:23-28, including shipwrecks, lashings, and sleepless nights. Peter, likewise, was jailed and eventually martyred. The physical tolls they bore testify to the cost of preaching the Gospel and not denying Christ, showing that physical endurance is a significant aspect of a soldier's calling. Their hardships demonstrate a commitment that transcends the physical body, relying on the hope of the resurrection.

2. **John the Baptist:** John's imprisonment by Herod culminated in his execution. Despite the confinement and eventual beheading, John stayed true to his prophetic calling, enduring the physical toll of confinement and isolation. His experience underscores the potential costs of faithfulness, where even the body can become a sacrifice for the sake of the Kingdom.

3. **Jesus:** Jesus endured physical suffering on a level that encapsulates the ultimate physical toll. From scourging to crucifixion, He bore the full weight of physical pain. His willingness to endure such suffering exemplifies the extreme lengths of sacrificial love and obedience. The physical toll He bore is a model for all believers, showing that, in Christ, even the body's suffering can have redemptive purpose.

Emotional Toll

Emotional struggles are a significant part of the journey for a soldier of Christ. Feelings of betrayal, abandonment, sorrow, and spiritual burden often accompany faithful service to God.

1. **Joseph:** Sold into slavery by his brothers and imprisoned unjustly in Egypt, Joseph experienced deep emotional trials. His isolation and betrayal by family and later by those in authority (Genesis 39-41) reflect the emotional toll of enduring injustices and maintaining faith. Yet, Joseph's emotional resilience, rooted in his trust in God's sovereignty, ultimately led to his elevation and reconciliation with his family. His story shows that God can use emotional wounds to shape and prepare His soldiers for greater purposes.

2. **John the Baptist:** John experienced moments of emotional struggle, particularly when he questioned whether Jesus was truly the Messiah while suffering in prison (Matthew 11:2-3). His uncertainty in a dark moment reveals the emotional toll even great believers face. John's faith was reaffirmed by Christ's assurance, illustrating that periods of doubt are met with divine encouragement for those who stand firm.

3. **Jesus:** Jesus experienced the emotional weight of sorrow and compassion throughout His ministry, feeling the pain of humanity's suffering and the spiritual blindness of those who rejected Him (Matthew 23:37). In Gethsemane, He felt the full emotional agony of impending separation from the Father, praying with "sweat like drops of blood" (Luke 22:44). His emotional burden demonstrates the deep love and compassion required of a soldier of Christ, willing to bear the heartbreak of humanity's sinfulness for the sake of redemption.

Enduring **Mental, Physical, and Emotional Trials**

Each of these dilemmas mental, physical, and emotional tolls demands unique resilience, focus and determination for a soldier of Christ.

> Mentally, soldiers remain steadfast, keeping their minds on God's promises and drawing strength from Scripture.

> Physically, they endure hardship, knowing that their bodies may suffer but that their spirits are strengthened through trials.

> Emotionally, they embrace the struggles and the heartbreak of their calling, knowing that God's comfort and assurance sustain them through it all.

The experiences of Daniel, Paul, Peter, Joseph, John the Baptist, and Jesus Himself demonstrate that each hardship faced has a significant purpose in God's plan, shaping , molding and fortifying them into faithful, resilient, profitable soldiers who overcome for the sake of the Kingdom and kingdom business itself. Their endurance and strength inspire believers to view their trials not as obstacles but as a path to deeper fellowship with God and a testament to the power of Christ at work in them.

PETERS ENDURING REMORSE: "BROKEN TO BE BUILT AGAIN"

Peter's journey is a powerful testament to the depth of remorse, regret, and sorrow one can experience, even while faithfully enduring in service. His story exemplifies how a soldier of Christ can carry the weight of past failures yet remain devoted and empowered by grace to fulfill a higher calling.

The Burden of Remorse and Regret

Peter's denial of Jesus, recounted in all four Gospels, was a moment of deep personal regret. As Jesus faced His darkest hour, Peter denied knowing Him three times (Matthew 26:69-75), fulfilling Jesus' prediction and causing Peter to break down in bitter weeping. This act left Peter with a deep sense of shame and remorse. To Peter, who had boldly proclaimed his loyalty, this denial was a devastating failure, especially knowing he had promised Jesus, "Even if I have to die with You, I will not deny You" (Matthew 26:35).

> ➢ Lasting Emotional Impact: Living with the memory of betraying Christ, especially as one of His closest disciples, likely weighed heavily on Peter. His regret would have been compounded by his awareness that he had failed Jesus in a defining moment. This regret likely stayed with him, surfacing as a continual reminder of his human weakness and need for forgiveness and grace.

Grace and Restoration by Jesus is fortified strength to the soul. After His resurrection, Jesus specifically sought to restore Peter, knowing the weight of sorrow and regret Peter bore. In John 21, Jesus asked Peter three times, *"Do you love Me?"* allowing Peter to affirm his love three times, an intentional mirroring of Peter's three denials. Each response from Peter was met with a command to "feed My sheep," effectively commissioning Peter to continue in his role as a leader among the disciples. Through this encounter, Jesus demonstrated His willingness to forgive, reinforcing Peter's calling and reminding him that his past failures would not define his future service. Jesus' grace transformed Peter's sorrow into a purpose-driven resolve, giving him the courage to lead with humility and compassion. Rather than remain paralyzed by regret, Peter's failure became a source of deep empathy and determination, motivating him to shepherd the early Church with rich wisdom, understanding and humility.

Faithful Endurance Despite Sorrow

After Jesus' ascension, Peter's life was marked by tireless devotion. He became a pillar of the early Church, enduring persecution, imprisonment, and even threats of death for the sake of Christ. Despite the sorrow that likely resurfaced, Peter used his past failure as a reminder of God's mercy and a basis for his boldness in preaching the Gospel.

➤ Strengthened by Grace: Peter's endurance demonstrates that he was strengthened by God's grace and forgiveness rather than held back by regret. In 1 Peter 5:10, he speaks of the God of "all grace" who will "restore, establish, strengthen, and settle" those who suffer, a reflection of his personal experience with Jesus' restoration. This grace became the foundation for his resilience, reminding him that God's mercy outweighed his failures.

➤ A Humble Leadership: Peter's letters, particularly 1 Peter, reflect a tone of humility, compassion, and encouragement. His exhortations to believers to remain steadfast and endure suffering echo the depth of his own repentance and growth. By focusing on his new purpose in Christ, Peter was able to channel his sorrow into service, leading the Church with a humility born out of failure and restoration.

Endurance Unto Death

Peter's faithfulness extended to his death, where, according to tradition, he was crucified upside down, feeling unworthy to die in the same manner as Christ. This act of humility and commitment encapsulates a life marked by enduring sorrow, redeemed by grace, and ultimately sealed by sacrifice. Peter's end reveals that his sorrow, though ever-present, served as a continual reminder of God's love and forgiveness, empowering him to give his all for the Kingdom. Peter's journey from denial to restoration is a vivid example of how

a soldier of Christ can live with the tension of regret while still embracing God's calling. His life teaches us that sorrow over past mistakes need not hinder service; instead, it can deepen a believer's empathy, humility, and resolve to serve faithfully. Peter's story shows that God's forgiveness not only redeems the broken but also commissions them to lead, love, and endure until the very end. His legacy encourages believers that even in their weakest moments, grace abounds, transforming sorrow into a powerful testimony of God's relentless mercy and strength.

Peter's journey is a powerful testimony to the depth of remorse, regret, and sorrow, one can experience during tribulations, even while faithfully enduring in service. His story exemplifies how a soldier of Christ can carry the weight of past failures yet remain devoted and empowered by grace to fulfill a higher calling. Peter's denial of Jesus, recounted in all four Gospels, was a moment of deep personal failure. As Jesus faced His darkest hour, Peter denied knowing Him three times (Matthew 26:69-75), fulfilling Jesus' prediction and causing Peter to break down in bitter weeping. This act left Peter with a profound sense of shame and remorse. To Peter, who had boldly proclaimed his loyalty, this denial was a devastating failure, especially knowing he had promised Jesus, "Even if I have to die with You, I will not deny You" (Matthew 26:35).

> **Lasting Emotional Impact:** Living with the memory of betraying Christ, especially as one of His closest disciples, likely weighed heavily on Peter. His regret would have been compounded by his awareness that he had failed Jesus in a defining moment. This regret likely stayed with him, surfacing as a continual reminder of his human weakness and need for forgiveness and grace.

Faithful Endurance Despite Sorrow

After Jesus' ascension, Peter's life was marked by tireless devotion. Later on following Pentecost he became a pillar of the early Church, enduring persecution, imprisonment, and even threats of death for the sake of Christ. Despite the sorrow that likely resurfaced, Peter used his past failure as a reminder of God's mercy and a basis for his boldness in preaching the Gospel. Undeniably, Peter became Strengthened by Grace; he did not allow his past to negatively affect his future in spite of the devils' devices. Peter's endurance demonstrates that he was strengthened by God's grace and forgiveness rather than held back by regret. In 1 Peter 5:10, he speaks of the God of "all grace" who will "restore, establish, strengthen, and settle" those who suffer, a reflection of his personal experience with Jesus' restoration. This grace became the foundation for his resilience, reminding him that God's mercy outweighed his failures. Serving God through faithful and sincere leadership Peter's letters, particularly in 1 Peter, reflect a tone of humility, compassion, and encouragement. His exhortations to believers to remain steadfast and endure suffering echo the depth of his own repentance and growth. By focusing on his new purpose in Christ, Peter was able to channel his sorrow into service, leading the Church with a humility born out of failure and restoration.

Endurance Unto Death

Peter's faithfulness extended to his death, where, according to tradition, he was crucified upside down, feeling unworthy to die in the same manner as Christ. This act of humility and commitment encapsulates a life marked by enduring sorrow, redeemed by grace, and ultimately sealed by sacrifice. Peter's end reveals that his sorrow, though ever-present, served as a continual reminder of God's love and forgiveness, empowering him to give his all for the Kingdom.

Peter's journey from denial to restoration is a vivid example of how a soldier of Christ can live with the tension of regret while still embracing God's calling. His life teaches us that sorrow over past mistakes need not hinder service; instead, it can deepen a believer's empathy, humility, and resolve to serve faithfully. Peter's story shows that God's forgiveness not only redeems the broken but also commissions them to lead, love, and endure until the very end. His legacy encourages believers that even in their weakest moments, grace abounds, transforming sorrow into a powerful testimony of God's relentless mercy and strength.

Each of these apostles Peter, Daniel, Paul, Joseph, John the Baptist, and even Jesus Christ himself demonstrated remarkable obedience and faithfulness and **endurance on the frontlines of faith**, serving as prime examples of devotion under intense trials. Their lives show how obedience often required sacrifice, courage, and a commitment to God's call above all else.

Peter: Redeemed and Steadfast

After denying Jesus, Peter was restored and recommissioned by Christ. His obedience grew from his deep repentance and was demonstrated in his unwavering leadership in the early Church.

➤ **Bold Preaching:** Peter was the first to publicly proclaim the Gospel after Pentecost, delivering a sermon that led to the conversion of thousands (Acts 2:14-41). Despite the risk of imprisonment, he fearlessly preached Jesus' resurrection and salvation, driven by his commitment to obey Christ's command to "feed My sheep."

➤ **Fearless Shepherd of the Church:** Peter became a pillar of the early Church, providing guidance, correction, and encouragement to new believers. His letters reflect a commitment to shepherd God's people humbly, encouraging others to endure suffering for the sake of Christ (1 Peter 5:1-4).

According to tradition, Peter was crucified upside down, choosing a death he believed was unworthy of his Savior. His willingness to die for the faith showed his ultimate obedience and loyalty to Jesus.

Daniel: Faithful Under Pressure

Daniel lived faithfully in Babylon as a captive under pagan rule, consistently choosing obedience to God over compliance with Babylonian conquest authorities.

➢ Refusal to Compromise, from refusing the king's food, to praying openly despite a royal edict, Daniel consistently obeyed God's law over Babylonian demands (Daniel 1, 6). His commitment to God's ways set him apart and earned him favor, demonstrating that obedience leads to both earthly influence and spiritual resilience.

➢ Wise Prophetic servant, through visions and dreams, Daniel was God's mouthpiece to kings and empires, faithfully relaying God's messages even when they were difficult or risky. His obedience in speaking truth to power exemplified his courage to serve God rather than men.

Faithful endurance even unto the Lion's Den. Facing death for his faithfulness, Daniel's obedience in prayer led to miraculous deliverance, showcasing God's power to protect those who remain true.

Paul: A Life Poured Out for the Gospel

Paul's conversion and obedience marked a radical transformation, with every aspect of his life devoted to proclaiming Christ.

➢ Paul obeyed Jesus Christ call by embarking on extensive missions spreading the Gospel to gentiles, enduring shipwrecks, beatings, persecutions and imprisonment. His letters to the churches reveal a heart fully committed to

building up the body of Christ, regardless of personal hardship (2 Corinthians 11:23-28).

➤ Authentic, bold and uncompromising doctrine; Paul was steadfast in preserving the purity of the Gospel, opposing false teachings and urging believers to hold to the truth of scripture. His letters demonstrate a commitment to God's Word, guiding believers toward sound doctrine and godly living (Galatians 1:6-10).

Faithful Unto Death, imprisoned in Rome, Paul continued to encourage the churches, seeing his suffering as a final act of obedience. His declaration, "I have fought the good fight, I have finished the race, I have kept the faith" (2 Timothy 4:7), reflects a life poured out fully in obedience to Christ.

Joseph: Obedience Through Integrity and Patience

Joseph's life in Egypt is a testament to obedience in adversity, maintaining integrity and trust in God even when circumstances were bleak.

➤ Integrity under adversity and disappointment. Sold into slavery by his brothers, Joseph served faithfully in Potiphar's house and resisted temptation, remaining true to God despite potential consequences. His response to Potiphar's wife, "How then could I do such a wicked thing and sin against God?" (Genesis 39:9), reflects his obedience and fear of the Lord.

➤ Wrongfully imprisoned, Joseph continued to serve diligently while serving his time, interpreting dreams for fellow prisoners, which eventually led to his elevation by Pharaoh. His obedience under unjust conditions shows faithfulness despite hardship, trusting that God was at work even in dark times.

Forgiveness yielding superior wisdom and profound leadership. Elevated to Pharaoh's right hand, Joseph showed compassion and forgiveness toward his brothers who sold him into slavery, understanding God's sovereign plan in his trials. His obedience to God's call enabled him to save many lives and reconcile his family (Genesis 50:20).

John the Baptist: Unwavering Prophetic Voice

John's ministry exemplified obedience through boldness and humility, even as he faced growing opposition.

> ➤ Calling Israel to Repentance faithfully paving the way of Jesus Christ; John obeyed his calling by fearlessly preaching repentance, preparing the way for Jesus, the promised messiah. His boldness in speaking truth to everyone, from religious leaders to rulers, demonstrated his commitment to God's message over popular opinion (Matthew 3:1-12).
> ➤ Obediently fulfilling his role, John baptized Jesus, humbling himself and recognizing that his purpose was to point to the Messiah. His willingness to decrease so Christ might increase (John 3:30) exemplifies a soldier of faith focused on God's glory.

Faithful Unto Death, imprisoned for confronting Herod's unlawful marriage, John held firm to his prophetic calling, ultimately dying for his obedience. His life shows the cost of standing for righteousness, even when it leads to personal sacrifice.

Jesus: The Ultimate Example of Obedience

Jesus' life is the epitome of perfect obedience, laying down His own will to fulfill the Father's redemptive plan.

> ➤ Obedience in ministry, every action in Jesus' ministry was aligned with His Father's will. From healing the sick to teaching about the Kingdom, He served as the obedient Son,

fulfilling prophecy and living as the model of righteousness (John 5:19).

➤ In Gethsemane, Jesus fully surrendered to the Father's will, praying, "Not my will, but Yours be done" (Luke 22:42). His obedience here represents the ultimate sacrifice, choosing the cross for humanity's sake despite knowing the pain it would bring.

➤ The strong arm and Lamb of God; obedient Unto death, Jesus' death on the cross exemplifies the highest form of obedience. Philippians 2:8 describes Jesus as "obedient to the point of death, even death on a cross," signifying that His entire mission was about fulfilling the Father's redemptive purpose.

Each of these "apostle-soldiers of Christ" served faithfully on the frontlines of faith through faithfully enduring pain, fiery trials, and tribulations with both their heart and mind on the kingdom.

✓ Peter's leadership after his restoration showcases obedience rooted in humility and dedication to the early Church.

✓ Daniel's resilience and commitment under foreign rule exemplify obedience in the face of cultural pressure.

✓ Paul's tireless missionary work and doctrinal integrity reflect obedience that transcends personal hardship.

✓ Joseph's integrity and patience reveal obedience that trusts in God's timing and purpose.

✓ John the Baptist's prophetic boldness and humility highlight obedience that prioritizes God's mission over personal safety.

✓ Jesus' life and sacrifice embody the ultimate obedience, fulfilling God's will even unto death.

Their obedience shaped not only their own spiritual journeys but also the faith of countless others, serving as powerful examples of what it means to be on the frontlines of faith. Through trials and triumphs, they reveal that obedience is both the call and the legacy of every soldier of Christ. Enduring hardship and standing against demonic opposition are foundational in the life of a "Soldier of Christ," capturing the strength and resolve required for a...

Kingdom-focused life.

Endurance is one of the defining qualities that Paul attributes to a faithful soldier of Christ. Here's why it's vital. Christ's Example, Jesus exemplified endurance in the face of suffering. He endured the cross, scorned shame, and faced immense rejection (Hebrews 12:2). Enduring hardship allows believers to mirror Christ's willingness to suffer for God's glory, embracing the trials that shape spiritual maturity. Spiritual Refinement, Hardships refine faith like fire refines gold. James 1:2-4 says that trials produce patience, and patience matures believers, completing their faith. In a soldier's life, endurance is a means of spiritual purification, bringing out a refined, resilient faith that relies on God's strength over human ability. Building resilience for kingdom work, trials prepare Christians to withstand future battles, reinforcing spiritual resilience. Just as earthly soldiers face rigorous training to strengthen them physically and mentally, God allows hardships to strengthen believers spiritually, shaping their faith into a sturdy foundation for advancing the Kingdom. Standing against demonic opposition "Recognizing and Resisting the Enemy" as soldiers of Christ, believers must also contend with spiritual warfare, which requires understanding the nature of demonic opposition and standing firm against it.

➤ Awareness of the Enemy's Tactics; Paul reminds us in Ephesians 6:12 that we wrestle not against flesh and blood, but against principalities, powers, and spiritual forces of evil. Recognizing that the Christian battle against the forces of darkness, is not against people but spiritual influences of demonic forces that to exalt themselves against the **TRUE** knowledge of God. Followers of Christ must prepare themselves to respond with spiritual, not worldly, weapons. Awareness of demonic tactics such as deception, temptation, and discouragement help believers remain vigilant and rooted in God's truth.

➤ In Ephesians 6:13-17, Paul instructs believers to "put on the full armor of God" to withstand evil. This armor includes the belt of truth, breastplate of righteousness, shield of faith, helmet of salvation, and the sword of the Spirit (God's Word). Each piece equips believers to stand firm and resist demonic schemes, grounding them in God's promises and protection. The Word of God is the primary weapon for countering spiritual deception and declaring truth amid lies.

➤ Relying on God's strength and power through prayer; prayer is an essential tool for standing firm. Paul emphasizes in Ephesians 6:18 the importance of praying "in the Spirit on all occasions." This is where a believer's strength is renewed, as they petition for God's guidance and protection. Prayer connects the soldier directly with God's power, bringing divine reinforcement against opposition.

➤ God grants his sheep courage to stand firm in the face of adversity. Like a soldier in battle, courage is needed to stand against the relentless attacks of the enemy. This courage stems from faith in Christ's victory over evil (Colossians 2:15). Believers can face opposition without fear, knowing Christ has already disarmed the powers of darkness. Courage is not about the absence of fear but about choosing to trust God's strength amid spiritual battles.

Kingdom Mindset! Seeing Hardships and Opposition as Part of the Soldiers Mission

For a "Soldier of Christ," enduring hardship and resisting opposition are not random isolated events but are integral to the mission. Trials and opposition often open doors for believers to witness to others through their resilience and unwavering faith. Paul, for instance, faced imprisonments and sufferings that seemed to hinder his ministry, yet he saw them as opportunities to advance the Gospel (Philippians 1:12-14). A Kingdom mindset embraces adversity as a chance to bear fruit, bringing God glory through faithfulness. The Bible promises a crown of life for those who remain steadfast under trial (James 1:12). This crown is not just a reward but a symbol of victory, a testament to enduring faith and loyalty to God. For soldiers of Christ, enduring opposition is not in vain; it builds an eternal reward and honors the call to faithfulness. Lastly, the soldier's confidence rests in Christ's ultimate victory. Romans 8:37 reminds believers that they are "more than conquerors" through Christ. Facing hardship and spiritual opposition with confidence in Christ's victory empowers believers to stand strong. This perspective shifts the battle from one of personal struggle to one of Kingdom purpose, where every challenge contributes to a greater, divine victory.

In essence, a soldier of Christ is called to endure with courage, resist with spiritual discernment, and fight with a Kingdom-focused heart. Every hardship and every encounter with opposition becomes an opportunity to manifest Christ's strength, glorify God, and bring forth the Kingdom's power in a world often at odds with it. This endurance shapes a soldier not only for this life but for eternal reward, securing a crown that reflects their dedication and faithfulness in the face of every trial.

Meaning of Enduring Hardship as Soldiers in Christ

Enduring hardship as a soldier in Christ involves staying steadfast, faithful, and resilient through difficulties and challenges in life, knowing that the Christian journey is not always easy. It includes

persevering through trials, suffering for the sake of righteousness, and remaining committed to God's purpose despite opposition, persecution, or suffering.

Being a soldier in Christ's Kingdom involves a commitment to a life of **discipline**, **faith**, and **steadfast loyalty** to God's mission. It's not a mere label, but a call to actively engage in the spiritual battle against darkness, uphold God's truth, and defend the values of His Kingdom and the integrity of His word with courage. This role is based on allegiance to Jesus as both Savior and Lord, meaning believers submit their lives fully to His guidance, following His example and obeying His commands, no matter the personal cost.

Equipped for Spiritual Battle

> Ephesians 6:10-18 describes the "armor of God" as the essential gear for a soldier of Christ, including biblical truth, righteousness, faith, and the Word of God.

As soldiers, believers are given spiritual armor to stand firm against the forces of evil. Each piece symbolizes a readiness to uphold truth and integrity, resist temptation, and actively defend their faith. Prayer, as emphasized in verse 18, is the lifeline of every soldier, aligning them with God's will and empowering them to overcome spiritual battles.

Steadfast Endurance and Perseverance

> 2 Timothy 2:3-4 - "Endure hardship with us like a good soldier of Christ Jesus. No one serving as a soldier gets involved in civilian affairs, he wants to please his commanding officer."

A soldier in Christ's Kingdom understands that challenges are part of the journey. This endurance is a mark of devotion and strength, allowing believers to remain focused on the mission without becoming entangled in worldly distractions. Just as soldiers live to please their commanding officer, believers strive to live in a way that honors and pleases God, maintaining a Kingdom-focused mindset.

Courage in the Face of Opposition

> ➤ Joshua 1:9 and 2 Timothy 1:7 emphasize God's command to be strong and courageous.

Courage is a defining trait of a soldier in Christ's Kingdom. This courage stems from faith in God's power and protection, allowing believers to speak truth, defend the faith, and share the gospel with love, even when faced with adversity. As soldiers, they are called to stand firm in their beliefs and not shrink back, becoming witnesses to the transforming power of the Kingdom in their lives.

Living with a Sacrificial Mindset

> ➤ Romans 12:1 - "Offer your bodies as a living sacrifice, holy and pleasing to God, this is your true and proper worship."

Like soldiers who serve their nation with loyalty and sacrifice, believers offer themselves fully to God's service. This sacrificial mindset means prioritizing God's will above personal desires, living for the Kingdom's advancement. Christ's sacrifice becomes their model, inspiring them to serve selflessly and commit fully to God's calling.

Advancing the Kingdom's Mission

> ➤ Matthew 28:19-20 calls believers to make disciples, baptizing and teaching them about Jesus.

A soldier in Christ's Kingdom is also a disciple-maker, active in sharing the gospel and helping others come to know Jesus. This mission goes beyond mere words, as soldiers are to embody the message of hope, redemption, and transformation found in Christ. They are called to be lights in the darkness, spreading God's love and truth to the world, regardless of the opposition they might face.

To be a soldier in Christ's Kingdom is to live a life marked by unwavering faith, obedience, and courage. It involves a readiness to endure hardship, a focus on God's mission, and a commitment to stand firm against any opposition to the gospel. With hearts set on

pleasing their Heavenly Father, soldiers of Christ move forward in spiritual resilience, knowing their ultimate reward is in heaven. This calling is a profound privilege, one that involves both sacrifice and deep spiritual purpose, as believers play a crucial role in advancing God's Kingdom on earth.

Real-Life Scenarios the Christ Soldiers are not exempt from facing!

Persecution for Faith: A believer might face ostracism from friends and family for their faith, similar to how early Christians were treated. Despite the emotional pain, they remain steadfast in their faith, sharing the Gospel whenever or Wherever possible.

Health Challenges: A Christian battling a chronic illness endures physical pain and limitations. They use their experience to minister to others facing similar challenges, encouraging them to rely on God's strength.

Financial Hardship: A believer loses their job and faces financial struggles. Instead of despair, they trust in God's provision, continuing to give and serve others, which strengthens their faith and testimony.

Grief and Loss: After losing a loved one, a Christian may wrestle with deep sorrow but finds solace in God's promises. They use their experience to comfort others who are grieving, exemplifying the hope found in Christ.

Conflict and Reconciliation: A church community experiences division due to differing opinions. A believer steps up to promote reconciliation and unity, demonstrating endurance in fostering peace amidst hardship.

Enduring hardship as soldiers in Christ involves a deep reliance on God, the practice of faith, and an unwavering commitment to the mission of spreading the Gospel. The trials believers face are opportunities for growth, character development, and ultimately glorifying God through their endurance and faithfulness.

Why bad things happen to good people?

A "Believer of God" or Soldier of Christ can explain why bad things happen to good people by using the Bible to reveal God's perspective on suffering and hardship. According to Scripture, the presence of hardship in the lives of believers is not a sign of God's abandonment, but rather a part of the believers' journey with God and often serves a greater purpose in God's divine plan. Here's how a believer might explain this using biblical principles.

The World is Fallen Due to Sin

Romans 5:12 (NIV) – "Therefore, just as sin entered the world through one man, and death through sin, and in this way death came to all people, because all sinned."

John 16:33 (NIV) – "In this world, you will have trouble. But take heart! I have overcome the world."

From a biblical standpoint, the reason bad things happen in the world, including to good people, is rooted in the fall of humanity. When sin entered the world through Adam and Eve, it introduced death, suffering, and brokenness into creation. As a result, even the most righteous people experience pain and hardship. However, Jesus warns that trouble is inevitable in this world, but He also promises hope by overcoming the world. So, bad things happen not because God is unjust, but because we live in a fallen, sinful world. A lot of current hardships faced today are man-made and man created.

God Allows Hardship to Develop Faith and Character

Scripture:

James 1:2-4 (NIV) – "Consider it pure joy, my brothers and sisters, whenever you face trials of many kinds, because you know that the testing of your faith produces perseverance. Let perseverance finish its work so that you may be mature and complete, not lacking anything."

Romans 5:3-4 (NIV) – "Not only so, but we also glory in our sufferings, because we know that suffering produces perseverance; perseverance, character; and character, hope."

God sometimes allows bad things to happen to "good" people as a way to refine their faith and build their character. Just as a soldier undergoes difficult training to be prepared for battle, believers endure hardships that strengthen their faith. Trials and sufferings help believers develop perseverance, resilience, and deeper trust in God. This process of growth is essential for becoming mature in Christ and fully equipped to fulfill God's purpose.

Suffering Draws Us Closer to God and His Purpose

2 Corinthians 1:8-9 (NIV) – "We were under great pressure, far beyond our ability to endure, so that we despaired of life itself... But this happened that we might not rely on ourselves but on God, who raises the dead."

Psalm 34:18 (NIV) – "The Lord is close to the brokenhearted and saves those who are crushed in spirit."

Sometimes, God allows suffering to draw us closer to Him. In times of hardship, we often realize our dependence on God more profoundly and learn to lean on Him for comfort and strength. Paul explains that suffering can drive us to rely on God rather than on our own strength. It is in our brokenness that God reveals His presence and faithfulness most clearly, and this intimacy with God strengthens our relationship with Him.

Trials serve a unique role in testing and strengthening the faith of a believer, building resilience and leading them to a deeper reliance on God. Here's how.

Revealing Genuine Faith

Scripture: 1 Peter 1:6-7 - "In this you rejoice, though now for a little while, if necessary, you have been grieved by various trials, so that the tested genuineness of your faith, more precious than gold that perishes though it is tested by fire, may be found to result in praise and glory and honor at the revelation of Jesus Christ."

Trials expose the true nature of a believer's faith, revealing whether it is dependent on circumstances or anchored in God. This refining process ensures that faith is genuine, enduring, and pleasing to God.

Deepening Dependence on God

Scripture: 2 Corinthians 12:9-10 - "But he said to me, 'My grace is sufficient for you, for my power is made perfect in weakness.' Therefore I will boast all the more gladly of my weaknesses, so that the power of Christ may rest upon me."

Trials often bring believers to the end of their own strength, prompting them to rely solely on God. Through reliance on His strength and grace, believers learn that God's provision is sufficient in all circumstances.

Developing Patience and Perseverance

Scripture: James 1:2-4 - "Count it all joy, my brothers, when you meet trials of various kinds, for you know that the testing of your faith produces steadfastness. And let steadfastness have its full effect, that you may be perfect and complete, lacking in nothing."

Enduring trials teaches patience and perseverance, both vital qualities in the Christian walk. Through repeated experiences of overcoming challenges, believers grow stronger, more resilient, and better equipped for future trials.

Purifying and Refining Character

Scripture: Romans 5:3-5 - "Not only that, but we rejoice in our sufferings, knowing that suffering produces endurance, and endurance produces character, and character produces hope, and hope does not put us to shame..."

Just as impurities are removed from metal in a furnace, trials work to purify and refine a believer's character. This process of sanctification is essential for growing closer to Christ and becoming more like Him.

Encouraging Spiritual Growth and Maturity

Hebrews 12:10-11 - "For they disciplined us for a short time as it seemed best to them, but he disciplines us for our good, that we may share his holiness. For the moment all discipline seems painful rather than pleasant, but later it yields the peaceful fruit of righteousness to those who have been trained by it."

God's discipline through trials is a sign of His love, pushing believers toward holiness and spiritual growth. Through these experiences, believers gain wisdom, perspective, and a deepened relationship with God.

Building Empathy and Compassion for Others

Scripture: 2 Corinthians 1:3-4 - "Blessed be the God and Father of our Lord Jesus Christ, the Father of mercies and God of all comfort, who comforts us in all our affliction, so that we may be able to comfort those who are in any affliction, with the comfort with which we ourselves are comforted by God."

Having endured trials, believers are better equipped to comfort and support others facing similar difficulties. This shared experience builds empathy and enhances the unity of the Body of Christ.

Enhancing Trust in God's Sovereignty and Goodness

Scripture: Romans 8:28 - "And we know that in all things God works for the good of those who love him, who have been called according to his purpose."

Facing challenges helps believers develop a stronger trust in God's sovereignty and goodness. Recognizing that God works all things for good, even in painful circumstances, strengthens their assurance of His perfect plan.

Trials are not merely tests but instruments of growth, drawing believers closer to God and shaping them into the image of Christ. Through trials, believers come to know God's character more deeply, trust Him more fully, and emerge as mature Christians ready to fulfill His purposes.

Believers Share in Christ's Sufferings

1 Peter 4:12-13 (NIV) – "Dear friends, do not be surprised at the fiery ordeal that has come on you to test you, as though something strange were happening to you. But rejoice inasmuch as you participate in the sufferings of Christ, so that you may be overjoyed when his glory is revealed."

Philippians 1:29 (NIV) – "For it has been granted to you on behalf of Christ not only to believe in him, but also to suffer for him."

As soldiers of Christ, believers are called to participate in the sufferings of Christ. Jesus Himself, who was perfectly good, suffered and died, not because He deserved it, but to fulfill God's redemptive plan. In the same way, believers may endure suffering as part of their journey to live for Christ and share in His mission. Suffering for the sake of righteousness aligns us with Jesus, and through it, we anticipate sharing in His glory when He returns.

Eternal Perspective: Earthly Suffering is Temporary

➤ **2 Corinthians 4:17 (nkjv)** – " For our light affliction, which is but for a moment, is working for us a far more exceeding and eternal weight of glory."

➤ **Romans 8:18 (nkjv)** – " 18 For I consider that the sufferings of this present time are not worthy to be compared with the glory which shall be revealed in us.."

While bad things happen to good people, Scripture encourages believers to have an eternal-kingdom perspective. The trials and hardships of this life are temporary and small in comparison to the eternal glory that awaits believers in heaven. Soldiers of Christ endure suffering on earth, knowing that their true reward is not in this life but in eternity with God. This hope sustains believers through even the most difficult circumstances.

God's Sovereignty! His Ways Are Higher Than Ours

➤ **Isaiah 55:8-9 (NIV)** – "'For my thoughts are not your thoughts, neither are your ways my ways,' declares the Lord. 'As the heavens are higher than the earth, so are my ways higher than your ways and my thoughts than your thoughts.'"

➤ **Romans 8:28 (NIV)** – "And we know that in all things God works for the good of those who love him, who have been called according to his purpose."

God's ways are often beyond human understanding. While believers may not always comprehend why certain hardships occur, they trust that God is sovereign and that He works all things for good. This doesn't mean that every situation will seem good from a mortal perspective, but that God uses even the most difficult circumstances for His purposes. Like a soldier following the command of a general, Christians trust God's wisdom, even when they don't fully understand it.

Rain falls on the Just and the Unjust

Believers can explain that bad things happen to good people due to the fallen nature of the world, and because suffering has a purpose in the life of a Christian. It refines faith, builds character, draws us closer to God, and allows us to share in the sufferings of Christ. As soldiers of Christ, we are called to endure hardship with the knowledge that our present sufferings are temporary and are preparing us for eternal glory. Ultimately, a soldier of Christ rests in the truth that God is sovereign and working all things for the good of those who love Him.

In James 1:2-4, the Apostle James encourages believers to "*count it all joy*" when they encounter trials because of the spiritual growth and maturity that trials produce. Here's why the Redeemed of God (believers) are called to find joy even in the midst of suffering and hardship.

1. Trials Test and Strengthen Faith

"Count it all joy when you fall into various trials, knowing that the testing of your faith produces patience. But let patience have its perfect work, that you may be perfect and complete, lacking nothing **James 1:2-4.** "

Trials are not random or meaningless in the life of a believer; they serve a purpose. When we face difficulties, our faith is tested. This testing reveals the strength of our faith and reliance on God. Just as physical exercise strengthens muscles, trials strengthen our spiritual muscles, faith, patience, and endurance. As a result, believers become more resilient and steadfast in their relationship with God.

Consider gold being refined by fire. The heat of the fire burns away impurities and makes the gold purer. In the same way, trials refine and purify our faith, removing weaknesses and helping us grow stronger in Christ.

2. Steadfastness (Endurance) Leads to Maturity

"But let patience have its perfect work, that you may be perfect and complete, lacking nothing. If any of you lacks wisdom, let him ask of God, who gives to all liberally and without reproach, and it will be given to him Romans 8:18. "

The ultimate goal of enduring trials is spiritual maturity. The word "perfect" in this context refers to being spiritually mature and whole, not lacking anything in our walk with God. As believers endure various trials with faith, their character is developed, and they grow in Christlikeness. Steadfastness allows us to handle future challenges with grace and to live fully as people of faith.

A soldier who undergoes rigorous training is prepared for battle. The training might be difficult, but it equips the soldier to face challenges with strength and confidence. In the same way, enduring trials makes believers spiritually "battle-ready" for the challenges of life.

3. Trials Bring Us Closer to God

Trials can deepen our dependence on God. During times of hardship, we realize that we are not self-sufficient. Instead, we must rely on God's strength, wisdom, and provision. This draws us into a closer relationship with Him and allows us to experience His grace and faithfulness in a deeper way. Think of how a child clings more tightly to a parent when scared or uncertain. In trials, believers are drawn closer to their Heavenly Father, finding comfort and strength in His presence.

4. Joy in Knowing God is at Work

The reason believers can "count it all joy" is because they understand that God is at work in every trial. Even though the trial itself may be painful or difficult, believers have the assurance that God is using it for their good, to build character, faith, and spiritual maturity. This divine purpose brings joy, even in the midst of suffering, because believers know that God's plans for them are good and intentional (Romans 8:28).

A gardener prunes plants to help them grow healthier and bear more fruit. The pruning process is cutting and painful, but it is necessary for growth. Similarly, trials can feel like "pruning" in our lives, but they are part of God's process to help us grow and bear more spiritual fruit.

5. Eternal Perspective

Believers can have joy in trials because they look beyond their present circumstances and focus on the eternal rewards. Trials are temporary, but the growth, maturity, and spiritual fruit that come from enduring them have eternal value. Knowing that trials will one day give way to eternal glory with Christ allows believers to rejoice in the midst of suffering (2 Corinthians 4:17).

A marathon runner endures the pain of the race because they are focused on the finish line. In the same way, believers endure trials with joy because they are focused on the eternal prize.

Cowardice in the Kingdom Revelation 21:8

Cowardice in the Kingdom is a severe deviation from God's standards, where fear overtakes and paralyzes faith and leads to disobedience, unfruitfulness, and ultimately separation from God. In Scripture, cowardice isn't viewed as mere hesitation but as a refusal to stand boldly in God's truth and trust in His promises. When fear takes precedence over faith, it perverts the believer's trust in God, rendering them ineffective in the spiritual battles they face and stunting their growth. The Bible repeatedly emphasizes that fear is a tool of the enemy, designed to weaken believers' resolve, isolate them from their God-given mission, and prevent them from fulfilling their divine calling.

God's response to cowardice is a consistent command to be **courageous, strong,** and **bold.** Scriptures such as (Joshua 1:9) and (Ephesians 6:10-11) illustrate that courage is not optional for believers; it is a requirement rooted in reliance on God's power and protection. True courage does not stem from personal confidence but from the knowledge that God is always present, providing the strength needed to face any challenge. This divine courage enables believers to conquer fear, uphold their faith, and live in obedience, regardless of the cost. When fear is replaced with courage, believers are able to fully step into God's promises, advancing the Kingdom and standing as powerful witnesses of His unfailing faithfulness.

The Bible's warnings against cowardice are sharp and explicit. (Revelation 21:8) categorizes the cowardly alongside the unbelieving, the immoral, and the idolatrous, those who ultimately will not enter God's eternal Kingdom. Cowardice here is portrayed as a rejection of God's truth, resulting in separation from His presence. This warning serves to underscore that the Kingdom of God requires a courageous commitment, where believers must place their trust fully in Christ rather than retreat into fear or self-preservation. Choosing courage in the face of opposition reflects a believer's true allegiance to God, demonstrating faithfulness even when it demands sacrifice or suffering.

Faith and fear cannot coexist. Faith drives believers forward, causing them to embrace God's promises and engage fully in His work, while fear and cowardice lead to stagnation and withdrawal. To be a soldier in the Kingdom means to embody a courage grounded in faith, rejecting fear as an obstacle that hinders spiritual victory and Kingdom advancement. God's commands to be bold serve as a reminder that believers are called to live victoriously, assured that He is with them, empowering them to overcome. In the Kingdom, courage is a mark of trust, a witness to the world, and an essential aspect of walking in the fullness of faith, ultimately preparing believers to enter into God's eternal glory.

Why Count it All Joy?

The Redeemed of God are called to "count it all joy" when they face trials because *trials test and strengthen their faith, develop steadfastness, and ultimately lead to spiritual maturity.* Through these hardships, believers are drawn closer to God, and they learn to rely more fully on His grace and power. While trials may be difficult, believers can have joy because they know that God is at work in their lives, refining and shaping them to become more like Christ. This eternal perspective allows them to embrace challenges with faith, hope, and joy.

How Fear Paralyzes Faith

Fear is a powerful emotion that can cripple a person's ability to act in faith. For believers, **fear often becomes a tool that the enemy uses to keep them from fulfilling God's purpose and calling.** When fear takes over, it paralyzes faith by causing doubt, hesitation, and a lack of trust in God's promises. Here's how fear paralyzes faith and how it affects the life of a believer.

1. Fear Causes Doubt in God's Promises

Matthew 14:29-31 (NIV) – "Then Peter got down out of the boat, walked on the water and came toward Jesus. But when he saw the wind, he was afraid and, beginning to sink, cried out, 'Lord, save me!' Immediately Jesus reached out his hand and caught him. 'You of little faith,' he said, 'why did you doubt?'"

When Peter stepped out in faith to walk on water, his focus was initially on Jesus. However, when fear took over, he began to doubt and sink. Fear distracts us from the power and presence of God, shifting our focus to the circumstances around us. When doubt enters the heart, it weakens faith, and believers begin to sink under the weight of their fears instead of walking confidently in God's promises.

2. Fear Leads to Disobedience

Numbers 13:31-33 (NIV) – "But the men who had gone up with him said, 'We can't attack those people; they are stronger than we are.'... We seemed like grasshoppers in our own eyes, and we looked the same to them."

Hebrews 11:6 (NIV) – "And without faith it is impossible to please God, he is a rewarder of them that diligently seek him.

When the Israelites were on the verge of entering the Promised Land, fear paralyzed their faith. The spies, except for Joshua and Caleb, were overwhelmed by the size and strength of their opponents, forgetting that God had already promised them victory. Fear led to their disobedience, causing an entire generation to miss out on God's promise. Fear can cause believers to hesitate or outright refuse to follow God's leading, which results in disobedience and forfeiture of God's blessings.

3. Fear Stops Forward Progress

Scripture:2 Timothy 1:7 (NIV) – "For God has not given us a spirit of fear, but of power, and of love, and of a sound mind."

Fear prevents us from moving forward in the things God has called us to do. **While faith pushes us to step out in confidence, fear tells us to stay where it feels safe.** A soldier in Christ who is gripped by fear cannot move forward in battle. Instead of advancing the Kingdom of God, they remain stagnant, hindered by their doubts and insecurities. This results in missed opportunities for ministry, personal growth, and kingdom impact.

4. Fear Leads to Spiritual Paralysis

Matthew 25:25-26 (NIV) – "So I was afraid and went out and hid your talent in the ground. See, here is what belongs to you.' His master replied, 'You wicked, lazy servant! So you knew that I harvest where I have not sown and gather where I have not scattered seed?'"

The parable of the talents shows that fear can lead to spiritual paralysis. The servant who was given one talent buried it out of fear, believing that failure would displease his master. However, it was his lack of faith and action that actually led to his condemnation. Fear causes believers to hide their gifts and abilities, preventing them from being effective for God's kingdom. A spiritually paralyzed believer is one who does not use their God-given talents, time, or opportunities because fear has immobilized them.

5. Fear Contradicts Faith in God's Sovereignty

Isaiah 41:10 (NIV) – "So do not fear, for I am with you; do not be dismayed, for I am your God. I will strengthen you and help you; I will uphold you with my righteous right hand."

Psalm 56:3-4 (NIV) – "When I am afraid, I put my trust in you. In God, whose word I praise, in God I trust and am not afraid. What can mere mortals do to me?"

Fear directly challenges the belief that God is in control and that He will provide and protect. Believers are called to trust in God's sovereignty, knowing that He is always present and in control of every situation. When fear overwhelms, it leads to a lack of faith in God's plan and provision. A soldier of Christ must trust that God is sovereign, even in the midst of trials and battles. Otherwise, fear will cause them to retreat rather than advance in spiritual warfare.

6. God Cannot Use a Coward Soldier

2 Timothy 1:7 – " For God gave us a spirit not of fear but of power and love and self-control".

In spiritual warfare, God calls for soldiers who are courageous, bold, and fully reliant on His strength. A soldier who is fearful or cowardly cannot effectively engage in spiritual battles or fulfill the Great Commission. In the Bible, God often calls out the need for bravery and condemns cowardice, especially when it comes to standing for truth and advancing His kingdom.

7. God Calls for Boldness, Not Fear

Joshua 1:9 (NIV) – "Have I not commanded you? Be strong and courageous. Do not be afraid; do not be discouraged, for the Lord your God will be with you wherever you go."

God consistently commands His people to be strong and courageous. Fear cripples soldiers and makes them ineffective in the battle. Joshua was commanded to lead the Israelites into the Promised Land, and for this, he needed to be bold and confident in God's promises. Similarly, God's soldiers today must be bold in their witness, unafraid to face challenges because God is with them.

8. Cowardice is a Sin That Displeases God

Revelation 21:8 (ESV) – "But as for the cowardly, the faithless, the detestable, as for murderers, the sexually immoral, sorcerers, idolaters, and all liars, their portion will be in the lake that burns with fire and sulfur, which is the second death."

This verse is significant because it shows that cowardice is listed alongside severe sins like murder, idolatry, and immorality. God cannot use a soldier who shrinks back in fear, and He condemns cowardice as a serious spiritual issue. The implication here is that cowardice comes from a lack of faith in God's power and sovereignty. If someone consistently chooses fear over faith, they are acting contrary to the life of a true believer.

9. Cowardice in Spiritual Battle Leads to Defeat

Judges 7:3 (NIV) – "Now announce to the army, 'Anyone who trembles with fear may turn back and leave Mount Gilead.' So twenty-two thousand men left, while ten thousand remained."

In the story of Gideon, God separated those who were fearful from those who were courageous. The fearful soldiers were sent home because God could not use them in battle. Fear leads to defeat even before the battle begins. God needs soldiers who trust in Him completely and are willing to engage in the fight, even when the odds seem impossible. Those who allow fear to control them cannot fulfill God's plan.

10. God Requires Trust and Boldness

Proverbs 28:1 (NIV) – "The wicked flee though no one pursues, but the righteous are as bold as a lion."

God's people are called to be bold and courageous. Like lions, the righteous stand firm in the face of danger and adversity, trusting in God's strength. Boldness in faith is a sign of righteousness and a deep trust in God's power and provision. Cowardice, on the other hand, indicates a lack of faith and prevents believers from standing up for truth and righteousness.

Cowards Shall not Enter the Kingdom of Heaven(Revelation 21:8).

Fear paralyzes faith by causing **doubt, disobedience,** and **spiritual paralysis**. A cowardly soldier cannot be effective in the spiritual battle because fear keeps them from acting on God's commands. The Bible makes it clear that cowardice is a sin that prevents someone from entering heaven, as seen in (Revelation 21:8), where the cowardly are condemned along with other grievous sins. God calls for boldness, courage, and unwavering trust in His power and promises. As soldiers of Christ, believers are to face challenges and spiritual battles with confidence, knowing that God is with them and will equip them to overcome every obstacle. Fear may be a natural human emotion, but it must be surrendered to God in order for faith to flourish and for believers to be victorious in their walk with Christ.

Courage's Soldiers who follow Gods Command will live a "Victorious Life"

In the Christian life, followers of Christ are called to live victoriously through faith, obedience, and reliance on God's strength. However, when believers give in to carnal, worldly ways, they can find themselves living defeated lives, spiritually weak, ineffective, and disconnected from the power of God. The Bible provides clear warnings and examples of how adopting carnal, worldly behaviors can lead to defeat. When the Apostle Paul urged believers to not "entangle themselves in civilian affairs" (2 Timothy 2:4), he was speaking metaphorically, using the imagery of a soldier's single-minded, devoted, dedication to duty. Paul wrote, "No one serving as a soldier gets entangled in civilian affairs, but rather tries to please his commanding officer" (2 Timothy 2:4, NIV). In this verse, *he compares the life of a Christian to that of a soldier, emphasizing the importance of focus, dedication, and discipline in serving Christ.* Just as a soldier prioritizes their orders above all else, Paul is encouraging believers to prioritize their relationship with God and their mission for the gospel above the distractions of everyday life.

By "civilian affairs," Paul means anything that distracts or pulls a believer away from their devotion to Christ and His purposes. This isn't to say that daily responsibilities, relationships, or work are unimportant; rather, he is urging Christians to be vigilant not to allow worldly concerns, personal ambitions, or temporal distractions to outweigh their ultimate commitment to God. A soldier's life requires sacrifices, and similarly, the life of a disciple may mean setting aside pursuits that do not align with or even hinder one's spiritual calling.

In essence, Paul's counsel is to avoid becoming so absorbed by worldly concerns that they compromise one's commitment to Christ. Just as a soldier answers to a commanding officer, Christians are called to live with a mindset that seeks to please God, staying focused on the greater spiritual battle rather than becoming sidetracked by temporary distractions. Persevering through hardships as a good soldier of Christ comes with profound rewards, both now and in eternity, which make the journey worth every sacrifice. The Bible speaks directly to these promises, underscoring why enduring trials has lasting significance.

Firstly, perseverance shapes our character and deepens our relationship with God. When we endure hardship, it refines us, teaches us patience, and develops resilience, shaping us into the image of Christ. James 1:2-4 explains this beautifully; "*Consider it pure joy, my brothers and sisters, whenever you face trials of many kinds, because you know that the testing of your faith produces perseverance. Let perseverance finish its work so that you may be mature and complete, not lacking anything.*" Here, James reveals that enduring hardships isn't just about survival; it's about growth. Each trial and struggle shapes us into stronger, more faithful believers who rely deeply on God. Moreover, heavenly rewards await those who persevere. Scripture promises crowns, such as the Crown of Life, for those who endure trials for their faith (James 1:12, Revelation 2:10). These crowns signify honor, victory, and eternal life, gifts beyond earthly comparison, given by God as a reward for our steadfast love and faithfulness. Jesus, in (Matthew 5:11-12), even reminds believers to "*rejoice and be glad, because great is your reward in heaven*" when they face persecution. In His Kingdom, our faithfulness will be rewarded with eternal joy, honor, and the satisfaction of having run the race well.

Another key reason to persevere is the powerful witness it provides to others. When we stand firm, our faith shines as a testimony to those around us. Our endurance may inspire someone else to turn to Christ or give strength to another believer facing hardship. As Paul says in Philippians 1:12-14, his imprisonment advanced the gospel because it encouraged others to speak boldly for Christ. Our perseverance can be a light to others, showing the world the strength and beauty of a life surrendered to God.

Finally, persevering keeps our eyes fixed on our eternal hope. In (2 Corinthians 4:17-18), Paul tells us, *"For our light and momentary troubles are achieving for us an eternal glory that far outweighs them all. So we fix our eyes not on what is seen, but on what is unseen, since what is seen is temporary, but what is unseen is eternal."* These words remind us that, though the journey is difficult, the glory of eternity with God will make every hardship worth it. To persevere means to keep our eyes on the prize; an eternity with Christ, free from pain, sorrow, or suffering. Consequently, suffering can deepen believers' connection with Christ. In times of hardship, Christians find comfort in knowing that Jesus fully understands their pain. (1 Peter 4:12-13 NIV) says, *"Dear friends, do not be surprised at the fiery ordeal that has come on you to test you, as though something strange were happening to you. But rejoice inasmuch as you participate in the sufferings of Christ, so that you may be overjoyed when his glory is revealed."* This passage encourages believers to embrace suffering, seeing it not only as a shared experience with Christ but as preparation for the glory to come.

Therefore, persevering to the end is worth it because of the transformation it brings, the heavenly reward it promises, the witness it provides, and the eternal hope that awaits. <u>The hardships of this life are temporary, but the rewards of steadfast faith are eternal. For a soldier of Christ, persevering to the end is not merely about enduring; it's about keeping faith alive, fighting the good fight, and looking forward to the day we stand before God, hearing those words: "Well done, good and faithful servant."</u>

" I have fought the good fight, I have finished the race, I have kept the faith. Finally, there is laid up for me the crown of righteousness, which the Lord, the righteous Judge, will give to me on that Day, and not to me only but also to all who have loved His appearing". **2 Timothy 4:7-8**

Notable Prisoners from the Bible

Their stories and why they were imprisoned

Genesis 39–41	**Joseph**	Imprisoned in Egypt after being falsely accused by Potiphar's wife of attempted assault.
Judges 16.	**Samson**	Captured by the Philistines after being betrayed by Delilah; they blinded him and put him in prison.
Jeremiah 37–38	**Daniel**	Although not in prison per se, Daniel was thrown into a lion's den as punishment for praying to God, defying King Darius' decree.
14:3-12, Mark 6:17-29.	**John the Baptist**	Imprisoned by King Herod for publicly condemning Herod's marriage to Herodias, his brother's wife. Later beheaded in prison.
Acts 4, Acts 5.	**Peter and John**	Imprisoned multiple times for preaching about Jesus and performing miracles in His name.
Acts 16:16-40.	**Apostle Paul and Silas**	Imprisoned in Philippi for casting a demon out of a slave girl, which disrupted local commerce. Miraculously freed after an earthquake.
(1 Kings 22:26-27)	**Micaiah**	Imprisoned by King Ahab for prophesying defeat in battle Micaiah's faithfulness to God's word highlighted the cost of
Daniel 3	**Shadrach, Meshach, & Abednego**	Like Daniel, they weren't in a traditional prison but were thrown into a fiery furnace for refusing to worship King Nebuchadnezzar's golden image.
Matthew 27:15-26, Mark 15:6-15	**Barabbas (Evil Soldier)**	A criminal and insurrectionist imprisoned by the Romans; he was released instead of Jesus when the people were given a choice.
(Revelation 1:9)	**John**	Exiled to the island of Patmos, essentially a prison, where he received the book of Revelation. His isolation became the backdrop for the powerful vision of Christ's ultimate victory
(Joshua 7)	**Joshua**	He led the Israelites into the Promised Land after Moses along with the battle of Jericho
Matthew 26:47-68, John 18.	**Jesus Christ**	Imprisoned briefly after his arrest in the Garden of Gethsemane before his trial and crucifixion.

Behold I'm Coming Quickly

1 Peter 4:12-13 1

CROWNED WITH PURPOSE

ANOINTED FOR GODS PROMISE

The anointed purpose of the believer along with Gods promised crowns to His faithful; speaks to the distinct calling and divine assignment that God gives each of us, alongside the assurance of His promises. Examining how devout men were anointed for their purpose and how that set them apart. Righteous men of God like David, who was anointed as a young shepherd before becoming king, show us that anointing marks both purpose and preparation for Gods divine plan.

Crowning as Symbols of God's Promises: Crowns represent the fulfillment of God's promises, whether in a literal sense for kings and queens or spiritually, as with the crowns in heaven mentioned in both the Old and New Testament.

Linking Purpose to Promise: Examining how purpose isn't just about our earthly assignments but is tied to eternal promises. For example, Paul's writings often speak of running the race and receiving a crown, suggesting that purpose here on earth is directly connected to eternal reward.

Living Out the Anointing Daily: The practical side of being "anointed" in our daily lives, aligning actions with purpose and promises. This could be how we steward what God has given us.

106

What It Means to Be Anointed by God?

Chosen by God: Specifically selected for a divine spiritual purpose or purposes, as seen in God's chosen ones such as **David, Moses,** and the **prophets.** Being chosen implies a personal and intentional selection by God for His divine purposes. Personally selected for a unique kingdom purpose.

> *"You did not choose Me, but I chose you and appointed you that you should go and bear fruit"* **(John 15:16)**.

***David* –** Anointed by Samuel at a young age, David's calling was a divine choice, setting him apart to lead Israel. His journey from shepherd to king represents a divine appointment where God saw his potential despite his humble beginnings.

Being chosen by God means receiving His approval and calling, even before we see it in ourselves. When God chooses, He qualifies the unqualified, ensuring that the chosen person can bear fruit for His kingdom. This choice is transformative, bringing identity, purpose, and often an unexpected path.

Divine Assignment: Anointing is a commissioning by God, where His call places the anointed on a designated, sacred path. This can involve specific roles in leadership, service, or ministry.

> "For we are His workmanship, created in Christ Jesus for good works, which God prepared beforehand that we should walk in them" (Ephesians 2:10).

Moses – Called to deliver Israel from Egypt, Moses was given a daunting mission. Though reluctant due to his speech impediment, God empowered him to fulfill his assignment with signs and wonders.

A divine assignment is an intentional calling from God to fulfill a specific mission. It's not based on personal ability but on God's provision, where He equips and sustains those He calls. Our divine assignments often lead us to rely on God fully, highlighting His power and our role as vessels.

Filled with the Holy Spirit: Empowered by the Holy Spirit to accomplish God's purpose, receiving strength, guidance, and wisdom (as demonstrated when Jesus received the Holy-Spirit at His baptism). This empowerment equips believers with what they need to walk in God's purpose, as seen when Jesus received the Spirit at His baptism. Empowerment from the Holy Spirit grants strength, guidance, and wisdom for fulfilling God's purpose, exemplified in Jesus' baptism.

1. **Scriptural Reference**: *"But you shall receive power when the Holy Spirit has come upon you; and you shall be witnesses to Me" (Acts 1:8).*
   Biblical Example: *Jesus at His Baptism* – The Holy Spirit descended upon Jesus, marking the beginning of His ministry with divine power and wisdom. It signified His anointing as the Messiah.
2. **Elaboration**: Being filled with the Holy Spirit is foundational to being anointed. This filling brings spiritual empowerment, discernment, and the ability to live out God's will with conviction. It transforms ordinary abilities into spiritual capacities, making one effective and fruitful in their calling.

Empowered to Lead: Anointing often involves leadership in God's kingdom, enabling one to lead with humility and divine strength, guiding others according to God's will. Those anointed by God are given divine strength and authority to lead. In the Kingdom of God, this leadership often involves humility, guidance, and support for others, with Christ as the ultimate example.

"The Spirit of the Lord shall rest upon Him, the Spirit of wisdom and understanding, the Spirit of counsel and might" (Isaiah 11:2).

Solomon – When Solomon asked for wisdom to govern Israel, God granted him unmatched wisdom and understanding. His leadership became a testament to God's anointing.

Leadership in God's kingdom is a call to serve with wisdom and integrity. God's anointing empowers leaders with abilities beyond their natural capacities, enabling them to guide others according to His ways. Such leaders model humility and reliance on God.

Set Apart for Service: Dedicated to God, living apart from worldly pursuits to fulfill His purpose. Being anointed means living a life dedicated to God's purpose, separated from worldly pursuits. This separation reflects holiness and commitment to God's will.

"You shall be holy, for I am holy" (1 Peter 1:16).

The Levites – Anointed and consecrated to serve in the tabernacle, the Levites were set apart for worship and sacrifice, representing a life wholly devoted to God.

To be set apart is to live a life dedicated to God's will, distinct from worldly pursuits. This separation brings holiness and purity, positioning the anointed as a vessel for God's purposes. It's a lifestyle that reflects

Spiritual Influence in Kingdom Ministry: Those who are anointed often experience the favor of God in their ministry, leading to visible results and impact.

"And the Lord was with him; he was successful in whatever he undertook" *(Genesis 39:2-3).*

Joseph – Despite hardships, Joseph's success in Egypt displayed God's favor upon him, bringing prosperity even in captivity.

Success in ministry often accompanies the anointed, not necessarily in worldly terms but in spiritual fruitfulness and God's blessing. Anointed success is marked by God's provision and His endorsement.

Supernatural Insight: With anointing comes spiritual discernment and wisdom, enabling believers to see beyond the natural and understand the deeper workings of God. Gifts like discernment and wisdom that empower the anointed to see beyond the natural.

> *"He reveals deep and hidden things; He knows what lies in darkness, and light dwells with Him" (Daniel 2:22).*

Daniel – Gifted with interpretation, Daniel had supernatural insight, revealing dreams and prophecies by God's power.

Supernatural insight allows the anointed to understand God's mysteries and discern His will. It serves as a guide in decision-making and often confirms God's purposes, enabling the individual to serve effectively.

Life Marked by God's Favor: Those anointed by God are often recognized by others for having a unique grace and favor over their lives. A distinguishing grace over their life, often evident and undeniable to others.

> *"Surely, Lord, you bless the righteous; you surround them with your favor as with a shield" (Psalm 5:12).*

Esther – Favored by the king, Esther's life reflects how God's favor places anointed individuals in positions of influence.

God's favor acts as a shield, protecting and advancing His anointed ones. It opens doors and provides opportunities to fulfill His purposes, often bringing recognition and respect from others.

Spiritual Gifts: Equip the anointed to fulfill their calling with divine ability, often enhancing ministry and impacting lives. These gifts are signs of God's active presence and grace. God grants unique abilities and gifts through the Holy Spirit, enabling the anointed to carry out their mission with divine aid. Unique spiritual abilities granted by the Holy Spirit that are used for God's purposes.

"There are different kinds of gifts, but the same Spirit distributes them" (1 Corinthians 12:4).

The Early Church of Pentecost – Believers were filled with various gifts of the Spirit, which strengthened the Church and demonstrated God's power.

Spiritual gifts are bestowed upon the anointed to empower them uniquely for their calling, ensuring they can serve, teach, encourage, and edify others with divine precision and strength. These gifts, distributed by the Holy Spirit, reveal God's grace in action, as seen in the Early Church, where believers utilized diverse gifts to build up the body of Christ and make His presence known. As (1 Corinthians 12:4) highlights, though the gifts vary, they all originate from the same Spirit.

Intimacy with God: Anointing fosters a closer, more personal relationship with God, where the individual experiences regular encounters and guidance from Him. A closer, more personal relationship with God, marked by frequent encounters with His presence.

"Draw near to God, and He will draw near to you" (James 4:8).

Moses – Known for his close relationship with God, Moses spoke to Him "face to face," representing profound intimacy.

Anointing brings believers into a deeper relationship with God, where they experience His presence, hear His voice, and feel His guidance. This intimacy is a source of strength, peace, and spiritual depth.

Relationship with God:

"Draw near to God, and He will draw near to you" (James 4:8).

A relationship with God is foundational for the anointed, as it fuels their faith, aligns their purpose with His, and cultivates intimacy through trust and obedience. This relationship, as

(James4:8) emphasizes, grows deeper as one earnestly seeks God, drawing near to Him through prayer, study, and worship. Moses exemplifies this closeness; his "face-to-face" encounters with God not only empowered his leadership but also revealed God's will to the people, illustrating how intimacy with God can profoundly impact and guide one's mission.

The 4 Principles of Gods Anointed

1. *Chosen by God:* The idea of divine selection, as seen in Men of God like David or the prophets, where God singles out individuals with a specific calling.
2. *Divine Assignment:* Anointing as a form of commissioning, where being anointed sets someone on a path unique to God's plans for them.
3. *Filled with the Holy Spirit:* Supernatural empowerment that strengthens the believer to fulfill their mission (like Jesus receiving the Holy Spirit at His baptism).
4. *Empowered to Lead:* Leadership in God's kingdom often means serving with humility and strength derived from anointing, much like the kings and prophets of the Bible.

Anointing fosters a close relationship with God, where believers experience His presence, hear His voice, and receive His guidance. This relationship is marked by trust, communication, and a deep spiritual connection that sustains and empowers the anointed for their calling.

Privileges of the Anointing

➢ **Success in Ministry and Supernatural Insight**: Anointing often comes with unique abilities, like discernment or spiritual insight, which support one's divine mission.
➢ **Favor and Spiritual Gifts**: These help fulfill the believer's calling and foster intimacy with God, creating a life distinguished by God's favor and closeness.

➤ **Jesus as the Promised Anointed One**: Reflecting on Jesus' anointing at His baptism and subsequent acts in His ministry offers a perfect example. He was anointed to fulfill His destiny as Savior, and His life exemplifies each characteristic of divine anointing.

Differentiating God's Promises from God's Covenants

Promises: God's promises are assurances that reflect His faithfulness and love for His people. These are often unconditional gifts, like offering peace, protection, or provision. For example, God promises to be with His people or to provide for their needs. Promises are a way God shows His consistent care and presence in the lives of His people, reminding them of His enduring commitment to bless and sustain them.

Covenants: On the other hand, are solemn, binding agreements, (which if broken may carry deadly consequences) that establish a formal relationship between God and His people. They carry both blessings for obedience and serious consequences for disobedience. Famous covenants, like those made with **Abraham**, **Moses**, and **David**, often include specific commitments or conditions. For instance, the covenant with Israel required obedience to God's laws to maintain His protection and blessing. Covenants, therefore, emphasize mutual responsibilities and reflect a deeper partnership, where God and His people agree to live in certain ways to uphold their bond.

While promises are God's generous gifts given out of love, covenants are structured relational commitments that shape how God and His people interact. This difference shows how God's relationship with His people includes both unwavering care and a call to faithful partnership. Every person's life holds inherent purpose within God's all-encompassing plan, regardless of their faith. God can use anyone, believer or nonbeliever, to fulfill His purposes, showcasing the significance of each individual in His grand design. God's purposes are extended to everyone, even those outside the faith, showcasing that all lives are inter-woven into His broader plan and bigger picture. Each person, whether they acknowledge it or not, can serve a role in God's Omnipotent narrative.

God's Will vs. Human Free Will

This could cover the tension between divine sovereignty and our own choices, emphasizing that while we're free to make our own decisions, true fulfillment comes when we align our will with God's. Free-will refers to the choice that every individual is their own "free-moral-agent", empowered to make their own personal choices pertaining to the faith direction they choose to go. At the end all will be held responsible for those choices, reflecting the God-given capacity to discern, choose, and act independently, free of coercion on God's behalf. Inevitably he honors your individual freedom to choose. This could include righteous men like Jonah, who initially resisted God's will but ultimately found purpose in surrendering to it.

Jesus as the Perfect Prototype of the Anointing

> **Anointed at His Baptism**: At Jesus' baptism, the Holy Spirit descended on Him, preparing Him for His public ministry (Luke 3:22).
> **Anointed with Ointment**: On three occasions, Jesus was anointed with fragrant ointment, symbolizing His role as Savior and His preparation for His sacrificial death.

Other Signs and Privileges of Being Anointed

Peace in the Midst of Trials: *"And the peace of God, which transcends all understanding, will guard your hearts and your minds in Christ Jesus"* (*Philippians 4:7*). *Paul and Silas* – When imprisoned, they sang hymns and praised God, demonstrating profound peace even in difficult circumstances.

> *Anointed individuals often experience supernatural peace, especially in times of trouble. This peace isn't based on circumstances but on God's presence, guarding their hearts and minds and sustaining them through hardships.*

Divine Protection: *"The angel of the Lord encamps around those who fear Him, and He delivers them"* (Psalm 34:7). Daniel in the Lion's Den – God protected Daniel by shutting the mouths of lions, showing divine protection over His anointed.

> *Those anointed by God are often shielded from harm in ways that reveal God's active protection. This doesn't mean they are immune to challenges, but God's hand of protection is evident, preserving them for His purposes.*

Increased Discernment *"For the Lord gives wisdom; from His mouth come knowledge and understanding"* (Proverbs 2:6).

> *Solomon* – Known for his exceptional discernment, Solomon could judge rightly and make wise decisions. *Anointing brings heightened spiritual discernment, allowing believers to recognize truth, avoid deception, and make decisions aligned with God's will. It's a valuable gift that helps in navigating complex situations with wisdom.*

Authority Over Spiritual Forces: *"I have given you authority to trample on snakes and scorpions and to overcome all the power of the enemy"* (Luke 10:19).

> *The Apostles* – When Jesus sent out the disciples, they exercised authority over demons and healed the sick, demonstrating spiritual authority. *Anointed believers often carry a sense of spiritual authority, empowered by God to confront and overcome spiritual darkness. This authority brings victory over the forces of evil and is a testament to God's power working through His people.*

Faith that Moves Mountains: *"If you have faith as small as a mustard seed, you can say to this mountain, 'Move from here to there,' and it will move"* *(Matthew 17:20).*

> ➤ ***Elijah*** – His prayers influenced nature, from withholding rain to calling down fire from heaven. *Anointed individuals are often marked by extraordinary faith, enabling them to trust God for the impossible. This faith encourages others and builds the community of believers, inspiring confidence in God's promises.*

Joy in Service: *"The joy of the Lord is your strength"* *(Nehemiah 8:10).*

> ➤ ***The Apostles*** – Even when persecuted, the apostles rejoiced for being considered worthy of suffering for Christ (Acts 5:41). *Anointed people experience a profound joy that empowers them in their service. This joy transcends external circumstances, arising from a deep connection with God and the fulfillment found in fulfilling His purposes.*

Fruitfulness in Impact: *"You did not choose Me, but I chose you and appointed you that you should go and bear fruit"* *(John 15:16).* The Early Church – Filled with the Holy Spirit, the apostles spread the gospel, leading to rapid church growth and spiritual fruitfulness.

> ➤ *Anointed individuals often see fruitful outcomes from their ministry and work, where God uses their efforts to multiply blessings and positively impact others. Their lives become a channel for God's grace, bringing transformation to those around them.*

Resilience and Perseverance *"But the one who stands firm to the end will be saved"* *(Matthew 24:13).*

> ➤ ***Job*** – Despite intense trials, Job's faith and resilience remained, ultimately leading to restoration. *Anointing gives believers the strength to persevere, even in the face of adversity. This resilience enables them to fulfill God's purpose, holding firm in faith and trust regardless of the circumstances.*

116

Favor in Unlikely Places: *"And Jesus increased in wisdom and stature, and in favor with God and man" (Luke 2:52). Joseph* – Despite being in a foreign land and facing hardship, Joseph found favor in the eyes of Pharaoh and was elevated to a position of authority.

> ➤ *Anointed individuals often find favor even in unexpected or challenging environments. This favor can open doors to opportunities that seem beyond reach, allowing them to fulfill their purpose effectively.*

Boldness in Witness: *"Now, Lord, consider their threats and enable your servants to speak your word with great boldness" (Acts 4:29).*

Peter and John – After Pentecost, they boldly proclaimed Jesus, despite opposition and threats.

> ➤ *Anointed people are bold in their witnessing because they rely on God's strength, not their own, to speak truth without fear, even in the face of opposition. With the Spirit's empowerment, they are compelled to proclaim the gospel courageously, trusting that God will guide their words and actions. Like the early disciples in (Acts 4:29), they pray for boldness and are unafraid to confront challenges, knowing that their message carries divine authority and purpose.*

Every life has purpose

Every God given life has purpose, regardless of faith, is an insightful biblical concept that speaks to God's sovereign design and the significance of each individual within His plan. Scripture reveals that God's purposes are not limited to believers alone; He often uses both believers and nonbelievers to achieve His will. This understanding reflects the vastness of God's wisdom and His control over all creation. Here's an in-depth look at how this purpose manifests for every individual.

God's Sovereignty Over All Creation: *"The Lord has made everything for its purpose, even the wicked for the day of trouble" (Proverbs 16:4).*

This verse underscores that God has created everything with a purpose. It shows that even those who do not walk with Him can still serve a role in His divine plan. God's purpose is not hindered by disbelief or opposition; rather, His sovereignty ensures that even those outside the faith can contribute to His overall design. This extends to world events, historical shifts, and individual lives, revealing God's power to use all things, even rebellion, to fulfill His purposes.

Examples of Nonbelievers Used by God

Pharaoh in Egypt: *"But for this purpose, I have raised you up, to show you my power, so that my name may be proclaimed in all the earth" (Exodus 9:16).*

Pharaoh, despite his hardened heart and resistance to God's commands, was still used by God to demonstrate His power and deliver Israel from bondage. Pharaoh's resistance only highlighted God's authority and magnified His sovereignty. This story illustrates that even opposition to God can be instrumental in His purposes, ultimately revealing His character to the world.

Cyrus, King of Persia: *"Thus says the Lord to His anointed, to Cyrus, whose right hand I have grasped, to subdue nations before him and to loose the belts of kings… For the sake of my servant Jacob, and Israel my chosen, I call you by your name, I name you, though you do not know me" (Isaiah 45:1, 4).*

Cyrus was a pagan king who did not know Yahweh, yet he was called God's "anointed" and chosen to free the Israelites from Babylonian captivity. Through Cyrus, God orchestrated the return of His people to their land and the rebuilding of the temple. This example demonstrates that God can anoint and assign purpose to nonbelievers to accomplish His redemptive work, showing His

absolute control over history and the lives of those who don't yet recognize Him.

Nebuchadnezzar of Babylon: *"Now I, Nebuchadnezzar, praise and exalt and glorify the King of heaven, because everything he does is right and all his ways are just. And those who walk in pride he is able to humble"* (Daniel 4:37).

Although initially prideful and dismissive of God, Nebuchadnezzar ultimately acknowledged God's sovereignty after a period of humility. His story shows how God used a powerful, prideful king as an example of His authority over all rulers. Nebuchadnezzar's life demonstrates that God can transform even the heart of a nonbeliever to serve as a witness to His greatness, illustrating that no one is beyond His reach or outside His purpose.

The Purpose of Nations and Rulers *"The king's heart is a stream of water in the hand of the Lord; He turns it wherever He will"* (Proverbs 21:1).

This verse reveals that God directs the actions of rulers and nations according to His will, often using them to fulfill His sovereign purposes, whether they acknowledge Him or not. Throughout the Bible, God raises and removes leaders, orchestrates nations' destinies, and influences world events, all for the fulfillment of His divine plan. This reinforces that every life and role has purpose, woven into God's greater story.

The Purpose of Individuals, Both Believers and Nonbelievers *"In him we were also chosen, having been predestined according to the plan of him who works out everything in conformity with the purpose of his will"* (Ephesians 1:11).

God's plan includes "everything"—from the life of each believer to the actions of nonbelievers. This truth shows that God's purpose is comprehensive, not limited by human acknowledgment or belief. Nonbelievers, knowingly or unknowingly, contribute to the unfolding of God's will, whether as instruments in others' spiritual journeys or through their influence on circumstances that lead to the fulfillment of His promises.

Joseph's Brothers as Unwitting Instruments of God's Purpose *"As for you, you meant evil against me, but God meant it for good, to bring it about that many people should be kept alive, as they are today" (Genesis 50:20).*

Joseph's brothers acted out of jealousy, intending to harm him. However, their actions were part of God's plan to place Joseph in Egypt, where he would save many lives during a famine. This example shows that God can use even the misguided actions of nonbelievers to bring about His good purposes, demonstrating that His will prevails even when others mean harm.

All Creation Is for God's Glory *"For from Him and through Him and to Him are all things. To Him be glory forever. Amen" (Romans 11:36).*

Every person, every event, and every life ultimately serves the purpose of glorifying God. Whether or not people recognize or acknowledge Him, all creation points to His majesty and authority. This verse emphasizes that all things exist by and for God, reinforcing that each life, regardless of belief, has an intrinsic role in reflecting His glory.

God's Desire for All to Come to Him and receive Salvation *"The Lord is not slow in keeping His promise, as some understand slowness. Instead, He is patient with you, not wanting anyone to perish, but everyone to come to repentance" (2 Peter 3:9).*

God's purpose extends to a desire for all people to come to repentance and relationship with Him. Even as He uses nonbelievers in His plan, He desires their transformation and salvation. This verse reveals that God's purpose is both sovereign

and redemptive, He works through everyone, yet He also calls each individual into a personal relationship with Him, hoping they will turn to Him.

Purpose in Believers' Influence on Nonbelievers *"You are the salt of the earth... You are the light of the world. A city set on a hill cannot be hidden" (Matthew 5:13-14).*

Nonbelievers' presence often strengthens believers by challenging them to live out their faith with boldness, as "salt and light" in a world that may not recognize God. Through interactions with nonbelievers, believers grow in compassion, resilience, and conviction. The presence of nonbelievers gives believers opportunities to witness, demonstrate God's love, and shine His light. This dynamic serves a dual purpose, edifying the believer while also pointing nonbelievers toward Christ.

The Bible provides ample evidence that God's purpose encompasses every life, regardless of faith. Each individual, knowingly or unknowingly, plays a role in His divine plan. From rulers to ordinary people, God's sovereignty uses everyone to fulfill His will, whether through orchestrating historical events, challenging believers to deepen their faith, or showcasing His power through those who oppose Him. God's desire, ultimately, is for all to come to know Him; however, even those who resist can still be instruments in His greater story. This understanding of universal purpose not only underscores God's control over all creation but also encourages believers to trust in His wisdom and redemptive power, even in the most unlikely places and people.

Anointed Ones are not our own

According to Scripture, our lives ultimately belong to God. The Bible teaches that we are created by Him, sustained by His provision, and redeemed through the sacrifice of Jesus Christ. This idea is powerfully captured in *1 Corinthians 6:19-20*, which states; "Do you not know that your bodies are temples of the Holy Spirit, who is in you, whom you have received from God? You are not your own; you were bought at a price. Therefore, honor God with your bodies." *1 Corinthians 6:19-20*

The Christian's identity and calling. Let's break it down.

"Your Bodies are Temples of the Holy Spirit":
This phrase emphasizes that, as believers, our bodies are sacred because God's Spirit dwells within us. Just as the ancient temple was set apart for worship and the presence of God, so are our bodies. This changes how we view ourselves; we are more than physical beings; we are sanctuaries for God's Spirit.

"You Are Not Your Own"
Here, Paul declares that our lives, including our bodies and spirits, are not solely under our control or possession. This truth challenges the common idea of personal ownership over one's life, affirming that Christians are accountable to God, not to their own desires or ambitions.

"You Were Bought at a Price"
This phrase refers to the redemptive sacrifice of Jesus on the cross. The "price" paid for believers was the life and blood of Christ, who gave Himself to redeem humanity from sin and death. The concept of being "purchased" denotes both a transfer of ownership and an incredible act of love and value. It signifies that God saw such worth in humanity that He was willing to pay the ultimate price, His own Son.

"Therefore Honor God with Your Bodies":

The concluding command calls believers to respond by honoring God with their lives. This means living in a way that reflects the holiness and purpose given by God, acknowledging His ownership and our role as stewards of the life He has entrusted to us.

Other Supporting Scriptures

Life was created by God, belongs to God and is to be utilized by His Solem purpose. He has full authority over our lives ultimately, he is in control.

Romans 14:8: *"If we live, we live for the Lord; and if we die, we die for the Lord. So, whether we live or die, we belong to the Lord."*

This verse underscores that every moment of a believer's life, whether in life or death, is dedicated to the Lord. Our identity and purpose are found in Him, and we are His, regardless of circumstances.

Galatians 2:20: *"I have been crucified with Christ and I no longer live, but Christ lives in me. The life I now live in the body, I live by faith in the Son of God, who loved me and gave Himself for me."*

Paul speaks here of the transformative identity believers receive in Christ. By faith, believers no longer live for themselves; rather, they live through Christ, whose sacrifice gives new life and purpose.

Psalm 100:3: *"Know that the Lord is God. It is He who made us, and we are His; we are His people, the sheep of His pasture."*

This verse reminds us of our Creator's authority over our lives. God not only created us but also cares for and guides us, like a shepherd with his flock. It reinforces that our lives are not our own but belong to the One who made us.

The truth that our lives belong to God carries rich significance in the Christian faith. We belong to God because we have been redeemed through Christ's sacrifice. When we receive Jesus as our Savior, our identity is redefined, **we are no longer our own but are adopted as children of God and co-heirs with Christ**. This relationship with Him transforms how we see ourselves and our place in His kingdom. Acknowledging that our lives belong to God influences every aspect of how we live. As His stewards, we are entrusted with our time, talents, and resources, calling us to use them faithfully to glorify Him. This awareness gives our lives purpose beyond our own desires, driving us to live in alignment with God's will. Recognizing that we are God's own chosen vessels, leads us to live with an eternal perspective, understanding that our earthly journey is preparation for eternal communion with Him. Our relationship with God is everlasting, and our lives here serve as a foundation for this eternal connection. Scripture teaches that our lives belong to God both by creation and redemption. In 1 Corinthians 6:19-20, Paul reminds us that we were "bought at a price" through Jesus' sacrifice, calling believers to honor God in every part of life. This knowledge reshapes our identity and purpose, as we live not for ourselves but as beloved children who reflect God's love, holiness, and purpose, honoring the One who gave everything for us.

Spiritual gifts are Special Abilities given by the Holy Spirit

Spiritual gifts are special abilities granted by the Holy Spirit to believers to build up the Church and advance God's kingdom, they cannot be bought, taught or accessed on consignment. Each gift is a unique expression of God's grace, intended to empower believers for ministry, strengthen the Church, and reveal God's power and presence. The New Testament provides lists and descriptions of these gifts, emphasizing their purpose in uniting the Church, fostering maturity, and glorifying God. Here's a deeper look into

what Scripture teaches about spiritual gifts, based on passages like *1 Peter 4:10-11, Romans 12:6-8, 1 Corinthians 12:7,* and *Ephesians 4:11-16.*

Spiritual Gifts as Expressions of God's Grace

"Each of you should use whatever gift you have received to serve others, as faithful stewards of God's grace in its various forms" (1 Peter 4:10).

Spiritual gifts are given as expressions of God's grace, and each believer has a role in stewarding these gifts responsibly. The gifts are diverse, reflecting God's manifold grace, and are meant to serve others within the body of Christ. Using these gifts is not for personal gain, profit or status but for serving others in love and humility. When believers use their gifts faithfully, they become channels through which God's grace flows to meet the Church's needs and fulfill His purposes.

Variety of Gifts and Their Functions *"We have different gifts, according to the grace given to each of us. If your gift is prophesying, then prophesy in accordance with your faith; if it is serving, then serve; if it is teaching, then teach; if it is to encourage, then give encouragement; if it is giving, then give generously; if it is to lead, do it diligently; if it is to show mercy, do it cheerfully." Romans 12:6-8:*

This passage lists several gifts, including **prophecy, serving, teaching, encouraging, giving, leading**, and **showing mercy**. Each gift corresponds to a specific function in the Church, highlighting that the body of Christ has many needs, met through the unique contributions of each member. When these gifts are exercised with love, humility, compassion and a spirit of excellence, they create a healthy and effective Church. This variety ensures that every need is met, from practical service to teaching, from leadership to compassion.

Manifestation of the Holy Spirit for the Common Good of Gods Kingdom *"Now to each one the manifestation of the Spirit is given for the common good" (1 Corinthians 12:7).*

Spiritual gifts are manifestations of the Holy Spirit, visible expressions of God's presence within the Ministry, Church and Fulfilling the Great Commission. Each gift is given not for individual gain but for the common good of the whole community. This means that when believers exercise their gifts, they contribute to the unity, health, and growth of the Church also in Gods kingdom on earth. The "common good" reminds believers that their gifts are meant to serve, encourage, and edify others, reflecting God's love and unity in the body of Christ.

Purpose of Gifts in Building Up the Church *"So Christ himself gave the apostles, the prophets, the evangelists, the pastors and teachers, to equip his people for works of service, so that the body of Christ may be built up until we all reach unity in the faith and in the knowledge of the Son of God and become mature, attaining to the whole measure of the fullness of Christ Ephesians 4:11-13."*

Paul identifies specific roles apostles, prophets, evangelists, pastors, and teachers are given to equip the Church for ministry. These gifts are vital for equipping believers, helping them grow in faith, knowledge, and unity. The purpose of these gifts is not only to spread the gospel but also to foster spiritual maturity within the Church. As believers grow in unity and maturity, they collectively reflect Christ more fully, becoming a powerful witness to the world of His love and grace.

Unity and Maturity in the Body of Christ *"Then we will no longer be infants, tossed back and forth by the waves, and blown here and there by every wind of teaching and by the cunning and craftiness of people in their deceitful scheming. Instead, speaking the truth in love, we will grow to become in every respect the mature body of him who is the head, that is, Christ Ephesians 4:14-16."*

The kingdom-use of spiritual gifts strengthens believers, making them resilient and grounded in truth. Through the use of gifts, the Kingdom of God grows in unity and maturity, enabling believers to discern truth from deception and to live out their faith with stability and conviction. This maturity is essential for the Church to function effectively, fulfilling God's purposes and resisting worldly influences. The result is a unified body that reflects Christ's character and reveals His truth to the world.

Glorifying God through Spiritual Gifts

"If anyone speaks, they should do so as one who speaks the very words of God. If anyone serves, they should do so with the strength God provides, so that in all things God may be praised through Jesus Christ. To him be the glory and the power forever and ever. Amen" (1 Peter 4:11).

Spiritual gifts, when exercised with a heart for God, bring glory to Him. Believers are encouraged to use their gifts with excellence, speaking and serving in ways that reflect God's character. This verse reminds believers that gifts are not only for edification but also for worship; each gift is an opportunity to honor God. When used with humility and faithfulness, spiritual gifts direct the Church's focus to God, as every act of service or teaching is supposed to point back to Yahweh as the source of strength and wisdom. The Bible emphasizes that spiritual gifts are divine enabling's, given to believers as acts of grace by the Holy Spirit. They serve distinct purposes within the Body of Christ, Ministry and Fulfilling the Great Commission.

> ➢ **To equip and edify** believers, helping each member grow in faith and maturity.
> ➢ **To strengthen unity**, fostering harmony as each gift complements the others.
> ➢ **To provide stability and discernment**, enabling the Church to resist false teachings and remain rooted in truth.
> ➢ **To glorify God**, as each gift reflects His power and presence.

These gifts are a testament to God's active involvement in the life of his Kingdom, Church and overall purpose as Sovereign God, demonstrating His power and love to the world. Each believer, by exercising their gift, participates in God's assignment to his chosen and helps manifest His kingdom on earth. This framework for spiritual gifts unites the Church as a body, where every part has purpose and value, each contributing to a larger whole under the leadership of Jesus Christ.

Purpose as promises and preparation for destiny

Here are three anointed men from the Bible **David, Moses,** and **Elisha**, each of whom exemplifies how anointing marked both their purpose and preparation for destiny. Through their lives, we see how God's anointing not only set them apart for a unique purpose but also prepares them for significant roles in His plan.

David

Anointed as King and Prepared Through Humility and Faithfulness *"Then Samuel took the horn of oil and anointed him in the midst of his brothers; and the Spirit of the Lord came upon David from that day forward"* (1 Samuel 16:13).

> **Purpose and Preparation**: David's anointing by the prophet Samuel marked him as the future king of Israel, setting him apart for a royal purpose. However, this purpose did not unfold immediately. David spent years as a shepherd and later served in King Saul's court as a musician and warrior. These roles prepared him for leadership, teaching him humility, courage, and reliance on God.

> **Journey to Destiny**: David's time as a shepherd taught him how to care for and protect his flock, skills that would later translate into leadership over Israel. His battles, especially his victory over Goliath (1 Samuel 17), demonstrated the faith and courage God

instilled in him. David's years of fleeing from King Saul refined his character, teaching him to trust in God's timing and justice.

Fulfillment: David's anointing ultimately led to his destiny as Israel's king, and his reign was marked by faith, worship, and a heart after God. His life demonstrates that anointing often includes seasons of preparation, where God shapes and molds the individual for future responsibilities.

Moses

Anointed as Deliverer and Prepared Through Wilderness Training and Divine Encounters

Scriptural Reference: *"Now go, for I am sending you to Pharaoh. You must lead my people Israel out of Egypt"* (Exodus 3:10).

Purpose and Preparation: Moses' anointing as the deliverer of Israel became evident when God called him at the burning bush. Although Moses was reluctant and felt unqualified, God assured him, saying, "I will be with you" (Exodus 3:12). This marked him as chosen for a divine mission. Moses' early life in Pharaoh's palace gave him insight into Egyptian culture, while his time in Midian as a shepherd prepared him for leading and caring for a large group of people.

Journey to Destiny: After his initial calling, Moses faced intense preparation. He learned humility in Midian, spent years tending sheep, and developed a heart of patience and endurance, qualities essential for leading Israel. Through signs and wonders, God empowered Moses to confront Pharaoh and lead the people out of Egypt, demonstrating God's power over all.

Fulfillment: Moses' anointing led to the deliverance of Israel and the establishment of the Law at Mount Sinai. His journey reveals that God's anointing includes equipping and shaping the individual, often through difficult circumstances, so they can carry out God's purposes with strength and faith.

Elisha

Anointed as Prophet and Prepared Through Service and Devotion

Scriptural Reference: *"So Elijah went from there and found Elisha son of Shaphat. He was plowing with twelve yoke of oxen, and he himself was driving the twelfth pair. Elijah went up to him and threw his cloak around him"* *(1 Kings 19:19)*.

Purpose and Preparation: Elisha's anointing began when Elijah placed his cloak (or mantle) on him, symbolizing the transfer of prophetic authority. This act signaled God's choice of Elisha as Elijah's successor, with a purpose to continue the prophetic ministry in Israel. Elisha left his livelihood to follow and serve Elijah, demonstrating his readiness for the call.

Journey to Destiny: Elisha's preparation came through years of faithful service to Elijah. He observed, learned, and supported the prophet in various tasks, developing humility, perseverance, and a deep understanding of God's work. When Elijah was taken up to heaven, Elisha received a "double portion" of Elijah's anointing (2 Kings 2:9-10), empowering him to carry out his prophetic mission.

Fulfillment: Elisha's ministry was marked by miracles and powerful prophetic acts, showing God's hand on him as a leader and prophet in Israel. His anointing prepared him not only for a life of service but for a ministry that would impact the nation, demonstrating God's power and presence among His people.

These three men, David, Moses, and Elisha illustrate that God's anointing is both a declaration of purpose and a period of preparation. Each was called for a significant role, but God refined them through experiences that shaped their faith, character, and abilities. The anointing on their lives reminds us that God's anointing is not immediate elevation but often a process of growth, where He

prepares individuals for the fullness of their destiny. This process of anointing and preparation ensures they are equipped and ready to fulfill their purpose in God's perfect timing.

Purpose and Preparation For Your Destined Crown.

The representation of crowns in the Bible is rich and complex, representing not only earthly authority, achievement but also the fulfillment of God's promises to His people. Crowns are used in Scripture to signify honor, reward, victory, and the completion of a purpose given by God. They remind believers of the hope of eternal life, the reward for faithful service, and the victory that comes through Christ. Here's a deep dive into the biblical significance of crowns as symbols of God's promises.

The Crown as a Symbol of Authority and Honor *"You have made them a little lower than the angels and crowned them with glory and honor" (Psalm 8:5).*

From the beginning, humanity was given authority over creation and honored with the role of God's representatives on earth. This "crown" of glory and honor speaks to the dignity God bestowed upon people as His image-bearers. Crowns are a mark of the honor and authority granted by God, and this promise is foundational; mankind is created with purpose, dignity, and a unique role in God's design.

Example in Kingship: In the Old Testament, kings were crowned to signify God's appointment and authority. For instance, *David was anointed and crowned as king over Israel,* representing God's promise to establish a lineage and kingdom that would eventually lead to the Messiah (2 Samuel 7:12-13). This crowning is a visible manifestation of God's promise and His faithfulness in raising leaders for His people.

Crowns as Rewards for Faithfulness

Scriptural Reference: *"Blessed is the one who perseveres under trial because, having stood the test, that person will receive the crown of life that the Lord has promised to those who love Him" (James 1:12).*

The "crown of life" is a reward promised to those who endure trials and remain faithful. This crown represents the promise of eternal life and the ultimate reward for a life devoted to God. It serves as a motivation for believers to persevere, knowing that their struggles on earth will be rewarded in eternity.

The Crown of Life in Revelation *Revelation 2:10* reiterates this promise, where Jesus tells the persecuted church in Smyrna, "Be faithful unto death, and I will give you the crown of life." This crown symbolizes not only survival through trials but also victory over spiritual opposition. It's a tangible reminder of the hope of resurrection and the unbreakable promise of eternal life for those who are steadfast in faith.

Crowns of Victory and Triumph in Christ *"Do you not know that in a race all the runners run, but only one gets the prize? Run in such a way as to get the prize… They do it to get a crown that will not last, but we do it to get a crown that will last forever" (1 Corinthians 9:24-25).*

Paul uses the imagery of a victor's crown to encourage believers to pursue their faith with discipline and endurance. In ancient times, athletes were awarded a laurel wreath or crown as a symbol of victory. Similarly, Paul describes the "imperishable crown" given to those who finish the race of faith. This crown is the reward for a life lived with purpose, discipline, and focus on Christ.

Victory through Faith The "crown of righteousness" (2 Timothy 4:8) is another example of a crown signifying victory, this time over sin and worldly influences. Paul declares that this crown awaits "all who have loved His appearing," pointing to the promise of eternal life for those who long for Christ's return. This crown

symbolizes the victory believers share through Christ and the promise of being made righteous and complete at His coming.

The Crown as a Symbol of Eternal Glory *"And when the Chief Shepherd appears, you will receive the crown of glory that will never fade away"* *(1 Peter 5:4).*

Peter encourages the leaders of the Church to shepherd the flock willingly and eagerly, with the promise that they will receive the "crown of glory" from Christ. This crown represents the honor and eternal reward awaiting those who serve faithfully. It also speaks to the eternal nature of God's promises, this crown will "never fade away," signifying that God's promises are everlasting.

Glory through Service This crown-of-glory reminds believers that service to others, done with a humble heart, will be rewarded in God's kingdom. Unlike earthly crowns that fade and lose value, this crown is eternal, symbolizing the honor God bestows on His faithful servants, reflecting His promise to recognize and reward every act of faithfulness.

The Crowns Cast Before God's Throne *"The twenty-four elders fall down before Him who sits on the throne and worship Him who lives forever and ever. They lay their crowns before the throne and say: 'You are worthy, our Lord and God, to receive glory and honor and power'"* *(Revelation 4:10-11).*

In Revelation, the twenty-four elders represent the redeemed, who cast their crowns before God's throne as an act of worship. This gesture of laying down their crowns signifies that all honor, victory, and reward belongs to God alone. It is a powerful symbol of surrender, acknowledging that every gift, every victory, and every reward comes from Him.

Symbol of Submission: By casting their crowns, the elders demonstrate that even the rewards of faithfulness are ultimately for God's glory. This image reminds believers that all crowns' are symbols of victory, honor, and reward are given by God and should be returned to Him in reverence and humility. This action encapsulates the promise of eternal worship and union with God, where the redeemed find their ultimate purpose in glorifying Him forever.

Promise of Future Crowns for Believers *"Now there is in store for me the crown of righteousness, which the Lord, the righteous Judge, will award to me on that day, and not only to me, but also to all who have longed for His appearing"* (2 Timothy 4:8).

Paul's confident expectation of the "crown of righteousness" underscores that crowns in the Bible are not just earthly symbols but divine promises. This crown signifies the completion of the believer's journey toward holiness and is a promise of God's acceptance and approval on the Day of Judgment. It represents the hope of being made fully righteous in Christ, completing the process of sanctification.

Fulfillment of God's Promise: This crown is a personal assurance of eternal reward, highlighting God's promise to every believer who lives in anticipation of His return. It reminds us that the life of faith leads to a future reward that is both personal and eternal, a "crown" that signifies being welcomed and honored by God Himself. *Crowns are profound symbols of God's promises, reflecting various facets of His relationship with believers.*

> ➤ **Authority and Honor**: Crowns signify the honor and authority granted by God to those who follow Him, from kings anointed for leadership to believers who live faithfully, demonstrating a life set apart for His glory.
> ➤ **Reward for Faithfulness**: God promises a "crown of life" to those who endure trials with steadfast faith, symbolizing His reward for perseverance and unwavering commitment.
> ➤ **Victory through Christ**: Crowns embody the victory believers have over sin, death, and worldly challenges

through their faith in Christ, representing triumph in spiritual warfare.

➢ **Eternal Glory and Service**: The "crown of glory" is a promise of everlasting honor, particularly for those who serve sacrificially, reflecting God's appreciation for a life of dedication.

➢ **Act of Worship**: Ultimately, crowns will be cast before God's throne, symbolizing the believer's eternal purpose in glorifying Him, acknowledging His sovereignty over all honor and reward.

Each crown is a tangible representation of God's deeper promises, reminding believers that their faithfulness, perseverance, and service are known and valued by Him. Throughout Scripture, the imagery of crowns provides encouragement and assurance of God's steadfast promises, pointing to a future of eternal life, honor, and worship in His presence. These crowns embody virtues like wisdom, faithfulness, stewardship, perseverance, and authority, inspiring believers to strive for excellence in every area of life, seeking the ultimate crown that is eternal.

21 Crowns that could be achieved!

The 7 Glorious Crowns on Earth

1. Crown of Your Head

➢ **Scripture References:** Genesis 49:26; Deuteronomy 33:16

➢ **Meaning and Relevance:** This crown represents a divine blessing and high honor, often connected to heritage, destiny, and the unique calling God places on an individual's life. Jacob's blessing over Joseph is a profound example of a legacy crown, signifying that God's favor follows and shapes the life paths of His chosen people, passing down blessings from faithful ancestors.

➢ **Significance:** This crown reminds believers that their lives are woven into a generational story of faith, where God's favor flows through their spiritual lineage. Embracing this inheritance, believers are encouraged to honor their God-given identity and purpose, knowing that they stand on a foundation of blessings passed down by faithful forebears.

2. Hoary Head Crown (Gray Hair of Wisdom and Age)

➢ **Scripture References:** Proverbs 16:31
➢ **Meaning and Relevance:** Gray hair is honored as a crown of wisdom and life experience, bestowed on those who have lived in reverence to God. It symbolizes the invaluable insight and spiritual maturity that only comes from a lifelong journey with God, reflecting dignity, wisdom, and earned respect.
➢ **Significance:** This crown calls believers to value spiritual longevity and maturity. As they grow older, they are reminded that each season of life brings wisdom, and they are called to serve as guides and mentors to younger generations, offering hard-won insights that glorify God.

3. Help Mate Crown (A Virtuous Wife as a Crown to Her Husband)

➢ **Scripture References:** Proverbs 12:4; Proverbs 31:10-12
➢ **Meaning and Relevance:** A virtuous wife is described as a crown to her husband, symbolizing the blessings, honor, and strength that a godly spouse brings to the marriage. This crown signifies the godly virtues of loyalty, integrity, and wisdom that enhance and support her husband's calling and, by extension, the well-being of the family.
➢ **Significance:** This crown speaks to the high value of a godly spouse, a source of spiritual and emotional strength. Believers are reminded that God's design for marriage includes partnership in faith, where each spouse's unique qualities contribute to a relationship that reflects God's love and strengthens the family's foundation.

4. Heritage/Ancestry Crown

➢ **Scripture References:** Proverbs 17:6; Psalm 127:3-5

➢ **Meaning and Relevance:** The crown of heritage represents the blessing of family legacy and the honor of raising children who continue the faith. It emphasizes that children and grandchildren are a tangible extension of one's values and commitment to God.

➢ **Significance for Believers:** This crown encourages believers to nurture their children's faith, creating a lasting legacy. They are called to see their offspring as gifts from God, worthy of investment and love, as they prepare the next generation to walk in God's ways and uphold a family legacy centered on Christ.

5. Home Affluence/Stewardship Crown

➢ **Scripture References:** Proverbs 27:24; Proverbs 24:3-4

➢ **Meaning and Relevance:** This crown signifies the peace, stability, and blessing that come from responsible stewardship and wise management of the home. The Bible often portrays the home as a sanctuary where godly principles provide order, harmony, and resourcefulness.

➢ **Significance for Believers:** Believers are encouraged to honor God in their stewardship of their homes, handling finances, family responsibilities, and relationships with diligence and integrity. By doing so, they demonstrate God's provision and make their households a testament to God's grace and faithfulness.

6. Honor Athlete (Incorruptible Crown for Spiritual Victory)

➢ **Scripture References:** 1 Corinthians 9:24-25

➢ **Meaning and Relevance:** Often called the "incorruptible crown," this reward celebrates those who, like dedicated athletes, have run their spiritual race with endurance, self-discipline, and faith. This crown points to the eternal reward waiting for those who overcome worldly distractions and persevere in their faith journey.

➤ **Significance:** This crown calls believers to approach their walk with Christ as a disciplined pursuit, developing perseverance, self-control, and focus on eternal reward. It reminds them that their faithful journey is an ongoing race, with the ultimate victory found in reaching the "finish line" of eternal life with God.

7. Highness, Headship, Authority Crown (Kingly Leadership)

➤ **Scripture References:** 2 Chronicles 23:11

➤ **Meaning and Relevance:** This crown symbolizes the responsibility and authority granted to those appointed by God to lead. Kingship in the Bible represents both privilege and accountability, where leaders are called to serve with justice, humility, and wisdom, reflecting God's rule and guidance.

➤ **Significance:** This crown reminds leaders within the faith to lead righteously and responsibly, serving others in humility and seeking God's wisdom. Believers in positions of influence are called to honor God in their leadership, knowing they are ultimately accountable to Him.

The 7 Crowns of Wickedness

1. Crown of Pride/Foolishness

➤ **Scripture References:** Isaiah 28:1-3; Proverbs 14:24; Proverbs 16:18-19

➤ **Meaning and Relevance:** This crown signifies the danger of pride, a self-centered arrogance that often precedes downfall. Pride elevates human will over God's and blinds

individuals to their need for His guidance, leading to spiritual ruin.

➢ **Significance:** Believers are cautioned to guard against pride, recognizing that humility before God is the path to true honor. This crown warns that unchecked pride not only leads to personal ruin but also disrupts spiritual clarity and separates us from God's favor.

2. Crown of Corruption (Profanity and Lawlessness)

➢ **Scripture References:** 2 Samuel 23:6-7
➢ **Meaning and Relevance:** This crown symbolizes moral and spiritual decay, representing a rejection of God's moral laws. Lawlessness distances individuals from God's protection and disrupts the lives of those around them, ultimately leading to chaos and destruction.
➢ **Significance:** This crown serves as a warning against compromising God's standards for short-term gain or worldly pleasure. Believers are reminded to live by God's commandments, understanding that true freedom and peace are found within His boundaries.

3. Crown of Agony (Crown of Thorns)

➢ **Scripture Reference:** Matthew 27:29
➢ **Meaning and Relevance:** Worn by Jesus during His crucifixion, this crown is a powerful symbol of mockery, suffering, and the price paid for humanity's redemption. It represents the humility and self-sacrifice of Christ, who bore this shame to secure victory over sin.
➢ **Significance:** Reflecting on this crown invites believers to grasp the depth of Christ's love and sacrifice. It serves as a call to live lives of gratitude and humility, knowing the cost of their redemption and the grace extended to them through Jesus' suffering.

4. Crown of Plunder (Greed and Exploitation)

> **Scripture References:** Revelation 6:2; Revelation 9:1
> **Meaning and Relevance:** This crown reflects the greed that drives people to pursue wealth and power at the expense of others. It signifies the empty pursuit of materialism, where selfish ambition causes harm to others and draws individuals away from God.
> **Significance:** Believers are warned about the dangers of prioritizing material wealth over spiritual wealth. This crown encourages them to focus on godly stewardship and integrity, avoiding the emptiness of greed and the exploitation of others.

5. Crown of Perverted Politics (One World Government and Blasphemy)

> **Scripture References:** Revelation 13:1-11; 1 John 4:3
> **Meaning and Relevance:** This crown represents the rise of political powers that reject God's sovereignty, manipulating systems and people for evil purposes. It serves as a warning against leaders and institutions that blaspheme God, often deceiving people with false promises of peace or unity.
> **Significance:** This crown calls believers to be spiritually discerning, aware of systems that operate without regard for God's truth. They are reminded to stay grounded in God's Word, recognizing that worldly authority is temporary and often at odds with God's eternal rule.

6. Crown of Pain and Injury

> **Scripture References:** Daniel 4:33-34; Jonah 1:4-17
> **Meaning and Relevance:** This crown represents the pain and trials that can come as a form of divine correction, leading individuals back to humility and obedience. It is

God's way of using hardship to cultivate growth and dependence on Him.

➤ **Significance:** Believers are encouraged to view pain and challenges as opportunities for spiritual refinement. This crown reminds them that God may allow hardship to shape their character and draw them closer to Him.

7. Crown of Iniquity (The Devil's Crown)

➤ Scripture References: Revelation 12:3-4
➤ Meaning and Relevance: Worn by Satan, this crown signifies rebellion, deception, and the desire to lead humanity away from God. It reflects the ultimate separation from God that comes through sin and resistance to His authority.
➤ Significance: This crown serves as a sobering reminder to resist evil influences and to remain committed to God. Believers are reminded that their steadfast faith is a defense against the forces that seek to separate them from God's love and truth.

The 7 Heavenly Crowns

1. The Incorruptible Crown (Sanctification and Self-Discipline)

➤ **Scripture Reference:** 1 Corinthians 9:24-25
➤ **Meaning and Relevance:** This crown is awarded to those who have practiced self-control and dedicated their lives to godliness. It signifies a life that resists the temptations of the flesh, choosing instead to walk in alignment with God's holiness.
➤ **Significance:** Believers are encouraged to develop spiritual discipline, knowing it leads to an eternal reward. This crown affirms that a life of self-restraint, focused on pleasing God, yields lasting spiritual benefits.

2. The Soldier's Crown (Spiritual Warfare)

➢ **Scripture References:** 2 Timothy 2:3-4; Romans 8:13
➢ **Meaning and Relevance:** Awarded to those who fight spiritual battles and remain committed to Christ despite challenges. This crown symbolizes resilience and faithfulness in the face of opposition, honoring the spiritual warrior who endures to the end.
➢ **Significance:** This crown reminds believers of the need for vigilance and endurance in their spiritual walk. They are called to resist temptation and persevere in faith, understanding that their trials contribute to their ultimate victory in Christ.

3. The Crown of Life (Endurance Through Suffering)

➢ **Scripture References:** James 1:12; Revelation 2:10
➢ **Meaning and Relevance:** This crown is given to those who endure suffering for Christ's sake, reflecting the joy and steadfast love that sustains them through hardship. It symbolizes the reward for unwavering faith in the face of trials.
➢ **Significance:** This crown reassures believers that God sees and honors their endurance. Through suffering, they are drawn closer to Him, trusting that their struggles hold eternal value.

4. The Crown of Glory (Faithful Service in Ministry)

➢ Scripture References: 1 Peter 5:2-4
➢ Meaning and Relevance: Awarded to those who faithfully serve in ministry, this crown honors their dedication to shepherding others. It reflects the unique honor given to those who serve God by leading His people with love and care.
➢ Significance: This crown encourages those in ministry to serve with joy and diligence, knowing their efforts are seen and rewarded by God. It affirms that faithful service is an eternal investment, impacting others and glorifying God.

5. The Crown of Righteousness (Longing for Christ's Return)

> ➤ **Scripture Reference:** 2 Timothy 4:8
> ➤ **Meaning and Relevance:** Awarded to those who eagerly await Christ's return, this crown reflects a life lived in hope and holiness. It symbolizes the deep longing for Jesus and a commitment to purity in preparation for His coming.
> ➤ **Significance for Believers:** This crown encourages believers to live with an eternal perspective, eagerly anticipating Christ's return. Their daily choices reflect their love for Jesus and their desire to be found faithful upon His arrival.

6. The Crown of Rejoicing (Soul-Winner's Crown)

> ➤ **Scripture References:** 1 Thessalonians 2:19
> ➤ **Meaning and Relevance:** Known as the "soul-winner's crown," it is awarded to those who have brought others to Christ. It represents the joy in heaven over each soul saved and reflects the fulfillment of the Great Commission.
> ➤ **Significance:** This crown motivates believers to share their faith, recognizing the eternal significance of evangelism. Every soul led to Christ adds to this crown, symbolizing the joy of participating in God's redemptive work.

7. The Martyr's Crown (Sacrifice for Faith)

> ➤ **Scripture References:** Revelation 2:10
> ➤ **Meaning and Relevance:** Given to those who sacrifice their lives for the sake of the gospel, this crown honors the ultimate act of faithfulness. It reflects the courage and devotion of those who choose Christ, even at the cost of their lives.
> ➤ **Significance:** This crown inspires believers to hold fast to their faith, even under persecution. It is a profound reminder of the strength and reward found in a life wholly dedicated to Christ, honoring those who choose loyalty to Him above all else

In the Christian faith, crowns symbolize the divine rewards granted by God to those who live with unwavering faith, obedience, and perseverance. These crowns are not earned through human effort or merit but are gifts of grace, bestowed upon those whose lives reflect commitment, sacrifice, and loyalty to God's purpose. Scripture reveals that the crowns believers receive in eternity are inseparably tied to the cross they bear in this life, embodying self-denial, resilience, and a deep alignment with God's will. Each crown represents not only honor but a life that has embraced the challenges and sacrifices of discipleship, echoing Jesus' call to *"take up your cross and follow Me"* (Matthew 16:24). These eternal rewards are God's powerful affirmation of lives devoted to His kingdom, transforming temporary trials into everlasting glory.

Crowns Cannot Be Purchased – They Are Given by Grace *"For it is by grace you have been saved, through faith—and this is not from yourselves, it is the gift of God—not by works, so that no one can boast" (Ephesians 2:8-9).*

The concept of "purchasing" a crown contradicts the biblical principle of grace. Salvation and its rewards are gifts from God, not something believers can acquire through wealth, status, or effort. Crowns are bestowed based on God's grace, reflecting His response to a life of faithful obedience. Just as salvation is a gift, so are the crowns believers may receive in heaven. They are signs of God's approval and reward, not of human merit or achievement.

Biblical Example – Simon the Sorcerer: In *Acts 8:18-20*, Simon the Sorcerer tried to "buy" the power of the Holy Spirit, and Peter rebuked him sharply: "May your money perish with you, because you thought you could buy the gift of God with money!" This example shows that spiritual gifts, including crowns, cannot be bought or obtained through human means. They are gifts from God, given only to those who live according to His purposes.

The Cross Before the Crown – Suffering and Perseverance Leads to Eternal Reward *"Then Jesus said to His disciples, 'Whoever wants to be my disciple must deny themselves and take up their cross and follow me. For whoever wants to save their life will lose it, but whoever loses their life for me will find it'"* *(Matthew 16:24-25).*

Jesus made it clear that following Him requires taking up one's cross. This "cross" symbolizes self-denial, sacrifice, and the willingness to endure hardship for the sake of Christ. Bearing the cross is the path to receiving the crown. In the Christian life, a crown is not achieved without enduring trials, suffering, and faithfully following Jesus. The cross precedes the crown; only through a life of surrender and service does the believer receive the promised reward.

Apostle Paul's Example: In *2 Timothy 4:7-8*, Paul reflects on his life of suffering and faithful service, saying, "I have fought the good fight, I have finished the race, I have kept the faith. Now there is in store for me the crown of righteousness." Paul's "crown of righteousness" was given in response to his perseverance and dedication to Christ, not because of earthly achievement or merit. His life exemplifies the necessity of enduring hardship for the sake of the gospel.

Crowns as Rewards for Faithfulness Amid Trials *"Blessed is the one who perseveres under trial because, having stood the test, that person will receive the crown of life that the Lord has promised to those who love Him"* *(James 1:12).*

The "crown of life" is promised to those who remain faithful through trials and challenges. This promise shows that crowns are rewards for perseverance, faith, and love for God, especially in the face of suffering. Trials are an essential part of the journey toward the crown, refining the believer's character and faith. Enduring hardship and trusting God amid adversity are marks of a life worthy of the crown.

The Refining Process: In *1 Peter 1:6-7*, Peter speaks of trials as a refining process: "These [trials] have come so that the proven genuineness of your faith, of greater worth than gold, may result in praise, glory, and honor when Jesus Christ is revealed." This "praise, glory, and honor" can be seen as a reward, akin to a crown. The process of enduring trials is what qualifies believers for these rewards, revealing that the crown comes through perseverance.

Following Jesus' Example: The Cross and Then the Crown *"Let us fix our eyes on Jesus, the author and finisher of our faith. For the joy set before Him, He endured the cross, scorning its shame, and sat down at the right hand of the throne of God" (Hebrews 12:2).*

Explanation: Jesus is the ultimate example of the cross before the crown. He endured the cross, embracing suffering and humiliation, to fulfill God's redemptive plan. Only after His crucifixion and resurrection did He "sit down at the right hand of the throne of God." His path to glory was through obedience, sacrifice, and self-denial. In the same way, believers are called to endure trials and follow Christ's example, knowing that their "crown" awaits in eternity.

Jesus' Invitation to Follow Him: In *Luke 9:23-24*, Jesus says, "Whoever wants to be my disciple must deny themselves and take up their cross daily and follow me." This invitation includes a promise; those who follow Christ will share in His reward. The way of the cross, though challenging, leads to eternal glory and the fulfillment of God's promises.

Eternal Crowns as Symbols of God's Approval and Fulfillment of His Promises *"Now there is in store for me the crown of righteousness, which the Lord, the righteous Judge, will award to me on that day, and not only to me, but also to all who have longed for His appearing" (2 Timothy 4:8).*

Crowns in Scripture, such as the "crown of righteousness," are symbols of God's promises fulfilled for those who live faithfully. This crown is a sign of God's approval and His fulfillment of His promise to reward those who persevere. The crown is not an achievement but a recognition of a life lived in alignment with God's will, reflecting His grace and approval.

The Heavenly Perspective: In heaven, believers cast their crowns before God's throne (Revelation 4:10-11), acknowledging that every reward ultimately belongs to Him. This act signifies that crowns, though received as rewards, are ultimately God's gifts, bestowed by His grace. In eternity, believers will lay down their crowns in worship, showing that the true reward is eternal communion with God.

Kingdom crowns are not prizes that can be purchased or earned through human means but rewards granted by God in response to faithful, obedient service and perseverance through trials. The path to the crown involves bearing a cross, symbolizing self-denial, sacrifice, and alignment with God's will and purposes. Just as Jesus endured the cross before receiving His crown of glory, believers are called to a life of sacrifice before receiving the eternal rewards that await them.

The message is clear: true spiritual crowns are attained not by wealth or status but by surrendering one's life to God, enduring hardship, and walking faithfully in His will. These crowns are symbols of God's promises fulfilled, signifying the honor, approval, and eternal joy that await those who persevere to the end.

Linking purpose to promise is intrinsically connected to God's eternal promises. In Scripture, purpose and promise go hand-in-hand, guiding believers toward a life of meaning that culminates in the fulfillment of God's promises. Our purpose here on earth is both a preparation and a precursor to the eternal rewards that await us in heaven. Let's explore how purpose is tied to promise, examining key biblical principles and examples.

Purpose and Promise as Part of God's Sovereign Plan *"For I know the plans I have for you," declares the Lord, "plans to prosper you and not to harm you, plans to give you hope and a future" (Jeremiah 29:11).*

God's declaration to Israel in captivity reflects His overarching plan for His people, where earthly purpose is woven into His promises of hope and restoration. This verse shows that God's plans (purpose) lead to a hopeful and prosperous future (promise), revealing that our earthly assignments are part of a larger, eternal plan.

As believers, our purpose is not random or without direction. Every step we take in faith serves as part of God's intricate plan, designed to bring us closer to the fulfillment of His promises. This perspective encourages believers to live purposefully, knowing that their lives and eternity are aligned with God's eternal intentions.

Purpose in the Present Leads to Promise in the Future *"And we know that in all things God works for the good of those who love him, who have been called according to his purpose" (Romans 8:28).*

Paul reassures believers that everything they experience—good or bad—serves God's purpose and ultimately works toward their eternal good. This verse reveals that our daily purpose and experiences are connected to the promise of God's divine orchestration and ultimate good. Life's trials, victories, and tasks are shaping us for a future that holds the fulfillment of God's promises.

Example: Joseph's life illustrates this beautifully. He endured betrayal, slavery, and imprisonment, but each hardship served God's purpose to place him in a position to save many lives. Joseph acknowledged this connection when he told his brothers,

"You intended to harm me, but God intended it for good" (Genesis 50:20). Joseph's earthly purpose, to preserve Israel during famine, was part of God's promise to Abraham to protect his descendants. Joseph's life was thus a bridge between earthly purpose and eternal promise.

Earthly Purpose as Preparation for Eternal Promise *"For our light and momentary troubles are achieving for us an eternal glory that far outweighs them all" (2 Corinthians 4:17).*

Paul encourages believers to view their earthly struggles as preparation for eternal glory. The trials we face on earth serve a purpose in preparing us for the "eternal weight of glory" that is the fulfillment of God's promises. Here, purpose isn't just about the tasks we accomplish but includes the shaping of our character and faith, which prepare us for eternity.

The life of the Apostle Paul embodies this principle. Despite facing persecution, imprisonment, and hardship, Paul embraced his earthly purpose as a servant of the gospel. He understood that his sufferings were molding him for eternal glory, which he would one day receive as a promise from God. Paul's life of purpose on earth was inextricably linked to his hope of future reward.

Living with Purpose Leads to the Fulfillment of God's Promises: *"Therefore, my dear brothers and sisters, stand firm. Let nothing move you. Always give yourselves fully to the work of the Lord, because you know that your labor in the Lord is not in vain" (1 Corinthians 15:58).*

Paul encourages believers to remain steadfast in their purpose, knowing that their efforts are not meaningless. The promise here is that every act of service, every sacrifice, and every step taken in faith holds eternal value and will be rewarded. Purpose in the Lord is directly tied to the promise of future reward, affirming that our work for Him contributes to His kingdom.

The parable of the talents (Matthew 25:14-30) illustrates how God values purposeful living. In the parable, the servants who invest their talents (earthly purpose) are rewarded by their master. The faithful servants are told, "Well done, good and faithful servant... Come and share your master's happiness" (Matthew 25:21). This "sharing in happiness" represents the fulfillment of God's promises for those who live with faithfulness and purpose.

Promise of Eternal Crowns for Purposeful Living *"Now there is in store for me the crown of righteousness, which the Lord, the righteous Judge, will award to me on that day—and not only to me, but also to all who have longed for his appearing" (2 Timothy 4:8).*

Paul speaks of the "crown of righteousness" as a reward for those who have lived purposefully in faith, looking forward to Christ's return. This crown signifies the fulfillment of God's promises and the culmination of a life lived in alignment with His purposes. It shows that our purpose on earth is part of God's eternal plan, with promises that will be fully realized in eternity.

Crowns are a symbol of God's approval and reward, granted to those who fulfill their purpose with faithfulness and endurance. Living with purpose is not only a matter of earthly impact but is directly connected to the eternal promises awaiting believers in heaven.

Eternal Promise Shapes Earthly Purpose *"But our citizenship is in heaven. And we eagerly await a Savior from there, the Lord Jesus Christ" (Philippians 3:20).*

Paul reminds believers that their true home and ultimate purpose are found in heaven. This eternal perspective shapes how they live on earth. Earthly purpose is not about achieving temporary goals or gaining worldly success but about living in alignment with the reality of heaven. The promise of eternal life and citizenship in heaven gives believers a divine purpose that transcends the temporary.

Abraham is a powerful example of living with an eternal perspective. Despite never seeing the complete fulfillment of God's promises in his lifetime, he lived by faith, "looking forward to the city with foundations, whose architect and builder is God" (Hebrews 11:10). Abraham's earthly purpose to be the father of a great nation, was rooted in God's eternal promises, and he trusted that God's promises extended beyond his earthly life.

The Role of Purpose in Inheriting the Promises *"We do not want you to become lazy, but to imitate those who through faith and patience inherit what has been promised" (Hebrews 6:12).*

This verse teaches that the promises of God are inherited through faith and patience. Earthly purpose requires active faith, perseverance, and dedication to God's will. Those who walk in purpose and live faithfully inherit the promises because they are aligned with God's covenant and will. Purpose on earth is a journey toward the promises of God, fulfilled in His timing.

The Israelites' journey to the Promised Land is a vivid illustration of **purpose linked to promise**. Although they wandered in the wilderness, their purpose was to follow God's guidance toward the land He promised to Abraham's descendants. This journey required faith, patience, and obedience. The purpose (following God) was integral to receiving the promise (the land), highlighting the connection between living in God's purpose and inheriting His promises.

The Bible reveals a consequential link between purpose and promise. Earthly purpose is not just about temporary achievements or fulfilling roles; it is preparation for the eternal promises God has made to His people. Our purpose aligns with God's greater plan and moves us toward the fulfillment of His promises, whether through our character development, acts of service, perseverance through trials, or faithfulness in waiting.

➢ **Purpose on Earth Is a Preparation for Eternal Rewards**: Earthly trials, service, and faithfulness prepare us for the "eternal weight of glory" that awaits in heaven.

➢ **Faithful Living Leads to Inheriting the Promises**: By living according to God's purpose, believers can look forward to eternal rewards, including crowns of righteousness, life, and glory.

➢ **An Eternal Perspective Gives Meaning to Earthly Purpose**: Knowing that we are citizens of heaven shapes how we live on earth, as every act of obedience, love, and service is a step toward the fulfillment of God's promises.

In summary, <u>purpose and promise are inseparable in the life of a believer. Our purpose is not only a calling for this life but also a journey toward eternal promises.</u> Every act of faithfulness, every trial endured, and every act of love carries us closer to the day when God's promises will be fulfilled in their entirety. This connection gives our earthly lives profound meaning and hope, as we live with the assurance that our purpose is part of God's unchanging promise for eternity.

Living Out the Anointing Daily

Living out the anointing daily means consciously aligning our lives with God's purposes and promises, actively embodying the calling and power He has placed within us. It's more than simply acknowledging that we are set apart; it is a daily commitment to act as His vessels, faithfully stewarding the resources, gifts, and opportunities He has given us. This daily anointing allows believers to live with purpose and intention, reflecting the character of Jesus in every aspect of life.

The concept of daily anointing is beautifully illustrated in the life of Jesus, who, as the Anointed One (Messiah), lived in total alignment with God's purpose and demonstrated what it means to walk under

divine anointing. Key events, like His baptism and the anointings at Bethany, underscore the significance and vitality of anointing for His mission and how this anointing prepared Him for His sacrificial role as Savior.

SPIRITUAL ASPECTS OF LIVING OUT THE ANOINTING DAILY

Stewardship of Gifts and Talents: To live out our anointing means to use our God-given abilities, spiritual gifts, and talents purposefully. This includes applying our skills, faith, works and resources to glorify God and serve others.

"Each of you should use whatever gift you have received to serve others, as faithful stewards of God's grace in its various forms" (1 Peter 4:10).Recognizing that our skills and resources are gifts from God, believers should view their abilities as tools to bless others and build God's Kingdom. This can look like volunteering, serving in ministry, or simply being a light in the workplace.

Integrity and Accountability: Living in daily anointing involves making choices that reflect God's holiness and love, maintaining integrity in our actions and interactions.

"So whether you eat or drink or whatever you do, do it all for the glory of God" (1 Corinthians 10:31). Anointing calls for a life of integrity, where every action, public or private is aligned with God's principles. This daily commitment to integrity honors the anointing within us and keeps us sensitive to the Spirit's leading.

Bearing Spiritual Fruit: The Holy Spirit empowers believers to bear fruit that reflects Christ's character, such as love, patience, kindness, and self-control.

"But the fruit of the Spirit is love, joy, peace, forbearance, kindness, goodness, faithfulness, gentleness, and self-control", (Galatians 5:22-23). Living out the anointing daily means allowing the Spirit to shape our character, enabling us to serve and love others as Christ does. The visible fruits of the Spirit are proof of a life lived under God's anointing.

Spiritual Discernment and Obedience: Daily anointing includes seeking God's guidance and being sensitive to His direction.

"Trust in the Lord with all your heart and lean not to your own understanding; in all your ways submit to him, and he will make your paths straight" (Proverbs 3:5-6). Believers anointed by the Spirit are encouraged to seek God's will in every decision, trusting Him to lead. This involves prayer, listening, and acting on His guidance, whether it is in relationships, career decisions, or ministry.

The Anointing of Jesus at Bethany

The anointing of Jesus at Bethany holds deep spiritual significance, symbolizing preparation, purpose, and the foreshadowing of His sacred atoning sacrifice at the cross. This event shows the powerful role anointing plays in both identifying and preparing someone for a divinely appointed mission. Jesus was anointed on multiple occasions, each with its own significance in preparing Him for His role as Savior and King.

"Then Mary took a pound of very costly oil of spikenard, anointed the feet of Jesus, and wiped His feet with her hair. And the house was filled with the fragrance of the oil." (John 12:3).

This anointing by Mary was a personal and symbolic act that recognized Jesus as the Messiah and prepared Him for His impending death. The perfume used, nard, was costly and symbolized great value, representing the priceless sacrifice Jesus was about to make for the sins of this world.

Mary's act of anointing Jesus was a recognition of His identity as the "Anointed One." By pouring out the costly perfume, Mary acknowledged Jesus' worth and the depth of her devotion. Jesus Himself recognized this act as preparation for His burial, highlighting the anointing's role in affirming both His purpose and the promise of His ultimate victory over sin and death.

Jesus' Anointing with the Holy Spirit at His Baptism: *"And the Holy Spirit descended on Him in bodily form like a dove. And a voice came from heaven: 'You are my Son, whom I love; with You I am well pleased'"* (Luke 3:22).

At His baptism, Jesus was anointed with the Holy Spirit, marking the beginning of His public ministry and signifying divine empowerment. This anointing equipped Jesus to perform miracles, preach the gospel, and ultimately fulfill His mission as the Savior.

The baptism anointing represents the empowerment believers receive through the Holy Spirit. Just as Jesus was equipped for His mission, believers are also anointed by the Spirit to fulfill God's purpose. Jesus' anointing with the Spirit serves as a model for us to live in obedience, humility, and reliance on God's strength in our daily lives.

Anointing as Preparation for Sacrifice: *"She has done a beautiful thing to me. The poor you will always have with you, but you will not always have me. She poured this perfume on my body beforehand to prepare for my burial"* (Matthew 26:10-12).

Jesus highlighted that Mary's act of anointing was a preparation for His burial, pointing to His sacrificial death. This act symbolized not only honor but also the readiness for His mission's fulfillment, His death and resurrection.

Just as Jesus' anointing prepared Him for His ultimate purpose, believers are called to live out their anointing in a way that honors

God and prepares them for the work He has called them to. This preparation often involves humility, sacrifice, and a willingness to be set apart, as Jesus was.

Anointing and Crowning with Purpose: Living as Kingdom Representatives *"But you are a chosen generation, a royal priesthood, a holy nation, His own special people, that you may proclaim the praises of Him who called you out of darkness into His marvelous light;" (1 Peter 2:9).*

This verse reminds believers that they are set apart, crowned with purpose and identity as representatives of God's kingdom. Being "anointed" in daily life is about living as a "royal priesthood," dedicated to showing God's love, compassion, and truth to the world. Living with the knowledge that we are crowned with God's promises should encourage believers to carry themselves with dignity, humility, and responsibility. ***Every action, decision, and interaction can reflect God's love and grace, serving as a witness to others.***

KEY TAKEAWAYS FROM LIVING OUT THE ANOINTING DAILY

➤ **Anointing Requires Stewardship**: Just as Jesus fulfilled His anointing by serving, healing, teaching, and sacrificing, believers are called to steward their anointing through faithful service, compassion, and obedience to God's Word. This daily anointing calls for intentional use of our time, resources, and spiritual gifts, as each is a tool for advancing God's Kingdom.

➤ **Anointing Prepares Us for Purpose**: The anointing isn't merely a mark of status; it is preparation for divine purpose. Every day offers a chance to grow, refine our character, and align with God's will. Just as Jesus was anointed and prepared for His mission, believers are equipped through the Spirit to fulfill the unique work God has entrusted to them.

➤ **Anointing and Sacrifice Go Hand in Hand**: Anointing often calls for sacrifice, mirroring Jesus' path to the cross. Living out our anointing means surrendering personal desires and comfort for the sake of God's Kingdom. Through sacrifice, believers embody Christ's love and mission, reflecting His dedication and selflessness.

Living out the anointing daily means recognizing that our lives are set apart for God's purpose and crowned by His promises. This anointing requires stewardship, integrity, and a commitment to sacrifice. Jesus' anointings, at His baptism, at Bethany, and in His ultimate sacrifice, demonstrate how divine anointing prepares believers for lives of purpose, service, and obedience. Just as Jesus was anointed for His mission, we are called to live in alignment with God's will, letting the Spirit guide every action and interaction. In essence, being anointed is about embodying Christ's love, wisdom, and grace, becoming a reflection of God's Kingdom in a world in need. Every day is an opportunity to walk in the Spirit's power, honor God's call, and fulfill our role as His anointed vessels, crowned with purpose and empowered to serve.

GODS PROMISES NEVER COME BACK VOID

Yes, Scripture confirms that God watches over His Word to perform it and that His promises are sure, never returning void. God's promises are grounded in His unchanging nature, His truthfulness, and His faithfulness. Both the Old and New Testaments reveal that when God speaks, He acts, and when He promises, He fulfills. Here's an in-depth look at what the Bible says about God's commitment to His Word and the certainty of His promises.

God Watches Over His Word to Perform It *"The Lord said to me, 'You have seen correctly, for I am watching to see that my word is fulfilled'"* *(Jeremiah 1:12).*

This verse shows God's vigilant commitment to His Word. In context, God is reassuring Jeremiah that His promises and His prophecies will come to pass. God actively oversees the fulfillment of His Word, ensuring that it accomplishes His purposes. God's promises are not idle or empty; they are declarations backed by His authority and power.

Believers can take comfort in knowing that God is actively engaged in bringing His Word to pass. He is not distant or indifferent; instead, He is personally involved in fulfilling every promise He has spoken. This assurance gives believers confidence to rely on His Word, knowing that He is faithful to fulfill it.

God's Promises Do Not Return Void *"So is my word that goes out from my mouth: It will not return to me empty, but will accomplish what I desire and achieve the purpose for which I sent it" (Isaiah 55:11).*

This verse declares the effectiveness and power of God's Word. When God speaks, His Word goes forth with purpose and will not return to Him without achieving its intended outcome. Just as rain and snow water the earth to produce growth, God's Word produces life, change, and fulfillment. This verse confirms that God's promises are powerful and will be accomplished, regardless of circumstances or obstacles.

Believers can trust that God's promises are reliable. They do not depend on human ability or circumstances but on God's sovereignty and faithfulness. No matter how impossible a promise may seem, God's Word will accomplish His purpose because He is the one who fulfills it.

Examples of <u>God's Promises in the Old Testament</u>

Abrahamic Covenant:

Promise: God promised to bless Abraham and make him the father of a great nation, ultimately blessing the world through his descendants (Genesis 12:2-3).

Fulfillment: This promise pointed to the coming Messiah, Jesus, who would bring salvation to all nations (Galatians 3:16). Despite Abraham's advanced age and Sarah's barrenness, God fulfilled His Word, and through Abraham's lineage, Jesus was born, blessing all who believe.

This covenant reminds us that God's promises may unfold over time, but they are certain. God's commitment to Abraham was based on His own character, not on Abraham's strength or ability.

God's Promise to Be Israel's God:

Promise: God promised Israel that He would be their God and they would be His people (Leviticus 26:12-13).

Fulfillment: Throughout the Old Testament, God repeatedly proved His faithfulness to Israel, even when they strayed. Despite Israel's failures, God remained their God, fulfilling His covenant promises.

God's faithfulness to Israel, despite their disobedience, shows that His promises are based on His character, not human perfection. God's commitment to His people is enduring, showing that He will not abandon His promises.

Promise of Protection:

Promise: God promised protection and care for His people (Psalm 121).

Fulfillment: Throughout Israel's history, God protected them from their enemies, guided them through the wilderness, and provided for them.

This promise reassures believers that God is their vigilant protector, watching over them with care and power. He guards His people and fulfills His promises of protection in countless ways.

Promise of Forgiveness and Restoration:

Promise: God promised Israel that repentance would bring forgiveness and restoration (2 Chronicles 7:14).

Fulfillment: Time and again, God forgave Israel when they turned back to Him, restoring their fortunes and their relationship with Him. This promise shows that God is always ready to forgive and heal.

God's readiness to forgive and restore is an enduring promise. His mercy and grace are constant, assuring believers that repentance opens the door to renewed fellowship with Him.

Examples of God's Promises in the New Testament

Promise of Salvation through Faith:

Promise: God promised salvation to all who believe in His Son (Romans 1:16-17).

Fulfillment: This promise is the foundation of the New Covenant, offering eternal life to all who place their faith in Jesus Christ. Salvation is God's gift, fulfilling His promise of redemption.

This promise assures believers that their salvation is secure in Christ. God has completed the work of salvation through Jesus, fulfilling His promise of eternal life.

Promise of All Things Working Together for Good:

Promise: God promised to work all things together for the good of those who love Him (Romans 8:28).

Fulfillment: Believers throughout history testify to God's ability to bring good from every situation, including trials and suffering. He turns difficulties into opportunities for growth and blessing.

This promise encourages believers to trust God in every circumstance, knowing that He is at work for their ultimate good, even when situations seem challenging or unclear.

Promise of New Life in Christ:

Promise: God promised a new identity and life in Christ (2 Corinthians 5:17).

Fulfillment: When a person believes in Christ, they are transformed, becoming a "new creation." This promise is fulfilled as believers experience God's transformative power in their lives.

This promise reassures believers that they are not bound to their past. God gives them a new identity and purpose, empowering them to live in freedom and victory.

Promise of Spiritual Blessings in Christ:

Promise: God promised every spiritual blessing in Christ (Ephesians 1:3).

Fulfillment: Through Christ, believers are blessed with spiritual riches, including forgiveness, redemption, and the Holy Spirit's indwelling.

This promise shows that believers have access to God's fullness and favor. They are spiritually blessed and empowered to live according to His will, assured that God has provided everything they need.

Promise of Peace:

Promise: God promised peace that surpasses all understanding (Philippians 4:6-7).

Fulfillment: Believers experience God's peace, especially in times of trouble. This peace guards their hearts and minds as they trust in Him.

God's peace is a protective promise, shielding believers from anxiety and fear. It is a constant reminder of His presence and care in every situation.

Jesus' Promises in the Gospels

Promise of Rest:

Promise: Jesus promised rest to those who come to Him (Matthew 11:28-30).

Fulfillment: Jesus offers rest for the soul, inviting those burdened to find relief and peace in Him.

This promise assures believers that they can find true rest in Jesus, free from the burdens of guilt, shame, and striving. His yoke is easy and His burden light.

Promise of Eternal Life:

Promise: Jesus promised eternal life to those who trust Him (John 4:14, John 10:28).

Fulfillment: Through His death and resurrection, Jesus fulfilled this promise, giving believers the assurance of eternal security.

Believers can rest in the knowledge that Jesus holds them securely, with a promise of eternal life that cannot be taken away.

Promise of His Return:

Promise: Jesus promised to return for His followers (John 14:2-3).

Fulfillment: While this promise is yet to be fulfilled, believers hold fast to the hope of His return, knowing that He is preparing a place for them.

This promise encourages believers to live with an eternal perspective, eagerly awaiting the day when they will be with Him forever.

God's promises, both in the Old and New Testaments, reveal His unchanging faithfulness and commitment to His people. He watches over His Word to perform it, and His promises never return void. Each promise, whether for provision, protection, salvation, or peace, is a testament to His trustworthy nature. As *2 Corinthians 1:20* says, "No matter how many promises God has made, they are 'Yes' in Christ." Through Jesus, every promise of God finds its fulfillment, giving believers full assurance that God's Word will accomplish His will, without fail.

Yahweh's anointing sets individuals apart with purpose, power, and divine alignment. Being anointed isn't merely a title or recognition; it is a rich spiritual experience that marks a believer for a unique mission. Anointing connects individuals to God's heart and mission, calling them into a life that rises above earthly pursuits and into a deep partnership with God Himself. Through His anointing, God communicates His faithfulness, purpose, and unwavering commitment to those He calls.

At the core of anointing lies **the principle of being chosen by God**. This divine selection is powerfully illustrated in the lives of chosen woman and men of God, like David and the prophets, whom God singled out for specific missions that would shape history. When God chooses someone, He does so with a particular calling in mind, often surpassing human understanding. This chosen status isn't about privilege alone; it is a weighty responsibility, reminding God's anointed that they are meant to accomplish things far beyond their own capacities. This calling reflects a sacred trust, placing believers in a role that calls for obedience, commitment, and readiness to fulfill the purposes of God.

Anointing also signifies a **divine assignment**, a commissioning by God that launches His chosen into unique paths prepared specifically for them. Just as David was anointed and then entered a journey of preparation for kingship, God's anointed are called to follow a unique path that unfolds over time, often requiring faith and patience. This assignment is not a one-time moment but a lifelong pursuit, carrying with it both promise and challenge. It means surrendering one's own plans in favor of divine direction, recognizing that God's purposes are higher and His strategies perfect. This divine assignment reflects God's intentional, hands-on guidance as He walks with His chosen through each season.

A critical aspect of anointing is being **filled with the Holy Spirit**, an empowerment that enables believers to carry out their divine assignment. Just as Jesus received the Holy Spirit at His baptism, God's anointed are infused with supernatural spiritual strength, wisdom, and guidance. The Holy Spirit is not just a helper but the active presence of God that leads, sustains, and fills believers with everything they need to succeed in their calling. This empowerment isn't optional, it's essential. It transforms the believer's abilities, helping them rise above limitations and doubts, instilling a confidence rooted not in themselves but in God's boundless power and promises.

Finally, anointing brings with it the **empowerment to lead**, especially when it comes to influencing others for God's kingdom. Leadership here isn't merely about authority; it's about humility, service, and alignment with God's will. Like the kings and prophets of the Bible, God's anointed lead through submission to God,

knowing that their strength and wisdom come from Him. God equips His anointed with spiritual gifts, unique abilities granted by the Holy Spirit, that enable them to carry out their tasks with purpose and precision. Each gift and every calling unfolds as part of a larger plan, revealing how God's promises are not just words but realities that never return empty or void. This chapter highlights <u>how crowns in Scripture serve</u>  <u>as symbols of divine promises, confirming that God's anointed are marked for victory, purpose, and destiny in His kingdom</u>

Crowned for Purpose

James 1:12

FROM BEGINNING TO END

In the Beginning, The Word and Creation expressed through John 1:1 *"In the beginning was the Word, and the Word was with God, and the Word was God"*. In the beginning, Yahweh's sovereign Word established all creation. The power and authority of His Word, which was with God and was God. Highlight how this eternal Word has remained unchanged and governs all things, underscoring Yahweh's decree as foundational.

Proverbs 19:21 ESV , Revelation 21:6 ESV , John 1:14 ESV , Hebrews 1:1-2 ESV , Genesis 1:1 ESV Colossians 1:16 ESV ,Revelation 1:8 ESV

Yahweh's Sovereignty: The Alpha and Omega

The Bible revealing Yahweh as the ultimate Sovereign, the Alpha and Omega, the beginning and the end. Through creation, redemption, and His eternal reign, God declares Himself the author and sustainer of all life, demonstrating His unmatched authority over all things. But what does it mean to call God sovereign, and why is He identified as the Alpha and Omega? Let's explore the biblical foundation for Yahweh's sovereignty and examine the significance of His eternal titles.

To say that God is sovereign is to acknowledge His ultimate authority and control over all creation. The word "sovereign" conveys God's rule, supremacy, and absolute right to govern as He wills. Unlike human leaders who govern with limited influence and authority, Yahweh's sovereignty is complete and unrestricted. Proverbs 19:21 (ESV) encapsulates this truth: "Many are the plans in the mind of a man, but it is the purpose of the Lord that will stand." Human intentions and schemes are subject to the supreme will of God, and nothing occurs outside His knowledge and decree.

Yahweh's sovereignty is eternal. From beginning to end, His purposes remain unchanged, untouched by worldly human agendas or the passage of time. His sovereignty means He has the power to bring about His will across generations, and nothing in creation can frustrate His intentions. This truth provides comfort and security to believers, as God's plans for the world and for individuals are founded on His perfect wisdom, righteousness, and love.

The book of Genesis opens with an extraordinary declaration: "*In the beginning, God created the heavens and the earth*" (Genesis 1:1 ESV). This verse establishes God as the ultimate source of all existence. Creation itself was brought forth by Yahweh's sovereign Word, underscoring His unparalleled authority. According to John 1:1-5 (ESV), *"In the beginning was the Word, and the Word was with God, and the Word was God."* The term "Word" (Greek: Logos) here reflects the very essence and power of God, active in creation. Through His Word, Yahweh not only formed the heavens and earth but set every aspect of creation into motion according to His will and purpose.

The idea of God's Word as both creative and sustaining is further highlighted in Colossians 1:16 (ESV), which says, "For by him all things were created, in heaven and on earth, visible and invisible, whether thrones or dominions or rulers or authorities, all things were created through him and for him." Every element of creation, seen and unseen, came into being by Yahweh's decree, and it exists for His glory. This profound truth reveals that no force, power, or entity in the universe exists outside of God's sovereign authority.

The power and authority of God's Word also reflects' His immutability, or unchanging nature. Hebrews 1:1-2 (ESV) reminds us that while God communicated in various ways in times past, He has ultimately spoken through His Son, Jesus Christ, "through whom also he created the world." This transition from prophetic revelation to direct manifestation in Christ underscores the consistency and fulfillment of God's sovereign plan. His Word, embodied in Christ, is the same Word that spoke creation into existence and governs all life with precision and purpose.

In Revelation 1:8 (ESV), God reveals Himself as the "Alpha and the Omega," a title that bookends the entirety of Scripture. As the first and last letters of the Greek alphabet, Alpha and Omega signify the beginning and the end, the origin and culmination of all things. This title emphasizes God's eternal nature and His supreme role in the history of creation. He is both the source and the ultimate goal of all existence.

God's identity as the Alpha and Omega further emphasizes His sovereignty in the unfolding of history. Revelation 21:6 (ESV) echoes this declaration; "It is done! I am the Alpha and the Omega, the beginning and the end. To the thirsty I will give from the spring of the water of life without payment." By declaring "It is done," Yahweh asserts His final word over creation and redemption. This divine proclamation not only emphasizes God's authority but also His faithfulness in fulfilling His promises. Everything God has purposed from the foundation of the world reaches its intended fulfillment in Him.

As the Alpha, Yahweh is the initiator of life, the One who spoke light into darkness and order into chaos. As the Omega, He is the ultimate Judge and Redeemer, the One who will bring all things to their completion. In between these points lies human history, which moves forward under His sovereign direction. God as the Alpha and Omega gives believers blessed assurance, reassuring them that their lives are secure within the providential care of the One who holds authority over all things.

John 1:14 (ESV) declares, *"And the Word became flesh and dwelt among us, and we have seen his glory, glory as of the only Son from the Father, full of grace and truth."* This momentous event, the Incarnation, demonstrates Yahweh's sovereignty in an unparalleled way. God, who existed before time began, chose to enter His creation as a man, Jesus Christ. Through Christ, God's sovereignty was revealed not only in power but in humility, grace, sacrifice and love.

The Incarnation embodies God's authority in human history, fulfilling promises spoken through the prophets and revealing His redemptive plan. Jesus, as the "heir of all things" (Hebrews 1:2 ESV), is appointed to bring about the fulfillment of God's kingdom, demonstrating that Yahweh's sovereignty is both personal and relational. Christ's life, death, and resurrection reveal the depth of God's commitment to redeem His creation, exercising His sovereign authority in a way that serves humanity's ultimate good.

Moreover, Jesus embodies the unchanging Word of God. In a world marked by instability and change, the aspect of Christ existence, blessed assurance and promise of return remains a constant, a sure foundation upon which believers can build their lives. By becoming flesh, the Word did not lose its authority; instead, it brought God's sovereignty to bear directly upon human history, affirming that every promise Yahweh made will find its "yes" in Christ (2 Corinthians 1:20).

While Yahweh's sovereignty extends over all creation, it also has direct implications for individual lives. Believers are called to live in submission to God's will, recognizing that every aspect of their lives falls under His care. Proverbs 19:21 (ESV) reminds us that while human beings may devise their own plans, it is "the purpose of the Lord that will stand." This scripture offers reassurance that God's

plan cannot be erased, even by the many twists and turns of human intentions.

This truth invites believers to rest in God's sovereignty, especially in times of uncertainty or suffering. Yahweh's purposes extend beyond our immediate understanding, often working in hidden ways to bring about His greater plan. Though humans cannot see the full picture, they can trust in the goodness and wisdom of God's sovereign decree. This confidence enables believers to face life's challenges with resilience and faith, knowing that their lives are held by the One who declared Himself the Alpha and Omega.

Recognizing Yahweh's sovereignty transforms how believers approach their relationship with Him. It calls for a life of full surrender, faith, and obedience. As the Alpha and Omega, Yahweh deserves the highest reverence, honor, praise and loyalty. Living in alignment with God's will requires yielding personal desires to His ultimate plan, trusting that His ways are higher than human understanding.

Moreover, Yahweh's sovereignty brings hope. Knowing that God has the final say over all things assures believers that evil will not have the last word. Yahweh, the Creator, and Redeemer, will restore and renew His creation, fulfilling every promise He has made. This confidence encourages believers to press on in faith, knowing that the God who began a good work in them will bring it to completion (Philippians 1:6).

In the grand narrative of Scripture, Yahweh's sovereignty is the thread that unites all things. As the Alpha and Omega, God reigns supreme, holding all creation in His hands and orchestrating every event according to His eternal purpose. From the foundations of the earth to the final judgment, Yahweh's decree stands unchallenged, guiding human history toward its ultimate fulfillment in Him.

The Bible reveals a God who is not only sovereign in power but also gracious in love. Through His Word, He created, sustained, and redeemed the world, bringing hope to all who trust in His unchanging authority. As believers embrace the sovereignty of Yahweh, they find strength, comfort, and purpose, assured that their lives are part of a divine plan that will reach its glorious completion in the One who is, and was, and is to come—the Almighty.

The Uniqueness in the identy of God His unique names)

The Bible reveals the character and nature of God in unique in nature and complex ways, helping believers to better understand who He is and how He relates to His creation. Among the richest aspects of this revelation are the names of God, each unique and filled with spiritual-depth. The names God chooses to reveal to His people provide insight into His attributes, intentions, and promises. Each name is not merely a title but a reflection of God's exceptional character, purpose, and the roles He fulfills in the lives of His people. Understanding the uniqueness of each of these names draws us into a deeper relationship with God, giving us a fuller comprehension of His majesty, power, and intimacy.

From the very beginning, we see God introducing Himself through names that reveal His distinct attributes. For example, when Moses encountered God at the burning bush, God revealed Himself as *Yahweh*, "I Am" (Exodus 3:14). This name highlights God's self-existence, His eternal presence, and His unchanging nature. Unlike human identities that can be fluid or influenced by external factors, *Yahweh* is foundational, representing God's essence as the one who simply *is*, the same yesterday, today, and forever. Knowing God as *Yahweh* gives believers a sense of security, knowing that God's presence is constant, even in changing circumstances.

The importance of God's names continues throughout the Bible. In Genesis, God reveals Himself as *El Shaddai*, meaning "God Almighty" or "The All-Sufficient One." This name reflects His boundless power and ability to sustain His creation. When we recognize God as *El Shaddai*, we understand that He is more than

172

capable of meeting our needs, whatever they may be. Similarly, other names like *Jehovah Jireh* ("The Lord Will Provide") and *Jehovah Rapha* ("The Lord Who Heals") show specific aspects of His care and provision, reassuring believers that He is both attentive to and capable of addressing their physical and spiritual needs.

These names do more than describe God; they invite believers to experience Him in specific ways. For instance, *Jehovah Shalom* ("The Lord Is Peace") emphasizes God as the source of peace, especially amid trials. In a world often marked by unrest, this name reminds us that true peace is found not in external circumstances but in God Himself. Similarly, *Jehovah Nissi* ("The Lord Is My Banner") represents God as our victory and rallying point in times of spiritual battles, reminding us that He stands with us, leading and empowering us.

As we explore these names, we find that each offers a unique invitation to know God on a personal level. They allow believers to draw near to God, not just in worship but also in trust, dependence, and surrender. Understanding the uniqueness of each name helps us comprehend God's **diverse** relationship with His people. He is our Creator (*Jehovah Elohim*), our Shepherd (*Jehovah Rohi*), and our Righteousness (*Jehovah Tsidkenu*). Each name reveals a particular aspect of God's love, power, and holiness.

The names of God, therefore, are not only about understanding who God is but about embracing who He desires to be in our lives. They remind us that God's presence is near, that He is actively involved, and that His attributes cover every dimension of human need. Engaging with God's names enriches our faith and deepens our relationship with Him, unveiling the **grandeur** of His character and the **varied** ways He chooses to connect with His creation.

1.Yahweh (YHWH) / Jehovah

Meaning: "I Am" or "The Self-Existent One" Scripture: *Exodus 3:14* — *"God said to Moses, 'I AM WHO I AM. This is what you are to say to the Israelites: I AM has sent me to you."* **Description:** The personal and covenant name of God, Yahweh underscores His self-existence and eternal presence, independent of anything or anyone.

2. El Shaddai

Meaning: "God Almighty" or "The All-Sufficient One"
Scripture: Genesis 17:1 — "When Abram was ninety-nine years old, the Lord appeared to him and said, 'I am God Almighty; walk before me faithfully and be blameless.'" ***Description:*** This name reveals God's power and sufficiency, affirming that He is more than capable of fulfilling every need and promise.

3.Adonai

Meaning: "Lord" or "Master" *Scripture: Psalm 8:1 — "O Lord, our Lord, how majestic is your name in all the earth!"* ***Description:*** Adonai reflects God's sovereign authority, reminding us that He reigns over all creation as the ultimate Master.

4.Jehovah-Jireh

Meaning: "The Lord Will Provide" *Scripture: Genesis 22:14 — "So Abraham called that place The Lord Will Provide."* **Description:** This name assures us of God's provision, highlighting His readiness to meet the needs of His people.

5.Jehovah-Rapha

Meaning: "The Lord Who Heals" *Scripture: Exodus 15:26 — "I am the Lord, who heals you."* ***Description:*** Emphasizing God as the healer, this name speaks to His power to restore both physically and spiritually.

6. Jehovah-Nissi

Meaning: "The Lord Is My Banner" *Scripture: Exodus 17:15 — "Moses built an altar and called it The Lord is my Banner."* **Description:** This name presents God as a symbol of victory, guiding His people to triumph and serving as their rallying point.

7. Jehovah-Shalom

Meaning: "The Lord Is Peace" Scripture: Judges 6:24 — "So Gideon built an altar to the Lord there and called it The Lord is Peace." **Description:** Jehovah Shalom embodies God as the source of true peace and completeness.

8. Jehovah-Tsidkenu

Meaning: "The Lord Our Righteousness" *Scripture: Jeremiah 23:6 — "This is the name by which he will be called: The Lord Our Righteous Savior."* **Description:** Signifying God's role as our righteousness, this name underscores His provision of moral and spiritual integrity.

9. Jehovah-Sabaoth

Meaning: "The Lord of Hosts" or "The Lord of Armies" *Scripture: 1 Samuel 1:3 — "Year after year this man went up...to worship and sacrifice to the Lord Almighty (Lord of Hosts) at Shiloh."* **Description:** This name reveals God as the commander of heavenly armies, showing His powerful presence in battles.

10. Jehovah-Shammah

Meaning: "The Lord Is There", *Scripture: Ezekiel 48:35 — "And the name of the city...will be: The Lord is there."* **Description:** Jehovah Shammah speaks to God's presence, assuring His people that He is always with them.

11. El-Elyon

Meaning: "The Most High God "*Scripture: Genesis 14:18-20 — "He was priest of God Most High, and he blessed Abram.* **"Description**: El Elyon emphasizes God's supremacy, highlighting His dominion over all things.

12. El-Roi

Meaning: "The God Who Sees" Scripture: Genesis 16:13 — "You are the God who sees me." **Description**: This name reveals God's awareness and compassion, assuring us that He sees and cares for each individual.

13. El-Olam

Meaning: "The Everlasting God" *Scripture: Genesis 21:33 — "He called on the name of the Lord, the Eternal God."* **Description**: El Olam signifies God's eternal nature, showing that He exists beyond the constraints of time.

14. Abba

Meaning: "Father" or "Daddy" *Scripture: Romans 8:15 — "By him we cry, 'Abba, Father.'"* **Description**: Reflecting an intimate, familial bond, this name represents God's closeness and loving care as a father.

15. Qanna

Meaning: "Jealous God", *Scripture: Exodus 34:14 — "The Lord, whose name is Jealous, is a jealous God."*
Description: Qanna speaks to God's zeal for His people's devotion, expressing His desire for exclusive worship.

16. Jehovah-Mekoddishkem

Meaning: "The Lord Who Sanctifies You", *Scripture: Leviticus 20:8 — "I am the Lord, who makes you holy."*
Description: This name reveals God as the one who purifies His people, setting them apart for His purposes.

17. Immanuel

Meaning: "God With Us", *Scripture: Isaiah 7:14, Matthew 1:23 — "They will call him Immanuel, which means 'God with us."* **Description**: Immanuel signifies God's presence among His people, realized through the person of Christ.

18. Jehovah-Rohi

Meaning: "The Lord Is My Shepherd", *Scripture: Psalm 23:1 — "The Lord is my shepherd; I shall not want."* **Description**: This name reflects God's care as a shepherd, guiding and protecting His flock.

19. Jehovah-Elohim

Meaning: "The Lord God" or "The Creator God", *Scripture: Genesis 2:4 — "When the Lord God made the earth and the heavens."* **Description**: Jehovah Elohim highlights God's power as the Creator, ruling over the heavens and the earth.

20. Jehovah-Hoshe'ah

Meaning: "The Lord Saves", *Scripture: Psalm 20:9 — "Lord, save the king! Answer us when we call!"*, **Description**: Emphasizing God's role as Savior, this name assures us of His power to deliver and save.

THE SABBATH: GODS ORDAIN DAY OF REST

The Edict of Milan, issued in 313 AD by Roman Emperors Constantine I and Licinius transformed the legal and social status of Christianity within the Roman Empire. Constantine enacted policies that favored Christians, such as <u>tax exemptions for the church</u> and clergy and the <u>promotion of Sunday as a day of rest in honor of the Christian Sabbath</u>. His Impact on Christianity bought an end of persecution of Christians and the church. The Edict of Milan brought an official end to centuries of brutal persecution. Christians could worship openly without fear, which encouraged the growth and development of the church. The legalization of Christianity gave it a newfound legitimacy, allowing it to flourish publicly. Christians gained political influence and began to integrate more fully into Roman society. Constantine did not make Christianity the official religion of the Roman Empire. While he played a crucial role in promoting and supporting Christianity, he did not establish it as their nation's religion. This official designation occurred later, under Emperor Theodosius I in 380 AD, with the issuance of the **Edict of Thessalonica**.

During Constantine's reign, he allowed a variety of religious practices to continue, even as he personally favored and supported Christianity. His policy was generally one of **religious tolerance and uniformity**, aiming for a peaceful coexistence of different faiths within the Roman empire. Here are some of the major religions and practices that continued during his rule:

1. Pagan Religions

> **Traditional Roman Pantheon**: Worship of the traditional Roman gods, such as **Jupiter, Mars,** and **Venus**, continued under Constantine. Temples remained open, and many Romans still practiced pagan rituals, which had deep cultural and historical roots in Roman society.

> **Imperial Cult**: The imperial cult, or the practice of worshipping the emperor as a deity, also persisted. Although Constantine did not encourage this cult, he did not actively dismantle it.

> **Sun God Cult (Sol Invictus)**: Constantine himself had a personal affinity for Sol Invictus, the Unconquered Sun, and maintained some association with this cult early in his rule. Some scholars believe his vision before the Battle of the Milvian Bridge might have merged his belief in Sol Invictus with the Christian God, contributing to his gradual adoption of Christianity.

2. Mithraism

> Mithraism, a mystery religion centered around the god Mithras, was especially popular among soldiers. Although exclusive to men and involving secretive rituals, it continued to have adherents, particularly in the Roman military, and Constantine did not prohibit its practices.

3. Judaism

> Judaism was tolerated under Constantine's rule, and Jews retained the right to practice their faith. While Constantine was less sympathetic to Jewish customs than to Christianity, he did not suppress the Jewish religion. Jewish communities were free to observe their traditions, worship in synagogues, and continue their religious practices.

4. Various Mystery Religions and Local Deities

> The Roman Empire was home to many mystery religions and local deities, such as the worship of Isis (from Egyptian religion) and other regional gods unique to specific provinces. Constantine allowed these cults and religious traditions to continue, as they posed little political threat and were often deeply ingrained in local cultures.

Constantine's Tolerance Policy

Constantine's approach was rooted in maintaining political, social and religious harmony. His Edict of Milan emphasized religious freedom, declaring that individuals could "follow the religion that each one wanted." This policy reduced the possibility of conflict between religious groups and kept the empire relatively stable as Christianity gained notoriety and prominence.

It wasn't until later, under Emperor Theodosius I, that non-Christian religions began to face significant restrictions. Constantine's policy was one of tolerance, setting the stage for Christianity's rise *but not mandating it at the expense of other faiths, religious or spiritual practices.* Non-Christian religions under Emperor Theodosius I rule began to face significant restrictions. Certain pagan festivals and customs survived, adapted, or merged with other Christian celebrations, even after paganism was officially banned by Theodosius I. Here's a breakdown to clarify how this process happened and why certain Pagan traditions continued and evolved in a new form:

Theodosius I's Ban on Pagan Practices

The Edict of Thessalonica (380 AD): Theodosius declared Christianity the official state religion and issued laws forbidding public pagan rituals and closing pagan temples. However, the reality on the ground was more intricate than expected. While formal, state-sponsored paganism was suppressed, many pagan customs and festivals continued to grow and flourish as they had strong cultural roots and were practiced privately or reinvented. It was difficult to enforce these bans across the vast Roman Empire, especially in remote or rural areas. People held onto their traditions, often finding ways to celebrate quietly or in forms that blended with emerging Christian customs.

Adaptation of Pagan Festivals and Practices Merged into Christian Traditions

Early Christian leaders found it beneficial to adapt and "Christianize" certain pagan festivals to make conversion and acceptance easier for the Roman public. By reinterpreting these festivals with Christian meanings, the church offered familiar celebrations that would ease the transition to Christianity. The church began to reframe pagan symbols, rituals and practices in a Christian context. This process allowed followers of the faith to keep certain customs while imbuing them with new, man-made Christian meanings.

Examples of Pagan Festivals Adapted by Christianity

Saturnalia rebranded to Christmas: The Roman festival of Saturnalia, celebrated around the winter solstice with feasting, gift-giving, and revelry, was gradually merged with Christmas. Although the actual birth date of Jesus isn't known, the Roman Catholic Church established December 25th as the celebration of His birth, overlapping with Saturnalia and Sol Invictus, making the transition smoother to accept and the mirage easier to swallow. The Roman Empire's integration of pagan customs with Christian practices allowed the commercialism of Christianity otherwise known as Christmas to spread more effectively, uniting a diverse population under Roman rule.

Lupercalia rebranded into Valentine's Day: Lupercalia was a fertility festival held in mid-February. The church later replaced it with the feast day of St. Valentine, a Christian martyr. Although different in meaning, certain themes of love and fertility carried over.

Vernal Equinox rebranded into Easter: Easter celebrates the Goddess Eostre as the goddess of fertility and sex. Other cultures celebrated the arrival of spring around the equinox, symbolizing renewal and life. Easter, a pagan holiday having nothing at all to do with Jesus Christ nor his resurrection was rebranded as celebrating

Jesus' resurrection, adopting some of the pagan seasonal symbols, like eggs and rabbits, as symbols of new life.

Samhain rebranded as **Halloween or All Saints' Day**: Samhain/Halloween is the most satanic and blasphemous holiday of all the pagan holidays, a Celtic festival marking the end of harvest and honoring demons and the dead, was Christianized by the Roman Catholic Church into All Saints' Day (November 1) and All Souls' Day (November 2), with Halloween otherwise known as mischief night or Devils Night evolving as a "night before" observance. Elements like honoring the dead overtly demonic persisted was pervertedly presented, packaged and sold as a Christian context.

Brumalia rebranded **New Year's**: Brumalia, honoring various gods associated with agriculture, wine, and the harvest. A pagan celebration, was observed in late December. As Christianity spread, this holiday slowly faded, but the timing around the year's end continued to be significant, eventually leading to New Year's celebrations.

Lemuria rebranded to **All Souls' Day**: A pagan Roman festival focused on appeasing the restless dead, or, to protect the household and community from malevolent demonic spirits. The Roman Lemuria, a day to honor deceased spirits (straight up witchcraft)was transformed into All Souls' Day, where Christians pray for the souls of the dead, retaining the theme of remembering the departed but in a camouflaged into Christianized framework.

Cultural Continuity and Syncretism

This is the blending of religious and cultural practices. Early Christianity combines spiritual, religious and witchcraft fundamentals of Roman, Celtic, and Germanic cultures, creating a syncretic mix. This approach allowed Christianity to spread more effectively, as it did not demand a total rejection of pre-existing cultural norms. The early church often chose to adapt and conform, rather than eradicate,

cultural heritage. By reinterpreting these paganistic customs, it allowed Christianity to become more inclusive of worldly carnality and less foreign the Roman culture and new converts, leading to more widespread acceptance and integration.

The Lasting Impact of Christianized Pagan Customs

Many modern holiday customs, such as Christmas trees, Easter eggs, and Halloween costumes, have roots in pagan secular pre-Christian traditions. These symbols have become secularized over time, with many people celebrating them as carnal tradition, rather than religious customs. In today's society, these holidays are celebrated both by the world, some churches and believers alike within and outside of religious contexts, with pagan secular traditions overlapping with religious observances. While these customs have pagan origins, they have been presented and marketed to fit a worldly, carnal cultural context appealing to both uninformed Christians and non-Christians.

The Deception that has stood the test of time

The Roman Empire skillfully integrated "**pagan rituals**" into the Christian religious tradition by reinterpreting and realigning their meanings, allowing a smoother cultural transition form of inclusivity base population under Roman Rule. Many of these festivals, such as Saturnalia (Christmas), Lupercalia (Valentine's Day), and Samhain (Halloween), have persisted in some sort of shape , form or fashion today sadly even in the church, carrying elements of their pagan origins into modern religious celebrations. These adaptations helped Christianity become more accessible and accepted to a predominantly pagan population while preserving elements of their cultural and spiritual practices. While Theodosius I officially banned pagan practices, the church adapted many popular pagan festivals by reinterpreting their meanings to fit Christian practices and traditions.

Although Constantine the Great is most famous for promoting and integrating Christianity into the Roman Empire, it is important to recognize the overt blending of certain pagan traditions, festivals and adaptations with Christian traditions, practices and symbols that also coincided with this breakthrough. His adaptation of Christianity did not completely excuse itself from pagan traditions but involved some degree of amalgamation.

There is no record of Constantine ever publicly declaring Jesus Christ as his personal Lord and Savior, nor Yahweh as the Sovereign God of the world. No historical document confirms that he viewed Jesus as the exclusive path to salvation in the way the bible defines. Constantine's relationship with Christianity was more than likely a combination of both **personal belief** and **political clout**. While he certainly played a critical role in Christianity's exoneration of persecution and rise  within the Roman Empire, his faith appears more as a favorable disposition toward the Christian God rather than a clear, personal confession of exclusive faith in Jesus as Lord and savior. Constantine continued to use titles and symbols associated with Roman paganism, including Pontifex Maximus, the chief priest of Roman religion, and even issued coins with pagan symbols alongside Christian imagery. This suggests he may have held a syncretic view of religion, valuing Christianity but also not denouncing other beliefs including paganism and witch-craft. As Constantine sought to unify his empire, which was still predominantly pagan when he came to power. Constantine's integration of pagan elements into Christianity was a pragmatic approach (people-pleasing) to unify a rising diverse empire. His promotion of Sunday worship, the use of solar imagery, and the incorporation of imperial cult practices helped align Christian

worship with existing pagan traditions, making the transition smoother for Roman converts. By allowing these pagan continuities, Constantine managed to simultaneously promote Christianity while regarding the deep historically rooted pagan heritage of the Roman world.

Yahweh declares and ordains the Sabbath Day, Not Man, King , Pope or Emperor

According to the Jewish calendar, the Sabbath day (Shabbat) officially begins at sunset on Friday evening and ends at nightfall on Saturday evening. This timing is based on the biblical principle that a day begins at sunset, drawn from *Genesis 1*, which states, *"And there was evening, and there was morning, the first day."*

Specifics of the Sabbath Start and End

The Sabbath begins approximately 18 minutes before sunset on Friday, allowing time to light the Sabbath candles and prepare for rest. This varies slightly by location and season. The Sabbath concludes when three stars are visible in the night sky on Saturday evening, which is around 40 minutes after sunset. This timing is based on Jewish law to ensure that the Sabbath is fully observed and extends slightly beyond sunset. Jewish tradition follows the concept that "evening" precedes "morning," as established in the creation account in Genesis, where each day is counted from evening to evening. This means the day begins at sunset and ends at the following sunset, so the Sabbath runs from Friday sunset to Saturday nightfall.

From a biblical perspective, changing the Sabbath from Saturday to Sunday could be seen as a departure from God's original command to observe the seventh day, and could be viewed as an example of conformity to human traditions or worldly influences. Here's an exploration of this question based on biblical commands, the historical change, and relevant scriptural warnings.

The Biblical Command to Observe the Sabbath on the Seventh Day

God's Commandment in Exodus elaborated in The Fourth Commandment, as given by Yahweh in Exodus 20:8-11, makes clear about observing the Sabbath on the **seventh day**. This commandment doesn't suggest flexibility in which day to keep; it specifically designates the seventh day (Saturday) as a day of rest to honor God's rest in creation. In Exodus 31:16-17, God describes the Sabbath as a "perpetual covenant" between Him and His people. This language indicates that the Sabbath observance on the seventh day was intended to be an enduring practice, a sign of Israel's unique relationship with Yahweh.

Biblical Basis for Seventh-Day Observance

Nowhere in the Bible is there a command to change the Sabbath to the first day of the week (Sunday). From a scriptural standpoint, the seventh-day Sabbath was directly instituted by God as a command to be observed. Constantine's Decree in 321 AD shifted the Christians Sabbath Day from Saturday to Sunday. **Constantine, a mere man in political authority**, played a major role in institutionalizing Sunday as a day of rest, Going against Gods commandment and decree, aligning it with his own political policies and agenda with the hopes of unifying and glorifying his Roman empire. Constantine's decree was not based on a biblical mandate but rather on a desire for a cohesive day of worship within the Roman Empire.

Constantine's endorsement of Sunday as the "respected day of the Sun" reflects Roman and pagan traditions, as much as any respect for Christian practice. The change can be seen as a political decision with religious implications, reflecting human authority over divine command. Theodosius I enforced Sunday worship as the official

Christian Sabbath through a decree that declared those who resisted, "*let them be anathema from Christ,*" where the term *anathema* signifies a severe curse or excommunication, cutting individuals off from the church. To ensure religious conformity, Theodosius imposed excommunication alongside financial fines, property confiscation, and restrictions on civil privileges, effectively isolating dissenters from community and societal participation. He closed non-compliant places of worship, used military force to suppress gatherings opposing the Nicene orthodoxy, and criminalized dissent as a state offense, leading to arrests, exile, and loss of assets. Through these measures, Theodosius employed the state's power to solidify religious unity and establish Sunday as the dominant day of worship across the empire in spite of Yahweh's direct decree that His Sabbath shall be honored and acknowledged on Saturday .

Stern Scriptural Warnings Against Conformity

Romans 12:2 – Conformity to the World: The Apostle Paul warns, "Do not be conformed to this world, but be transformed by the renewing of your mind, that you may prove what is that good and acceptable and perfect will of God" (Romans 12:2). Conforming to the practices of the world, especially when they contradict God's commands, is viewed as inconsistent with biblical teaching.

Warnings Against Human Traditions: In Matthew 15:9, Jesus criticizes the Pharisees for placing human traditions above God's commandments, saying, "*In vain they worship Me, teaching as doctrines the commandments of men*." This principle suggests that following human-established practices in place of God's explicit commands can lead to misplaced priorities.

Paul's Guidance on Remaining Faithful to God's Law: Throughout his letters, Paul emphasizes the importance of staying true to God's commands and not allowing cultural or political pressures to take precedence over biblical truth. For example, in

Colossians 2:8, he warns believers to *beware of "philosophy and empty deceit, according to the tradition of men."*

Implications of Conformity , Changing the Sabbath A critical Departure of Divine Instruction:

By shifting Sabbath observance to Sunday, Christians adopted a practice that was not biblically commanded. This can be viewed as conforming to cultural, political, and societal pressures rather than remaining strictly obedient to the original command of Yahweh to observe the Sabbath on the Seventh day.

Conformity vs. Faithfulness; the change may illustrate a departure from faithfulness to God's original decrees and a shift toward human tradition and authority. The shift reflects an adaptation to a Roman context rather than adherence to the scriptural Sabbath. The Sabbath was instituted at inception of creation by God himself, long before the giving of the law to Israel, and its observance is rooted in God's own actions (Genesis 2:2-3). This indicates that the Sabbath was meant as a universal-biblical-principle, not just a cultural one. Nowhere in the New Testament do we see an explicit change of the Sabbath to Sunday. Jesus himself observed the seventh-day Sabbath, as did the apostles, suggesting continuity with the original command rather than a shift to another day. From a biblical standpoint, changing the Sabbath from Saturday to Sunday can be seen as conformity to human, cultural and political influences, rather than adherence to God's clear command. **The shift is not supported by scriptural decree but by human decision,** specifically through Roman Emperor Constantine and later church tradition. Roman emperor Constantine, the Pope, Kings, Queens or princess do NOT HAVE, nor was ever GRANTED, the authority to change, alter or reconstruct Gods emphatical word. Paul's warning in Romans 12:2 and other biblical passages emphasize the importance of remaining true to God's commands, rather than adopting practices for political or societal convenience. Therefore, those who advocate for seventh-

day Sabbath observance argue that the biblical command remains unaltered and should be honored as originally given by God.

God's Covenant with His People: Blessings and Curses (Deuteronomy 28)

Covenant as Yahweh's decree in action, revealing blessings for obedience and curses for disobedience. This section showcases how God's principles were established to guide His people and emphasize the unchanging nature of His will across generations.

Deuteronomy 28 provides a vivid description of the blessings and curses tied to Israel's covenant relationship with God. This chapter demonstrates Yahweh's expectations for His people and the outcomes of either upholding or breaking His commands. It underscores that the covenant is more than a list of rules; it is a relational commitment, illustrating the principles of God's Nature as Creature, His justice, and the consistency of His will across generations. Here's a breakdown of Deuteronomy 28, touching on the covenant, blessings for obedience, and curses for disobedience.

God's Covenant with His People

Foundational Covenant Structure: The covenant in Deuteronomy 28 is a solemn agreement between Yahweh and Israel. It is based on a **two-way commitment**: God promises blessings if the Israelites obey, and warns of curses if they disobey. This reflects God's steadfast nature, where obedience brings alignment with His will and sustains a harmonious relationship, while disobedience severs that bond. Through this covenant, God's principles are enacted. His decrees serve as clear, unwavering guidelines to protect, prosper, and sanctify His people. They reveal His holy standards and demonstrate the intended blessings for living in obedience. This covenant isn't only for the Israelites of Moses' time; it exemplifies God's enduring principles, showcasing how His will remains consistent. His blessings and curses in Deuteronomy 28 are expressions of His justice and remain foundational to understanding His character.

Blessings in Obedience (Deuteronomy 28:1–14)

If Israel fully obeys Yahweh's commands, He promises immense blessings that permeate every aspect of life. Here's a summary of these blessings.

> ➤ **Personal and Communal Prosperity**: God assures personal blessings, such as good health, safety, and peace, along with communal blessings like increased population and agricultural productivity. Obedience fosters a thriving society under His care.
> ➤ **Abundant Provision and Prosperity**: God promises to bless their cities, fields, and homes with abundance. The land would yield crops plentifully, livestock would multiply, and storehouses would overflow (vs. 3–6).
> ➤ **Protection from Enemies**: God declares His protective power, promising to shield Israel from threats and to cause their enemies to be defeated before them (vs. 7).
> ➤ **International Reputation and Leadership**: Obedience would make Israel a model nation, respected and admired globally, and would grant them economic leadership, lending rather than borrowing (vs. 12–13).
> ➤ **Spiritual Favor and Relationship with God**: Obedience secures a close relationship with Yahweh, and His favor rests upon Israel, who will be set above all other nations as His treasured people.

Curses in Disobedience (Deuteronomy 28:15–68)

The chapter's second half, in stark contrast, outlines the dire consequences of forsaking God's commands. These curses show the depth of God's justice and His intolerance for disobedience among His covenant people.

> ➤ **Personal and National Suffering**: Just as obedience brings prosperity, disobedience leads to suffering, sickness, and poverty. God warns of plagues, diseases, and physical afflictions as a direct result of breaking the covenant (vs. 21–22, 27–29).

> ➤ **Agricultural and Economic Devastation**: Disobedience would cause the land to fail. The once fruitful fields would be barren, livestock would perish, and economic ruin would ensue (vs. 16–18, 38–42).

> ➤ **Defeat and Subjugation by Enemies**: Disobedience would lead to military defeat and oppression by foreign nations. Instead of being victorious, Israel would become subject to other nations, scattered among them, and made into slaves (vs. 25, 36–37, 49–52).

> ➤ **Social and Familial Collapse**: Disobedience leads to societal breakdown. Families would experience separation and loss, and there would be deep betrayal and mistrust within the community (vs. 30–34).

> ➤ **Mental and Emotional Distress**: There would be intense mental anguish and instability among the people, leading to confusion, fear, and despair (vs. 28, 34, 66–67).

> ➤ **Spiritual Estrangement**: Persistent disobedience would lead to spiritual alienation from Yahweh. They would experience the consequences of breaking covenant with God, resulting in spiritual emptiness and isolation (vs. 58–59).

The Unchanging Nature of God's Will

Deuteronomy 28 exemplifies the immutability of God's character. His blessings and curses are not arbitrary but serve a dual purpose of encouraging righteousness and deterring sin. Through this chapter, we observe God's justice in honoring His promises and holding His people accountable to His commands. His decrees in Deuteronomy 28 remain a timeless reminder of His consistent standards for living in accordance with His will.

The Atonement of Sin and Fulfillment in Christ

Scripture Foundations: Romans 5:8-11, Hebrews 9:12-14, *1 Peter 2:24, Leviticus 17:11, Hebrews 9:22, Revelation 5:9 , 1 Peter 3:18 , 2 Corinthians 5:21 , 1 John 4:10 , John 1:29 , Matthew 20:28 Romans 5:11, Galatians 3:13, Revelation 1:5, Hebrews 9:28 , Ephesians 1:7 , 1 Timothy 2:6, Colossians 1:14*

Jesus Christ provided atonement for sin through sacrifices and ultimately fulfilled this through Christ's sacrifice. The atonement of sin is one of the most sacrificial events of the ages, embodying God's unmatched divine love, mercy, and justice as fulfilled in Jesus Christ, the promised Messiah. In understanding the atonement, we glimpse into God's heart and His plan to reconcile humanity to Himself through Jesus. From the earliest sacrificial systems established in the Old Testament to the ultimate sacrifice of Christ on the cross, the atonement serves to restore our relationship with God, affirm His love and justice, and secure the salvation of believers under His sovereign plan. The following sections will delve into the purpose, fulfillment, and implications of the atonement of sin, with emphasis on key scriptures.

The concept of atonement originates in the Old Testament, where sacrifices and offerings were instituted by God to cover the sins of His people. According to Leviticus 17:11, "the life of a creature is in the blood, and I have given it to you to make atonement for yourselves on the altar; it is the blood that makes atonement for one's life." The shedding of blood was thus central to the atonement, symbolizing the giving of life to cover sin, which separates humanity from God. This system underscored the gravity of sin and the necessity of blood to cleanse and bring about reconciliation with God.

Atonement, at its core, was about bridging the gap between a holy God and sinful humanity. The sacrificial system established a way for God's people to approach Him, highlighting that reconciliation

required a sacrifice. Yet, the animal sacrifices, as Hebrews 10:4 states, were not ultimately effective to take away sin; they served as a foreshadowing of the perfect sacrifice to come. They were a temporary measure under God's covenant with Israel, pointing forward to the coming Messiah who would provide a final, once-for-all atonement for sin.

Jesus Christ fulfilled the promise of atonement as the perfect, sinless Lamb of God. In John 1:29, John the Baptist exclaims upon seeing Jesus, *"Look, the Lamb of God, who takes away the sin of the world!"* Jesus' coming signified the fulfillment of the Old Testament sacrifices. Unlike animal sacrifices, which were repeated and imperfect, Jesus' sacrifice was once for all, complete and perfect. Hebrews 9:12-14 describes how Christ, by His own blood, entered the Most Holy Place, "obtaining eternal redemption" for believers. This sacrifice was able to "cleanse our consciences from acts that lead to death, so that we may serve the living God."

The significance of Jesus' sacrifice is unmatched throughout the ages. As God incarnate, He was able to bear the full weight of human sin and guilt. 1 Peter 2:24 explains that "He himself bore our sins in His body on the cross, so that we might die to sins and live for righteousness." Jesus' atonement was not merely a covering but a complete removal of sin, allowing believers to stand justified before God. This act of sacrificial love demonstrated God's desire to restore the broken relationship caused by sin. Romans 5:8-11 encapsulates this truth, *"But God demonstrates His own love for us in this; While we were still sinners, Christ died for us...We also rejoice in God through our Lord Jesus Christ, through whom we have now received reconciliation."*

The atonement reveals both God's love and justice. Sin incurs a debt that demands justice, as sin is an offense against a holy God. This is clearly stated in Hebrews 9:22, which declares, "without the shedding of blood there is no forgiveness." God's justice required that the penalty of sin and death be paid. Yet His love was so great that He provided a way for this penalty to be met without condemning humanity. In 1 John 4:10, it says, *"This is love: not that we loved God, but that He loved us and sent His Son as an atoning sacrifice for our sins."*

Jesus' sacrificial death satisfied God's justice while manifesting His love. This balance between justice and love is further emphasized in *2 Corinthians 5:21: "God made Him who had no sin to be sin for us, so that in Him we might become the righteousness of God."* Jesus, though sinless, took upon Himself the guilt of sin, absorbing the wrath of God on behalf of humanity. In doing so, He became the perfect substitute, the ultimate expression of divine love and justice meeting in perfect harmony.

SECURING BELIEVERS UNDER YAHWEH'S SOVEREIGN PLAN

The atonement of Jesus Christ secures believers in God's sovereign plan of salvation. Through His death and resurrection, Jesus not only conquered sin but also granted believers the promise of eternal life and reconciliation with God. Revelation 5:9 speaks of Christ's worthiness to open the scroll and redeem people from every tribe, language, people, and nation by His blood. This redemption encompasses all who believe in Him, uniting them as one people under God's kingdom.

Through the atonement, believers are brought into a covenant relationship with God, where they are covered by Christ's righteousness and empowered by the Holy Spirit. Ephesians 1:7 confirms this, saying, *"In Him, we have redemption through His blood, the forgiveness of sins, in accordance with the riches of God's grace."* Believers are not only forgiven but are made heirs of God's promises, secure in the salvation purchased by Jesus' blood.

This assurance is further illustrated in 1 Peter 3:18, which states, "For Christ also suffered once for sins, the righteous for the unrighteous, to bring you to God." Jesus' suffering was purposeful; it reconciled believers to God and granted them access to His presence. The

atonement anchors believers in the certainty of their salvation, for it is based not on their own works but on the finished work of Christ.

The atonement through Jesus brings freedom from sin and death, offering believers a new identity and purpose in Christ. Galatians 3:13 declares, *"Christ redeemed us from the curse of the law by becoming a curse for us."* Through His sacrifice, Jesus broke the power of sin and its curse, enabling believers to live in the freedom of God's grace. This liberation from sin empowers Christians to pursue a life of holiness and devotion to God, no longer bound by the chains of guilt and condemnation.

Furthermore, the atonement calls believers into a life of purpose and mission. *In Matthew 20:28, Jesus states, "the Son of Man did not come to be served, but to serve, and to give His life as a ransom for many."* As recipients of Christ's redemptive work, believers are called to reflect His love and serve others, bearing witness to the transformative power of the gospel. 1 John 4:10 emphasizes that believers are to love others as God has loved them, demonstrating the impact of Christ's atoning work in their lives.

Finally, the atonement inspires worship and gratitude. In Revelation 1:5, believers are reminded that Jesus loves us and has "freed us from our sins by His blood." The response to this act of divine love is one of reverence and worship, as Christians acknowledge the cost of their salvation and the depth of God's mercy. Colossians 1:14 affirms this gratitude, recognizing that "in Him we have redemption, the forgiveness of sins." The atonement compels believers to live lives of worship, grounded in the knowledge that they have been redeemed at a great cost.

The atonement of sin through Jesus Christ is central to the Christian faith, fulfilling God's promise to redeem and restore His people. By offering Himself as the ultimate sacrifice, Jesus bridged the divide between humanity and God, paving the way for eternal reconciliation. The atonement underscores God's love and justice,

His desire to draw humanity to Himself, and His commitment to upholding His holy standards. In Christ, believers find forgiveness, freedom, purpose, and an unshakeable hope.

Scriptures like *Romans 5:11*, which declare, *"We also rejoice in God through our Lord Jesus Christ, through whom we have now received reconciliation,"* ricochets' the joy and peace that flow from this atonement. Jesus' fulfillment of the atonement reveals Yahweh's sovereign plan, a plan where love and justice meet, where the broken are restored, and where believers are secured under the grace of God. This profound act of love is not only a testament to God's character but a foundation for the Christian life, calling believers to live in the light of His mercy and to share this gospel of reconciliation with the world.

Through the atonement of Christ, God's sovereign plan is revealed and fulfilled, culminating in the ultimate hope for believers, the promise of eternal life with God. This atoning sacrifice invites all to experience the depth of God's love and to enter into a restored relationship with Him, affirming that, indeed, Jesus is the promised Messiah, the Lamb of God who takes away the sin of the world.

Jesus as the Author of the New Covenant
Luke 22:20, Hebrews 8:6-13

Jesus, the Mediator of a new covenant, fulfilled Yahweh's decree by securing eternal redemption. This section can discuss Jesus' role in establishing a covenant of grace, one that calls believers into a relationship with God and ensures His eternal promises.

In the New Covenant, Jesus is the Mediator who bridges the gap between God and humanity, fulfilling Yahweh's decree through His sacrificial death and resurrection. The foundation of this covenant rests in the promise of grace, a divine gift that offers eternal redemption and reconciliation with God. In *Luke 22:20*, Jesus declares, *"This cup is the new covenant in my blood, which is poured out for you,"* signifying His blood as the seal of this new relationship. His

sacrifice replaces the need for the repetitive animal sacrifices of the Old Covenant, as Jesus' perfect offering was sufficient to cover all sin for all time.

Hebrews 8:6-13 highlights the supremacy of the New Covenant by stating that Jesus has a "more excellent ministry" because He mediates an "improved covenant" established on better promises. Under the Old Covenant, the law written on stone tablets by Yahweh, then delivered through Moses, adherence was required for fellowship with God. However, the New Covenant promised in Jeremiah 31:31-34 and reiterated in Hebrews ensures that the law is now written on believers' hearts. This shift signifies a move from external obligation to internal transformation, where believers are invited into a deep, personal relationship with God through Christ.

Through His role as the Author of the New Covenant, Jesus not only fulfills the prophecies of the Old Testament but also offers a path to salvation based on grace, not works. This covenant calls believers into an everlasting relationship, secured by His promise to remember their sins no more. In accepting Jesus' sacrifice, believers embrace a covenant of love and forgiveness, an enduring relationship marked by God's faithfulness. By establishing this New Covenant, Jesus assures believers of their inheritance as children of God and co-heirs in His kingdom, a promise that is as eternal as God's love.

Jesus' Final Warning Before Ascension Matthew 28:18-20, Acts 1:8-11

Jesus' final instructions and warnings to His disciples, underscored the urgency of living under Yahweh's decree. Emphasize how His commands call believers to uphold God's ways, marking the transition from His earthly ministry to the Spirit-led mission of the Church.

Jesus' final warning to His disciples before His ascension was a sobering reminder of the spiritual challenges they would face and the judgment awaiting those who rejected His message. In the hours and days leading up to His departure, He spoke words that warned His disciples about the weight of their mission, the coming hardships, and the reality of His imminent return.

One of the strongest warnings Jesus left to his disciples is found in Matthew 24:4-14, where He foretold the trials that would come upon the world and the Church before His return. Jesus warned of false prophets, wars, persecutions, and the love of many growing cold. He urged His disciples to remain vigilant, reminding them that they would face deception and hardship as they spread His message. This warning highlighted the need for discernment and perseverance; they were not only to preach the gospel but also to guard their own hearts and remain faithful amid adversity.

Jesus also warned His disciples that He would return "like a thief in the night" (1 Thessalonians 5:2), encouraging them to always be prepared. In Matthew 25, through the parables of the Ten Virgins and the Talents, Jesus warned them about the importance of being spiritually ready and active. The parable of the Ten Virgins emphasizes readiness for His return, as the unprepared virgins found themselves shut out from the wedding banquet. This served as a metaphor for the spiritual state of His followers, encouraging them to keep their "lamps" filled with oil, symbolizing a life sustained by faith and the Holy Spirit, so they would be ready when He returned.

In *Acts 1:7*, Jesus issued a final caution, saying, *"It is not for you to know the times or dates, the Father has set by his own authority."* This warning reminds the disciples to focus not on trying to predict His return, but on fulfilling the mission He had given them. Jesus emphasized that their energy should be directed toward spreading the gospel, not speculating on His timing. This instruction was crucial in keeping their focus on their purpose rather than being sidetracked by curiosity or distractions.

The overall theme of Jesus' final warnings to His disciples was one of urgency, faithfulness, and vigilance. He called them to be ready at

all times, to stay faithful to the end, and to live with a sense of expectancy for His return. This warning, intended not only for His disciples but for all believers, underscores the reality that the end could come at any moment. Jesus' words serve as a powerful call to live each day in alignment with His teachings, actively preparing for the day He will return in judgment and glory. In these final warnings, Jesus impressed upon His disciples the seriousness of their mission, the cost of discipleship, and the promise of His return, urging them to carry out their calling with unwavering devotion until they would meet Him again.

God's Will or Your Will Be Done: The Believer's Freedom to Choose

Matthew 26:39, Romans 12:1-2, Romans 12:2 , Matthew 6:10, Ephesians 5:17 , Proverbs 3:5-6 , Jeremiah 29:11, Hebrews 10:36, Psalm 119:105, 1 Timothy 2:4, 1 John 2:16-17, 1 Peter 3:17 , Mark 3:35, 1 Peter 4:19, Proverbs 19:21,

The choice believers face between surrendering to Yahweh's will or pursuing their own. Human free will forever wages war against the divine sovereignty of Gods will. We examine the importance of aligning with God's will to receive His promises.

The pursuit of "God's Will or Your Will Be Done" reveals one of the most wrestled-with aspects of a believer's journey; the freedom to choose one's path while ultimately recognizing that God's sovereignty reigns supreme. Throughout Scripture, God grants humanity free will, making us "free moral agents" who can make our own choices. Yet, God's will is supreme, and His purposes will prevail. This balance between human free will and divine sovereignty invites believers to constantly seek alignment with God's purposes. Scripture describes God's will as pure, perfect, and pleasing (Romans 12:2). It is more than a set of rules; it is a path to true purpose and peace. God's will is rooted in His love, wisdom, and desire for humanity's fullness of life. In Jeremiah 29:11, God assures, *"For I know the plans I have for you…plans to prosper you and not to harm you, plans for a hope and a future."* God's will is ultimately for our highest good, leading to a purpose-filled life aligned with His kingdom.

In Ephesians 5:17, Paul encourages believers to "understand what the Lord's will is," stressing that understanding God's will is crucial for those who follow Him. ***This guidance comes through Scripture, prayer, the prompting of the Holy Spirit, and godly counsel***. Believers are called to surrender their lives to God's plan, even when it challenges personal desires. From the beginning, God gave humans the ability to choose, as seen in Eden (Genesis 2-3). This freedom allows us to follow God's will or pursue our own paths. Proverbs 19:21 recognizes this reality: "Many are the plans in a person's heart, but it is the Lord's purpose that prevails." Though we can choose our path, God's will holds eternal significance.

This freedom carries responsibility. Choosing our own will over God's can distance us from His purpose. God invites us to yield our will to Him, not as a form of control but as an expression of love. Romans 12:1 urges believers to "offer [themselves] as a living sacrifice, holy and pleasing to God," symbolizing a willing submission of one's will. The tension between following God's will and pursuing personal desires is a familiar struggle. In Matthew 26:39, Jesus expresses this conflict in Gethsemane, praying, "My Father, if it is possible, may this cup be taken from me. Yet not as I will, but as you will." Here, Jesus models the surrender of personal desire to God's plan, even in the face of suffering.

Believers often face similar choices, balancing aspirations with God's calling. Pursuing our own will may seem satisfying momentarily, but it can lack fulfillment. Jesus warns in *Matthew 7:21-23: "Not everyone who says to Me, 'Lord, Lord,' shall enter the kingdom of heaven, but he who does the will of My Father in heaven."* This statement highlights the gravity of choosing God's will over self-will. Jesus indicates that words alone are insufficient; true faith is evidenced by obedience to God's will.

Those who claim to follow Jesus but reject His commands are warned of the consequences of self-deception. Their choices may lead them to stand before Christ only to hear, "I never knew you; depart from Me, you who practice lawlessness." Jesus' warning underscores that doing God's will is essential to enter His kingdom.

Aligning with God's Will: Seeking Divine Guidance

Aligning with God's will, requires intentionality, humility, and seeking His direction over our own. Proverbs 3:5-6 urges, *"Trust in the Lord with all your heart and lean not on your own understanding; in all your ways submit to him, and he will make your paths straight."* This submission is not passive acceptance but active pursuit, requiring us to release control and trust His wisdom. To discern God's will, believers are encouraged **to renew their minds through Scripture (Romans 12:2), to pray, and to remain sensitive to the Holy Spirit.** God's Word is a lamp to our feet (Psalm 119:105), guiding us in uncertainty. The Holy Spirit within believers helps us navigate decisions and align with God's purposes. Choosing to follow our own will over God's leads to spiritually costly consequences. When believers pursue desires misaligned with God's plan, they may experience emptiness or spiritual stagnation. *Proverbs 14:12* warns, *"There is a way that appears to be right, but in the end, it leads to death."* This death may be spiritual, causing separation from God's blessings and the peace that comes with walking in His purpose. In Matthew 6:10, Jesus teaches that our daily prayer should include, "Your kingdom come, your will be done on earth as it is in heaven." This expresses a commitment to place God's will above our own, prioritize His kingdom, and seek alignment with His plans. It reminds believers that fulfilling God's will on earth is a collective and individual calling, requiring daily surrender and long-term commitment.

God's Sovereignty: The Final Say

While believers are free to choose their paths, God's sovereignty ensures that His purposes will ultimately be fulfilled. Proverbs 19:21 assures, *"Many are the plans in a person's heart, but it is the Lord's purpose that prevails."* Even when humans exercise their free will away from God's intended path, He can redeem and redirect their course, accomplishing His greater plan.

Romans 8:28 reveals, *"And we know that in all things God works for the good of those who love him, who have been called according to his purpose."* This speaks to God's ability to work through both our successes and failures, bringing about His purposes even when our choices lead us away from His will. Though we may stray, God's grace draws us back, and His sovereignty ensures that His ultimate plan is never thwarted.

THE REWARD OF CHOOSING GOD'S WILL

For those who choose to align their lives with God's will, there is a profound reward; the experience of true purpose, peace, and eternal life. Hebrews 10:36 reminds believers that "you need to persevere so that when you have done the will of God, you will receive what he has promised." Aligning with God's will opens the door to blessings that far surpass the fleeting rewards of pursuing personal desires. Inevitably, the choice between "God's will or your will be done" reflects a fundamental aspect of the believer's journey; the freedom to choose as a free moral agent and the responsibility to submit to God's purposes. While we have autonomy to follow our desires, true fulfillment lies in surrendering to God's perfect will. The journey of faith calls believers to trust in God's wisdom, seek His guidance, and embrace His purposes over their own. Ultimately, God's will reigns supreme, and aligning with it allows believers to experience the

fullness of life that comes with walking in His light, purpose, and promise.

THE FINAL TRUMPET! ANNOUNCING THE END

1 Corinthians 15:51-52, Revelation 11:15

The final trumpet as Yahweh's declaration of the end of the age and the fulfillment of His sovereign plan. <u>This event signifies the culmination of prophecy, the resurrection of believers, and the establishment of His eternal kingdom.</u> The sounding of the final trumpet is a momentous event in biblical prophecy, marking the end of the age and the fulfillment of Yahweh's sovereign plan. Rooted in Scriptures like 1 Corinthians 15:51-52 and Revelation 11:15, the final trumpet announces the resurrection of believers and the establishment of God's eternal kingdom. It signals the culmination of God's promises to His people, gathering those who have accepted His call and aligning creation under His eternal reign. For those who have heeded the call of repentance, this moment brings the promise of transformation, as they are clothed in immortality and meet their Savior. This trumpet call is God's ultimate declaration that His judgment has arrived and that His Word has been fulfilled in its entirety. <u>Repentance remains a vital invitation while we have life,</u> yet the final trumpet serves as a reminder that this offer is not indefinite. God, in His mercy, has extended the gift of salvation and the chance to turn from sin while we live, but once the trumpet sounds or one's earthly life concludes, no further appeals will be heard. This closing of the door to grace underscores the importance of choosing God now, as no one can claim ignorance at this stage. The Scriptures are clear that after death or at the final trumpet, there is no opportunity to negotiate or bargain with God's justice. The decisions we make in life seal our fate in eternity, underscoring the urgency of repentance and the acceptance of salvation before it is too late.

The final trumpet is not merely a Biblical event but a line of separation between God's mercy and His judgment. In this climactic moment, there is a definitive end to the opportunity for grace, as the eternal kingdom is set and judgment is rendered. Revelation 11:15 proclaims the victory of Christ's kingdom, where He reigns forever and all earthly authority is made subject to Him. This profound moment affirms that God's patience, though abundant, has a purpose and a limit. For those who ignored His call or dismissed His Word, the final trumpet brings the sobering reality of an eternal separation from God, with no possibility for appeals or reconsideration. It is, therefore, a call for all to turn to God now, while the opportunity for forgiveness and reconciliation remains.

The White Throne Judgment Revelation 20:11-15

Yahweh's decree fulfilled in judgment, where each person is judged according to their deeds. Describe the justice and righteousness of Yahweh, whose judgment is final and reveals the outcome for the righteous and the wicked.

The White Throne Judgment is a climactic event in biblical prophecy, representing the fulfillment of Yahweh's decree and the ultimate moment of divine justice as described in Revelation 20:11-15. At this throne, Yahweh sits in purity and holiness, with all creation laid bare before Him. This is a day of reckoning, where each person is judged according to their deeds, both the hidden and the seen. The righteousness of God shines through this judgment, affirming that His standard is perfect, His wisdom unfailing, and His justice unerring. As the Creator and ultimate Lawgiver, Yahweh alone has the authority to determine each person's eternal destiny, and at the White Throne, there is no bias or favoritism only pure, divine justice that cannot be appealed or altered.

This exponentially reveals Yahweh's unchanging character and His commitment to justice within His kingdom. It serves as the final separation between the righteous, whose names are found in the Book of Life, and the wicked, who are cast into the lake of fire. For the righteous, the White Throne Judgment confirms the fullness of

Yahweh's promises, affirming their faith and faithfulness in life as they enter His eternal kingdom. For the wicked, this judgment is a solemn declaration that their choices have brought them eternal separation from God. In this way, the White Throne Judgment emphasizes the gravity of our choices on earth and serves as a powerful reminder of Yahweh's sovereignty, holiness, and the inescapable reality of His justice. The relevance of the White Throne Judgment to the Kingdom of God lies in its role as the final establishment of God's order, where all rebellion, sin, and opposition are removed from His creation. It marks the ultimate purification of His kingdom, ensuring that only those who have embraced His love, righteousness, and truth dwell in His eternal presence. This judgment is Yahweh's final act of restoration, establishing peace, holiness, and joy in His kingdom without the stain of sin. Through this judgment, Yahweh confirms that His kingdom is one of truth and justice, with the redeemed experiencing the fullness of God's promises, and His authority reigning supreme forever.

Yahweh's Way, The Final Say

Revelation 21:1-7, Isaiah 46:10

Yahweh's sovereignty from the beginning to the end. His Word is the final authority, and His kingdom will stand eternally. The hope and glory found in Yahweh's eternal plan is priceless to those who are His. In the end, God's Word will stand unchallenged, for Yahweh's sovereignty is eternal, and His decrees are unbreakable. Isaiah 46:10 declares, *"My counsel shall stand, and I will accomplish all my purpose,"* underscoring that from the beginning of time to its end, God's will prevail over all things. Every prophecy, every promise, and every warning in Scripture is fulfilled according to His timing and purpose. This ultimate authority assures believers that Yahweh's kingdom, unlike the fleeting kingdoms of this world, is unshakable and everlasting. God has the final say, not only in individual lives but over the entire course of history, times-past and the future, guiding it toward His glorious conclusion where His Word is fulfilled in every detail. Yahweh's final declaration will usher in a new creation, where sin, death, and sorrow have no place. Revelation 21:1-7 paints a picture of the new heaven and new earth, where God's people dwell with Him in perfect peace and joy. *"Behold, the dwelling place of God is with man. He will dwell with them, and they will be His people."* This statement affirms that the ultimate fulfillment of His Word is not only a kingdom but a relationship, an eternal bond with those who have remained faithful. In this restored creation, every tear is wiped away, every pain is removed, and the former things have passed. This is Yahweh's final, triumphant declaration over creation, that His Word brings life, restoration, and unbreakable fellowship with His people.

__Nothing else will matter in that final day but Yahweh's Word and His eternal decree. Earthly achievements, human philosophies, and all alternative paths will fade in the light of His glory__, as Philippians 2:10-11 declares that every knee will bow, and every tongue confess that Jesus Christ is Lord. At this final moment, there is no competing voice or opinion, only the truth and authority of God's Word. In John 12:48, Jesus Himself states, "The word that I have spoken will judge him on the last day," emphasizing that our lives are measured by the divine standard alone. For believers, this is a source of hope and strength, a promise that despite life's trials, <u>Yahweh's Word is unchanging and His kingdom awaits those who cling to it. His promises are our inheritance, and His truth will reign supreme eternally, assuring us that in the end, it is indeed Yahweh's way and His final say that will endure forever.</u>

John 16:33 *"These things I have spoken to you, that in Me you may have peace. In the world you will have tribulation; but be of good cheer, I have overcome the world."*

Matthew 5:10 *"Blessed are those who are persecuted for righteousness' sake, for theirs is the kingdom of heaven,"*

Crowned for Purpose

John 1:1

Crown of Life

Hebrews 1:1-2

Names of the Most-High God

21 Unique Names of God, Yahweh's Sovereignty

Yahweh	The self-existing, eternal God	(Exodus 3:14)
Elohim	God the Creator	(Genesis 1:1)
Adonai	Lord, Master	(Psalm 8:1)
El Shaddai	God Almighty	(Genesis 17:1)
Jehovah Jireh	The Lord Will Provide	(Genesis 22:14)
Jehovah Rapha	The Lord Who Heals	(Exodus 15:26)
Jehovah Nissi	The Lord Is My Banner	(Exodus 17:15)
Jehovah Shalom	The Lord Is Peace	(Judges 6:24)
Jehovah Tsidkenu	The Lord Our Righteousness	(Jeremiah 23:6)
Jehovah Mekoddishkem	The Lord Who Sanctifies	(Exodus 31:13)
Jehovah Sabaoth	The Lord of Hosts	(1 Samuel 1:3)
Jehovah Raah	The Lord Is My Shepherd	(Psalm 23:1)
Jehovah Shammah	The Lord Is There	(Ezekiel 48:35)
El Elyon	God Most High	(Genesis 14:18-20)
El Roi	The God Who Sees	(Genesis 16:13)
El Olam	The Everlasting God	(Genesis 21:33)
Yahweh Tsuri	The Lord Is My Rock	(Psalm 18:2)
Yahweh Nakeh	The Lord Who Strikes	(Ezekiel 7:9)
Yahweh Bore	The Lord Creator	(Isaiah 40:28)
Abba Father	Father, of intimacy and relationship	(Romans 8:15; Galatians 4:6)
Ancient of Days	Eternal One, referenced in the Book of Daniel	(Daniel 7:9-22)

Isaiah 53: *"And He was wounded for our transgressions, He was bruised for our iniquities; The chastisement for our peace was upon Him, And by His stripes we are healed. All we like sheep have gone astray; We have turned, every one, to his own way; And the Lord has laid on Him the iniquity of us all..."*

"Then the seventh angel blew his trumpet, and there were loud voices in heaven, saying, "The kingdom of the world has become the kingdom of our Lord and of his Christ, and he shall reign forever and ever." **Revelation 11:15**

Daniel 2:44 "And in the days of those kings the God of heaven will set up a kingdom that shall never be destroyed, nor shall the kingdom be left to another people. It shall

break in pieces all these kingdoms and bring them to an end, and it shall stand forever."

Matthew 11:12 "From the days of John the Baptist until now the kingdom of heaven has suffered violence, the violent take it by force.

JEHOVA SHAMAH

BEARING THE CROSS, EMBRACING
THE PAIN , REFINED AS PURE GOLD

Jehovah Shammah – God is Present in Every Trial. Ezekiel 48:35 – "The Lord is there." God, Jehovah Shammah, is present in every aspect of the believer's journey, through bearing the cross, enduring trials, and receiving the crown. This presence provides assurance and strength".

Ezekiel 48:35 – "The Lord is <u>there</u>."

In every season, Jehovah Shammah, "The Lord is there" remains an unwavering source of hope and blessed-assurance for the believer. This divine presence was not only promised to the Israelites in their restoration but extends to every follower of Christ today. The journey of faith is one marked by peaks and valleys, seasons of rejoicing and seasons of deep trial. Yet, through it all, God's presence is constant.

When believers are called to bear their cross, facing personal struggles, doubts, and pains, they are not alone. Jehovah Shammah is there, providing strength to endure the journey. As Jesus bore His cross, He embodied the promise that <u>God walks with us through suffering.</u> Just as Christ endured His darkest hours for the joy set before Him, we are encouraged by the reminder that God's presence brings purpose and meaning to our trials.

In the midst of every storm, Jehovah Shammah stands as our steady refuge, reassuring us that His hand remains upon us. This presence does not remove the hardships but instead infuses them with divine strength, peace, and comfort. Through every hardship, God shapes us, refining our faith as pure gold, preparing us for the eternal crown of life.

Finally, as we press toward the reward of faith, the crown promised to those who endure, Jehovah Shammah is not only there at the finish line; He is present every step along the way. The God who declares, "I am with you," remains our close companion from the first steps of faith to the moment we meet Him face to face. Jehovah Shammah, our ever-present God, is the sustaining power in every trial, our strength, and the reason we press on.

BEARING THE CROSS: THE PATH OF ENDURANCE

The Call to Follow Christ *"If anyone would come after me, let him deny himself and take up his cross and follow me." Following Christ requires self-denial and willingness to endure trials Mark 8:34.*

Strength Through Trials

➤ **John 19:17** *"And He, bearing His cross, went out to a place called the Place of a Skull, which is called in Hebrew, Golgotha"*, Jesus' example of bearing His cross shows the ultimate act of obedience and sacrifice.

➤ **1 Corinthians 1:18** *" For the message of the cross is foolishness to those who are perishing, but to us who are being saved it is the power of God"*. For those who are saved, the cross is the power of God, even if the world sees it as foolishness.

➤ **James 1:2-4** *" My brethren, count it all joy when you fall into various trials, knowing that the testing of your faith produces patience. But let patience have its perfect work, that you may be perfect and complete, lacking nothing"* "Count it all joy…when you meet trials…for the testing of your faith produces steadfastness." Bearing the cross builds endurance and steadfast faith, foundational for spiritual maturity.

A Believers' Call, The Civil Duty of Following Christ
Bearing the Cross, The Path of Discipleship and Endurance

The call to follow Christ is more than a private faith; it is a sacred duty that shapes how believers interact with the world. It is a "civil duty" in the sense that followers of Jesus are ambassadors of His love, justice, and truth in society, standing as visible representatives of God's kingdom on Earth. This duty requires believers to embrace the path of discipleship with commitment and resilience, just as Jesus described in *Mark 8:34: "If anyone would come after me, let him deny himself and take up his cross and follow me."*

This call entails self-denial, a challenging but essential aspect of the Christian life. In a world that often celebrates self-gratification, believers are called to live counter-culturally by putting God's will above personal desires. Self-denial means setting aside pride, worldly ambition, and selfish motivations to seek first the kingdom of God. This path is difficult, but it is part of bearing the cross, enduring hardship and staying faithful even when the journey is tough.

In John 19:17, we see Jesus Himself bearing His cross, a powerful example of obedience and sacrifice. His path was one of humiliation and suffering, yet He took it willingly out of love and submission to the Father's will. As His followers, we are invited to walk a similar path, enduring trials and suffering, when necessary, as a testament to our devotion to Him. Our trials, though often painful, are not without purpose. They refine us, deepen our faith, and align us more closely with the heart of Christ, who endured the ultimate trial on our behalf.

The Apostle Paul understood this power in the cross, explaining in 1 Corinthians 1:18 that *"the word of the cross is folly to those who are perishing, but to us who are being saved, it is the power of God."* While the world may see our faith as foolish, those who experience the transformative work of the cross understand its power. The cross is more than a symbol; it is the pathway to new life, where we find the strength to endure life's hardships and persevere in faith. James 1:2-4 also reminds us that trials are opportunities for growth. "Count it all joy," he writes, "when you meet trials…for the testing of your faith produces steadfastness." These words speak directly to the heart of bearing the cross. Trials are not obstacles but building blocks in our spiritual maturity, shaping us into people of endurance and deep faith. When we face challenges with joy and perseverance, we grow in steadfastness, becoming better equipped to fulfill our calling as Christ's followers.

In essence, the believer's "civil duty" is to reflect Christ in every facet of life. As we carry our cross, following His example, we contribute to the kingdom building of Gods ministerial calling on earth, as kingdom-lights that shine in darkness, love, and truth. Bearing the cross may lead us through trials, but it also grants us the strength to endure and the privilege of walking with Christ. Through self-denial, steadfast faith, and unwavering devotion, we fulfill our duty to God and to the world, embodying the kingdom values that make a lasting impact.

"The Process of Spiritual Refinement for the Follower of Christ" **Refinement, Purified Through Trials.**

THE PROCESS OF SPIRITUAL REFINEMENT

- ➢ **1 Peter 1:6-7** *"In this you greatly rejoice, though now for a little while, if need be, you have been grieved by various trials, that the genuineness of your faith, being much more precious than gold that perishes, though it is tested by fire, may be found to praise, honor, and glory at the revelation of Jesus Christ"* Trials test the genuineness of faith, purifying it as gold, resulting in praise and honor.
- ➢ **Isaiah 48:10** *"Behold, I have refined you, but not as silver; I have tested you in the furnace of affliction.* This speaks to God's intention to refine through hardship, not to destroy, but to purify.
- ➢ **Zechariah 13:9** *The refining pot is for silver and the furnace for gold, But the Lord tests the hearts.* God refines as silver and gold, assuring His people that they are His.

Purposeful Testing by God

- ➤ **Proverbs 17:3** *"The refining pot is for silver and the furnace for gold, But the Lord tests the hearts".* The crucible tests silver, and the furnace tests gold, but the Lord tests hearts.
- ➤ **Job 23:10** *"But He knows the way that I take; When He has tested me, I shall come forth as gold".* Affirming the result of refinement is purity and resilience.

The Process of Spiritual Refinement for the Follower of Christ

Purified Through Trials

The journey of spiritual refinement is essential to the life of a believer. God, as a wise and loving Father, uses trials and hardships to refine His chosen ones; shaping them into vessels of honor and maturity. This refining process, often uncomfortable, serves to purify and strengthen faith, proving its authenticity and preparing believers to fulfill God's purposes.

In 1 Peter 1:6-7, Peter describes trials as the means by which faith is tested and refined, *"so that the tested genuineness of your faith, more precious than gold that perishes though it is tested by fire, may be found to result in praise and glory and honor at the revelation of Jesus Christ."* Here, Peter equates the believer's faith to gold, which is purified through intense heat. Just as gold, once refined, displays greater value and brilliance, so too does faith become purer and stronger when it endures trials. Through testing, believers are not only made stronger but also more aligned with the character and will of Christ, which brings honor to God.

Isaiah 48:10 emphasizes that God refines us *"in the furnace of affliction."* This imagery of the furnace speaks to the depth and intensity of some of our trials. God's purpose in allowing hardship is not to harm but to purify to strip away impurities like selfishness, fear, and doubt, ultimately producing a heart that fully trusts in Him. It is through affliction that we become more deeply dependent on God's grace, and our faith is sharpened, ready to withstand life's challenges. In

Zechariah 13:9, God reassures His people, saying, *"I will refine them like silver and test them like gold. They will call on my name, and I will answer them; I will say, 'They are my people,' and they will say, 'The Lord is our God."* This refinement is personal. God is deeply invested in the transformation of His people, refining them not as a distant observer but as an intimate guide and sustainer. By purifying their hearts, He affirms His love and ownership, establishing a profound connection where His people recognize Him fully as their God. Purposeful testing is echoed in Proverbs 17:3: *"The crucible for silver and the furnace for gold, but the Lord tests the heart."* This comparison highlights that while gold and silver are refined by earthly means, the heart undergoes refinement by God Himself. This process is often about revealing hidden motives, fears, or dependencies that hinder spiritual growth, allowing believers to experience greater spiritual freedom and purity.

The story of Job also illustrates this truth. In Job 23:10, he states, "When he has tried me, I shall come forth as gold." Despite the depth of his suffering, Job recognizes the refining hand of God at work. His trials, while painful, yield resilience and purity, ultimately preparing him for deeper understanding and blessing.

Spiritual refinement is a continual process, whereby God lovingly removes impurities and strengthens faith. Though painful, it is purposeful, leading to greater intimacy with Him, resilience in faith, and readiness to fulfill His will. The result is a faith purified by trials, a life that brings honor to God, and a heart fully devoted to Him.

The Process of Refinement: Purified for the Crown

Purpose of Refinement

> ➤ **1 Peter 1:6-7** *"In this you greatly rejoice, though now for a little while, if need be, you have been grieved by various trials, that the genuineness of your faith, being much more precious than gold that perishes, though it is tested by fire, may be found to praise, honor, and glory at the revelation of Jesus Christ"* Trials serve to refine and purify faith,

likened to gold tested by fire, to bring glory and honor to Christ.

➢ **Isaiah 48:10** *Behold, I have refined you, but not as silver; I have tested you in the furnace of affliction.* God refines His people through affliction, using trials not as punishment but as a purifying process.

God's Testing of Hearts

➢ **Proverbs 17:3** *The refining pot is for silver and the furnace for gold, But the Lord tests the hearts.* Just as silver and gold are refined in fire, the Lord tests and refines the hearts of His people.

➢ **Zechariah 13:9** *I will bring the one-third through the fire, Will refine them as silver is refined,*
And test them as gold is tested. They will call on My name, And I will answer them. I will say, 'This is My people'; And each one will say, 'The Lord is my God.' "I will put them into the fire and refine them as silver…" God uses trials to confirm His people's identity and devotion.

Outcome of Spiritual Refinement:

➢ **Job 23:10** *But He knows the way that I take; When He has tested me, I shall come forth as gold.* After testing, believers emerge as pure gold, refined and resilient.

THE PROCESS OF REFINEMENT: PURIFIED FOR THE CROWN

<u>The process of spiritual refinement is integral to the life of a believer, preparing them not only for earthly service but also for the crown of eternal reward.</u> Through trials and affliction, God purifies the faith of His people, shaping them to reflect His character and honor His name. This process of refinement, though often challenging, reveals the depth of God's love and His purpose for each believer, aligning them closer to His will and strengthening their identity in Christ.

The purpose of refinement is beautifully captured in 1 Peter 1:6-7, where Peter compares trials to a purifying fire that tests and strengthens faith. Just as gold is refined to reveal its purity, trials purify the believer's faith, removing impurities such as fear, doubt, and self-reliance. Peter emphasizes that this refined faith "may be found to result in praise and glory and honor at the revelation of Jesus Christ." When believers endure hardship, they not only bring honor to Christ but are also prepared to receive His eternal crown. God's purpose in allowing these trials is not punishment; rather, it is to draw believers closer to Him, transforming them to bear a closer resemblance to Christ.

Isaiah 48:10 echoes this idea, with God proclaiming, "I have refined you, but not as silver; I have tried you in the furnace of affliction." This imagery of affliction as a refining furnace underscores <u>that trials are a necessary part of spiritual growth. God uses hardship as a tool to purify His people,</u> burning away what hinders their relationship with Him and purging anything that keeps them from fulfilling their divine calling. It is a process of love, not anger, meant to cleanse the heart and prepare believers for the greater blessings of faith.

God's testing of hearts further illuminates the role of refinement in deepening devotion and confirming identity in Him. *Proverbs 17:3* states, *"The crucible for silver and the furnace for gold, but the Lord tests the heart."* Just as fire exposes the nature of precious metals, God tests hearts to reveal the strength and purity of faith. These tests are not

intended to harm but to reveal areas where believers need to grow, encouraging a deeper reliance on Him and a more genuine expression of faith. Zechariah 13:9 reinforces this truth, with God declaring, "I will put them into the fire and refine them as silver is refined." This act of refinement confirms believers as His own, assuring them of their identity and value in Him. Through trials, God shapes their hearts, reinforcing their devotion and resilience as they grow in faith. The outcome of refinement is beautifully summarized in Job 23:10, where Job proclaims, "When he has tried me, I shall come forth as gold." After enduring life's trials, believers emerge purified and resilient, reflecting God's glory. Refined for the crown, they are equipped to carry out His purposes and to ultimately receive the reward of eternal life with Him.

Through this refining journey, God's love and purpose shine through, drawing believers closer to Him and preparing them for the crown that awaits, a reward of faith tested, purified, and made radiant by the fires of spiritual refinement.

God's Presence Through Refinement and Bearing the Cross

Endurance with Jehovah Shammah

Psalm 66:10-12 *"For You, O God, have tested us; You have refined us as silver is refined. You brought us into the net; You laid affliction on our backs. You have caused men to ride over our heads; We went through fire and through water; But You brought us out to rich fulfillment".* Even through testing and burdens, God leads His people to a place of abundance, demonstrating that trials refine us for greater blessings.

The Assurance of God's Presence

Romans 5:3-5 *And not only that, but we also glory in tribulations, knowing that tribulation produces perseverance; and perseverance, character; and character, hope. Now hope does not disappoint, because the love of God has been poured out in our hearts by the Holy Spirit who was given to us.* Suffering produces endurance, which shapes character and leads to hope, reinforcing that God's love and presence carries us through every trial, refining us for His purposes.

Jehovah Shammah: God's Presence Through Refinement and Bearing the Cross

In the believer's journey, Jehovah Shammah, "The Lord is there", is the assurance of God's steadfast presence through every moment of refinement and suffering. The process of bearing the cross, enduring trials, and undergoing spiritual refinement can be daunting, but it is marked by God's continual presence, empowering believers to persevere and emerge stronger.

Psalm 66:10-12 captures this promise beautifully: "For you, God, tested us; you refined us like silver…we went through fire and water, but you brought us to a place of abundance." These words reveal that while God allows testing, He is actively leading His people through each trial. As believers endure hardships, they are purified, like silver in the refiner's fire. The process is intense and often painful, yet it produces a purer faith, preparing the believer for greater spiritual abundance and maturity. God does not merely observe this process from afar; He is intimately involved, guiding and sustaining His people through it all.

The Apostle Paul, in Romans 5:3-5, affirms the power of suffering in a believer's life. He writes, "Not only that, but we rejoice in our sufferings, knowing that suffering produces endurance, and endurance produces character, and character produces hope." This chain reaction, suffering leading to endurance, endurance to character, and character to hope, reveals the intentionality behind trials. Each step in the refining process builds upon the last, strengthening the believer's faith and deepening their hope in God. The end result is a hope that is "poured out in our hearts through the Holy Spirit," demonstrating that even in suffering, God's love is actively at work within us. His presence is a source of comfort, reminding us that every hardship has purpose and that we are being shaped for His glory.

Jehovah Shammah's presence is especially meaningful when believers are called to bear their cross, a symbol of self-denial, sacrifice, and perseverance. Just as Christ bore His cross for the joy set before Him, believers are invited to endure trials with the assurance of God's presence and strength. <u>Every hardship, whether physical, emotional, or spiritual, becomes an opportunity to draw closer to God, who walks with us in every circumstance. Bearing the cross is not simply about enduring suffering but about embracing the journey of faith, trusting that God is refining us through it.</u>

God's presence transforms the refining fire and the weight of the cross into a means of growth. He does not abandon His children in their trials; instead, He refines them, purifying their hearts, strengthening their character, and leading them to a place of spiritual abundance. In the furnace of life's challenges, Jehovah Shammah stands alongside His people, providing them with endurance, shaping their character, and anchoring their hope. As they walk through fire and bear their cross, they are assured that God is there, guiding them toward the fulfillment of His purposes and the joy of His everlasting presence.

Bearing Real-World Crosses for Christ

The Apostle Paul's words in *2 Corinthians 6:4-8* capture the essence of what it means to live a life of faith in a world full of suffering, injustice, and relentless trials. He doesn't speak of a life sheltered from hardship, but instead, he emphasizes endurance in the face of unimaginable pain and turmoil. Paul's depiction of "afflictions, hardships, calamities... sleepless nights, hunger... slander and praise" resonates deeply with the harsh realities many believers face today, often quietly, often unseen, and sometimes even misunderstood by the very communities they seek refuge in.

The Hidden Crosses Christians Bear in the Modern World

Homelessness and Poverty

For some believers, bearing the cross means enduring the dehumanizing experiences of homelessness, struggling for basic needs like food and shelter. This isn't a "temporary setback" but a long, isolating road where the world can turn its back. Sleeping on sidewalks, bearing cold winters without shelter, relying on the kindness of strangers for a meal—these are the realities many face alone, often unseen by society and sometimes even judged rather than helped by the church. *"In sleepless nights and hunger"* is a phrase that defines their existence, a cross borne in the shadows.

Drug Addiction and Recovery

For others, addiction is the cross they bear, a constant battle against cravings and the weight of guilt. Addiction can arise from past traumas, attempts to numb pain, or simply from the harshness of life. In these moments, the stigma of addiction and the painful path of recovery can be isolating, misunderstood, and stigmatized. Yet, those who fight this battle often cling to faith as their lifeline, their only hope for deliverance, embodying *"great endurance"* in a struggle that most will never fully comprehend.

Survivors of Abuse and Violence

Many believers carry the silent cross of surviving physical, sexual, or domestic abuse. They've endured injustices that have scarred them in ways words cannot describe. To bear the name of Christ while carrying the weight of these traumas is to live in a paradox of brokenness and hope. Their faith is forged in the fires of *"afflictions and calamities"* that others may never see, but that are nonetheless real, painful, and deeply personal. Bearing this cross means trusting in a God who sees their pain, even when others don't.

Victims of Human Trafficking

Human trafficking is a tragic reality that often feels too painful to mention. Yet there are believers who have escaped this horror or are still ensnared in it. Their lives are a testament to resilience, to the power of survival, and to a deep, unspeakable pain. Bearing this cross requires them to hold on to the slimmest thread of hope, trusting that Christ sees their suffering. Paul's phrase, *"treated as impostors, and yet are true,"* speaks to those who live hidden lives, bearing a truth few can understand but that God Himself honors.

Mental Illness and Inner Struggles

The cross of mental illness is one that is often misunderstood within the church. Depression, anxiety, PTSD, and other mental health challenges are real, heavy burdens that many believers carry. Enduring each day, holding on to faith when the mind itself feels like an enemy, requires extraordinary endurance. These believers embody *"great endurance, in afflictions, and sleepless nights"* as they wrestle with invisible battles. Bearing the cross in this way is an act of profound faith and resilience, even when others may not understand.

Everyday Realities of Dishonor and Slander
For many, the cross also means facing social rejection, slander, and dishonor for their faith. In workplaces, family gatherings, or friend groups, holding to one's beliefs can mean facing ridicule or isolation. Just as Paul mentions being *"treated as impostors,"* these believers live with the pain of being judged, misunderstood, or even ostracized. Bearing this cross means standing firm in faith, knowing that they may never receive the world's approval, yet trusting that God's approval is worth every moment of dishonor.

Enduring with Faith Amid Unseen Crosses

Paul's list of trials in *2 Corinthians 6:4-8* goes beyond mere words, it is a raw acknowledgment of the crosses believers carry daily, in circumstances that often go unnoticed by society. These aren't just "spiritual metaphors" but real-life burdens; homelessness, addiction, abuse, trauma, mental illness, poverty, and social isolation. And through it all, Paul reminds us that our crosses aren't borne alone. With *"the Holy Spirit, genuine love… and the power of God,"* believers can find strength in their suffering, purpose in their pain, and resilience that only God can give.

God is There in Every Trial

Through the afflictions and injustices, Jehovah Shammah, The Lord Who Is There, stands with each believer, intimately aware of every struggle. He sees the hidden wounds, understands the silent tears, and is present in each trial. These crosses aren't signs of divine abandonment but rather profound opportunities to experience God's sustaining power, grace, and comfort. As Paul declared, *"We commend ourselves in every way"* through these trials, knowing that God's presence transforms suffering into strength, pain into purpose, and sorrow into a testimony of His enduring love. This is the real-life gospel, raw, unvarnished, and full of God's sustaining power amidst the most difficult of crosses. Believers who endure these crosses are walking testaments to the power of faith, standing as testimonies to a world that often overlooks the unseen battles they fight each day.

The Promise of the Crown: Rewards for the Refined and Faithful

- ➤ **Crown of Life:**
  - ❖ **James 1:12** – Those who remain steadfast through trials will receive the crown of life promised by God.
- ➤ **Crown of Righteousness:**
  - ❖ **2 Timothy 4:7-8** – Paul's example of completing the race and fighting the good fight to receive the crown of righteousness, which is promised to all who are faithful.

> ➢ **Enduring to Share in Christ's Glory:**
> - ❖ **1 Peter 4:12-13** – Embrace fiery trials as a means of sharing in Christ's sufferings, leading to ultimate joy and glory when His presence is fully revealed.

The promise of the crown is a profound reward given to those who remain steadfast through life's trials, bearing their cross with faith and integrity. <u>In the Bible, the crown is a symbol of victory, honor, and eternal reward for those refined by suffering and committed to living a life of faithful endurance.</u> These crowns, not material but spiritual, are marks of honor that God bestows on His faithful, those who have endured, grown in righteousness, and shared in Christ's sufferings.

Crown of Life

The Crown of Life is a promise God gives to those who persevere under the weight of trials. *James 1:12* says, *"Blessed is the man who remains steadfast under trial, for when he has stood the test he will receive the crown of life which God has promised to those who love him."* This crown represents a life victorious over suffering, a reward for those who have walked faithfully through hardship without abandoning their love for God. This is not an earthly reward but an eternal acknowledgment of a life well-lived in the face of adversity. For believers, the Crown of Life serves as a reminder that every painful moment, every sacrifice, and every act of resilience will not go unnoticed by God.

Crown of Righteousness

The Crown of Righteousness is promised to those who long for Christ's appearing and remain steadfast in their faith journey, as the Apostle Paul exemplifies in 2 Timothy 4:7-8: *"I have fought the good fight, I have finished the race, I have kept the faith. Now there is in store for me the crown of righteousness..."* This crown is granted to those who actively pursue righteousness, fighting against sin and persevering in their commitment to the gospel. The Crown of Righteousness is a testament to lives lived in faithful anticipation of Christ's return, embodying a desire for His kingdom and an unwavering commitment to His truth. It reminds believers that their faithfulness is not in vain and that their love for God's righteousness will be rewarded with eternal honor. Together, these crowns represent the fullness of God's promises to those who remain faithful. The Crown of Life assures believers of their eternal inheritance, the Crown of Righteousness rewards lives committed to the faith journey, and the promise of glory invites believers to see trials as a pathway to a deeper union with Christ. In God's eternal kingdom, these crowns symbolize His acknowledgment of faithfulness, endurance, and love, qualities He cherishes and will reward eternally.

Enduring to Share in Christ's Glory

Lastly, 1 Peter 4:12-13 invites believers to *"rejoice insofar as you share Christ's sufferings, that you may also rejoice and be glad when his glory is revealed."* This speaks to the unique privilege of sharing in Christ's sufferings, an honor that allows believers to experience a deeper connection to Him. Through fiery trials, they are refined, becoming more like Christ and, ultimately, prepared to share in His glory. The joy and glory awaiting believers are not just for surviving trials but for enduring them with faith that reveals the power of God in their lives. Sharing in Christ's glory is the ultimate fulfillment of every sacrifice made for His name.

The promise of these crowns reflects God's faithfulness to reward His people, acknowledging not just the endurance of trials but the character, righteousness, and faithfulness cultivated through them. These crowns are symbols of His love, affirmations of lives lived for His glory, and reminders of the eternal joy awaiting those who remain faithful to the end.

Refined as Pure Gold, Crowned for Glory

The journey of bearing the cross and enduring God's refining process are deeply intertwined, not separate aspects of the Christian life. Together, they form a unified path that molds believers into the likeness of Christ and prepares them for the ultimate reward; the crown of glory. God, as Jehovah Shammah, the God who is present walks alongside His people every step of the way, providing the strength and guidance they need to persevere through hardship and emerge victorious.

Bearing the cross signifies a life of self-denial and dedication to Christ, an essential part of following Him. Jesus Himself declared in *Mark 8:34, "If anyone would come after me, let him deny himself and take up his cross and follow me."* Bearing the cross is a call to live sacrificially, to endure suffering, and to remain faithful despite adversity. It is a journey that challenges believers to look beyond themselves and see God's purpose at work even in difficult circumstances. This act of taking up the cross is a profound expression of trust and obedience, a willingness to follow Christ regardless of the cost. Yet, the call to bear the cross does not stand alone; it is closely linked to the refining process, a journey where faith is tested and purified.

Refinement is God's way of preparing believers for the crown. As gold is purified in the furnace to remove impurities, so believers are refined through trials to remove the hindrances that may weaken their faith. Scripture reassures believers of the purpose behind this process. In 1 Peter 1:6-7, Peter explains that *"though now for a little while you may have had to suffer grief in all kinds of trials,"* these trials come so that *"the proven genuineness of your faith of greater worth than gold…may result in praise, glory and honor when Jesus Christ is revealed."* Trials are not random or meaningless; they are purposeful and deeply transformative. Each hardship, every painful experience, and every act of perseverance serves to make believers spiritually resilient, preparing them for the crown that awaits those who have remained steadfast.

Throughout this journey of cross-bearing and refinement, Jehovah Shammah is present, faithfully guiding His people. God does not leave His children to navigate these challenges alone; His presence is the source of their strength. He is the One who sustains them when they feel weary, the One who comforts them in sorrow, and the One who assures them that their suffering is not in vain. Through the refining fire and the weight of the cross, God's presence is a constant reminder that He has a purpose for every trial and that He is preparing His people for an eternal reward.

As believers endure these refining trials and faithfully bear their cross, they are called to look forward to the promise of crowns, which relate as symbols of God's faithfulness and reward for those who persevere. The Crown of Life, promised in James 1:12, honors those who remain steadfast under trial. The Crown of Righteousness, which Paul speaks of in 2 Timothy 4:8, celebrates a life lived faithfully in anticipation of Christ's return. And the promise of sharing in Christ's glory, as mentioned in 1 Peter 4:13, assures believers that they will experience ultimate joy in God's presence. Each of these crowns is not simply a prize, but a profound expression of God's acknowledgment of faith, love, and endurance.

In conclusion, the journey of bearing the cross and undergoing refinement is one of spiritual transformation and preparation for eternal glory. God uses both processes to mold His people, to purify their hearts, and to deepen their dependence on Him. As they persevere, believers can take joy in the knowledge that these crowns are more than just symbols, they are eternal reminders of God's love, His refining work, and His promise to reward the faithful. Refined as pure gold and crowned for glory, believers are ultimately drawn into a deeper relationship with God, sharing in His glory and rejoicing in His presence forever.

Behold I'm Coming Quickly

John 1:1

Crowned for Purpose

2 Timothy 4:8

PURPOSE IN THE PAIN

ALLOWED BY GOD: SUBDUED BY GRACE!

Pain For the believer, pain is often perceived as an adversary, something to evade at all costs, a force that unsettles life and threatens our sense of peace and purpose. Yet, in the divine economy of God's Kingdom, pain is not an interruption but a tool in the hand of the Almighty. It is permitted, not to break us, but to **mold us**, **refine us**, and **prepare us** for His sovereign purposes. Scripture is complete with examples of faithful servants, Apostles, prophets, and men and women of God, who endured trials of staggering intensity. These were not random hardships but divine appointments, intricately integrated into the Hallmark of God's redemptive plan. From the Apostle Paul, who bore a thorn in his flesh while proclaiming, *"My grace is sufficient for you, for my power is made perfect in weakness"* (2 Corinthians 12:9), to Job, who declared in his anguish, *"When He has tested me, I will come forth as gold"* (Job 23:10), the consistent theme is one of transformation through grace.

Their victories were not marked by an absence of suffering but by the abundant presence of God's grace. This grace empowered them to endure, to trust in the unseen, and to press forward in hope when all seemed lost. It was grace that transformed their ashes into beauty, their mourning into joy, and their trials into triumphs. Through their journeys, we see that pain, though bitter in the moment, is often the precursor to a deeper faith, a renewed purpose, and a clearer revelation of God's glory. Pain is not the end of the story for the believer; it is the crucible through which we are prepared for the eternal weight of glory yet to be revealed (2 Corinthians 4:17).

Joseph, who was betrayed and imprisoned; **David**, who was pursued by enemies; and **Job**, who lost everything, all testify that pain does not have the final say. In His sovereignty, God allows certain trials to enter our lives, yet He also provides grace to subdue them, turning what was meant to harm into a source of growth, resilience, and strength. This subject-matter explores the purpose woven into our pain and the grace available to us in every season of suffering. By looking closely at the lives of these Apostles and Men of God, we uncover a divine truth; pain is allowed by God, but it is subdued and transformed by His grace, giving our lives a testimony that brings hope, power, and glory to Him. Many devout individuals from both the old and new testament faced unique and significant painful struggles, demonstrating how God's grace operated in their lives despite immense pain.

Joseph: Betrayed by his brothers, sold into slavery, and unjustly imprisoned. Despite the deep betrayal and loss, Joseph's story in Genesis reveals how God used his suffering to position him as a savior for his family and Egypt (Genesis 50:20).

Job: A powerful example of undeserved suffering. Job's numerous losses, his family, health, and wealth, allowed him to encounter God more deeply, learning that trust in God supersedes understanding (Job 42:5-6).

Daniel: Taken into captivity as a young man, Daniel faced continuous challenges to his faith. His steadfastness through trials like the lion's den demonstrated that God's grace sustains those who refuse to compromise (Daniel 6).

Paul and Silas: Imprisoned for preaching the Gospel, yet they chose to worship in their chains. Their story shows how grace empowers

us to rejoice in the midst of hardship, ultimately leading to a miraculous deliverance and conversion of others (Acts 16:25-34).

Mary Magdalene: Her deliverance from demonic oppression and her devoted discipleship with Christ exemplify how God's grace can restore purpose and identity through pain, transforming her into a devoted witness to His resurrection (Luke 8:2, John 20:11-18).

Jeremiah, the Weeping Prophet: Called to deliver hard truths to an unheeding nation, Jeremiah faced rejection, isolation, and sorrow. Yet, his obedience amid suffering reflects grace that fuels faithfulness even when the world turns against us (Jeremiah 20:7-9).

Peter: From denying Christ to becoming a foundational leader, Peter's journey shows how grace reshapes failure into purpose, granting strength and resilience through repentance and restoration (John 21:15-17).

Esther: Risking her life for her people, Esther's story highlights how God's grace gives courage to face danger, fulfilling purpose in the face of death (Esther 4:14-16).

John, on Patmos: Exiled and isolated, John's visions revealed difficult truths about humanity's end. The mental and emotional strain of transcribing the book of Revelation shows grace as a sustaining force amid the weight of divine revelation (Revelation 1:9).

The divine perspective on pain and human suffering is branded throughout scriptures history, revealing both the _consequences of disobedience_ and the _promise of ultimate restoration_. From the curse in the Garden of Eden to the promise of a pain-free eternity in the book of Revelation, the Bible illustrates that suffering as an integral part of a human being living a spiritual experience; not without purpose, nor endured without divine companionship.

The Origin of Pain and
The Divine Design of Consequence

In Genesis, the curse following Adams disobedience and sin marks the triumphant entry of pain into our world. For Eve, pain in childbirth became part of her experience; for Adam, the toil of being evicted from the "Garden of Edon" and pain cultivating the desolate earth became his reality. These physical pains are symbols of a deeper spiritual reality; separation from God leads to inner turmoil and struggle. All of creation now groans under the weight of this curse, as Paul explains in *Romans 8:22*, *"the whole creation groans and labors with birth pangs,"* a statement that speaks to the collective burden of sin that humanity and creation bear together.

Yet, from a divine perspective, these pains are not arbitrary punishments but a means to shape and prepare. Like the pain of labor that eventually yields the joy of new life, these struggles remind us of the hope for renewal and restoration. This hope is poignantly described in Revelation 21:4, where God promises to wipe away every tear and banish pain forever. Until then, we endure, <u>knowing that even our suffering has a purpose</u>; a significant purpose that is sometimes hidden but always held by a loving Creator. Among all biblical figures, Job is perhaps the ultimate example of unrelieved suffering. A "blameless and upright" man (Job 2:3), he experiences a level of loss and despair that few could endure. Through Satan's direct attack, Job loses his family, wealth, health, and the support of his wife, who advises him to "curse God and die." Job's suffering, though permitted by God, is not without divine objective or purpose. His struggle shows us that even the most righteous are not exempt from pain, nor does pain necessarily signal divine abandonment. As his pain intensifies, Job isolates himself, turning inward to question and plead for understanding. His journey through loss is deeply human, reflecting our own impulse to seek meaning in our suffering. Job's story serves as a stimulant for those moments when pain isolates us, making us feel unseen and unheard. And yet, in his darkest hours, Job learns that God's presence remains with him. Through a

long and painful journey, he ultimately encounters God in a new way, gaining a deeper revelation of God's majesty and sovereignty. This encounter reveals that suffering, though often shrouded in mystery and beyond human understanding, serves as a divine catalyst for transformation, drawing the believer into a deeper and more intimate fellowship with God. The New Testament brings element of understanding to the nature of pain, especially as it is transformed through the life and teachings of Jesus Christ. Pain, rather than being solely a consequence of sin, becomes a doorway to joy and a means of spiritual refinement. Just as a woman's labor pains bring forth the joy of new life, so do our spiritual struggles prepare us for the joy of God's kingdom.

Paul and Silas's imprisonment is a striking example of this principle. Though beaten and bound, they pray and sing hymns, their praises rising as a testament to the redemptive power of suffering (Acts 16:23-25). Their joy in suffering brings about miraculous deliverance, not only for themselves but also for the jailer and his household, who come to salvation. Paul's ability to find strength and even joy in suffering is rooted in his understanding of God's grace; he writes, "My grace is sufficient for you, for my power is made perfect in weakness" (2 Corinthians 12:9). This grace does not remove the suffering but transforms it, allowing it to serve a higher purpose.

At the heart of the Christian faith is the ultimate demonstration of purpose in pain; the life, death, and resurrection of Jesus Christ. Jesus endured physical, emotional, and spiritual agony, bearing a crown of thorns, weeping at Lazarus's grave, and feeling the weight of human brokenness and suffering. He carried not only His own pain but also the collective suffering of all humanity. His three days in the earth, likened to Jonah's three days in the belly of the whale, signify a period of unimaginable darkness and isolation. Jesus knows pain intimately. He who was sinless bore the ultimate consequence of sin so that we might find life in Him. In His suffering, Jesus offers us a model of redemptive endurance. He did not avoid pain but embraced it, transforming it into a pathway to our redemption. Through Jesus, we find that pain is not an end but a bridge to grace. His presence with us in our darkest hours, as Paul affirmed, "But the Lord stood with me" (2 Timothy 4:17), is a reminder that we are never alone in our suffering. Ultimately, the divine perspective on suffering is one of companionship and redemption. While pain is a reality of this fallen world, it is also the means through which God refines us, draws us closer to Him, and reveals His sustaining grace. Pain, permitted by God, is subdued by His grace, which empowers us to endure and transforms our suffering into a testimony of faith. Through the lives of Job, Paul, and Christ Himself, we learn that suffering, though difficult, has a divine purpose, to bring us into a deeper relationship with God and to prepare us for the joy of His kingdom, where pain will finally cease, and we will be fully restored in His presence.

Pain as the "Ultimate Test of Faith"!

Pain is the believer's ultimate test of faith because it challenges the very foundations of trust, endurance, and devotion in a way that few other experiences do. Pain whether physical, emotional, or spiritual, pushes us beyond our comfort zones, confronting us with questions about God's nature, His promises, and His presence in our lives. This experience strips away the superficial layers of belief, leaving behind the core of who we are and what we truly believe about God.

HERE'S WHY PAIN SERVES AS THIS ULTIMATE TEST

Pain Challenges Our Perception of God's Goodness and Love

When believers face suffering, especially prolonged or intense pain, it can feel as though God is distant or, at worst, unloving. In these moments, the character of God is questioned, not because God changes, but because our perception does. Pain creates a situation where the believer must choose whether to trust that God is still good and that His promises hold true, even when the evidence around us

might suggest otherwise. Job's story epitomizes this struggle. Though his life crumbled, he famously declared, "Though he slay me, yet will I trust in him" (Job 13:15). Job's pain forced him to confront his understanding of God's goodness, yet he chose to trust despite his suffering.

Pain Tests Our Willingness to Surrender

In pain, believers confront their own limitations and are reminded that they are not in control. This is especially true when pain is unrelenting or seems undeserved. <u>Pain invites believers to surrender their need for control and yield to God's will, even when His will includes suffering.</u> Jesus in Gethsemane is a powerful example of this. Knowing the agony that awaited Him, He prayed, *"Not my will, but yours be done" (Luke 22:42)*. The act of surrender in the midst of pain is an ultimate test of faith, as it demands that we relinquish our desires and place our trust entirely in God's plan.

Pain Exposes the Depth of Our Faith

When all is well, faith can appear strong and steadfast. But pain exposes the true strength and depth of a believer's trust in God. In times of blessing, we might find it easy to praise God and speak of His faithfulness. Yet, when faced with hardship, the superficial faith falls away, revealing either genuine trust or wavering doubt. Pain requires us to exercise our faith muscles, often in ways we never anticipated, drawing us closer to God as we lean on Him for strength we do not have on our own.

Pain Refines Us Spiritually

Pain has a refining power, often compared to a purifying fire in scripture. The Apostle Peter wrote, *"These [trials] have come so that the proven genuineness of your faith of greater worth than gold, which perishes even though refined by fire may result in praise, glory, and honor when Jesus Christ is revealed"* (1 Peter 1:7). Just as gold is refined through intense heat, our faith is purified and strengthened through suffering. Pain strips away distractions and superficial attachments, leaving us with a clearer focus on God and a more profound sense of dependence on Him.

Pain Teaches Dependence on God's Grace

Pain reveals human limitations and drives believers to seek strength beyond themselves. The Apostle Paul, who endured immense suffering, experienced this firsthand. He wrote, *"My grace is sufficient for you, for my power is made perfect in weakness" (2 Corinthians 12:9).* In pain, believers often reach the end of their own "carnal devices", learning that God's grace is not just an abstract idea but a present reality that sustains them when nothing else can. Pain allows believers to experience God's presence and strength in a uniquely intimate way, deepening their faith as they learn to rely on His grace.

Pain Demonstrates the Reality of Eternal Hope

Pain reminds believers that this world is not their final destination. Every instance of suffering reinforces the hope of eternity with God, where there will be no more pain, sorrow, or loss (Revelation 21:4). The believer's ability to endure pain, sustained by faith in this promise, becomes a testament to the world of the reality of eternity. Paul eloquently captured this perspective, saying, "For I consider that the sufferings of this present time are not worthy *to be compared* with the glory which shall be revealed in us." (Romans 8:18). Pain shifts the believer's gaze from temporary affliction to the promise of eternal joy, reinforcing faith in God's ultimate plan of redemption.

Pain Serves as a Testimony to Others

When believers endure suffering with faith and grace, their lives become a testimony to others. Pain often makes room for God's glory to be displayed, as others witness the strength, peace, and hope that can only come from Him. The story of Paul and Silas in prison (Acts 16:23-25) is a powerful example; their decision to sing and pray in the midst of pain not only brought about their deliverance but also led the jailer and his household to faith. Enduring pain with faith shows the world that God's presence transcends circumstances and that He is trustworthy even in hardship.

In every way, pain challenges believers to hold onto their faith in the unseen promises of God, making it the ultimate test. When faith endures through pain, it produces a maturity, resilience, and intimacy with God that cannot be cultivated any other way. Pain draws believers closer to God, teaches them dependence on His grace, refines their faith, and serves as a powerful witness to the hope found in Christ. <u>Through this test, the believer not only grows spiritually but also stands as a living testimony that faith can withstand even the fiercest storms, rooted firmly in the God who remains faithful through it all.</u>

PAINS ABILITY TO PREPARE, GROW, REFINE, DEVELOP YOU!

Pain, though hurtful and often unwelcome, can be one of the most powerful forces for transformation in a believer's life. It serves as a spiritual-receptacle where character is forged, faith is refined, and a deeper dependence on God is developed. While pain challenges us to our core, it can also be a hidden gift that shapes us in ways that "<u>comfort</u> and <u>ease</u>" cannot. Here's a deep dive into how pain, rather than being merely an obstacle inevitably prepares, grows, refines, and develops believers and their character. Pain has a way of revealing what we're made of and what we still lack. It's as if God allows these hardships to strengthen us for the greater calling He has prepared for us. Pain strips away self-reliance and compels us to lean into God, preparing us for future challenges and service. It readies us to handle more profound tasks in His Kingdom with a tested and fortified spirit. Consider Joseph, who endured betrayal, slavery, and imprisonment before he rose to a position of influence in Egypt. Each painful experience prepared him with the resilience, humility, and wisdom needed to lead a nation through famine. Without those hardships, Joseph may not have been prepared for such an immense task. Pain readied him for his ultimate purpose. Just as plants grow by breaking through the soil and reaching toward the sun, believers often grow most when breaking through hardship toward God. <u>Pain</u>

demands that we seek God earnestly, pray fervently, and delve deeper into His Word for comfort and guidance. In this way, pain becomes a fertile ground for spiritual growth, pushing us beyond a shallow, circumstantial faith into one that is steadfast and mature. When life is easy, growth can become stagnant. But pain disrupts complacency, requiring us to examine our beliefs, motives, and character. In Romans 5:3-4, Paul tells us that "suffering produces perseverance; perseverance, character; and character, hope." Pain challenges our preconceived ideas and stretches our faith, allowing us to grow spiritually and gain a more profound understanding of God's nature.

Scripture frequently employs this example of a "refining fire" to illustrate how God uses trials to purify His people. Just as gold and silver are subjected to intense heat to separate the waste and reveal their true worth, so too does God permit the fires of suffering to consume the impurities within our hearts, whether pride, selfish ambition, fear, or unbelief. These trials are not punitive but transformative, instruments of His love and wisdom designed to conform us to the image of Christ. Through this refining process, He forges within us a character that is steadfast, unshakable, and fully aligned with His divine will, preparing us to reflect His glory and fulfill His purpose. Job's story is a vivid illustration of this refining process. Although he was already described as blameless, his trials stripped away his self-righteousness and led him to a new, humbling understanding of God's majesty. By the end of his suffering, Job's faith was purified and strengthened, leaving him with a deeper reverence and love for God.

Pain as the Catalyst for Christ-like Character

Pain doesn't merely teach us to endure, it also develops the core qualities that define Christian character. Compassion, empathy, humility, patience, and endurance are often born out of hardship. It's through experiencing our own suffering that we learn to identify with the suffering of others, becoming vessels of God's love and comfort to a hurting world.

Jesus Himself was described as *"a man of sorrows and acquainted with grief"* *(Isaiah 53:3).* His experience with pain developed a heart of compassion that allowed Him to minister to the broken, sick, and outcasted. Through our own struggles, we become more Christ-like, able to walk alongside others in their pain with genuine empathy and understanding. Pain deepens our character, making us capable of loving as Jesus loved. Pain has a unique way of

cutting through our illusion of self-sufficiency. When everything is going well, it's easy to rely on our own strength and resources, forgetting our need for God. Pain forces us to confront our limitations and recognize that we cannot do life alone. This dependence is not a sign of weakness but of strength, as it shifts our reliance onto God's power and provision. Paul's "thorn in the flesh" *(2 Corinthians 12:7-10)* is a prudent example. Despite praying for relief, he accepted God's answer: *"My grace is sufficient for you, for my power is made perfect in weakness."* Through this experience, Paul learned to depend on God's grace, realizing that his weakness allowed God's strength to be displayed. Pain becomes a pathway to surrender, leading us to trust in God's unfailing support. Pain teaches us to endure. When we face hardship and choose to continue in faith, we build spiritual resilience. Each trial we overcome strengthens our ability to face future difficulties with courage and hope. This endurance is a crucial aspect of our walk with God, as it prepares us to navigate the uncertainties and struggles of life without wavering. The Apostle James wrote, "Let perseverance finish its work so that you may be mature and complete, not lacking anything" (James 1:4). Pain has a way of creating resilience that comfort never could. Each experience of hardship trains us to trust God more deeply, helping us to stand firm in the face of adversity. Finally, pain can develop our character by giving us a testimony of God's faithfulness. When we endure suffering and remain steadfast, our lives become a testament to the power of faith and the sustaining grace of God. Pain allows us to experience God's presence in a unique way, equipping us to share our story of hope and redemption with others. Paul and Silas's response to pain, singing hymns while imprisoned, did more than uplift their spirits; it became a testimony that led to the salvation of their jailer and his family. Their faith in the midst of suffering revealed the power of God to those around them. Pain has the potential to transform not only our lives but also the lives of those who witness our journey, providing a testimony that speaks of God's goodness and faithfulness.

In essence, while pain is often hurtful, it is far from purposeless. It prepares us for greater service, grows our faith, refines our character, and develops a Christ-like heart within us. Pain teaches us to depend on God, builds our endurance, and ultimately allows us to bear witness to His sustaining grace. Although painful experiences are challenging, they are often where God does His most transformative work, shaping us into the image of Christ and equipping us to fulfill our divine purpose. In God's hands, even pain becomes a tool for profound spiritual growth and preparation, transforming us in ways that ease and comfort never could.

REFINEMENT-FAITH STRENGTHENING TO WALK THROUGH THE FIRE

The story of Shadrach, Meshach, and Abednego is a powerful illustration of God's sovereign purpose in allowing His believers to *walk through* the fire rather than escape it. In their refusal to bow to Nebuchadnezzar's golden image, these men demonstrated absolute loyalty to God, even at the cost of their lives. God could have miraculously delivered them before they ever entered the furnace, but He chose instead to allow them to walk through it. Here's a deeper look at why a sovereign God would allow His faithful to walk

through the fire rather than avoid it altogether. God allowed Shadrach, Meshach, and Abednego to enter the fire to demonstrate His unparalleled power and presence with His people. By being present *in* the fire with them, God revealed that His protection transcends circumstances. As they stood unharmed in the flames, they provided an undeniable witness to Nebuchadnezzar and all who watched, proving that the God of Israel was not just another god but the sovereign Creator who controlled all elements, even fire. This visible demonstration of God's power made an indelible mark on those present, leading Nebuchadnezzar to proclaim, "There is no other god who is able to deliver in this way" (Daniel 3:29). Walking through the fire revealed to the world that God is sovereign, not just over His people but overall creation, including kings and empires. In scripture, fire often symbolizes refinement. By walking through the fire, Shadrach, Meshach, and Abednego experienced a literal and spiritual refining process. They emerged from the furnace not only unharmed but also with a faith that had been proven and strengthened. God allowed them to endure the flames as a way of solidifying their faith and deepening their reliance on Him. It demonstrated that true faith is not just professed; it is tested and refined, much like gold purified in a furnace (1 Peter 1:7).

Their walk through the fire was a journey of spiritual refinement. Facing their trial head-on showed that God's people don't need to escape adversity to prove their faith. Instead, enduring the flames brought them closer to God, building a resilience that comfort or ease could never foster. One of the most remarkable aspects of this story is the fourth figure seen walking in the fire, one who had "the appearance of the Son of Man" (Daniel 3:25). This was likely a manifestation of God's presence. Rather than rescuing them from outside the fire, God chose to enter into it with them. This act reveals a profound truth about His character. God doesn't leave His people to suffer alone; He joins them in their suffering. The experience of God's presence in the midst of their trial showed Shadrach, Meshach, and Abednego, and all believers, that God is intimately involved in our lives, even in our darkest moments. The flames that might have separated them from life instead became a place of communion and fellowship with God Himself, demonstrating that there is no place too perilous for God to reach His people.

By allowing His servants to walk through the fire, God emphasized the power of faithful resistance in the face of oppression. Shadrach, Meshach, and Abednego's choice to stand firm, despite the threat of a fiery death, exemplified what it means to serve God with an uncompromising faith. They declared, "Our God whom we serve is able to deliver us...but if not, be it known to you, O king, that we will not serve your gods" (Daniel 3:17-18). Their willingness to endure the consequences of their faith serves as a timeless reminder that allegiance to God outweighs earthly power or safety. Walking through the fire provided a visible example of unwavering faith and courage that has inspired believers throughout history. By choosing faith over fear, these men showed that God's people are called to live with conviction, even when obedience may lead to suffering. Their decision to go through the fire underscores that faith isn't always about seeking escape but about trusting God regardless of the outcome.

Walking through the fire created a powerful story of deliverance that would not have existed had they avoided the furnace. Their trial became a testimony that brought glory to God, challenged idolatry, and changed the heart of a king. The very flames that were meant to consume them became the setting for a miracle that proclaimed God's supremacy. This narrative reminds believers that our greatest trials can become our greatest testimonies. God often allows us to go through difficult circumstances not only for our growth but to reveal His power to others. When we endure trials, especially those meant to harm us, with faith and resilience, we proclaim God's faithfulness to those around us, sometimes in ways that words alone cannot express.

MODELING CHRIST'S WILLINGNESS TO SUFFER

The story of Shadrach, Meshach, and Abednego foreshadows Christ's own willingness to enter into human suffering and endure the ultimate "fire" on behalf of humanity. Just as God joined these men in the flames, Jesus entered our world, fully embracing suffering and death so that we might be saved. Their experience in the furnace serves as a powerful illustration of God's love, a love willing to walk into our pain, even to the point of death on a cross. By allowing His people to endure trials rather than escape them, God models the same sacrificial love He later demonstrates in Christ. Walking through the fire symbolizes God's commitment to walk with us in suffering, and it prepares believers to understand the depth of love and sacrifice shown in Jesus' life and death. God allowed Shadrach, Meshach, and Abednego to walk through the fire not as an act of abandonment, but as a demonstration of His power, presence, and purpose. This act underscores that faith isn't a shield from hardship but a foundation upon which we stand through it. By facing the fire head-on, they discovered that God was not just a deliverer but a companion in their suffering, a purifier of faith, and a witness to the watching world. This story reminds us that sometimes the fire is exactly where we are meant to be, not to escape it, but to walk through it, fully trusting that God's purpose, grace, and presence will meet us in every flame.

GRACE AS DIVINE PROTECTION
IN THE FLAMES

God's grace subdued Nebuchadnezzar's attack on Shadrach, Meshach, and Abednego in an astonishing and multifaceted way, turning an act of aggression into an extraordinary testimony of His power and favor. Here's how God's grace transformed what could have been a deadly encounter into a story of divine deliverance and victory. God's grace was most visibly present in the miraculous protection that shielded the three men from the flames. When

Nebuchadnezzar ordered the furnace heated "seven times hotter than usual" (Daniel 3:19), it was intended to ensure their immediate death. However, God's grace rendered the fire harmless to them. Though the flames consumed the soldiers who threw them in, Shadrach, Meshach, and Abednego walked through the furnace without any harm. Not a hair on their heads was singed, nor was there even the smell of smoke on them (Daniel 3:27). This divine protection showcased God's grace in action, demonstrating that no earthly power, even one as mighty as Nebuchadnezzar's, could override God's will or harm His people. God's grace shielded them in His divine, all so powerful-protection, nullifying the king's violent intentions and leaving them untouched by the flames. In the midst of the fire, Nebuchadnezzar saw a fourth figure who appeared to be "like a son the Son of Man" (Daniel 3:25). This fourth figure, understood by many to be either an angel or an appearance of Jesus Christ, the King, was a direct manifestation of God's grace. Rather than simply removing the men from danger, God's grace was expressed through His presence *with them* in the fire. This act showed that God doesn't always spare us from the flames, but His grace ensures that we're never alone in our suffering. The presence of this divine figure subdued the terror of the flames, transforming the furnace from a place of death to one of divine fellowship and deliverance. God's grace didn't remove the trial but entered it, assuring the three men of His steadfast presence and support.

Nebuchadnezzar, in his pride and anger, tried to assert his absolute authority by issuing a decree that demanded death for anyone defying his command. However, God's grace overruled Nebuchadnezzar's power by rendering his orders powerless. Though the king intended to intimidate and enforce allegiance, God's grace ensured that His

people would not fall victim to human authority that contradicted divine law. By preserving Shadrach, Meshach, and Abednego, God displayed His supreme authority over all rulers and kingdoms. His grace undercut Nebuchadnezzar's intentions, showing that earthly authority has limits when it comes to His people. Through grace, God demonstrated to Nebuchadnezzar, and all present, that His sovereignty supersedes human power, subduing the king's plans and humbling him in the process.

God's grace turned an intended execution into a testimony that impacted the heart of Nebuchadnezzar himself. Witnessing the miraculous protection of Shadrach, Meshach, and Abednego, Nebuchadnezzar was moved to acknowledge the greatness of their God. He declared, *"Blessed be the God of Shadrach, Meshach, and Abednego, who has sent his angel and delivered his servants who trusted in him" (Daniel 3:28).* This transformation in the king's perspective was a direct result of the grace that preserved the three men and revealed God's power to all who were watching. God's grace subdued Nebuchadnezzar's attack by converting a moment of punishment into a profound declaration of faith. Nebuchadnezzar's heart was softened, and he publicly acknowledged the sovereignty of the Hebrew God Yahweh. This transformation demonstrates how God's grace can work through trials to bring about unexpected changes, even in the hearts of those who seem opposed to Him.

The grace of God was also revealed in how He honored the unwavering faith of Shadrach, Meshach, and Abednego. They went into the fire fully aware of the risks, declaring, "Our God whom we serve is able to deliver us…But even if he does not…we will not serve your gods" (Daniel 3:17-18). Their faith was an expression of absolute trust, and God's grace rewarded that trust by sparing them from harm. By delivering them, God demonstrated that His grace is sufficient to reward faithfulness, even in the face of deadly threats. This preservation served as an affirmation of the power and reliability of placing trust in God over human authorities. The grace extended to them reinforced the truth that God honors those who remain true to Him, providing supernatural protection and validation of their commitment.

Grace in the Repeal of the King's Decree

God's grace not only spared the three Hebrew men but also led to a "repeal" of Nebuchadnezzar's decree. Following the miraculous events, Nebuchadnezzar issued a new proclamation: *"Therefore I make a decree: Any people, nation, or language that speaks anything against the God of Shadrach, Meshach, and Abednego shall be torn limb from limb…for there is no other God who is able to deliver in this way"* (Daniel 3:29). What began as an attempt to force conformity ended as a public declaration of God's supremacy. The decree that once condemned Shadrach, Meshach, and Abednego was replaced with a mandate that honored their God. This repeal was a profound act of grace, showing that God's intervention can completely transform circumstances and even bring about favor and freedom in place of condemnation. In a broader sense, this story of deliverance through God's grace foreshadows the ultimate deliverance found in Jesus Christ. Just as the fourth figure appeared in the fire, Jesus came into the world to walk through the fires of human suffering and sin alongside us. The grace that subdued Nebuchadnezzar's wrath and saved the three men points forward to the grace that redeems all believers through Christ's sacrifice. In allowing Shadrach, Meshach, and Abednego to endure the fire but preserving them within it, God illustrated His power to save His people not only from earthly trials but from eternal separation. The grace shown in the furnace is a shadow of the greater grace offered through Jesus, who delivers us not just from physical harm but from sin and death itself. Through every aspect of this event, God's grace subdues the attack of Nebuchadnezzar, transforming a furnace of death into a setting for divine deliverance, testimony, and transformation. By protecting His faithful servants, transforming Nebuchadnezzar's decree, and revealing His presence in the fire, God's grace turned an act of aggression into a victory that brought glory to His name and set an enduring example of His power to save.

THE RELEVANCE OF PAIN IN
A BELIEVERS' LIFE!

The relevance of pain in a believer's life is deeply transformative, serving a purpose far reaching beyond the immediate discomfort or struggle it may convey. Pain, rather than being a force that inevitably leads to bitterness, has the potential to make us better, if we allow it to draw us closer to God and refine our character. Through pain, God often works to deepen our faith, mature our perspective, and align us more closely with His purposes. Here's why pain, while challenging, holds relevance in the journey of faith.

Pain tests and strengthens faith. In times of difficulty, believers are challenged to rely on God more fully, moving from a surface-level faith to a deep-rooted trust without borders or guard-rails. When life is easy, it can be tempting to grow complacent, but pain forces us to confront our doubts, questions, and even fears. It pushes us to cling to God in ways that comfort cannot. Just as a muscle grows stronger through resistance, faith grows stronger as we persist through hardship. Through pain, God shapes resilient believers who stand firm even in adversity. James 1:2-4 speaks to this, saying, "Consider it pure joy, my brothers and sisters, whenever you face trials of many kinds, because you know that the testing of your faith produces perseverance. Let perseverance finish its work so that you may be mature and complete, not lacking anything." <u>Pain is not a random occurrence but a tool that God uses to mature and complete our faith.</u>

PAIN REFOCUSES PRIORITIES AND
REALIGNS US WITH GOD'S PURPOSE

Pain often has a way of recalibrating our hearts and minds. It reveals what truly matters and can strip away distractions that keep us from focusing on God. In the midst of suffering, we are reminded of our need for God and are more likely to seek Him wholeheartedly. Pain reveals the fleeting nature of worldly comforts and draws us to eternal values, realigning us with God's purpose.

The Apostle Paul, who endured countless hardships, wrote in Philippians 3:8, "*I consider everything a loss because of the surpassing worth of knowing Christ Jesus my Lord, for whose sake I have lost all things.*" Pain has a way of shifting our perspective, helping us prioritize our relationship with God and the things that matter eternally over the temporary comforts we often cling to. Experiencing pain can foster compassion and empathy for others who suffer. When we go through trials, we become more aware of the struggles others face, making us more sensitive and willing to extend grace and support. Pain allows believers to become conduits of God's love and comfort to those in need, as we learn firsthand the value of compassion. Paul describes this in *2 Corinthians 1:4: "[God] comforts us in all our troubles, so that we can comfort those in any trouble with the comfort we ourselves receive from God.*" Our experiences with pain enable us to reach out to others with genuine understanding, making us agents of God's healing and grace.

PAIN CAN DRAW US CLOSER TO GOD

Pain has a way of breaking down walls and bringing us to our knees before God. In suffering, we often recognize our own limitations and need for God's strength. Pain becomes a powerful catalyst for a deeper, more intimate relationship with Him. Through struggles, believers are often drawn closer to God as they seek His presence, comfort, and guidance in ways they might not otherwise.

Psalm 34:18 assures us, "The Lord is close to the brokenhearted and saves those who are crushed in spirit." In our lowest moments, God's presence can become more real and more precious. Rather than driving a wedge between us and God, pain can deepen our dependence on Him, helping us experience His love and faithfulness more intimately. Pain is often a tool God uses to shape and mold our character. Through hardships, believers learn patience, humility, perseverance, and self-control. These qualities are often hard-won, developed only through

the challenges that pain brings. By enduring hardship with faith, we allow God to transform our character, making us more like Christ. Romans 5:3-4 captures this process: *"We also glory in our sufferings, because we know that suffering produces perseverance; perseverance, character; and character, hope."* The refining process isn't easy, but it leads to a depth of character that glorifies God and enables us to walk in His purpose with greater integrity and strength.

PAIN HIGHLIGHTS OUR DEPENDENCE ON GOD'S GRACE

Pain often brings us to a point of dependency on Gods power and strength, where we realize that we cannot rely on our own strength or understanding. This dependence isn't weakness; it's an opportunity to experience God's grace in a profound way. When we recognize our need, we open ourselves to receive God's sustaining grace, which carries us through even the darkest valleys.

In 2 Corinthians 12:9, Paul reflects on God's response to his suffering: *"My grace is sufficient for you, for <u>my power is made perfect in weakness</u>."* Pain allows us to experience God's power and grace in our lives, reminding us that His strength is more than enough to sustain us.

Pain can serve as a prelude to joy. Just as the struggle of labor leads to the joy of new life, the hardships believers endure can give way to greater blessings and fulfillment. Suffering often gives way to spiritual growth, deeper relationships, and increased faith. It prepares us for the joy and reward of God's presence and promises. Jesus Himself exemplifies this perspective in Hebrews 12:2, which says, *"For the joy set before him he endured the cross, scorning its shame, and sat down at the right hand of the throne of God."* Jesus endured suffering not for suffering's sake, but because He knew the joy that lay ahead. Pain, when endured with faith, can transform us, drawing us closer to the joy and fulfillment found in Christ.

While pain has the potential to make us bitter, God's intent is to use it to make us better. The relevance of pain in a believer's life is ultimately about transformation. It shapes our faith, focuses our hearts on God, builds our character, and draws us into closer relationship with Him. Pain challenges us, but when we allow God to work through it, it can become a path to deeper spiritual growth and a more profound experience of His grace and love.

<u>God doesn't waste our pain; He redeems it, using it to make us more like Christ and to prepare us for His eternal promises.</u> In His hands, pain serves as a refining tool not to destroy us, but to strengthen us, to deepen our faith, and to draw us into the fullness of life He has for us.

The equation *Pain + Perseverance + Purpose = Refinement* represents a powerful journey of spiritual and personal transformation. Let's break down how each component contributes to the process of **total-refinement**, yielding a deeper understanding of God's work in our lives.

1. Pain as the Catalyst for Growth

➢ **Role of Pain**: Pain often serves as the starting point in the refinement process. It disrupts our comfort zones, confronts us with our limitations, and can be a catalyst that moves us toward God and inner transformation. Without pain, we might never be motivated to change or grow.

➢ **Challenge to Face**: Pain can feel overwhelming, even discouraging, but when it's approached as a necessary part of growth, it becomes a tool rather than a torment. Embracing pain with a willingness to learn from it is the first step in the refining journey.

2. Perseverance as the Sustaining Force

➢ **Role of Perseverance**: Perseverance is what keeps us moving forward, even when the journey is difficult. It's the ability to endure hardship with resilience, holding on to faith

and hope through trials. Perseverance transforms pain from a temporary experience into a meaningful process of growth.

➤ **Challenge to Face**: Perseverance requires endurance, especially when results or relief are not immediately visible. This phase can feel like a prolonged season of waiting or struggling, but it's crucial. Perseverance refines character and strengthens faith, helping us to stand firm under pressure.

3. Purpose as the Guiding Vision

➤ **Role of Purpose**: Purpose gives pain and perseverance a meaningful direction. Knowing that there's a purpose, whether it's God's ultimate plan, personal growth, or fulfilling a calling that motivates us to endure hardship with hope. Purpose turns adversity into an opportunity to fulfill a larger, meaningful role in God's plan.

➤ **Challenge to Face**: Sometimes, purpose is not immediately clear, which can lead to frustration or discouragement. Discovering purpose often requires prayer, reflection, and patience. Purpose also invites us to realign our goals with God's will, seeing beyond the temporary struggle to the lasting impact it can have.

THE OUTCOME OF SPIRITUAL REFINEMENT

➤ **What is Refinement?** Refinement is the process of being purified, strengthened, and transformed. Just as precious metals are refined in fire to remove impurities, the combination of pain, perseverance, and purpose works together to strip away what is not essential, leaving a stronger, purer character.

➤ **How it Transforms Us**: Through refinement, we become more resilient, compassionate, humble, and faithful. It deepens our relationship with God and shapes us into the image of Christ. The challenges we face lead to spiritual maturity and a greater understanding of God's faithfulness.

Pain + Perseverance + Purpose = Refinement Each component plays a critical role:

1. **Pain** forces us to confront the areas in need of growth.
2. **Perseverance** gives us the strength to endure and press forward.
3. **Purpose** provides the motivation and meaning behind our suffering.

Together, they create refinement, a divine process that shapes us into people of character, depth, and resilience. *This equation encourages us to view trials not as mere obstacles, but as opportunities to be molded by God into the people He created us to be.*

THE PAIN OF PAUL'S "THORN IN THE FLESH"

This meant that God's sustaining presence and strength would enable Paul to endure, even as the thorn remained. Paul's weakness was not a limitation in God's eyes; rather, it became a platform for displaying God's strength and grace. By allowing the thorn to remain, God taught Paul and all believers that His strength is best revealed in moments of human weakness. The thorn was not a barrier to God's power; it was a vehicle through which God's power could be manifested more fully. This principle that strength comes through weakness is central to the Christian voyage. Paul came to understand and embrace this truth, saying, *"Therefore I will boast all the more gladly about my weaknesses, so that Christ's power may rest on me" (2 Corinthians 12:9).* He recognized that his weakness, rather than hindering his ministry, actually magnified God's glory and power. Through grace, Paul was able to persevere, empowered by a strength that was not his own. God's choice not to remove the thorn redefined Paul's understanding of suffering. While he initially sought deliverance, he came to realize that God's grace was even more valuable than relief. The thorn transformed his perspective, teaching him that God's presence and grace were sufficient, even if his circumstances didn't change. This shift from seeking deliverance to embracing

dependence is a powerful lesson in faith. Paul learned to see his suffering not as a punishment or failure but as a unique opportunity to experience God's grace in ways he might not have otherwise. His weakness became a pathway to deeper intimacy with God and a greater reliance on His provision. Paul's thorn became a powerful testimony to the sufficiency of God's grace. He continued his ministry despite his suffering, demonstrating to others that human limitations could not hinder God's work. His ability to persevere, empowered by grace, showed that God's power is not constrained by human weakness but is often revealed most clearly through it. In this way, Paul's thorn became a meaningful source of encouragement for all who suffer. It taught the early church and us today that suffering is not a sign of God's absence but often an avenue through which His presence and strength are revealed. In his final reflections on the thorn, Paul reaches a place of acceptance, even joy, in his weakness. He declares, "For when I am weak, then I am strong" (2 Corinthians 12:10). Paul's journey with his thorn led him to a place where he could find contentment not in the removal of his suffering, but in the realization that God's grace was more than enough. This contentment reflects the heart of faith; a trust in God's wisdom, a reliance on His strength, and a surrender to His will. Through his thorn, Paul learned that God's grace was the greatest gift, one that could sustain him through any trial, filling his life with divine strength despite human frailty.

By virtue of the thorn in his flesh, Paul's journey teaches us that God doesn't always deliver us *from* our suffering but often chooses to strengthen us *through* it. God's grace became Paul's lifeline, offering him the strength to continue his mission, a deeper humility, and a testimony of God's faithfulness. The thorn may have been painful, but it became a source of profound spiritual growth and a vivid reminder that God's grace is sufficient for every challenge. **In our own trials, Paul's experience assures us that while deliverance may not always come, God's grace will always be enough to carry us through.**

ROOTED AND GROUNDED IN GOD

The Bible has much to say about being rooted in God, especially during times of pain, testing, and difficulty. Being rooted in God means having a firm, unshakeable foundation in Him that enables believers to endure hardship with faith and perseverance. The Word of God provides both guidance and encouragement for staying connected to Jesus Christ and remaining anchored to His cross. Here's an exploration of what the Bible says about this steadfast connection and how believers can cultivate it. In Colossians 2:6-7, Paul exhorts believers, *"So then, just as you received Christ Jesus as Lord, continue to live your lives in him, rooted and built up in him, strengthened in the faith as you were taught, and overflowing with thankfulness."* Being rooted in Christ means drawing spiritual nourishment and strength from Him, much like a tree draws sustenance from its roots. The deeper the roots, the stronger the believer can stand during storms. Being deeply rooted in God is essential because trials and hardships are an inevitable part of life. Jesus Himself said, "In this world you will have trouble. But take heart! I have overcome the world" (John 16:33). Knowing that pain and testing are part of the journey, believers are encouraged to build a foundation in Christ that can withstand adversity.

Staying Connected to Jesus Christ Through Spiritual Disciplines

1. **Abiding in Christ**: Jesus teaches His followers the importance of staying connected to Him in John 15:4-5: "Remain in me, as I also remain in you. No branch can bear fruit by itself; it must remain in the vine... apart from me, you can do nothing." Abiding in Christ means maintaining a constant connection with Him, like branches to a vine, drawing life and strength from Him every day.

2. **Prayer**: Prayer is one of the primary ways to stay rooted in God. Through prayer, believers communicate with God, bringing their needs, struggles, and praises before Him. Philippians 4:6-7 encourages us to "not be anxious about

anything, but in every situation, by prayer and petition, with thanksgiving, present your requests to God." Prayer helps us to remain focused on God's presence and to receive peace and strength in times of difficulty.

3. **Reading and Meditating on God's Word**: Psalm 1:2-3 describes the blessed person as one who "delights in the law of the Lord and meditates on his law day and night. That person is like a tree planted by streams of water, which yields its fruit in season." The Word of God is a source of wisdom, comfort, and guidance. Regular engagement with scripture allows believers to internalize God's truths, enabling them to stand firm when life is challenging.

ANCHORING TO THE CROSS OF CHRIST

<u>Understanding the Sacrifice of Jesus</u>: The cross of Jesus Christ represents the ultimate demonstration of God's love, grace, and redemption. In times of testing, believers are called to remember what Jesus endured for their sake, taking comfort in the fact that He knows pain, betrayal, and suffering firsthand. Hebrews 12:2 urges believers to "*fix our eyes on Jesus, the pioneer and perfecter of faith. For the joy set before him, he endured the cross.*" Keeping our focus on the cross reminds us of the price Jesus paid and the victory He secured.

<u>Finding Strength in His Example</u>: Jesus's perseverance through suffering is an example for all believers. In Matthew 16:24, Jesus said, "Whoever wants to be my disciple must deny themselves and take up their cross and follow me." Anchoring ourselves to the cross means committing to follow Jesus, even when it's hard, and finding strength in His example of obedience and love.

PERSEVERING THROUGH TRIALS AND TESTING

<u>Counting Trials as Joy</u>: James 1:2-4 teaches that "the testing of your faith produces perseverance." Rather than seeing trials as setbacks, believers are encouraged to view them as opportunities for <u>growth</u>

and <u>refinement.</u> Enduring trials with faith builds character and spiritual maturity, helping believers to become more rooted in God.

Relying on God's Strength: Isaiah 40:31 promises that "those who hope in the Lord will renew their strength. They will soar on wings like eagles; they will run and not grow weary, they will walk and not be faint." During painful or difficult times, believers can trust that God will sustain them with His strength, even when their own strength fails. Staying connected to Christ through prayer and worship brings His empowering presence into every struggle.

FELLOWSHIP WITH OTHER BELIEVERS

The Strength of Community: Hebrews 10:24-25 encourages believers "not giving up meeting together, as some are in the habit of doing, but encouraging one another." Being rooted in God also means being connected with His body, the Church. In times of hardship, the support, prayers, and encouragement of other believers can be invaluable. God often uses others to speak life, hope, and truth into our lives.

Accountability and Encouragement: Fellowship provides accountability and encouragement, helping believers stay focused on God's promises. When rooted in a Bible-Believing community of faith, believers are better equipped to remain steadfast during trials, knowing they are supported and lifted up by others who share their faith.

EMBRACING THE HOPE OF ETERNAL LIFE

Keeping an Eternal Perspective: Hardships can feel overwhelming, but the Bible encourages believers to look beyond temporary trials to the eternal hope found in Christ. In 2 Corinthians 4:17-18, Paul writes, "For our light and momentary troubles are achieving for us an eternal glory that far outweighs them all. So we fix our eyes not on what is seen, but on what is unseen." Anchoring

to the cross includes holding onto the promise of eternal life, knowing that God's ultimate plan is to bring His people to Himself in a place where there is no more pain or sorrow.

The Promise of God's Presence: Finally, the Bible assures believers that God is always with them, even in their darkest moments. Psalm 23:4 reminds us, "Yea, though I walk through the valley of the shadow of death, I will fear no evil; For You *are* with me; Your rod and Your staff, they comfort me." Being rooted in God means trusting His promise to be with us, comforting and guiding us, no matter what we face.

PRACTICAL STEPS TO STAY ROOTED IN GOD THROUGH PAIN AND DIFFICULTY

➢ **Daily Prayer and Devotion**: Commit to spending time in God's presence, bringing your struggles, needs, and praises to Him.

➢ **Consistent Bible Reading**: Engage with scripture daily, meditating on God's promises and truths that strengthen faith.

➢ **Remember the Cross**: Regularly reflect on Jesus's sacrifice and find strength in His example of enduring suffering with love and obedience.

➢ **Seek Fellowship**: Stay connected with other believers, building relationships that encourage faith, accountability, and support.

➢ **Hold Onto God's Promises**: Keep an eternal perspective, focusing on the hope of eternal life and the reality of God's presence with you through every trial.

By staying rooted in God and anchored to the cross, believers can endure pain, testing, and difficulty with hope and resilience. Through every trial, God promises to be with us, sustaining us with His grace, refining our faith, and bringing us closer to Himself.

PAIN CANNOT STOP THE PURPOSES OF GOD, BUT IT CAN SHAPE THE OUTCOME OF THE JOURNEY

Pain, negative attitudes, and rebellious spirits can create significant obstacles in a believer's life, but they *cannot* ultimately stop the purposes of God. Scripture is filled with examples showing that God's plans are sovereign, and while our responses to pain, challenges, and commands can affect our journey, they cannot override His divine will. However, a negative response to pain, such as adopting a bad attitude, a rebellious spirit, or focusing solely on self, can hinder our growth, delay blessings, and distance us from the crowns God has promised.

Here's a deeper look at how pain and our responses to it interact with God's purposes, and why it is crucial to live and respond to pain in God's way rather than the world's way.

PAIN CANNOT STOP THE PURPOSES OF GOD, BUT IT CAN SHAPE OUR JOURNEY

God's Sovereign Purposes: God's plans are ultimately unstoppable. Isaiah 46:10 states, "My purpose will stand, and I will do all that I please." Even in a world filled with pain and suffering, God's purposes prevail. Pain is part of the fallen world, but God uses it to bring about His greater plans. Joseph's journey from betrayal and suffering to becoming a ruler in Egypt is a powerful example of God's sovereign purpose prevailing despite intense pain and hardship. In Genesis 50:20, Joseph declares, "You intended to harm me, but God intended it for good to accomplish what is now being done, the saving of many lives."

While pain cannot stop God's plans, it is often used by God to refine, redirect, and deepen a believer's faith. God uses pain not as a barrier, but as a catalyst for growth. In Romans 8:28, we are reminded that "in all things God works for the good of those who love him, who have been called according to his purpose." Pain may challenge us, but it is never outside of God's redeeming hands.

A NEGATIVE ATTITUDE AND REBELLIOUS SPIRIT CAN HINDER OUR JOURNEY AND DELAY BLESSINGS

The Danger of a Negative Outlook: A negative attitude, especially when directed toward God's commands, can harden the heart and hinder our spiritual growth. The Israelites provide a vivid example of this. Despite God's promises, their constant complaints, rebellion, and lack of faith delayed their entry into the Promised Land. What should have been an 11-day journey became a 40-year wandering because of their negative response to hardship and testing. While God's purpose for Israel eventually came to pass, many missed the blessing because they chose grumbling and rebellion over trust and obedience.

A negative attitude or rebellious spirit can distance us from God. Hebrews 3:12-13 warns us, "See to it, brothers and sisters, that none of you has a sinful, unbelieving heart that turns away from the living God." If we allow bitterness or rebellion to take root, it can cloud our faith and rob us of the blessings God desires for us to experience on earth, affecting our spiritual vitality and joy.

A REBELLIOUS SPIRIT CAN PREVENT US FROM ACHIEVING THE CROWN

Crown as a Reward for Faithfulness: In scripture, the crown is often a reward for perseverance, faithfulness, and steadfastness. Paul speaks of a "crown of righteousness" reserved for those who have "fought the good fight" and "finished the race" (2 Timothy 4:7-8). A rebellious spirit, however, can lead us away from this path of obedience and perseverance, threatening to rob us of the crown.

God is patient, but a persistent rebellious spirit can have serious consequences. Saul, the first king of Israel, was given a divine mandate to lead God's people, yet his disobedience cost him the kingdom. In 1 Samuel 15:23, Samuel tells him, "Rebellion is like the sin of divination, and arrogance like the evil of idolatry. Because you have rejected the word of the Lord, he has rejected you as king." While God's plans for Israel continued, Saul missed out on his calling and blessings due to his disobedience. This highlights that rebellion can indeed prevent us from fully achieving God's promises, including the crowns reserved for faithful servants.

RESPONDING TO PAIN IN GOD'S WAY VERSUS THE WORLD'S WAY

<u>God's Way</u>: The Bible teaches that we should respond to pain with <u>faith</u>, <u>patience</u>, and a <u>steadfast commitment to God's principles</u>. *Romans 12:12* instructs, *"Be joyful in hope, patient in affliction, faithful in prayer."* God calls us to endure pain with an eternal perspective, trusting that He is working through it for our good and His glory. When we respond to pain with trust and obedience, we allow God's grace to shine through us, revealing His strength in our weakness.

The world often responds to pain with bitterness, resentment, escapism, or self-pity. These reactions may offer temporary relief, but they ultimately lead to further pain and distance from God's presence. If believers adopt this approach, they risk becoming hardened and unable to see the purpose and growth that God intends. James 1:2-4 urges us to consider trials as opportunities for growth, saying, "Let perseverance finish its work so that you may be mature and complete, not lacking anything."

LIVING THROUGH PAIN AS A TESTIMONY OF GOD'S GRACE

<u>Grace as a Sustaining Power</u>: Pain is an unavoidable part of life, but when endured with grace, it becomes a powerful testimony to God's faithfulness. Paul's experience with his "thorn in the flesh" exemplifies this. God did not remove Paul's pain but promised, "My grace is sufficient for you, for my power is made perfect in weakness" (2 Corinthians 12:9). By accepting his limitations and relying on God's grace, Paul turned his pain into a testament of God's strength.

Believers are called to let grace abound in their lives, even in the face of adversity. Peter encourages us in 1 Peter 4:16 to "not be ashamed, but praise God that you

bear that name" when we suffer as Christians. Living through pain in a way that reflects God's grace and goodness serves as a testimony to others, showing that God's purposes are greater than any trial we face.

THE ETERNAL PERSPECTIVE: PAIN HAS A PURPOSE IN GOD'S PLAN

One of the most encouraging promises in scripture is that our earthly pain is temporary compared to the eternal glory that awaits us. Paul affirms this in 2 Corinthians 4:17, "For our light and momentary troubles are achieving for us an eternal glory that far outweighs them all." Embracing this perspective helps believers endure pain with hope, knowing that God's purposes will prevail, and that He will reward faithfulness in the end.

Even though pain is often difficult to understand, believers are reminded that God can use it to accomplish His will in our lives. Romans 8:28 tells us that "in all things God works for the good of those who love him, who have been called according to his purpose." Pain, therefore, becomes part of God's transformative process, drawing us closer to Him, strengthening our faith, and refining our character.

Pain, negative attitudes, or a rebellious spirit cannot ultimately stop God's purposes, but they can hinder our spiritual growth, delay blessings, and cause us to miss out on the full rewards of obedience. Believers are called to respond to pain in *God's way*; with faith, patience, and a reliance on His grace; so that we may grow, testify of His faithfulness, and live lives that reflect His purposes.

By staying anchored in God's truth and responding to pain with a surrendered heart, we open ourselves to His transforming grace and ensure that His plans and purposes abound in our lives. Even in a world filled with unavoidable pain, God's grace is sufficient to carry us, guide us, and prepare us for the eternal glory that awaits. Through faith, endurance, and humility, we keep our eyes fixed on Jesus, allowing His grace to shine brightly as we journey toward the crowns He has promised.

THE CONSEQUENCES OF GIVING IN TO PAIN!

Yes, the Bible is clear about the consequences of giving in to pain without perseverance and refusing to trust in God's strength through trials. Throughout scripture, examples and teachings reveal what can happen when believers choose to give in to despair, bitterness, or rebellion instead of enduring faithfully. Here are <u>ten biblical consequences of failing to persevere through pain according to God's way.</u>

1. Loss of Spiritual Growth and Maturity

James 1:2-4 emphasizes the importance of persevering through trials, stating, "Consider it pure joy, my brothers and sisters, whenever you face trials of many kinds, because you know that the testing of your faith produces perseverance. Let perseverance finish its work so that you may be mature and complete, not lacking anything."

When believers choose not to persevere, they miss the opportunity for growth, maturity, and the "completeness" God desires for them. Avoiding or succumbing to trials can leave a believer spiritually immature and unprepared for future challenges, lacking the resilience needed to thrive in their walk with God.

2. Hindrance to God's Blessings and Promises

The story of the Israelites wandering in the wilderness is a vivid example of how failing to trust God through hardship can delay or even forfeit blessings. In Numbers 14:22-23, God says, "Not one of those who saw my glory and the signs I performed in Egypt and in the wilderness but who disobeyed me and tested me ten times, not one of them will ever see the land I promised."

The Israelites' lack of faith, perseverance, and trust in God's promises led them to miss entering the Promised Land. Similarly, refusing to persevere can result in missed blessings, opportunities, or promises that God intended to fulfill in our lives.

3. Bitterness and Spiritual Hardening

Hebrews 3:12-13 warns against letting hardship or unbelief harden our hearts; "See to it, brothers and sisters, that none of you has a sinful, unbelieving heart that turns away from the living God. But encourage one another daily…so that none of you may be hardened by sin's deceitfulness."

When believers refuse to persevere and choose bitterness, it can lead to a hardening of the heart. This hardening distances us from God and can make it difficult to respond to Him in faith. Bitterness, when left unchecked, can grow and eventually separate us from God's fellowship and blessings.

4. Loss of Eternal Rewards and Crowns

In Revelation 3:11, Jesus says, "I am coming soon. Hold on to what you have, so that no one will take your crown." Similarly, James 1:12 promises, "Blessed is the one who perseveres under trial because, having stood the test, that person will receive the crown of life that the Lord has promised to those who love him."

The Bible speaks of rewards and crowns for those who endure faithfully. When believers give up in the face of pain and fail to persevere, they risk losing these eternal rewards. Perseverance is part of the journey toward the "crown of life" and other rewards God promises to His faithful followers.

5. Increased Vulnerability to Temptation and Sin

In Galatians 6:9, Paul encourages believers not to "grow weary in doing good, for at the proper time we will reap a harvest if we do not give up." Weariness in the face of difficulty can lead to giving in to temptation and making unwise decisions.

When believers do not persevere through pain, they may be more prone to compromise their values, seek worldly comforts, or fall into sin as a form of escape. Giving in to pain can create vulnerability, making it easier to stray from God's commands and adopt attitudes or actions that hinder spiritual growth.

6. Broken Fellowship with God and Missed Intimacy

Psalm 34:18 reminds us that "The Lord is close to the brokenhearted and saves those who are crushed in spirit." In times of pain, believers have an opportunity to draw closer to God and experience His presence. However, when they reject this opportunity, they may miss the intimacy that God offers in hardship.

Refusing to persevere can lead to broken fellowship with God, causing believers to miss the unique comfort, strength, and intimacy that He offers during times of suffering. Pain can be a doorway to deeper fellowship with God, but rejecting perseverance can prevent us from experiencing that closeness.

7. Potential Loss of Witness and Testimony

Matthew 5:16 calls believers to "let your light shine before others, that they may see your good deeds and glorify your Father in heaven." How believers respond to hardship can serve as a powerful testimony of faith and God's grace.

Failing to persevere and giving in to despair or bitterness can damage a believer's witness to others. Pain, when endured with faith, can bring hope to those who observe our lives, but a negative response may instead discourage others or lead them to question the sincerity of our faith.

8. Loss of Peace and Joy in Christ

Romans 5:3-4 teaches that "we also glory in our sufferings, because we know that suffering produces perseverance; perseverance, character; and character, hope." God's desire is for perseverance to lead to peace, joy, and hope.

When believers refuse to persevere, they miss out on the peace and joy that God offers even amid trials. A refusal to endure with faith can lead to feelings of despair, discouragement, and a loss of hope, as believers cut themselves off from the sustaining power of God's promises.

9. The Risk of Judgment and Discipline

Hebrews 12:6 reminds us that "the Lord disciplines the one he loves, and he chastens everyone he accepts as his son." God disciplines His children to bring them back to a place of faithfulness.

When believers refuse to persevere and choose instead to walk away from God, they may experience His discipline. God's discipline is always intended for restoration, but it can be painful and often involves consequences that could have been avoided through faithful perseverance.

10. Missing the Fullness of God's Purpose and Calling

In Philippians 3:13-14, Paul speaks about pressing on toward the goal to win the prize. He writes, "Forgetting what is behind and straining toward what is ahead, I press on toward the goal to win the prize for which God has called me heavenward in Christ Jesus."

By refusing to persevere, believers risk missing the fullness of God's purpose and calling in their lives. Pain can be part of God's process of preparing us for greater purpose, but if we refuse to press forward, we may never achieve the goals He has set before us.

The consequences of refusing to persevere in pain, according to scripture, are profound. They can include missed spiritual growth, delayed blessings, vulnerability to sin, broken fellowship with God, loss of testimony, and <u>even the forfeiture of eternal rewards. God calls believers to respond to pain with perseverance, not only for their own spiritual growth but to fulfill His purposes and bring glory to Him.</u>

Pain and testing are part of the believer's journey, but God's grace is always sufficient to carry us through. By remaining steadfast, believers not only avoid these consequences but also position themselves to receive the fullness of God's blessings, maturity, and eternal rewards. The promise of God's Word is clear, for those who persevere, there is hope, peace, and a crown of life awaiting them.

PAIN AS A BRIDGE TO SALVATION AND GROWTH RATHER THAN CONDEMNATION

Pain in a believer's life can indeed be a means of *salvation* and *growth* rather than condemnation. Scripture reveals that God often allows or even sends pain not as punishment but as a tool to draw us closer to Him, refine our faith, and align our lives with His purposes. Pain, though challenging and uncomfortable, can ultimately save our souls by stripping away attachments to this temporary world and anchoring us in eternal truth. This understanding is rooted in the recognition that our bodies are temporary, but our souls are eternal. God's priority is always the soul, which endures forever, while the body is temporary. Jesus emphasizes this in Matthew 10:28, saying, "Do not be afraid of those who kill the body but cannot kill the soul. Rather, be afraid of the One who can destroy both soul and body in hell." This verse underscores that God is more concerned with the eternal state of our souls than our temporary physical condition. Pain often redirects our focus from the temporary comforts of the world to the eternal truths of God's Kingdom. It reminds us of our mortality and dependence on God, helping us prioritize our souls' welfare over earthly desires or comfort. In doing so, pain serves as a call to examine our relationship with God, our faith, and our commitment to His ways. In 2 Corinthians 12:7-10, Paul describes a "thorn in the flesh," a painful affliction that kept him humble and dependent on God. Despite pleading with God to remove it, Paul was given this response; "My grace is sufficient for you, for my power is made perfect in weakness" (2 Corinthians 12:9). Paul's thorn, though painful, was allowed by God to prevent spiritual pride and keep him close to the source of true power, God's grace. Paul's pain was a form of spiritual protection, guarding him from pride, which could have led to spiritual ruin. The thorn in his flesh kept him humble, anchored in God's strength rather than his own. Through this pain, Paul learned a profound truth; that God's strength is magnified in our weaknesses. Pain, then, became a pathway to experiencing God's grace more fully, saving Paul from self-reliance and drawing him nearer to Christ. The fact that God chose to sustain Paul with grace

rather than remove his affliction illustrates that the eternal welfare of the soul is more significant than the temporary comfort of the body. God was more interested in using Paul's pain to keep him spiritually vigilant, aware of his need for grace, and anchored in faith. In Romans 8:18-23, Paul writes, "For I consider that the sufferings of this present time are not worthy *to be compared* with the glory which shall be revealed in us." He explains that all of creation is groaning under the effects of sin, waiting for the "redemption of our bodies." Pain and suffering serve as reminders that this world is fallen and temporary, leading believers to hope for the eternal glory that awaits them in God's Kingdom. The "groaning" of creation, and of believers who await redemption, teaches us to long for the eternal rather than cling to the temporary. Pain, in this sense, creates a spiritual hunger for heaven, for a place where suffering will cease. By enduring suffering with faith, believers are reminded that pain is temporary and that their souls are destined for an eternity of peace and joy with God. Paul reassures believers that while suffering is difficult, it is minor compared to the eternal glory that God has promised. Pain becomes a saving influence when it reminds us that our true citizenship is in heaven. This hope in future glory anchors the believer's soul in the promises of God, drawing us away from the fleeting pleasures of the world and closer to the eternal joy that awaits. Proverbs 17:3 states, *"The crucible for silver and the furnace for gold, but the Lord tests the heart."* Just as precious metals are refined in the fire to remove impurities, pain can serve to purify our souls by revealing and removing sinful habits, idols, and misplaced priorities. Through this process, believers are drawn into a closer relationship with God, becoming more aware of their dependence on Him.

Pain can also serve as a wake-up call, leading to repentance and spiritual renewal. Psalm 119:67 says, *"Before I was afflicted, I went astray, but now I obey your word."* In this way, pain acts as a divine intervention that redirects us to the path of obedience. By enduring pain and learning from it, believers are saved from further spiritual harm, as the experience brings them back into alignment with God's will. Pain fosters humility, teaching believers to surrender their will to God and seek His guidance. When believers experience pain, they often turn to God with a new awareness of their limitations, cultivating a heart of humility and dependence. This dependency, rather than self-reliance, strengthens the soul's connection to God, securing its eternal well-being.

PAIN AS PREPARATION FOR ETERNITY AND ASSURANCE OF SALVATION

Purification for Future Glory: Pain helps purify believers, preparing them for eternity in God's presence. In 1 Peter 1:6-7, Peter explains that trials refine faith like fire refines gold, proving it "genuine" and resulting in "praise, glory, and honor" when Christ is revealed. This purification process is essential because it readies the soul for heaven, where nothing impure can enter (Revelation 21:27).

Assurance of Salvation Through Suffering: In Hebrews 12:5-7, believers are reminded that suffering is part of God's discipline, a sign of His love and our legitimate sonship. "The Lord disciplines the one he loves, and he chastens everyone he accepts as his son." Far from condemnation, pain becomes a means by which God assures us of His care and commitment to our growth. Pain then becomes a marker of our belonging to God and His refining love, assuring us of our salvation and future inheritance.

✓ **God's Way: Acceptance and Surrender**: When we view pain as part of God's plan to refine and save our souls, we respond with acceptance and surrender, knowing that it's working for our ultimate good. Rather than despairing, we can lean into God's grace, trusting Him to use our suffering for His purposes. Paul's response to his thorn in 2 Corinthians 12:10 captures this beautifully: "That is why, for Christ's sake, I delight in weaknesses, in insults, in hardships, in persecutions, in difficulties. For when I am weak, then I am strong."

✓ **The World's Way: Resentment and Escape**: The world often views pain as something to avoid at all costs, leading many to react with resentment, bitterness, or escapism. This approach can separate us from God, causing spiritual harm rather than growth. Resisting God's purposes in pain can harden the heart and prevent the soul from experiencing the deeper work God intends.

Living with the Eternal in Mind: For believers, pain is temporary and serves a greater purpose in light of eternity. While our bodies are subject to decay and suffering, our souls are being prepared for a glorious future with God. Paul's words in Romans 8:18 remind us that, "our present sufferings are not worth comparing with the glory that will be revealed in us." Pain, then, becomes a temporary affliction that refines us for an eternal inheritance.

The Eternal Reward of Faithful Endurance: Revelation 21:4 offers the hope that in eternity, God "will wipe every tear from their eyes. There will be no more death or mourning or crying or pain." The eternal joy of God's presence far outweighs the temporary pain of this life, and enduring hardship faithfully anchors our souls in that promise.

Pain, while difficult, is often sent into a believer's life not to condemn but to save, refine, and prepare the soul for eternity. God allows pain to help us shed attachments to this temporary world and deepen our dependence on Him. Through pain, God redirects our focus to what truly matters, our relationship with Him and our eternal destiny.

By viewing pain as a means of salvation and refinement, believers can respond with faith and perseverance, knowing that God's grace is sufficient and His purposes are perfect. The soul, eternal and infinitely precious to God, is shaped through suffering, purified for an everlasting life with Him. Through this lens, pain becomes not a curse, but a blessing that leads us closer to the heart of God, securing our hope and future in Him. Painful circumstances are an undeniable reality for believers and non-believers alike. Mental illness, sexual abuse, broken homes, unemployment, poverty, addiction, abandonment, homelessness, divorce, betrayal, imprisonment, chronic illness, and the loss of loved ones, these are just some of the crushing burdens that people face every day. <u>The Bible makes it clear that choosing to follow Jesus does not exempt us from these hardships. In fact, walking with Christ often means facing deeper, refining trials. Yet, through it all, we are assured that God's grace is more than sufficient.</u>

BELIEVERS ARE NOT EXEMPT FROM
PAIN AND SUFFERING

Jesus Himself stated, "In this world, you will have trouble" (John 16:33). Accepting Christ doesn't remove life's burdens; it changes how we bare them. As believers, we are not immune to mental illness, abuse, betrayal, poverty, or any other form of suffering. In fact, the Bible teaches that we should "count it all joy…when you meet trials of various kinds, for you know that the testing of your faith produces steadfastness" (James 1:2-4). Pain and trials are a part of God's refining process, shaping us to be more like Christ and drawing us closer to Him.

Just as Jesus endured rejection, persecution, betrayal, and unimaginable physical pain, we too are called to share in His sufferings (Philippians 3:10). His suffering reminds us that pain is not a sign of divine abandonment, but an invitation to join Him in a deeper way, trusting in God's sovereignty even when we cannot see His purpose. Jehovah Shammah, "The Lord is There," assures us of God's presence even in our darkest valleys. Mental illness, abuse, broken homes, and other devastating realities can make us feel isolated and forgotten. But God's promise is that He is ever-present, even when we cannot sense Him. Psalm 34:18 tells us, "The Lord is close to the brokenhearted and saves those who are crushed in spirit." No matter how heavy the burden or how alone we feel, God

is with us, sustaining and comforting us through every painful moment.

Sometimes the Teacher is silent during the test. But God's silence is not absence; it is a deepening of our faith. His quiet presence is an invitation to rely more fully on His promises rather than our perceptions. Many times, pain is used by God to refine us, to shape us into His likeness, and to reveal His strength within our weakness. James 1:2-4 reminds us that trials and hardships are tools for producing steadfastness, so that we may become "perfect and complete, lacking in nothing." Pain is not sent to destroy us but to strengthen us, grow our resilience, and deepen our faith.

Consider the struggles of those facing chronic illness, addiction, or poverty. These hardships challenge us to rely on God alone, breaking down our reliance on ourselves or the world. Each trial is an opportunity to experience God's grace, as He meets us in our weakness and provides the strength we need to persevere. As Paul testifies, "My grace is sufficient for you, for my power is made perfect in weakness" (2 Corinthians 12:9). Pain equips believers to minister to others with compassion and understanding. Survivors of abuse, illness, betrayal, and other sufferings often find that their pain becomes a tool for serving others who are struggling. God does not waste our suffering; instead, He transforms it into a source of empathy and strength that enables us to walk alongside others with grace and understanding.

Paul writes in 2 Corinthians 1:4 that God "comforts us in all our troubles, so that we can comfort those in any trouble with the comfort we ourselves receive from God." As believers, we are called to be a light in a dark world, offering hope and compassion to those who are hurting, even as we ourselves carry our own burdens.

TRUSTING GOD'S WILL ABOVE OUR OWN

We may not be able to control what happens to us, but we can control how we respond. Trusting God through pain requires us to surrender our need for answers and instead place our faith in His perfect will. Jesus Himself modeled this when He prayed, "Not my will, but yours be done" (Luke 22:42). This surrender is not easy, especially in situations that seem unbearable, such as the loss of loved ones or chronic illness. But it is through this surrender that we find peace, knowing that God is working for our good, even in the darkest circumstances.

As believers, we are called to choose faith over despair, to respond with resilience rather than bitterness. When we rely on God's strength, we can fearlessly without doubt, climb the mountain rather than praying for it to be removed. This choice, this holy perseverance, is how we align ourselves with God's purposes, allowing Him to refine and shape us. God's grace is the sustaining power that carries us through every trial. It is not just a concept; it is a divine strength that empowers us to endure the hardships that would otherwise overwhelm us. Paul's testimony in 2 Corinthians 12:9, "My grace is sufficient for you, for my power is made perfect in weakness," reveals that God's grace is strongest when we are weakest.

For those struggling with addiction, mental illness, or poverty, God's grace offers hope and the promise of His strength to overcome. He may not always deliver us *from* the trial, but He always gives us the strength to endure it and emerge stronger, wiser, and closer to Him.

Living Through and Overcoming Pain in God's Way vs. the World's Way

The world offers temporary solutions to pain, numbing, avoidance, or bitterness, but God calls believers to a higher response. He calls us to trust, to forgive, to hold fast to His promises. In doing so, we reflect His grace, love, and peace to a world that desperately needs it.

Pain and suffering in the believer's life are not pointless; they are purposed by God to make us stronger, more compassionate, and more like Christ.

> ➤ **Choosing Faith Over Bitterness**: Instead of becoming bitter, we choose to trust that God is using our suffering for a greater purpose (Romans 8:28).
> ➤ **Finding Hope in Eternity**: Earthly pain is temporary, but God promises an eternity free from suffering (Revelation 21:4).
> ➤ **Embracing God's Refinement**: Rather than resisting, we allow pain to shape us, knowing that trials produce endurance, maturity, and completeness (James 1:2-4).

Hope in God's Eternal Promise

Finally, as believers, we hold onto the promise that our pain is temporary, and that a day is coming when "He will wipe every tear from their eyes. There will be no more death or mourning or crying or pain" (Revelation 21:4). This hope anchors us through every trial, reminding us that God's ultimate plan is for our redemption and eternal joy. When we live with this eternal perspective, pain no longer has the final word. Instead, it becomes part of the journey that refines us for an eternal life with Christ. We may face abandonment, poverty, illness, betrayal, and countless other sorrows, but we are sustained by a hope that transcends this world. We are promised that God's grace is sufficient, and that through it all, He is there, Jehovah Shammah, the God who never leaves us.

Pain is often seen as an enemy to be avoided, something that disrupts life and derails our sense of peace and purpose. Yet, the journey of faith reveals that pain can be an instrument in God's hands, allowed not to destroy us, but to shape and refine us for His purposes. Throughout Scripture, we find story after story of Apostles and Men and Women of God who faced unimaginable suffering but emerged with stronger faith, renewed purpose, and a clearer vision of God's plan. The difference in their lives wasn't a lack of suffering, it was grace. This grace, freely given by God, enabled them to endure, to hope, and ultimately, to triumph over their circumstances. Joseph, who was betrayed and imprisoned; David, who was pursued by enemies; and Job, who lost everything, all testify that pain does not have the final say. In His sovereignty, God allows certain trials to enter our lives, yet He also provides grace to subdue them, turning what was meant to harm into a source of growth, resilience, and strength. We've intricately explored the purpose woven into our pain and the grace available to us in every season of suffering. By looking closely at the lives of these Apostles and Men of God, we uncover a divine truth; pain is allowed by God, but it is subdued and transformed by His grace, giving our lives a testimony that brings hope, power, and glory to his name.

Painful circumstances are inevitable, even for believers, but they are not purposeless. *God uses every trial to refine us, strengthen our faith, and prepare us for eternity.* Though we live in a world where pain cannot be avoided, we have a God who is present with us in every trial, providing grace, comfort, and strength. Our faith is tested, our endurance is built, and our character is shaped through pain, all for the purpose of making us complete in Christ.

In our darkest moments, we are reminded that God is more concerned with our souls than our bodies. While our physical bodies may suffer, our souls are being prepared for eternal glory. In every trial, we are given a choice; to trust God's will above our own, to allow Him to work through our pain, and to emerge refined, strengthened, and closer to Him. God's grace is indeed sufficient, and His purpose is always to bring us closer to Him, making us ready to one day enter into His eternal presence.

Crowned for Purpose

2 Corinthians 12:9

MANIFOLD GRACE

GODS PROVISION THROUGH TRIALS AND AFFLICTION

Yahweh has abundantly graced (gifted) his first born Isreal, the nations, as well as non-believers, not just believers with grace! He sent his son Jesus Christ to die for us, He gave us salvation which is the gift of life. He's giving all the opportunity of repentance, His covenant promises, grace in answered and even unanswered prayers, scripture and revelation, presence and work of the Holy Spirit, patience and forbearance with sin, the gift of life, and creation. Ultimately, He is our heavenly provider and our sustainer but most importantly <u>He has graced us beyond measure</u>. Grace is an essential part of God's design and character. Grace is closely related to God's benevolence, love, and mercy. Grace can be variously defined as "God's favor toward the unworthy" or "God's benevolence on the undeserving." In His grace, God is willing to forgive us and bless us abundantly, in spite of the fact that we don't deserve it nor often do we deserve to be dealt with so generously. To fully understand grace, we need to consider who we were without Christ and who we become with Christ. We were born in sin (Psalm 51:5), and we were guilty of breaking God's holy laws (Romans 3:9–20, 23; 1 John 1:8–10). We were enemies of God (Romans 5:6, 10; 8:7; Colossians 1:21), deserving of death (Romans 6:23). We were unrighteous (Romans 3:10) and without means of justifying ourselves (Romans 3:20). Spiritually, we were destitute, blind, unclean, and dead. Our souls were in peril of everlasting punishment.

But then came grace. God extended His favor to us. Grace is what saves us (Ephesians 2:8). Grace is the essence of the gospel (Acts 20:24). Grace gives us victory over sin (James 4:6). Grace gives us "eternal encouragement and good hope" (2 Thessalonians 2:16). Paul repeatedly identified grace as the basis of his calling as an apostle (Romans 15:15; 1 Corinthians 3:10; Ephesians 3:2, 7). Jesus Christ is the embodiment of grace, coupled with truth (John 1:14).

God's Grace can be defined as the unmerited favor, lovingkindness, and divine enablement that God extends to this broken world. It encompasses His provision, protection, and power, given not based on human merit but out of His character of love, mercy, and righteousness. Grace is God is giving us what we do not deserve, such as salvation, forgiveness, and eternal life. *(Ephesians 2:8-9)* "For by grace you have been saved through faith, and that not of yourselves; it is the gift of God, not of works, lest anyone should boast." *(Romans 3:23-24)* *"For all have sinned and have fallen short of the glory of God, being justified freely by His grace through the redemption that is in Christ Jesus."* Grace is an expression of God's deep compassion and love, extended to humanity despite sinfulness. *(Titus 3:5-7)* *"Not by works of righteousness which we have done, but according to His mercy He saved us, through the washing of regeneration and renewing of the Holy Spirit."* Grace is God's power and strength given to believers to accomplish His will and endure life's challenges known as Divine Empowerment *(Philippians 2:13)* "For it is God who works in you both to will and to do for His good pleasure." Grace initiates salvation and sustains believers in their journey of becoming more like Christ as a gateway to Means of Salvation and Sanctification. *(Titus 2:11-12)* *"For the grace of God has appeared that offers salvation to all people. It teaches us to say 'No' to ungodliness and worldly passions, and to live self-controlled, upright, and godly lives in this present age. (Romans 6:14)"For sin shall no longer have dominion over you, for you are not under the law but under grace."* Yahweh's Manifold Grace is many-sided, providing for every need, spiritually, emotionally, and physically by way of multiple diverse provisions. *(1 Peter 4:10)"As each has received a gift, use it to serve one another, as good stewards of God's varied grace. (Hebrews 4:16)* "Let us then approach God's throne of grace with confidence, so that we may receive mercy and find grace to help us in our time of need." God's grace is most vividly expressed through the life, death, and resurrection of Jesus Christ. He is the embodiment of grace, offering redemption to all who believe in Him. (John 1:14) *"The Word became flesh and made his dwelling among us. We have seen his glory, the glory of the one and only Son, who came from the Father, full of grace and truth."* Through Christ, grace becomes not just an abstract concept but a tangible reality that reconciles us to God. Yahweh's grace is reflective of His omniscient character, love, and provision. It saves, sustains, empowers, and teaches believers, making it a foundational aspect of the Christian faith. God's grace is both the foundation of our salvation and the fuel for our daily walk with Him. It is a demonstration of His boundless love, a source of empowerment, and an invitation to transformation. By understanding and embracing God's grace, we are not only reconciled to Him but also inspired to reflect His character in our lives. Grace, in essence, is God reaching down to people with a love so vast and a gift so profound that it changes everything.

The term "manifold" generally means many and varied, expressing the idea of something with multiple forms, layers, or aspects. In a spiritual or theological context, "manifold" often refers to the diverse and abundant ways in which God's grace, wisdom, and works are revealed through His word, works and prophesies. In its simplest definition, *manifold* speaks to multiplicity, many and varied in form, layer upon layer of diverse expressions. Yet, in the context of faith, this word ascends to greater heights, inviting us to ponder the vast, inexhaustible nature of God's essence and works. It reflects the boundless creativity of the Creator, who reveals Himself through a multitude of channels, each uniquely beautiful yet harmoniously unified in purpose.

Consider the manifold wisdom of God, a wisdom that transcends human comprehension, manifesting in ways that challenge our finite

understanding. <u>This is the wisdom that weaves mercy into justice, sovereignty into humility, and grace into discipline.</u> It's the divine paradox where strength is perfected in weakness and the last are made first. Each piece in this divine puzzle is a revelation of His marvelous makeup, inviting us to explore the depths of His mysteries and the riches of His glory.

Equally unique is the manifold grace of God, which meets us in every circumstance with an answer tailored to our need. Like the layers of the atmosphere, His grace surrounds us, shielding, sustaining, and sanctifying us in ways we often fail to see. It is the grace that forgives, empowers, restores, and transforms; always sufficient, always abundant, always timely.

In the natural world, the concept of *manifold* is reflected in creation itself; a testimony to the Creator's infinite ingenuity. From the vibrant creation of <u>time</u>, <u>space</u> and <u>matter</u>, to the diversity of ecosystems, to the intricate design of a single cell, all of this magnificent creation whispers of God's manifold creativity. Similarly, in our lives, His works are manifold. They unfold through seasons of joy and sorrow, shaping us through blessings and trials, orchestrating even the smallest details for His eternal purposes.

To examine the unique manifold nature of God, is to step into a symphony of "divine revelation". It calls us to marvel at His infinite complexity while resting in the assurance of His singular, unchanging love. Every layer of His grace, wisdom, and work testifies to a truth that is both simple and fundamental; God is with us, for us, and in us, in countless ways, beyond what we can ask, think, or imagine.

20 WAYS YAHWEH HAS GRACED (GIFTED) MANKIND NOT JUST BELIEVERS!

➢ **Manifold Grace of God** – Grace that appears in many forms, offering comfort, strength, forgiveness, protection, and provision.

➢ **Manifold Wisdom of God** (Ephesians 3:10) – Refers to the complex, multi-layered wisdom of God that is beyond human comprehension.

So, "manifold" conveys richness and diversity, implying that God's blessings, purposes, and wisdom are not limited to one form but are vast and multi-dimensional. Yahweh's grace is generously poured out on all creation, extending beyond believers to all of creation. Here is a comprehensive list capturing 20 major ways Yahweh has graced or gifted This world, His people and Nations with Grace.

1. The Gift of Jesus Christ for All Humanity

John 3:16 – "For God so loved the world that he gave his one and only Son, that whoever believes in him shall not perish but have eternal life."

Jesus was given for the redemption of all people, a universal invitation to be reconciled to God.

Jesus' sacrifice reveals Yahweh's immense love, showing that He values every human life enough to offer His Son for our redemption. This gift extends to everyone, demonstrating that Yahweh desires to reconcile all people to Himself, transcending backgrounds, sins, and disbelief.

2. The Offer of Salvation and Eternal Life

Romans 6:23 – "For the wages of sin is death, but the gift of God is eternal life in Christ Jesus our Lord."

God's grace offers salvation and eternal life freely to all who choose to believe in Jesus, bridging the gap between humanity and Himself.

This is a gift of ultimate hope, showing Yahweh's desire for everyone to live beyond earthly limitations. By offering eternal life, He invites everyone into His presence forever, transforming human destiny and removing the fear of death for those who accept this grace.

3. The Opportunity for Repentance

2 Peter 3:9 – "The Lord is not slow in keeping his promise…not wanting anyone to perish, but everyone to come to repentance."

God's patience extends to all, providing the opportunity for repentance and a restored relationship with Him.

Yahweh's patience, allowing people time to turn back to Him, underscores His mercy. Rather than judging instantly, He gives people countless opportunities to change and embrace a new path, demonstrating His understanding of human struggles and His compassionate heart.

4. The Covenant Promises

Genesis 9:12-16 (Noahic Covenant), **Genesis 12:1-3** (Abrahamic Covenant), and others.

Yahweh's covenants are not just for Israel but carry blessings for all humanity. For example, His promise never to flood the earth again is a universal covenant of preservation.

*Through covenants, Yahweh makes binding promises that often benefit all humanity. For instance, the Noahic Covenant (promise never to flood the earth again) gives everyone assurance that **certain** natural devastations will never happen. These covenants show Yahweh's consistency, reliability, and commitment to creation.*

5. Grace in Answered and Unanswered Prayers

Matthew 7:7-11 – Jesus teaches that God graciously answers prayers according to His will, and even when prayers seem unanswered, He acts for ultimate good, often protecting us in ways we may not immediately understand.

Yahweh's responsiveness to prayers, even when not answered as expected, reflects His perfect wisdom. He knows what is ultimately best, often protecting us through unanswered prayers. This grace shows Yahweh as a loving Father who listens and answers according to His plans for our good.

6. Scripture and Revelation

Psalm 119:105 – "Your word is a lamp for my feet, a light to my path."

God has gifted all humanity with His Word, offering guidance, wisdom, and insight into His character and will, accessible to all who seek Him.

Yahweh's Word is accessible to all, providing truth, wisdom, and guidance. The Bible sheds light on Yahweh's character and teachings, helping people find purpose, morality, and understanding. It's a gift that can shape lives positively and lead people toward deeper knowledge of Him.

7. The Presence and Work of the Holy Spirit

John 16:8 – The Holy Spirit "will convict the world concerning sin and righteousness and judgment."

The Holy Spirit actively works in the world, guiding, convicting, comforting, and revealing truth, touching the lives of both believers and non-believers.

The Holy Spirit's role in guiding, convicting, and comforting extends beyond believers, nudging even non-believers toward truth and change. His universal presence shows Yahweh's grace at work in every heart, drawing all closer to divine understanding and righteousness.

8. Patience and Forbearance with Sin

Romans 2:4 – "Do you show contempt for the riches of his kindness, forbearance and patience, not realizing that God's kindness is intended to lead you to repentance?"

God's patience with human sinfulness is an act of grace, allowing time for individuals to come to repentance and seek reconciliation.

Yahweh's patience with human sinfulness exemplifies His profound mercy. Rather than immediately punishing, He waits, giving people time to recognize errors, turn to Him, and experience His forgiveness, demonstrating His desire for restoration over retribution.

9. The Gift of Life

Genesis 2:7 – "Then the Lord God formed a man from the dust of the ground and breathed into his nostrils the breath of life."

Life itself is a gift from Yahweh, who gives life and sustains it. Every breath is an extension of His grace.

Life itself is a profound gift from Yahweh, and each day is a testimony to His grace. Every heartbeat and breath underscores His sustaining power, making life sacred and valuable. This reminds humanity of the sanctity of life and Yahweh's hand in every living soul.

10. Creation as a Universal Gift

Psalm 19:1 – "The heavens declare the glory of God; the skies proclaim the work of his hands."

Creation itself, filled with beauty and resources, is a gift for all mankind to enjoy, pointing all people to the Creator.

Nature's beauty and resources are a reflection of Yahweh's care for all humanity. Creation not only sustains life but also inspires awe, leading hearts to recognize the Creator. Nature's abundance is a constant reminder of Yahweh's generosity and His provision for all.

11. God as Provider and Sustainer

Matthew 5:45 – "He causes his sun to rise on the evil and the good, and sends rain on the righteous and the unrighteous."

God provides essentials like sunlight, rain, food, and shelter to all people, caring for His creation regardless of their belief.

Yahweh provides necessities like sunlight, rain, and food, not only for believers but for all people. This shows His impartial kindness and care for all, offering humanity the essentials needed for survival and thriving, a true expression of divine grace.

12. Wisdom and Knowledge

Proverbs 2:6 – "For the Lord gives wisdom; from his mouth come knowledge and understanding."

God imparts wisdom, understanding, and creativity to humanity, enabling advancements in science, art, medicine, and society.

Yahweh imparts wisdom and understanding to humanity, enabling societal and cultural advancements. These gifts empower individuals and communities to grow, solve problems, and enhance quality of life. Wisdom and knowledge are divine treasures that guide humanity toward truth and purpose.

13. Human Conscience and Moral Awareness

Romans 2:14-15 – "They show that the requirements of the law are written on their hearts, their consciences also bearing witness..."

God has instilled a conscience in all people, a moral compass that guides humanity towards justice, compassion, and kindness.

Yahweh has inscribed a basic moral code in every human heart, making justice, kindness, and compassion universally understood. This gift enables societies to establish laws, uphold justice, and promote empathy, reflecting Yahweh's concern for righteousness and harmony.

14. Freedom and Free Will

Deuteronomy 30:19 – "I have set before you life and death, blessings and curses. Now choose life, so that you and your children may live."

God has graced humanity with the ability to make choices, honoring human agency and allowing personal decisions regarding faith, relationships, and life.

By granting free will, Yahweh honors human dignity and agency. He does not force people to follow Him but allows each individual to make choices, experience consequences, and seek Him willingly. This freedom reflects His respect for humanity's uniqueness and potential.

15. Seasons and Order in Creation

Genesis 8:22 – "As long as the earth endures, seedtime and harvest, cold and heat, summer and winter, day and night will never cease."

God has set the natural world in order, providing seasons and cycles that allow for growth, food, and sustainability for all.

Yahweh established natural rhythms like the seasons to ensure life's sustenance and predictability. The consistency of these cycles provides stability for humanity, allowing agriculture, food production, and life itself to flourish in harmony, demonstrating Yahweh's careful planning.

16. Mercy and Compassion in Judgments

Lamentations 3:22-23 – "Because of the Lord's great love we are not consumed, for his compassions never fail."

Even when humanity deserves punishment, God often withholds His judgment, extending mercy and giving second chances.

Yahweh's frequent withholding of judgment showcases His mercy. While humanity often falls short, He chooses to extend compassion, offering second chances and new beginnings. This grace is a demonstration of His unfailing love and readiness to forgive.

17. Hope and the Promise of Renewal

Revelation 21:4 – "He will wipe every tear from their eyes. There will be no more death or mourning or crying or pain, for the old order of things has passed away."

God's promise of a new heaven and new earth is a future hope for all creation, with the removal of suffering, an invitation to all who seek Him.

Yahweh's promise of a new heaven and earth, free from suffering and death, gives hope to all creation. This assurance of renewal encourages perseverance, lifting hearts with the knowledge that Yahweh's ultimate plan is to redeem and restore all things.

18. Common Grace for Societal Flourishing

Acts 17:26-27 – "From one man he made all the nations…he marked out their appointed times in history and the boundaries of their lands. God did this so that they would seek him."

God's grace extends to societal order and cultural advancement, allowing humanity to develop laws, government, and community structures for mutual benefit.

Yahweh's grace underpins the development of societies, cultures, and governments, providing order, safety, and community life. Through this, He allows humanity to experience peace, progress, and cooperation, enabling societies to reflect His order and justice.

19. Redemption and Restoration of Creation

Romans 8:21 – "The creation itself will be liberated from its bondage to decay and brought into the freedom and glory of the children of God."

God's grace involves the ultimate restoration of creation, not just for believers but for all existence, removing the curse of decay and bringing renewal.

Yahweh's redemptive plan includes all of creation, promising to renew the world. This restoration shows His care for every aspect of His creation, aiming to remove the effects of sin and decay, bringing everything into alignment with His perfect will.

20. The Gift of Community and Relationships

Genesis 2:18 – "The Lord God said, 'It is not good for the man to be alone. I will make a helper suitable for him.'"

Human relationships, families, friendships, and communities are gifts that reflect God's relational nature and allow people to experience love, companionship, and support.

> *Yahweh created humans to be in relationship, reflecting His own relational nature. Community, friendship, and family provide support, love, and shared purpose. Relationships fulfill humanity's deep need for connection, reflecting Yahweh's image in the love and unity found in human interactions.*

Yahweh's deep love and His desire for everyone to experience life beyond earthly limits is enriched in blessed assurance. This invitation to be part of His eternal kingdom underscores a grace that is patient, as Yahweh continually offers time and opportunities for repentance, illustrating His compassion and desire for restored relationships.

Beyond spiritual gifts, Yahweh's grace is seen in the tangible blessings He provides to humanity as a whole. The gift of life itself, the beauty and resources of creation, and the order within nature, such as seasons and cycles are all divine provisions that sustain and enrich life. Every breath, every ray of sunlight, and every harvest reflects His goodness. Yahweh's provision goes further in the form of wisdom and knowledge, guiding humanity's advancement in various fields, and the moral awareness He inscribes on every heart, which shapes societies to value justice and compassion. His common grace, supporting societal structures and encouraging progress, demonstrates His caring about the well-being of all people.

Ultimately, Yahweh's plan is not just for set individuals but for all creation, as He promises redemption and renewal of the world itself. His mercy in withholding judgment and the gift of free will allow humanity to come to Him by choice, experiencing love, community, and purpose. His vision of a restored heaven and earth, free from pain and suffering, is a future hope that extends to all who seek Him. Each of these facets of Yahweh's grace spiritual, physical, relational, and universal together paint a picture of a God who is deeply invested in humanity's flourishing, offering constant guidance, care, and an open invitation to everlasting relationship with Him.

God's grace, then and now, is abundant, multi-faceted, and continuously available to all who seek him. His compassion, provision, and desire for restoration shine through His many gifts, extending opportunities for connection, growth, and purpose to every individual. This comprehensive outpouring reflects a God who loves His creation deeply and seeks to draw all people into His grace. Yahweh's grace toward humanity is overwhelmingly evident in His gift of Jesus Christ, who embodies divine love and sacrifice. Jesus' life, death, and resurrection reveal Yahweh's deep commitment to redeeming every person, transcending past failures, sins, and backgrounds. This is a powerful reminder that Yahweh desires an intimate relationship with humanity, offering the path of reconciliation to all who would accept it. Through Christ, Yahweh bridges the gap between human imperfection and divine perfection, showing His boundless grace and His desire for none to be lost but all to be restored.

The gift of salvation and the promise of eternal life are pillars of Yahweh's grace, demonstrating His will for humanity to transcend earthly suffering and limitations. By extending salvation to all, Yahweh opens the door to a future in His presence, transforming our fear of death into a hope-filled anticipation of everlasting life. Additionally, Yahweh's patience in allowing time for repentance reflects His compassionate heart and understanding of human

struggles. Rather than passing immediate judgment, He offers countless opportunities for people to turn toward Him, signifying that His justice is also tempered with mercy.

Through His creation and the daily blessings within it, Yahweh sustains humanity with care and provision that extends to all people, regardless of belief. The beauty and order of nature, the seasons, and the gift of life itself testify to His grace, continually reminding humanity of His creativity and nurturing presence. The Holy Spirit, too, is at work, convicting, comforting, and guiding all hearts toward truth. By giving people, the wisdom to make moral choices and the free will to pursue them, Yahweh honors your "carnal-human-ability" to choose right & wrong, showing His respect for each individual's unique journey. His abundant grace shines in every heartbeat, breath, and opportunity to seek Him, providing a profound framework of divine love and purpose for this world.

Yahweh's grace toward human creation is overwhelmingly evident in His gift of Jesus Christ, who embodies divine love and sacrifice. Jesus' life, death, and resurrection reveal Yahweh's deep commitment to redeeming every person, transcending past failures, sins, and backgrounds. This is a powerful reminder that Yahweh desires an intimate relationship with His creation, offering the path of reconciliation to all who would accept it. Through Christ, Yahweh bridges the gap between human imperfection and divine perfection, showing His boundless grace and His desire for none to be lost but all to be restored.

The gift of salvation and the promise of eternal life are foundational building blocks of Yahweh's grace, demonstrating His will for humanity to transcend earthly suffering and limitations. By extending salvation to all, Yahweh opens the door to a future in His presence, transforming our fear of death into a hope-filled anticipation of everlasting life. Additionally, Yahweh's patience in allowing time for repentance reflects His compassionate heart and understanding of human struggles. Rather than passing immediate judgment, He offers countless opportunities for people to turn toward Him, signifying that His justice is also tempered with mercy.

Through His creation and the daily blessings within it, Yahweh sustains civilization with care and provision that extends to all people, regardless of belief. The beauty and order of nature, the seasons, and the gift of life itself testify to His grace, continually reminding humanity of His creativity and nurturing presence. The Holy Spirit, too, is at work, convicting, comforting, and guiding all hearts toward truth. Yahweh honors free will and your ability to choose eternal life or eternal separation from God for all of eternity, showing His respect for each individual's selective decision while we navigate this journey under His command. His abundant grace shines in every heartbeat, breath, and opportunity to seek Him, providing a profound framework of divine love and purpose for humanity.

God's grace is the foundation upon which believers stand in the face of spiritual warfare. It is not merely a passive kindness but an active, empowering force that enables us to confront and overcome the battles of _Spiritual Manipulation_, _Brainwashing_ and _Witchcraft-Attacks_ launched by the unseen realm. Grace meets us in our weakness, reminding us that <u>victory is not achieved through human strength but through divine intervention</u>. As Paul declares in 2 Corinthians 12:9, _"My grace is sufficient for you, for my power is made perfect in weakness."_ This sufficiency of grace means that no matter the depth of the struggle or the ferocity of the enemy's attacks, God's provision is more than enough. His grace becomes the source of both our courage and endurance, ensuring that we are never left defenseless or defeated.

Furthermore, God's grace equips us with the tools and spiritual insight needed to discern the enemy's schemes. It sharpens our spiritual senses, allowing us to identify and resist deception. Grace transforms us from passive recipients into active participants in God's redemptive plan, giving us the authority to stand firm against darkness. It is by grace that we wield the armor of God effectively,

for without His unmerited favor, our efforts would falter. Grace reminds us that spiritual warfare is not fought in isolation but in partnership with the Holy Spirit, who intercedes, empowers, and guides us to triumph. This divine empowerment is both humbling and inspiring, as it underscores that the victory belongs to God, yet He graciously invites us to share in it.

Perhaps most profoundly, God's grace in spiritual warfare assures us of His unshakable presence. Grace is not a distant gift; it is a constant companion, an ever-present reminder of God's commitment to His people. Even when the battle feels overwhelming, grace whispers the truth of Romans 8:37: *"In all these things, we are more than conquerors through Him who loved us."* This conquering grace doesn't merely carry us through the storm, it refines us, drawing us closer to God and strengthening our faith. It shifts our perspective, transforming spiritual battles into opportunities for deeper reliance on Him. Through His grace, we are not just survivors of spiritual warfare but overcomers, testifying to the power of God's unfailing love and faithfulness.

GOD'S PROVISIONS FOR OVERCOMING SPIRITUAL ATTACKS

The Armor of God

Ephesians 6:10-18 – The "armor of God" includes the belt of truth, breastplate of righteousness, shield of faith, helmet of salvation, and sword of the Spirit.

The armor of God is a complete spiritual defense system, equipping believers to stand firm against all forms of spiritual assault. Each piece serves a specific purpose, reminding believers of the strength and security found in God's truth, righteousness, faith, salvation, and the Word. Putting on this armor enables believers to remain steadfast in faith and resist the enemy's schemes effectively.

Divine Strength and Defense

Psalm 91:1-7 – "Whoever dwells in the shelter of the Most High will rest in the shadow of the Almighty... He will cover you with his feathers, and under his wings you will find refuge."

God Himself is a refuge and fortress for His people, offering divine strength and protection against all evil. This imagery of shelter and shadow represents the nearness and security God provides to those who seek Him. By dwelling in His presence, believers find rest and safety, trusting that He is their unwavering protector during spiritual conflicts.

God's Angels as Spiritual Guardians

Psalm 34:7 – "The angel of the Lord encamps around those who fear him, and he delivers them."

Angels are part of God's provision for spiritual protection, positioned as guardians and warriors in the unseen realm. God sends His angels to surround, protect, and deliver His people from spiritual threats, assuring believers that they are never alone in battle. This unseen angelic presence reinforces that God's protection extends beyond the visible, surrounding His people with supernatural defense.

Authority in Jesus' Name

Luke 10:19 – "I have given you authority to trample on snakes and scorpions and to overcome all the power of the enemy; nothing will harm you."

Jesus grants believers His authority over the forces of darkness, a powerful gift that enables them to rebuke and overcome spiritual threats. This authority in His name is an essential tool for resisting demonic forces, emphasizing that victory is part of the believer's inheritance. It reminds believers that Jesus' power, exercised through faith, is greater than any opposition they may face.

The Holy Spirit as the Defender and Guide

Key Scripture: *John 14:26* – "But the Helper, the Holy Spirit, whom the Father will send in My name, He will teach you all things, and bring to your remembrance all things that I said to you

The Holy Spirit, referred to as the "Advocate" or "Helper," strengthens, teaches, and reminds believers of the truth during spiritual challenges. The Holy Spirit resides within believers, guiding and defending them against spiritual deception and attack. He grants discernment, wisdom, and boldness, enabling believers to recognize and counteract the enemy's strategies. As a constant presence and teacher, the Holy Spirit empowers believers to stand in truth, reminding them of God's Word and strengthening their faith in times of trial.

Victory through the Blood of Christ

Key Scripture: *Revelation 12:11* – "They triumphed over him by the blood of the Lamb and by the word of their testimony."

Jesus' sacrificial blood is the foundation of believers' victory over evil. By His blood, believers are redeemed and protected, and the enemy's hold is broken. The power of Christ's sacrifice assures believers of victory in spiritual battles, instilling confidence that the enemy has already been defeated. The blood of Jesus is a constant reminder of God's grace, securing their triumph and providing an unshakeable assurance in warfare.

God's Promises of Deliverance

Key Scripture: *2 Thessalonians 3:3* – "But the Lord is faithful, and he will strengthen you and protect you from the evil one."

God's faithfulness ensures that He will protect and deliver His people from spiritual harm. His promises of deliverance are rooted in His unchanging character, giving believers confidence that He will stand as their defender. By holding onto God's promises, believers are strengthened in faith, trusting that He will not only protect but also deliver them from the schemes of the evil one.

God's grace, ever-present and abounding effortlessly, becomes a unbreakable anchor of hope and strength during spiritual warfare. Spiritual battles are inevitable in the life of a believer, but the assurance of God's grace transforms these trials from overwhelming challenges into opportunities for growth, victory, and deeper reliance on Him. Spiritual warfare often brings moments of intense weakness, fear, or uncertainty. In these times, God's grace sustains His people, providing strength that far exceeds human ability. As Paul learned when he pleaded for the removal of his thorn in the flesh, God's response, "My grace is sufficient for you, for my power is made perfect in weakness" (2 Corinthians 12:9) reminds us that His grace is not just enough; it is more than enough. It fills the gaps of our limitations, empowering us to persevere and stand firm when our strength fails. God's grace is a shield that defends us from the fiery darts of the enemy (Ephesians 6:16). This grace doesn't only protect us from external attacks; it also fortifies us internally. <u>It strengthens our resolve, renews our faith, and equips us with discernment to recognize and resist the enemy's lies.</u> Just as David declared, "You are my hiding place; you will protect me from trouble and surround me with songs of deliverance" (Psalm 32:7), God's grace surrounds us as a fortress, offering both external protection and internal peace. Through Jesus Christ, God's grace assures us of ultimate victory in every spiritual battle. By the blood of the Lamb and the word of our testimony (Revelation 12:11), believers triumph over the schemes of the enemy. Grace reminds us that the battle is not ours but the Lord's (2 Chronicles 20:15), and His power is already at work to secure our deliverance. The victory through Christ is not merely future but present, manifesting as the ability to stand firm and remain unshaken even in the fiercest storms. God's grace doesn't leave us passive in the fight; it equips and empowers us. The "armor of God" (Ephesians 6:10-18) is an embodiment of His grace, truth, righteousness, faith, salvation, the gospel, and His Word are all gifts given to us to stand against spiritual opposition. His grace gives us the courage to wield the sword of the Spirit (His Word) boldly and

the faith to extinguish every fiery dart aimed at our hearts and minds. Perhaps the most astonishing aspect of God's grace in spiritual warfare is that it draws us closer to Him. Battles push us into His presence, where we find peace, strength, and guidance. Grace invites us to approach the throne of God with confidence (Hebrews 4:16), to lay our burdens at His feet, and to trust in His unfailing love. In the midst of the fight, His grace whispers, "Be still, and know that I am God" (Psalm 46:10), reminding us that He is sovereign over every battle. Spiritual warfare is not just about defending against the enemy but about being refined through the struggle. God's grace works within us during these battles to deepen our faith, sharpen our discernment, and strengthen our dependence on Him. Each trial becomes a means of sanctification, molding us more into the image of Christ and preparing us for the glory that lies ahead. God's grace in the midst of spiritual warfare is a lifeline, a fortress, and a source of power. It sustains, shields, and transforms, reminding us that no matter how fierce the battle, we are never alone. His grace ensures that we not only survive but thrive, emerging from each trial stronger, more refined, and more deeply anchored in His love. Through His grace, we are victorious, not because of our strength, but because of His unwavering presence and power.

The Bible addresses the potential for people to misuse or take God's grace for granted, warning against attitudes and actions that abuse this precious gift. Here's key examples of **abusing or taking God's grace for granted** .

ABUSING GOD'S GRACE: WARNINGS AGAINST TAKING GRACE FOR GRANTED

The Word of God provides sobering warnings against the misuse of His grace, urging believers to approach it with reverence and humility. <u>Grace is not a license to sin but a gift to lead us into holiness.</u> Paul's emphatic question in Romans 6:1-2 confronts this error: *"What shall we say then? Shall we go on sinning so that grace may increase? By no means! We are those who have died to sin; how can we live in it any longer?"* Similarly, Jude 1:4 warns of individuals who distort grace into a justification for immorality, turning what is sacred into a tool for self-indulgence. The dangers of abusing God's grace are both dangerous and perilous. When grace is taken for granted, the believer risks spiritual stagnation, a state where growth in Christ is hindered, and the heart becomes indifferent to the call of  righteousness. Moreover, such neglect can lead to broken fellowship with God, <u>as unrepentant sin distances the believer from the fullness of His presence.</u> Beyond these consequences, Scripture reminds us that God's corrective discipline awaits those who misuse His grace. The author of Hebrews writes, *"The Lord disciplines the one He loves, and He chastens everyone He accepts as His son"* (Hebrews 12:6), affirming that even discipline is an act of grace meant to draw us back to the path of life. God's grace demands not complacency but accountability. Galatians 6:7 declares, *"Do not be deceived: God cannot be mocked. A man reaps what he sows."* This is not a denial of grace but a reminder of its holy purpose, to transform and sanctify us. To persist in sin while presuming upon God's mercy is to trample on the very gift meant to restore us. Instead, grace calls us to a life of gratitude and obedience. True understanding of grace inspires reverence, compelling us to honor God by pursuing righteousness. Through grace, we are not only forgiven but empowered to live holy lives. It is only by humbling ourselves before the magnitude of God's mercy that we can respond rightly, echoing Paul's exhortation in **Titus 2:11-12**: *"For the grace of God has appeared that offers salvation to all people. It teaches us to say 'No' to ungodliness and worldly passions, and to live self-controlled, upright, and godly lives in this present age."*

Let us, therefore, take to heart the immense privilege of grace, not as a veil for sin but as the power to walk in newness of life, glorifying the One who freely gave it.

Do Not Pervert the Grace of God

As we reflect on the boundless provisions of God's grace, it is critical to confront a sobering truth; the misuse and perversion of God's grace carry severe consequences. In today's world, where spiritual warfare is ever-present, some twist and distort the meaning of grace, turning it into a justification for sin, a tool for personal gain, or a diluted message that erodes the true Gospel. Scripture is clear; abusing or misrepresenting God's grace is not only very dangerous but invites judgment.

The Danger of Abusing Grace as a License for Sin

Paul's words in *Romans 6:1-2* are a direct rebuke to those who take God's grace for granted; "Shall we go on sinning so that grace may increase? By no means! We are those who have died to sin; how can we live in it any longer?" Grace is not an excuse to live in rebellion or continue in sin. Those who abuse grace in this way mock the sacrifice of Jesus Christ and misunderstand its purpose, to transform, not indulge.

False Prophecy and Deceptive Leadership

God's grace is often perverted by false prophets and teachers who twist Scripture for personal gain or to tickle the ears of their followers. *Jude 1:4* warns of those who "pervert the grace of our God into a license for immorality and deny Jesus Christ our only Sovereign and Lord." These individuals lead others astray, exploiting God's name for financial prosperity or worldly influence. Such actions not only dishonor God but also lead many into spiritual destruction.

The Spiritual Poison of Conformity

In an age when conformity to cultural norms is prized over adherence to God's truth, the Gospel of grace is often watered down to accommodate the world. *James 4:4* starkly reminds us, "Don't you know that friendship with the world means enmity against God?" Conforming to the world under the guise of grace betrays the Gospel, reducing it to a hollow, powerless shell. True grace calls for repentance, transformation, and obedience, not compromise.

The Desecration of Prosperity Gospel

Perhaps one of the most dangerous distortions of grace is the prosperity gospel, which equates God's blessings with material wealth and personal success. This false gospel cheapens and desecrates the riches of God's grace, turning it into a transactional relationship based on greed, the hope of selfish prosperity, and my personal favorite, vain ambition. *2 Peter 2:1-3* warns of such teachers. "They will exploit you with fabricated stories. Their condemnation has long been hanging over them, and their destruction has not been sleeping." The grace of God was never meant to be a tool for selfish ambition but a pathway to righteousness and eternal life.

God's Judgment of the Abuse of Grace

The Bible repeatedly warns that God will not tolerate the misuse of His grace. *Hebrews 10:29* speaks of those who "trample the Son of God underfoot" and "insult the Spirit of grace," declaring that such people face a fearful expectation of judgment. Grace is sacred, it was purchased with the blood of Jesus Christ. To abuse it is to treat that sacrifice with contempt, a grievous offense that invites divine discipline or eternal separation from God.

A CALL TO HONOR GRACE

God's grace is a precious gift, given not to be abused but to lead us into a deeper relationship with Him. As stewards of His grace, we are called to live lives of holiness, proclaim the true Gospel boldly, and reject teachings or practices that pervert its beauty. Let us remember the solemn words of *Galatians 1:8*, "But even if we or an angel from heaven should preach a gospel other than the one we preached to you, let them be under God's curse."

God's grace is powerful, transformative, and sacred. To misuse it is to walk a dangerous path, one that leads away from His presence. Let us honor His grace, live by His truth, and ensure that we never compromise the Gospel for the fleeting five-minute-approval of the world. For in doing so, we hold fast to the unshakable foundation of His grace, truth, love, and salvation through Jesus Christ.

Crowned for Purpose

Titus 2:11-12

THE DEVILS DEVICES !

Protecting Your Crown! Guarding Against the Devil's Devices and Worldly Thievery

I n a presant age where distractions enslave and deceit forever thrives, the believer's journey to secure the eternal crown of life is marked by defiance, vigilance and spiritual warfare. The Bible specifically warns that the enemy of our souls, Satan, is a deceiver who works tirelessly to blind the minds of those who do not believe, lest the light of the gospel of Christ should shine upon them (2 Corinthians 4:4). His schemes are not always overt; instead, they often manifest through subtle manipulations, worldly pleasures, and distorted truths designed to lead believers astray. Revelation declares him as *"the great dragon...who deceives the whole world"* (*Revelation 12:9*). Thus, the call to protect your crown is not merely an invitation, it is an urgent and active command for every follower of Christ to stand firm against his devices.

The devil's tactics have not changed since the beginning. He remains a liar and the father of all lies, crafting his strategies to exploit human weakness and draw us into sin (John 8:44). He whispers through false teachings, enticing philosophies, and compromised morals. The Apostle Paul warns of a time *"when some will depart from the faith, giving heed to deceiving spirits and doctrines of demons"* (*1 Timothy 4:1*). Such spirits seek to erode your spiritual foundation, sow seeds of doubt, and lead you to exchange the truth of God for a lie. This is why we are exhorted to "submit to God, resist the devil, and he will flee from you" (James 4:7). Submission to God is not passive; it requires a conscious commitment to remain steadfast in truth and righteousness, even when the world offers easier paths.

The world itself is a fertile ground for the enemy's deceptions. It glorifies self-indulgence, undermines godly principles, and breeds confusion. Scripture describes those who embrace deceit as the wicked, who "shall not dwell within [God's] house" and "shall not continue in [His] presence" (Psalm 101:7). Deception manifests through pride, division, and perversions of truth, which God detests, as outlined in Proverbs: "A lying tongue, hands that shed innocent blood...and one who sows discord among brethren" (Proverbs 6:16-19). If we are not careful, we risk becoming entangled in the very snares that the enemy lays before us, forfeiting the crown that Christ offers to those who endure in faith.

Despite these challenges, the promise of victory remains for those who cling to Christ. The Son of God was manifested to *"destroy the works of the devil" (1 John 3:8)*, and by His death, He rendered powerless "him who had the power of death, that is, the devil" (Hebrews 2:14). This truth is our assurance, but it also demands that we stay awake and alert. Paul reminds us, "It is high time to awake out of sleep; for now our salvation is nearer than when we first believed" (Romans 13:11). Clothed in the armor of light, we are called to walk in holiness, rejecting the works of darkness and putting on the Lord Jesus Christ (Romans 13:12-14).

Ultimately, the battle for your crown is about allegiance, whether to God or to the lies of the enemy. Scripture warns, "Do not be deceived, God is not mocked; for whatever a man sows, that he will also reap" (Galatians 6:7-8). To sow to the Spirit is to embrace eternal life, while sowing to the flesh leads only to corruption. Protecting your crown demands a proactive faith that refuses to compromise with worldly thievery. As John reminds us, "Many deceivers have

gone out into the world who do not confess Jesus Christ as coming in the flesh" (2 John 1:7). These deceivers and their falsehoods must be recognized and resisted. Only by anchoring ourselves in God's Word and walking in the Spirit can we safeguard the priceless inheritance that awaits those who endure to the end. Protect your "Crown of Life". Refuse the lies. Embrace the truth. The stakes are eternal, and the reward is incomparable.

Kingdom Identity Confusion

The enemy's primary tactic is attacking our identity in Christ. He whispers lies that our worth is tied to achievements, education, success, self-reliance appearance, or others' approval. A young believer might chase social validation, unaware that their true value is as a child of God, "fearfully and wonderfully made" (Psalm 139:14). When we seek affirmation outside of Christ, we exchange eternal promises for fleeting applause. To guard our crown, we must stand firm in the truth of who God says we are, refusing to let worldly identities define us. When we forget this, we trade the eternal crown for temporary applause.

> ➤ The devil loves to sow seeds of carnal-deceit, such as, the false insinuation tht our value is tied to worldly achievements, beauty, or approval. A believer may strive for career success, thinking it defines them, or seek validation through relationships or social media. As believers there's a higher call and an invaluable purpose as we are co-heirs with Christ" (Romans 8:17). This identity directly ties us to our eternal inheritance.

Guard your identity in Christ by rejecting worldly labels and embracing God's truth about who you are.

Temptation with Sinful Pleasures

The devil entices believers by minimizing the seriousness of sin, saying, "Just one time won't hurt." This could look like falling into sexual immorality, substance abuse, or gossip. A Christian struggling with pornography might believe they can control it, only to find themselves enslaved by shame and secrecy. King David's sin with Bathsheba began with a glance but escalated into adultery and murder (2 Samuel 11). The enemy's goal is to keep believers in cycles of sin, robbing them of intimacy with God. But through repentance, Christ offers restoration (1 John 1:9).

> ➢ Satan downplays the seriousness of sin, whispering, "It's just one time; it won't matter." A believer may indulge in gossip, pornography, or substance abuse, thinking they can control it, only to become enslaved by shame. King David's sin with Bathsheba began with a glance but ended in adultery and murder (2 Samuel 11). Sin seeks to sever intimacy with God, but through repentance, Christ restores us (1 John 1:9). *Do not give sin a foothold; instead, flee from it and seek restoration in Christ.*

Busyness and Demonic Distractions

Life's responsibilities, work, family, social events, collectively, can overwhelm us, leaving little time for God. Imagine a parent who wakes up early, works all day, handles family obligations, and ends the day binge-watching Netflix. They may love God but feel too tired to read their Bible or pray. The story of Martha and Mary in Luke 10 shows how busyness, even in good things, can rob us of what's most important, time with Jesus. The enemy delights when we trade prayer for productivity, knowing we can't fight spiritual battles on an empty soul.

> ➢ The devil keeps us so busy with responsibilities and entertainment, that keeps us so socially imprisoned and enslaved that we neglect time with God. Like Martha, we get

distracted by "good" things, missing the better choice of sitting at Jesus' feet (Luke 10:41-42). A weary soul cannot fight spiritual battles effectively. *Choose intimacy with God over the noise of life. Your spiritual strength depends on it.*

Discouragement and Doubt

In moments of hardship, such as losing a job or a loved one, the enemy whispers, "God has abandoned you." A believer facing financial struggles may begin doubting God's provision, questioning whether He sees their needs. This is exactly how Satan approached Job, hoping his suffering would drive him to curse God (Job 1:11). Doubt can make us feel isolated from God's promises, but we must remember that He "will never leave or forsake us" (Deuteronomy 31:8). Holding on to faith, even in the valley, ensures we don't lose our crown.

> ➤ In trials, the enemy whispers that God has abandoned us. A believer facing financial struggles may question God's provision, or one grieving a loved one may doubt His goodness. Job faced this tactic, yet he declared, "Though He slay me, yet will I trust Him" (Job 13:15). God's promises are unchanging, He will never leave us (Deuteronomy 31:8). *When doubt arises, anchor yourself in God's faithfulness.*

Comparison , Envy and Covetness

Scrolling through social media, a believer may feel envious seeing others with seemingly perfect lives; marriages, careers, or ministries. This spirit of comparison leads to resentment, making them feel as though God's blessings are passing them by. Cain's envy of Abel caused him to commit the first murder (Genesis 4:5-8). In the same way, envy steals joy, shifting focus from God's unique plan for us. We must remember that God's promises are personalized, and our journey is not meant to mirror anyone else's (Jeremiah 29:11).

➤ Scrolling through social media, believers may feel envious of others' "perfect" lives, from their careers to their ministries. Comparison breeds resentment, as seen in Cain's envy of Abel, which led to murder (Genesis 4:5-8). God has a unique plan for each of us (Jeremiah 29:11). *Celebrate others' blessings while trusting God's perfect timing for your own life.*

Spiritual Apathy and Lukewarmness

The enemy's subtle strategy is convincing believers that they've "done enough" spiritually. A churchgoer may attend service weekly but stop pursuing personal prayer, Bible study, or outreach. Over time, their passion for Christ cools. In Revelation, Jesus rebukes the church in Laodicea for being lukewarm, warning them to rekindle their spiritual fervor (Revelation 3:15-16). Apathy is dangerous because it goes unnoticed until spiritual decline sets in. Renewing our passion for God ensures we stay on fire for Him (Romans 12:11).

➤ The enemy convinces believers that they've done "enough" spiritually. Over time, their passion fades, leaving them lukewarm, like the Laodicean church (Revelation 3:15-16). Apathy is dangerous because it often goes unnoticed until it leads to spiritual decline. *Rekindle your zeal for Christ to stay spiritually alive and on fire.*

False Doctrines and False Teachers

Believers today are exposed to teachings that sound spiritual but contradict God's Word. This might include beliefs that Jesus isn't the only way to salvation or that God's blessings always equate to material wealth. These false teachings dilute the gospel and lead believers astray. Paul warned Timothy about people who would turn away from the truth to follow myths (2 Timothy 4:3-4). We must test every teaching against Scripture to guard our crown and stay rooted in truth (1 John 4:1).

> Satan introduces teachings that distort the truth, such as denying Christ as the only way to salvation or equating blessings with material wealth. Paul warned Timothy of people who would follow myths instead of sound doctrine (2 Timothy 4:3-4).*Test every teaching against Scripture to stay rooted in God's truth (1 John 4:1).*

Fear and Anxiety

Fear often creeps in through life's uncertainties. A Christian waiting on medical test results may be overwhelmed with anxiety, thinking the worst-case scenario. Another may avoid witnessing about Christ for fear of rejection. This is exactly what Peter faced when he denied Jesus to protect himself (Matthew 26:69-75). Fear is one of the enemy's strongest tools to paralyze believers. But God promises that "perfect love drives out fear" (1 John 4:18). Leaning into God's peace helps us fight fear and hold onto our crown.

> Fear silences believers, making them ineffective in their witness. Peter denied Christ out of fear (Matthew 26:69-75). Yet God's Word assures us that "perfect love drives out fear" (1 John 4:18).*Lean into God's peace and boldly stand firm in your faith.*

Unforgiveness and Bitterness

Holding onto grudges feels justified, but it chains us to bitterness. A believer hurt by a church leader might harbor resentment, refusing to forgive. This hinders their spiritual growth, as Jesus taught that unforgiveness blocks us from receiving God's forgiveness (Matthew 6:14-15). The enemy uses bitterness to poison relationships and harden hearts. Choosing to forgive, though difficult, sets us free and aligns us with Christ's example on the cross (Luke 23:34).

> Unforgiveness chains believers to bitterness, blocking their spiritual growth. Jesus warns that refusing to forgive others

hinders us from receiving God's forgiveness (Matthew 6:14-15).*Choose forgiveness to break free from the enemy's grip and walk in Christ's freedom.*

Division and Offense

The devil works tirelessly to sow division within families, churches, and communities. Imagine a small disagreement in a church ministry growing into a major conflict, causing members to leave in anger. Offense can seem harmless, but it fractures unity, which is vital for spiritual power (Psalm 133:1). Jesus warned that in the last days, many would be offended, leading to betrayal and division (Matthew 24:10). Forgiveness and love are essential to protect our crown from being stolen by offense.

> ➤ The enemy sows division in families, churches, and communities. A small offense can grow into major conflict, fracturing unity. Jesus warned that offense would abound in the last days (Matthew 24:10).*Forgiveness and unity are weapons against the enemy's schemes (Psalm 133:1).*

Pride and Self-Reliance

Success can tempt believers to think, "I've achieved this on my own." A Christian business owner might rely on personal skills and neglect seeking God's wisdom. This attitude reflects the same pride that caused Satan's fall (Isaiah 14:12-14). Pride blinds us to our need for God, setting us up for spiritual failure. Humility keeps us grounded, reminding us that everything good comes from the Lord (James 4:6).

> ➤ Success tempts believers to think they no longer need God. Pride blinds them to their dependence on Him, mirroring Satan's downfall (Isaiah 14:12-14). *Humility draws God's grace and keeps you rooted in His provision (James 4:6).*

Addictions and Strongholds

Addictions, whether to alcohol, drugs, or even technology, enslave believers and stunt spiritual growth. For example, a Christian struggling with a gaming addiction may spend hours in front of a screen, neglecting prayer or Bible reading. Jesus came to set us free from every form of bondage (John 8:36), but the enemy wants us chained. We must confront addictions through prayer, accountability, and practical steps to break free.

> Addictions enslave and weaken believers. Jesus came to set captives free (John 8:36). Confronting strongholds with prayer, fasting, and accountability brings victory.*Confront addictions with prayer, accountability, and reliance on the Holy Spirit.*

Isolation from the Body of Christ

When hurt by church members or facing personal struggles, believers might withdraw from fellowship. A Christian who stops attending church because of offense or discouragement becomes an easy target for the enemy. Ecclesiastes 4:9-12 teaches that we need community to stay strong in faith. Isolation weakens us spiritually, but staying connected to the body of Christ guards us from falling away.

> Isolation leaves believers vulnerable. Ecclesiastes 4:9-12 reminds us of the strength found in community and fellowship. Staying connected shields us from spiritual attacks. When believers withdraw from fellowship due to hurt or discouragement, they become easy targets. *Stay connected to the Church for encouragement and spiritual strength.*

Neglecting the Word of God

A believer may think, "I've read the Bible enough; I know what it says." However, spiritual battles require fresh revelation from God's Word daily. Neglecting Scripture leaves us vulnerable to deception and sin. Jesus resisted Satan's temptations by quoting Scripture

(Matthew 4:1-11). Staying rooted in God's Word equips us to discern lies and stand firm.

> Without the Word of God, believers lack discernment. Jesus resisted Satan's temptations with Scripture (Matthew 4:1-11). Daily immersion in God's Word equips us to stand firm. The Bible equips us to discern truth and resist deception. Neglecting it leaves believers vulnerable. *Immerse yourself in God's Word daily to strengthen your spiritual armor.*

Impatience and Impulsiveness

Waiting on God is hard, especially when circumstances feel urgent. A single Christian might rush into a relationship, believing they can't wait any longer for God's choice. Abraham and Sarah's impatience led them to create Ishmael, resulting in long-term consequences (Genesis 16). Acting prematurely often causes regret. Trusting God's timing brings His best blessings (Isaiah 40:31).

> Rushing ahead of God's timing, like Abraham and Sarah (Genesis 16), leads to avoidable consequences. Trusting God's perfect timing brings His best blessings (Isaiah 40:31). Impatience leads to rash decisions, as seen with Abraham and Sarah creating Ishmael (Genesis 16). *Trust God's timing—it brings blessings without regret (Isaiah 40:31).*

Persecution and Suffering

The enemy uses suffering to convince believers that following Christ isn't worth the cost. A student mocked for their faith may be tempted to compromise to fit in. But Jesus warned, "In this world, you will have trouble" (John 16:33). Persevering through trials secures our crown, for God rewards those who stand firm (James 1:12).

> Trials tempt believers to abandon their faith. Standing firm through persecution secures the crown of life (James 1:12). The enemy uses suffering to convince believers that

following Christ isn't worth the cost. Yet Jesus promises a crown to those who endure (James 1:12). *Persevere through trials to secure your eternal reward.*

Love of Money, Vanity and Materialism

The enemy deceives believers into thinking that wealth equals success. A believer obsessed with chasing financial success may neglect their spiritual life. Jesus cautioned that we cannot serve both God and money (Matthew 6:24). True riches are found in Christ, not material things.

> ➤ Building life on unstable foundations, like wealth or status, leads to spiritual collapse. Christ alone provides lasting security. The pursuit of wealth distracts believers from God. Jesus warned that we cannot serve both God and money (Matthew 6:24). *Store up treasures in heaven, not on earth.*

False Security in Worldly Things

Building security on careers, savings, or relationships offers a false sense of stability. When these things crumble, so can faith. Jesus taught that those who build their lives on worldly things are like a house built on sand, vulnerable to collapse when storms come. (Matthew 7:24-27). For example, a believer who puts their trust in a high-paying job may feel lost when facing sudden unemployment. The enemy wants us to anchor our security in temporary things, but our true foundation must be Jesus Christ. Only by focusing on eternity and God's promises can we withstand life's uncertainties without losing our crown (Colossians 3:2).

> ➤ Building life on unstable foundations like wealth or status leads to collapse. Jesus compared this to a house built on sand (Matthew 7:24-27). *Anchor your life in Christ for lasting security.*

Manipulating Emotions

The enemy often manipulates our emotions to steer us off course. We might feel overwhelmed with guilt, frustration, or sadness and make poor decisions in those moments. For instance, someone experiencing heartbreak might distance themselves from God, thinking, "If He loved me, He wouldn't let this happen." The Bible warns us that "the heart is deceitful above all things" (Jeremiah 17:9), meaning emotions can mislead us if they aren't grounded in truth. When we rely only on feelings, we become susceptible to doubt, confusion, and despair. However, God calls us to renew our minds with His Word, so our decisions reflect His will, not fleeting emotions (Romans 12:2).

> ➤ Prayer is essential to staying aligned with God's will. Neglecting it weakens spiritual strength (A disciplined prayer life fortifies faith. Prayerlessness disconnects believers from God's power. Jesus modeled the importance of prayer (Luke 5:16).*Commit to daily prayer to stay spiritually aligned and empowered.*

Neglect of Prayer and Intimacy with God

The enemy subtly convinces believers that prayer isn't urgent or that they can skip it without consequence. Over time, prayerlessness drains spiritual strength, making it harder to resist temptation and discern God's will. For example, a believer might prioritize work and hobbies over prayer, saying, "I'll pray tomorrow," only to find days and weeks have passed. This neglect separates us from the source of our power. Jesus Himself withdrew often to pray (Luke 5:16), modeling how vital prayer is. Without prayer, we cannot stay aligned with God's purpose, and the enemy is quick to exploit that distance to steal our crown.

> ➤ Prayer is essential to staying aligned with God's will. Neglecting it weakens spiritual strength. A disciplined prayer life fortifies faith. Prayerlessness disconnects believers from

God's power. Jesus modeled the importance of prayer (Luke 5:16).*Commit to daily prayer to stay spiritually aligned and empowered.*

Laziness in Spiritual Disciplines

The enemy uses laziness to keep believers from engaging in the spiritual practices needed for growth. It often looks like procrastination,"I'll pray later," or "I'll read my Bible tomorrow." Days turn into weeks, and soon believers feel distant from God. A Christian who once served actively in ministry might become complacent, falsly thinking they can slide-by spiritually. This is dangerous because a passive faith becomes a weak faith. Proverbs warns, "A little sleep, a little slumber... and poverty will come on you like a thief" (Proverbs 6:10-11). Just as physical laziness leads to material lack, spiritual laziness results in lack of wisdom, power, and victory. Over time, it dulls our discernment, leaving us vulnerable to temptation.

Like athletes discipline their bodies, believers must train themselves for godliness (1 Timothy 4:7-8). Laziness robs us of our crown by blocking our growth and weakening our connection with Christ. Procrastination weakens faith. Proverbs 6:10-11 warns against slothfulness.

> ➢ Laziness hinders spiritual growth. Proverbs 6:10-11 warns against slothfulness. Consistency in prayer and study builds resilience.*Discipline in prayer and study builds resilience and growth.*

Listlessness and Spiritual Apathy

Listlessness is deeper than laziness; it's a lack of passion, energy, or interest in the things of God. A believer may find themselves thinking, "What's the point?" and losing motivation to attend church, pray, or study Scripture. This apathy can set in after disappointments, when prayers seem unanswered or life feels stagnant. The devil's goal here is to make believers spiritually numb so they stop pursuing God altogether. Jesus warned against lukewarmness, saying, "Because you are neither hot nor cold, I will spit you out of my mouth" (Revelation 3:16).

> Rekindling spiritual fire requires intentional steps, asking the Holy Spirit to reignite our zeal, surrounding ourselves with godly influences, and remembering the joy of our salvation (Psalm 51:12).Disappointments can numb passion for God. Jesus warns against lukewarmness (Revelation 3:16).*Intentionally seek the Holy Spirit to rekindle your zeal for God.*

Social Detachment from Fellowship

The enemy isolates believers, weakening their faith. Hebrews 10:25 calls us to remain in fellowship.The enemy knows that believers are stronger when they're united with the body of Christ, so he works hard to isolate us. Hebrews 10:25 urges, "Do not forsake the assembling of yourselves together." When Christians cut themselves off from fellowship; whether due to offense, fatigue, or shame, they miss the encouragement and accountability that only community can provide. A believer might say, "I can follow Jesus on my own," but faith was never meant to be lived in isolation.

> Social detachment might also result from church hurt or relational conflicts. When unresolved offense causes someone to withdraw, it opens the door for bitterness and spiritual stagnation. The devil loves to prey on isolated believers, much like a predator targets animals that have separated from the herd. Staying connected to the body of Christ through small groups, church services, or prayer meetings helps us persevere in our walk and guard our crown from deception. *Community strengthens and encourages believers to persevere.*

Neglecting Prayer

The devil knows that prayer connects us to God's power, so he works overtime to make believers neglect it. Prayerlessness leads to spiritual dryness, confusion, and an inability to resist temptation. A Christian might say, "I don't know what to pray about," or "I'm too busy to pray," gradually allowing distractions to replace communication with God. But Jesus taught that prayer is essential, saying, "Watch and pray, so you will not fall into temptation" (Matthew 26:41).

➢ Prayerlessness disconnects believers from God's power. Jesus modeled the importance of prayer (Luke 5:16).When we stop praying, we drift further from God's will and become more susceptible to fear, anxiety, and worldly influences. Setting a regular prayer schedule, even if it starts small, helps build discipline and reignite intimacy with Christ. Prayer is where God speaks, strengthens, and aligns us with His purpose, without it, we become easy prey for the enemy. *Commit to daily prayer to stay spiritually aligned and empowered.*

Neglecting Fasting

Fasting is a powerful weapon that sharpens our spiritual sensitivity and humbles us before God, yet it is often neglected. The devil convinces us that "fasting is too hard" or unnecessary in today's busy world. But Jesus emphasized the importance of fasting, saying, "When you fast..." not "if" (Matthew 6:16-18). In moments of intense spiritual warfare or life decisions, fasting clears the noise of the world, aligning our hearts with God's voice.

➢ Fasting sharpens spiritual focus, but the enemy convinces us it's unnecessary. Jesus emphasized fasting's power (Matthew 6:16).For example, a believer struggling with confusion about their next steps in life may find clarity through fasting and prayer. The devil's strategy is to keep us comfortable, relying on food, entertainment, and pleasures instead of the Spirit.

Choosing to fast reminds us that we depend on God, not worldly comforts, and it brings breakthrough where ordinary prayers fall short (Isaiah 58:6-9). *Fasting brings spiritual breakthroughs (Isaiah 58:6-9). The enemy discourages fasting to keep believers spiritually stagnant. Use fasting as a weapon to align with God and gain breakthrough.*

Neglecting the Word of God

Without regular engagement with God's Word, believers cannot discern truth from lies. The enemy exploits biblical ignorance by distorting Scripture, just as he did with Eve in the Garden of Eden (Genesis 3:1-5). A Christian might feel too tired or uninterested to read the Bible daily, thinking, "I already know the basics." But the Word of God is living and active (Hebrews 4:12), and it feeds our souls in ways we don't always realize.

In real life, neglecting Scripture leads to confusion about moral choices, identity, and purpose. Daily reading builds spiritual resilience, offering strength to stand firm in trials. When believers know God's promises, they can confidently resist the enemy's lies and maintain their crown.

> ➤ Gradual neglect of spiritual practices leads to distance from God. Prioritizing time with Him restores closeness Small compromises, skipped prayers or missed church, create distance from God. Revelation 3:20 calls us back to intimacy with Him. *Prioritize time with God to restore closeness and fortify faith.*

The Drift from Intimacy with God

All these distractions, laziness, listlessness, social detachment, and neglect of prayer, fasting, and God's Word, ultimately lead to one thing, a drift from intimacy with God. Relationships, including our relationship with God, require intentionality. Just as neglecting

communication weakens friendships or marriages, neglecting our relationship with God leads to spiritual distance. A believer might say, "God feels far away," when in reality, it is they who have drifted.

The enemy works hard to keep us busy with life's demands, leaving little room for quiet time with the Lord. However, God desires intimacy with us. He knocks on the door of our hearts, waiting for us to invite Him in (Revelation 3:20). When we prioritize time with God, we experience the joy and peace that come from knowing Him deeply. Spiritual intimacy restores our soul, keeps us aligned with God's purpose, and strengthens us to resist the enemy's schemes.

> ➢ Small compromises lead to spiritual decline. Staying alert and armored in God's Word ensures victory (Ephesians 6:10-18).

REGULAR PRAYER, STUDY, AND WORSHIP KEEP YOU ROOTED AND VIGILANT.

Guard Your Crown By All means Necessary. The devil's tactics are subtle, but vigilance, prayer, and intentional pursuit of God keep us on the path to victory. Hold fast, resist deception, and fight for your eternal reward (Revelation 3:11). Keep chasing Yahweh, your crown is worth the fight. The devil's strategy is subtle, he doesn't often drag believers away from God in one dramatic moment. Instead, he uses small, gradual shifts; a skipped prayer here, missed church there, and slowly, intimacy with God fades. These distractions, laziness, listlessness, social detachment, and neglect of spiritual disciplines. are all designed to rob us of the crown that God has prepared for us.

However, through intentional pursuit of God, praying, fasting, fellowshipping, and studying the Word, we can reignite our passion and protect what God has given us. Staying close to Christ keeps us strong, and with His help, we can overcome every deception and finish our race with joy. Through distraction, deceit, and discouragement, the devil works to derail believers from finishing their race. Revelation 3:11 reminds us to "hold fast what you have, that no one may take your crown." Stay armored up, stay vigilant, and fight for your eternal reward. Guard your heart and mind with all diligence. The enemy's schemes are subtle, but with God's Word, prayer, and the Holy Spirit, victory is certain. Press on, stay alert, and protect your crown, it is worth the fight!

The devil's strategies are deceptively elusive and deeply personal, targeting our thoughts, emotions, and daily choices. His ultimate goal is to derail us from finishing our race and receiving the crowns that await us; the crown of life, righteousness, and glory (James 1:12, 2 Timothy 4:8, 1 Peter 5:4). But we are not without defense. By staying vigilant, immersing ourselves in God's Word, remaining in prayer, and walking closely with fellow believers, we can recognize these deceptions and overcome them through the power of the Holy Spirit (Ephesians 6:10-18). Christ calls us to "hold fast what you have, that no one may take your crown" (Revelation 3:11). With God's help, we can persevere, staying faithful and focused until the end. Stay alert, stay armored, and keep chasing Yahweh, your crown is worth the fight! Keep pressing forward! Your crown is within reach, don't let the enemy steal it. Stay rooted, stay disciplined, and never stop chasing Yahweh. While the devil schemes to rob believers of their crown, Christ has already secured victory for us. We are more than conquerors through Him who loves us (Romans 8:37). Armed with His Word, guided by His Spirit, and surrounded by His people, we can confidently resist every tactic and finish our race. <u>Let us persevere, fix our eyes on Jesus, and hold fast to what is promised. Your crown is worth it!</u>"

THE CRUCIAL VITALITY OF DESTROYING THE WORKS OF THE DEVIL, CRUCIFYING THE FLESH, AND BINDING DISTRACTIONS TO GUARD OUR CROWN OF SALVATION

The spiritual battle believers face is not one to be taken lightly. The works of the devil operate on multiple fronts, **morally**, **physically**, **intellectually**, and **spiritually,** seeking to rob us of the crown of salvation and hinder our growth in Christ. As the Bible teaches, the devil uses deceit, temptation, and distractions to gratify the flesh and divert our attention from God (Ephesians 2:3). However, through Christ's victory on the cross, believers have the power to destroy these works, crucify their flesh, and remain focused on their calling. This requires diligence, discipline, and the binding of every distraction that could hinder our walk with God. The works of the devil are targeted not only at unbelievers to keep them away from salvation, but also at believers to blunt their effectiveness for Christ. The devil entices people with sin, making it appear attractive and desirable (James 1:14). This moral deception convinces many to indulge in sinful pleasures that gratify the cravings of the flesh, such as addiction, immorality, and greed. These cravings leave people spiritually bankrupt and distanced from God.

Physically, the devil can afflict people with illness, as seen in the case of Job, whom Satan struck with painful sores to provoke him to curse God (Job 2:7). The enemy uses trials not only to attack the body but also to discourage believers, hoping they will abandon their faith in frustration. Intellectually, the devil clouds the minds of unbelievers, blinding them to the truth of the gospel (2 Corinthians 4:3-4). False doctrines and confusion keep them bound in error, making it difficult for them to see the path to salvation. Spiritually, the enemy snatches away the Word of God sown in hearts, causing believers to drift from truth and fall into spiritual apathy (Matthew 13:19). In the lives of believers, Satan's tactics become more subtle but equally destructive. His goal is to cool our love for Christ (Revelation 2:4) and disrupt our unity with other believers (John 13:34-35). He draws believers into sin through distractions, addictions, and worldly pursuits, entangling them in behaviors that separate them from the presence of God. If the enemy can lure us into spiritual stagnation, laziness, or compromise, we become ineffective in our witness and purpose in Christ.

CRUCIFYING THE FLESH: A DAILY DISCIPLINE FOR VICTORY

Though Christ has secured victory, believers are called to actively participate in this spiritual battle by crucifying the flesh. This means putting to death the sinful desires that wage war against our souls (Galatians 5:24). The flesh represents our fallen nature, with its cravings for comfort, pleasure, and self-indulgence. If left unchecked, these desires lead to spiritual decay and distance from God.

In practical terms, crucifying the flesh involves saying no to sinful habits, resisting temptations, and choosing to walk in the Spirit daily (Galatians 5:16-17). For instance, a believer struggling with addiction to entertainment or social media must consciously limit their exposure and redirect their attention to prayer, fasting, and Bible study. This daily act of self-denial strengthens our spirit and weakens the hold of the flesh, aligning us more closely with God's purposes.

The Apostle Paul described the Christian life as a race, urging believers to run in such a way as to obtain the prize (1 Corinthians 9:24-27). Part of running this race effectively is disciplining our bodies and minds, so they are not controlled by the flesh. Laziness, procrastination, and listlessness are all tactics the devil uses to weaken our resolve, but through the Holy Spirit, we have the strength to persevere.

BINDING THE DEMON OF DISTRACTIONS

Distractions are among the most effective tools in the devil's arsenal. <u>The enemy does not need to convince us to reject Christ outright; he only needs to keep us too busy, entertained, or overwhelmed to prioritize God.</u> Distractions come in many forms; social media, endless entertainment, unhealthy relationships, or even excessive work. These things aren't inherently evil, but when they consume our time and attention, they rob us of the opportunity to develop intimacy with God.

The Bible warns believers to stay alert and sober-minded, for the devil prowls around like a roaring lion, seeking someone to devour (1 Peter 5:8). One of the ways we resist the enemy is by binding the spirit of distraction through prayer and intentional living. Binding distractions means setting boundaries around our time and ensuring that nothing takes precedence over our relationship with God. For example, this might involve scheduling regular times for prayer and Bible reading, fasting from social media, or participating in fellowship with other believers.

In the story of Mary and Martha, Jesus highlights the importance of focusing on what truly matters. While Martha was "distracted by all the preparations," Mary sat at Jesus' feet, listening to His teaching. Jesus affirmed that Mary had chosen the better portion, which would not be taken away from her (Luke 10:38-42). Similarly, we must choose to prioritize God above all else, recognizing that our crown of salvation is too precious to forfeit for temporary distractions.

STAYING ARMORED FOR SPIRITUAL BATTLE

To stand firm against the devil's schemes, believers must be equipped with the full armor of God (Ephesians 6:10-18). This armor includes truth, righteousness, faith, salvation, the Word of God, and prayer. Each piece is essential in guarding against the enemy's attacks and remaining focused on our heavenly calling. The devil will attempt to exploit our weaknesses, but if we are clothed in God's armor, we can resist him and stand firm.

One of the most powerful weapons believers have is prayer. Jesus taught His disciples to "watch and pray so that you will not fall into temptation" (Matthew 26:41). Prayer keeps us connected to God's strength and enables us to discern the devil's deceptions. Fasting enhances this discipline by quieting the flesh and heightening spiritual sensitivity. Through prayer and fasting, we bind the forces of darkness and invite God's power into our lives to overcome distractions and temptations.

THE CRUCIAL VITALITY OF DESTROYING THE WORKS OF THE DEVIL, CRUCIFYING THE FLESH, AND BINDING DISTRACTIONS TO GUARD OUR CROWN OF SALVATION

The spiritual battle believers face is not one to be taken lightly. The works of the devil operate on multiple fronts and are relentless in their pursuit of your "eternal seperation from God", morally, physically, intellectually, and spiritually, seeking to rob us of the crown of salvation and hinder our growth in Christ. As the Bible teaches, the devil uses deceit, temptation, and distractions to gratify the flesh and divert our attention from God (Ephesians 2:3). However, through Christ's victory on the cross, believers have the power to destroy these works, crucify their flesh, and remain focused on their calling. This requires diligence, discipline, and the binding of every distraction that could hinder our walk with God. The works of the devil are targeted not only at unbelievers to keep them away from salvation, but also at believers to blunt their effectiveness for Christ. The devil entices people with sin, making it appear attractive and desirable (James 1:14). This moral deception convinces many to indulge in sinful pleasures that gratify the cravings of the flesh, such as addiction, immorality, and greed. These cravings leave people spiritually bankrupt and distanced from God.

Physically, the devil (with permission from God) can afflict people with illness, as seen in the case of Job, whom Satan struck with painful sores to provoke him to curse God giving way to sin (Job 2:7). The enemy uses trials not only to attack the body but also to discourage believers, hoping they will abandon their faith in frustration. Intellectually, the devil clouds the minds of unbelievers, blinding them to the truth of the gospel (2 Corinthians 4:3-4). False doctrines and confusion keep them bound in error, making it difficult for them to see the path to salvation. Spiritually, the enemy snatches away the Word of God sown in hearts, causing believers to drift from truth and fall into spiritual apathy (Matthew 13:19). In the lives of believers, Satan's tactics become more subtle but equally destructive. His goal is to steal our love for Christ (Revelation 2:4) and disrupt our unity with other believers (John 13:34-35). He draws believers into sin through distractions, addictions, and worldly pursuits, entangling them in behaviors that separate them from the presence of God. If the enemy can lure us into spiritual stagnation, laziness, or compromise, we become ineffective in our witness and purpose in Christ. Though Christ has secured victory, believers are called to actively participate in this spiritual battle by crucifying the flesh. This means putting to death the sinful desires that wage war against our souls (Galatians 5:24). The flesh represents our fallen nature, with its cravings for comfort, pleasure, and self-indulgence. If left unchecked, these desires lead to spiritual destruction and distance from God.

In practical terms, crucifying the flesh involves saying no to sinful habits, resisting temptations, and choosing to walk in the Spirit daily (Galatians 5:16-17). For instance, a believer struggling with addiction to entertainment or social media must consciously limit their exposure and redirect their attention to prayer, fasting, and Bible study. This daily act of self-denial strengthens our spirit and weakens the hold of the flesh, aligning us more closely with God's purposes.

The Apostle Paul described the Christian life as a race, urging believers to run in such a way as to obtain the prize (1 Corinthians 9:24-27). Part of running this race effectively is disciplining our bodies and minds, so they are not controlled by the flesh. Laziness, procrastination, and listlessness are all tactics the devil uses to weaken our resolve, but through the Holy Spirit, we have the strength to persevere.

Distractions are among the most effective tools in the devil's arsenal. The enemy does not need to convince us to reject Christ outright; he only needs to keep us too busy, entertained, or overwhelmed to prioritize God. Distractions come in many forms, social media addictions, laziness, lust of the flesh, pornography, endless entertainment, unhealthy relationships, or even excessive-enslaving-work. When they consume our time and attention, they rob us of the opportunity to develop intimacy with God.

The Bible warns believers to stay alert and sober-minded, for the devil prowls around like a roaring lion, seeking someone to devour (1 Peter 5:8). One of the ways we resist the enemy is by binding the spirit of distraction through prayer and standing firm on the Word of God. Binding distractions means setting boundaries around our time and ensuring that nothing takes precedence over our relationship with God. For example, this might involve scheduling regular times for prayer and Bible reading, fasting from social media, or participating in fellowship with other believers. In the story of Mary and Martha, Jesus highlights the importance of focusing on what truly matters. While Martha was "distracted by all the preparations," Mary sat at Jesus' feet, listening to His teaching. Jesus affirmed that Mary had chosen the better portion, which would not be taken away from her (Luke 10:38-42). Similarly, we must choose to prioritize God above all else, recognizing that our crown of salvation is too precious to forfeit for temporary distractions.

To stand firm against the devil's schemes, believers must be equipped with the full armor of God (Ephesians 6:10-18). This armor includes **truth, righteousness, faith, salvation,** the **Word of God,** and **prayer**. Each piece is essential in guarding against the enemy's attacks and remaining focused on our heavenly calling. The devil will attempt

to exploit our weaknesses, but if we are clothed in God's armor, we can resist him and stand firm.

One of the most powerful weapons believers have is prayer. Jesus taught His disciples to *"watch and pray so that you will not fall into temptation" (Matthew 26:41)*. Prayer keeps us connected to God's strength and enables us to discern the devil's deceptions. Fasting enhances this discipline by quieting the flesh and heightening spiritual sensitivity. Through prayer and fasting, we bind the forces of darkness and invite God's power into our lives to overcome distractions and temptations.

Each of these acts as devices the devil uses to rob believers of their crowns by distorting their relationship with God, drawing them away from His truth, and undermining their spiritual integrity. Let's explore how these can act as ***vehicles for spiritual sabotage***.

1. Pride

Pride is a root of many sins, leading individuals to exalt themselves above God's authority. It was the sin of Lucifer that caused his fall (Isaiah 14:12-15) and is a continual trap for believers. Pride blinds individuals to their need for God, making them rely on their own strength, wisdom, and righteousness instead of His grace. This self-centered mindset prevents true humility and submission to God's will, thereby forfeiting the crown promised to those who persevere in faith and obedience (James 4:6; Revelation 3:11).

2. Rebellion Against God

Rebellion, whether open or subtle, is a direct rejection of God's sovereignty and commandments. It manifests in disobedience, idolatry, or choosing the ways of the world over God's Word. This attitude is similar to witchcraft, as 1 Samuel 15:23 warns; "Rebellion is as the sin of witchcraft." By rebelling, believers sever themselves from the blessings of submission and obedience that secure their crowns, leaving them vulnerable to spiritual defeat.

3. Hypocrisy

Hypocrisy erodes the authenticity of a believer's faith and witness, creating a façade of godliness while denying its power (2 Timothy 3:5). It misrepresents the character of Christ and leads to judgment (Matthew 23:27-28). A hypocritical life hinders spiritual growth, allowing the enemy to sow doubt and confusion, ultimately preventing believers from receiving the crown of life reserved for those who remain faithful and true.

4. Pride and Self-Righteousness

While pride and self-righteousness are interconnected, self-righteousness uniquely involves the belief that one's own deeds are sufficient for salvation. This attitude contradicts the Gospel of grace and diminishes the sufficiency of Christ's sacrifice (Ephesians 2:8-9). Self-righteousness leads to judgmentalism and legalism, alienating others and forfeiting the crown of righteousness reserved for those who live by faith and grace.

5. Spiritual Exploitation

Spiritual exploitation occurs when leaders or systems misuse God's Word for personal gain or manipulation, leading believers astray (2 Peter 2:1-3). This includes false teachings, abusive authority, and twisting Scripture to serve selfish ambitions. Such exploitation steals the joy, peace, and spiritual rewards meant for faithful believers, robbing them of the incorruptible crown given to those who run the race with integrity (1 Corinthians 9:24-25).

6. Brainwashing

Brainwashing involves systematic manipulation to distort truth and impose false beliefs. This tactic often replaces God's Word with doctrines of men or ideologies contrary to Scripture (Colossians 2:8). When believers fail to test everything against God's Word, they risk forfeiting their spiritual inheritance, as their faith becomes rooted in lies instead of truth.

7. Lukewarmness

A lukewarm faith, a state of spiritual apathy, is condemned by Christ in Revelation 3:15-16: "Because you are lukewarm... I will spit you out of my mouth." This indifference toward God and His commandments leads to a compromised, ineffective faith that lacks the enthusiasm required to overcome the enemy. Believers who remain lukewarm jeopardize their crowns, as they fail to endure and bear fruit.

8. Dabbling in the Occult and Witchcraft

Engaging in occult practices or witchcraft directly opposes God's commandments (Deuteronomy 18:10-12). These practices invite demonic influence, sever fellowship with God, and place believers in spiritual bondage. The enemy uses such tactics to distract and enslave believers, leading them away from the path of righteousness and the crown of life promised to the faithful.

9. Spiritual Blindness

Spiritual blindness prevents believers from perceiving God's truth and understanding His will. This blindness can result from sin, pride, or the devil's deception, as described in 2 Corinthians 4:4: "The god of this age has blinded the minds of unbelievers." When believers fail to discern spiritual realities, they risk being led astray, losing their rewards for faithfully walking in the light of Christ.

10. Ignorance (Lack of Knowledge)

Hosea 4:6 warns, "My people are destroyed for lack of knowledge." Ignorance of God's Word and His promises leaves believers vulnerable to false teachings and spiritual defeat. Without the knowledge of Scripture, believers cannot effectively wield the sword of the Spirit (Ephesians 6:17), leaving them unequipped to resist the devil and secure their crowns.

Each of these devices reflects the devil's strategy to <u>distract</u>, <u>deceive</u>, and <u>destroy</u>. Believers must remain vigilant, grounded in God's Word, and fully armored with His truth to overcome these tactics and protect their eternal inheritance. The works of the devil are relentless, but Jesus has already secured victory on the cross. As believers, our task is to walk in that victory by crucifying our flesh, resisting distractions, and staying vigilant in prayer. The enemy's goal is to keep us from receiving our crown of salvation, whether through temptation, laziness, or distraction. But through the Holy Spirit, we are empowered to stand firm, pursue righteousness, and finish the race set before us. The Bible exhorts us to "hold fast what you have, that no one may take your crown" (Revelation 3:11). This requires intentional effort, binding the spirit of distraction, crucifying sinful desires, and staying connected to God through prayer, fasting, and His Word. As we persevere, we fulfill our purpose as ambassadors for Christ and secure the eternal reward that awaits us in heaven.

In this spiritual journey, our crown is worth the fight. Let nothing hinder your pursuit of Christ, stay focused, stay armored, and keep chasing Yahweh! The enemy may try to deceive and distract, but through the power of Jesus, we can destroy the works of the devil and walk victoriously in the promise of eternal life.

Warfare of the Mind

THE BATTLEFIELD OF THOUGHTS

The mind is the central battlefield in spiritual warfare. It is the seat of thoughts, emotions, and decisions, making it the enemy's primary target. Through lies, deceit, and temptation, Satan seeks to infiltrate the minds of believers, drawing them away from God's truth and will. This tactic is as ancient as God's Word itself, beginning with his deceptive approach in the Garden of Eden. From the beginning, Satan has employed lies as a powerful weapon to manipulate the

human mind. In Genesis 3:1-5, he approached Eve with a simple yet insidious question, "Did God really say...?" By planting doubt in her mind, he began to distort God's truth. Satan's lie suggested that God's instructions were restrictive rather than protective, implying that disobedience would lead to enlightenment and godlike status. This deception caused Eve to doubt God's character and His Word, leading to her disobeying God and inevitably the vehicle of sin corrupting humanity. In *John 8:44*, Jesus describes Satan as "*a liar and the father of it.*" Lies are not just a tactic but the very essence of Satan's nature. When the enemy speaks, his words are designed to twist truth, creating confusion and spiritual vulnerability. Lies about identity, purpose, and God's promises are particularly effective in leading believers astray. For instance, many fall prey to the lie that their worth is tied to their performance, possessions, or past sins, rather than their identity in Christ.

DECEIT AS THE DEVILS WEAPON

Deceit goes beyond simple lies; it involves crafting a convincing facade to obscure reality. In 2 Corinthians 11:14, Paul warns that "Satan himself masquerades as an angel of light." This highlights the subtlety of his approach. He often presents evil as good, cloaking sin in appealing narratives that align with human desires. For example, the world's messages about success, pleasure, or freedom often contradict God's truth but are presented in a way that seems harmless or even beneficial. The mind, when unguarded, becomes fertile ground for such deceit. Without discernment, believers can easily accept worldly philosophies or ideologies that subtly erode their faith. *Colossians 2:8* cautions against being "*taken captive through hollow and deceptive philosophy,*" reminding us of the need to measure all thoughts against the truth of Scripture.

TEMPTATION A GATEWAY TO SIN

Temptation is another key element of Satan's strategy to infiltrate the mind. He preys on natural human desires, distorting them to lead individuals into sin. As described in James 1:13-15, temptation begins with inner desires that, when acted upon, give birth to sin and eventually death.

Consider Satan's temptation of Jesus in the wilderness (Matthew 4:1-11). Each temptation appealed to physical needs, pride, or power, but Jesus resisted by countering with Scripture. This underscores the importance of a mind fortified with God's Word. Unlike Eve, who entertained Satan's lie, Jesus demonstrated the power of standing firm in truth.

THE MIND AS A SPIRITUAL BATTLEFIELD

The enemy's ultimate goal is to establish strongholds in the mind, places where lies take root and influence behavior. 2 Corinthians 10:3-5 describes spiritual warfare as pulling down these strongholds and "taking every thought captive to obey Christ." Recognizing the mind as the battlefield helps believers approach their thoughts with intentionality.

Daily renewal of the mind is essential in this battle. *Romans 12:2* urges believers, "*Do not conform to the pattern of this world, but be transformed by the renewing of your mind.*" Renewing the mind involves immersing oneself in Scripture, prayer, and worship, allowing God's truth to reshape thought patterns and guard against the enemy's infiltration. The enemy's strategy to target and infiltrate the mind is a deliberate assault on a believer's faith and relationship with God. Lies, deceit, and temptation are his weapons, but the Word of God is the ultimate defense. By understanding these tactics, believers can stand firm, guarding their minds and embracing the renewal that comes through Christ. The battlefield is real, but victory is promised to those who

trust in the Lord and wield the sword of the Spirit, which is the Word of God. The mind is the gateway to the soul, and the devil's purpose is clear! infiltrate this sacred space, manipulate thoughts, and ultimately take them hostage through lies, deceit, and sinful strongholds. Now we intricately explore the devil's motives and methods, exposing his strategies and equipping believers with the knowledge to stand firm against his schemes.

THE DEVIL'S STRATEGY TO INFILTRATE THE MIND

Satan's primary objective is to corrupt the mind, knowing it governs decisions, emotions, and spiritual awareness. By infiltrating thoughts, he creates doubt, fear, and confusion, effectively diverting the believer from God's truth. In Genesis 3:1-5, the serpent's first recorded act was to twist God's Word. He asked Eve, "Did God really say…?" questioning God's authority and reliability. By manipulating her perception, Satan planted seeds of doubt about God's goodness, leading to her disobedience. This strategy has not changed; the enemy continues to question God's truth and promises, aiming to distort the believer's understanding. Paul warns in *2 Corinthians 11:3*, *"But I fear, lest somehow, as the serpent deceived Eve by his craftiness, so your minds may be corrupted from the simplicity that is in Christ."* Satan's goal is to move believers away from the purity of the gospel, replacing it with complex lies that obscure the truth. In John 8:44, Jesus calls Satan the *"father of lies,"* underscoring the devil's intrinsic connection to deception. Every lie he sows is designed to corrupt the mind, leaving believers vulnerable to his schemes. His lies often mimic truth, making them harder to discern without God's Word as a filter. The battlefield is explicitly spiritual, as outlined in *Ephesians 6:11-12* *"Put on the full armor of God so that you can take your stand against the devil's schemes."* Satan's infiltration is not random; it is part of a calculated strategy to exploit human weaknesses, particularly mental vulnerabilities. In *Revelation 12:9*, we see the scope of his deception: *"The great dragon… deceives the whole world."* This passage reveals that Satan's plan extends beyond individuals to entire societies, spreading false ideologies, doctrines, and beliefs to capture minds altogether in a fowl attempt to <u>corrupt itself against the "True Knowledge of God"</u>.

MANIPULATING THOUGHTS
WITH LIES AND DECEIT

Once inside the mind, Satan manipulates thoughts through lies and deceit, twisting perceptions to lead people away from God. In Matthew 4:1-11, the devil tempts Jesus by twisting Scripture, trying to exploit His physical hunger, authority, and trust in God. Though Jesus was perfect, Satan's attempts show that even the sinless are not immune to the enemy's targeted manipulation. Believers must be equally vigilant, responding as Jesus did by exerting Scripture as their primary source of defense. The manipulation of thoughts often leads to sinful strongholds. 2 Corinthians 10:3-5 describes the enemy's work as creating *"arguments and every high thing that exalts itself against the knowledge of God."* Satan's lies build barriers in the mind, designed to block God's truth and establish patterns of sinful thinking. Temptation plays a crucial role in this manipulation. James 1:13-15 explains the progression; "Each one is tempted when he is drawn away by his own desires and enticed. Then, when desire has conceived, it gives birth to sin; and sin, when it is full-grown, brings forth death." Satan lures the mind into considering sin, often by presenting it as harmless or beneficial, before it spirals into spiritual death. Deception can make sin appear desirable or even righteous. *Proverbs 14:12* warns, *"There is a way that seems right to a man, but its end is the way of death."* Satan preys on human reasoning, twisting logic to justify actions contrary to God's will. 1 Peter 5:8 reminds believers to remain alert, *"Be sober, be vigilant; because your adversary the devil walks about like a roaring lion, seeking whom he may devour."* Satan's constant prowling underscores the need for mental vigilance and spiritual discernment.

When Satan's lies take root, they form strongholds entrenched patterns of sinful thought or behavior. *Romans 8:5-6* describes the conflict between fleshly and spiritual mindsets, *"For those who live according to the flesh set their minds on the things of the flesh, but those who live according to the Spirit, the things of the Spirit. For to be carnally minded is death, but to be spiritually minded is life and peace.."* The devil's purpose is to keep believers focused on the flesh, trapping them in worldly thinking that stifles spiritual growth. *Romans 12:2* commands believers to *"be transformed by the renewing of your mind."* This renewal breaks Satan's hold by replacing sinful strongholds with God's truth. Without renewal, the mind remains vulnerable to captivity. Colossians 2:8 warns against hollow and deceptive philosophies that take believers "captive." These strongholds often masquerade as harmless ideologies or cultural norms but lead to spiritual bondage. Finally, 2 Timothy 2:25-26 highlights the importance of repentance, "That they may come to their senses and escape the snare of the devil." Repentance and submission to God are essential for breaking free from the enemy's grip.

The devil's purpose in targeting the mind is deliberate and systematic. Through lies, deceit, and the creation of sinful strongholds, he aims to manipulate and ultimately take the mind hostage. However, Scripture equips believers to recognize these tactics, counteract them with God's truth, and renew their minds daily. Armed with vigilance and the Word of God, believers can stand firm, ensuring that their minds remain aligned with Christ and safeguarded against the enemy's schemes.

LET US HAVE THE MIND OF CHRIST

1 CORINTHIANS 2:16: "BUT WE HAVE THE MIND OF CHRIST."

To have the mind of Christ is to align our thoughts, decisions, and actions with His will and commands. The mind of Christ is a spiritual gift granted to believers through salvation, allowing us to perceive the world, trials, and temptations from a heavenly perspective. It equips us to discern between divine testing, which refines faith, and satanic temptation, which seeks to lead us astray.

Testing vs. Temptation

Testing and temptation may feel similar but differ significantly in origin, purpose, and outcome.

Testing: A divine process designed by Yahweh to refine a believer's character, strengthen their faith, and deepen their relationship with Him.

Purpose: Testing builds endurance and reveals areas of growth, allowing believers to trust God more deeply.

> **James 1:2-4**: "Consider it pure joy, my brothers and sisters, whenever you face trials of many kinds, because you know that the testing of your faith produces perseverance. Let perseverance finish its work so that you may be mature and complete, not lacking anything." *1 Peter 1:7: "These [trials] have come so that the proven genuineness of your faith of greater worth than gold, which perishes even though refined by fire may result in praise, glory and honor when Jesus Christ is revealed."* Divine testing is never meant to harm but to elevate the believer spiritually and draw them closer to God.

Temptation :A deliberate snare from the enemy, designed to exploit weaknesses and lead believers into sin and rebellion against God.

Purpose: Temptation's goal is separation from God's will, often achieved by appealing to human desires, pride, or fear.

> *James 1:13-15:* "*When tempted, no one should say, 'God is tempting me.' For God cannot be tempted by evil, nor does He tempt anyone; but each person is tempted when they are dragged away by their own evil desire and enticed. Then, after desire has conceived, it gives birth to sin; and sin, when it is full-grown, gives birth to death.*" Understanding these distinctions equips believers to respond appropriately to both testing and temptation.

Biblical Examples

1. Testing: Abraham's Faith with Isaac (Genesis 22:1-19)

Yahweh tested Abraham by asking him to sacrifice his son Isaac, the child of promise. This test was not to harm but to prove Abraham's obedience and trust in God's plan. Abraham demonstrated faith in God's sovereignty, even declaring, "*God Himself will provide the lamb*" *(Genesis 22:8)*. The outcome was a profound blessing and reaffirmation of God's covenant with Abraham, "*In your seed all the nations of the earth shall be blessed*, because you have obeyed My voice" (Genesis 22:18). Testing is designed to strengthen faith and produce obedience, bringing believers into closer alignment with God's will.

2. Temptation: Jesus Resisting the Devil (Matthew 4:1-11) After fasting for 40 days, Jesus was tempted by Satan in three ways:

> ➤ **Physical Need**: Turn stones into bread (Matthew 4:3-4).
> ➤ **Pride**: Throw Himself down to prove His divinity (Matthew 4:5-7).
> ➤ **Power**: Worship Satan in exchange for worldly kingdoms (Matthew 4:8-10).

Jesus resisted by wielding the Word of God, declaring, "It is written," each time. *Temptation seeks to exploit vulnerability, but reliance on Scripture and unwavering trust in God are powerful defenses.*

Encouragement for Believers

Testing and temptation are part of the Christian journey, but the outcomes differ based on our responses.

Testing Strengthens Faith

James 1:2-4 assures us that trials refine us, producing perseverance and spiritual maturity. Testing may be uncomfortable, but it ultimately deepens our reliance on God.

1 Peter 1:7 encourages believers to view trials as a means of glorifying Christ, whose strength is made perfect in our weakness.

God Provides Escape from Temptation

1 Corinthians 10:13: "No temptation has overtaken you except what is common to mankind. And God is faithful; He will not let you be tempted beyond what you can bear. But when you are tempted, He will also provide a way out so that you can endure it." *Believers are never left defenseless against temptation. God's Word, prayer, and the Holy Spirit equip us to resist the enemy's schemes.*

Having the Mind of Christ

To overcome testing and temptation, believers must embrace the mind of Christ. 1 Corinthians 2:16 reminds us that we are not left to our own devices; the Holy Spirit renews our minds to think, act, and respond as Jesus did. *The mind of Christ empowers believers to discern between testing and temptation, to trust God during trials, and to resist the enemy's lures.*

Testing refines and elevates, while temptation seeks to corrupt and destroy. Believers are called to navigate these spiritual realities with the mind of Christ, discerning the source and purpose of their

experiences. By anchoring their thoughts in Scripture, relying on God's strength, and walking in obedience, they can emerge victorious over both testing and temptation. In Christ, the battlefield of the mind becomes a place of triumph rather than defeat.

FULL SURRENDER TO YAHWEH VS. REDEDICATION TO RELIGIOUS DOGMA

The difference between full surrender to Yahweh and rededication to religious dogma is the difference between genuine relationship and hollow routine, between transformative faith and lifeless tradition. Understanding this distinction is vital for believers who desire to walk authentically with God rather than being trapped in systems that offer form without substance. Full surrender to Yahweh is a wholehearted commitment to God that stems from love and trust, not obligation. It is a relational response to the truth of who God is and what He has done. Surrender begins with the recognition of God's sovereignty and the believer's total dependency on Him. It requires laying aside self-will and embracing God's purpose, as Jesus declared in Matthew 22:37: "Love the Lord your God with all your heart and with all your soul and with all your mind. "This surrender is not about following rules or traditions but about cultivating a relationship with God that transforms every aspect of life. Psalm 51:17 reminds us that "the sacrifices of God are a broken spirit; a broken and contrite heart, O God, you will not despise." Yahweh desires humility and genuine repentance over ritualistic offerings.

When a believer surrenders fully to Yahweh, the Holy Spirit works within them to bring about sanctification; a process of becoming more like Christ. *2 Corinthians 3:18* explains this transformation: "*We all, who with unveiled faces contemplate the Lord's glory, are being transformed into His image with ever-increasing glory, which comes from the Lord, who is the Spirit.*" Full surrender allows the Holy Spirit to lead, guide, and reshape the believer's life into alignment with God's will.

In contrast, rededication to religious dogma emphasizes outward conformity to rules, traditions, and rituals often established by human institutions rather than God. While traditions can serve as reminders of faith, when divorced from genuine devotion, they become lifeless routines that hinder spiritual growth. *Mark 7:6-9* records Jesus' rebuke of the Pharisees: "*These people honor me with their lips, but their hearts are far from me. They worship me in vain; their teachings are merely human rules.*" The Pharisees prioritized adherence to traditions over a relationship with God, creating a legalistic system that stifled true worship.

Religious dogma often promotes external appearances of righteousness while neglecting the heart. Paul warns against such practices in *Colossians 2:20-23: "Since you died with Christ to the elemental spiritual forces of this world, why, as though you still belonged to the world, do you submit to its rules*; 'Do not handle! Do not taste! Do not touch!'? These rules... are based on merely human commands and teachings. Such regulations indeed have an appearance of wisdom... but they lack any value in restraining sensual indulgence." Man-made rules may appear spiritual but lack the power to transform the heart, mind or soul back to God. *Clinging to a dogma can lead to a stagnant faith where believers rely on tradition for their sense of righteousness, rather than on the grace and guidance of God. It also risks creating a false sense of security, where one's faith is measured by adherence to religious routines rather than the fruit of the Spirit or the ovrall authenticity of Gods Word.*

CALL TO AUTHENTIC WORSHIP : FOR GOD IS A SPIRIT AND HE WHO WORSHIPS HIM MUST WORSHIP HIM IN BOTH "SPIRIT AND IN TRUTH"

The remedy to dogma is authentic worship, pursuing a personal, intimate relationship with Yahweh. Authentic worship transcends rituals and focuses on knowing God deeply and obeying Him out of love. *John 4:23-24* declares, "*The hour is coming, and now is, when the true worshipers will worship the Father in spirit and truth; for the Father is seeking*

such to worship Him. God is Spirit, and those who worship Him must worship in spirit and truth." Authentic worship involves seeking God's presence through prayer, studying His Word, and allowing the Holy Spirit to direct one's life. It prioritizes relationship over routine, emphasizing that worship is not confined to specific practices but is a lifestyle of obedience and surrender. Believers are called to examine their hearts and ensure their faith is grounded in relationship with God, not in religious systems. Full surrender to Yahweh leads to joy, transformation, and intimacy with the Creator, while rededication to religious dogma risks falling into spiritual emptiness. By choosing surrender over routine, believers experience the fullness of life that Jesus promised in *John 10:10: "I have come that they may have life, and have it more abundantly.*

FROM DEATH SENTENCE TO REDEMPTION

Sin, by its very nature, is devastating and leads to death; both physical and spiritual. Its origin in the Garden of Eden introduced separation from God, pain, and mortality into the world, leaving humanity under the weight of sin's curse. Yet, thanks to the atonement and acceptable sacrifice of Jesus Christ, sin doesn't have to be a death sentence. For those who repent and turn to God, there is redemption, restoration, and eternal life. Sin's entrance into the world is chronicled in Genesis 3, where Adam and Eve disobeyed God's command by eating from the forbidden tree. This act of rebellion brought immediate spiritual death, separation from God and eventual physical death. As God pronounced judgment, He declared the consequences of sin; toil, pain, and the inevitability of returning to dust (Genesis 3:16-19). Paul reinforces this truth in *Romans 5:12: "Therefore, just as sin entered the world through one man, and death through sin, and in this way death came to all people, because all sinned."* Adam's disobedience set in motion a generational curse, condemning all humanity to experience the wages of sin. *Romans 6:23* bluntly states the consequence: "*For the wages of sin is death.*" Sin, like a cruel master, demands payment, and its payment is death. This truth highlights the gravity of sin's power to enslave and destroy. Every sin, no matter how small it seems, carries the weight of death because it violates God's holiness.

SIN DOESN'T HAVE TO BE A DEATH SENTENCE

While sin earns death, the story doesn't end there. God's grace offers a path to life through Jesus Christ. The second half of *Romans 6:23* proclaims the good news, "*But the gift of God is eternal life in Christ Jesus our Lord.*" Jesus Christ, through His atonement on the cross, bore the punishment that humanity deserved. *Isaiah 53:5* foretold this sacrifice: "*But He was pierced for our transgressions, He was crushed for our iniquities; the punishment that brought us peace was on Him, and by His wounds we are healed.*" Jesus' death satisfied the justice of God, paying the penalty for sin, and His resurrection broke the power of death. Because of Christ's work, sin no longer has to define a person's destiny. **Believers are given the opportunity to repent and turn back to God, exchanging death for eternal life**. *2 Peter 3:9* reminds us of God's heart: "*The Lord is not slow in keeping His promise, as some understand slowness. Instead, He is patient with you, not wanting anyone to perish, but everyone to come to repentance.*" Repentance is the key to escaping sin's death sentence. To repent is to acknowledge sin, turn away from it, and submit to God's will. *1 John 1:9* promises, "*If we confess our sins, He is faithful and just and will forgive us our sins and purify us from all unrighteousness.*" Through repentance, believers receive forgiveness, cleansing, and restoration to fellowship with God.

A CALL TO REDEMPTION

Sin does not have to be the final chapter of anyone's story. The atonement of Jesus Christ ensures that no sin is beyond redemption. God's love is so profound that He offers grace to all who turn to Him. Romans 5:8 captures this truth: "But God demonstrates His own love for us in this; While we were still sinners, Christ died for us." Rejecting sin and embracing Jesus is not just about avoiding death but about stepping into a new life. 2 Corinthians 5:17 declares,

"If anyone is in Christ, the new creation has come; The old has gone, the new is here!" In Christ, believers are no longer condemned but are given the power to live victoriously over sin through the Holy Spirit.

For those who feel trapped by sin's grip, the message is clear: turn to Christ. Repentance leads to redemption, and redemption leads to life. Sin may have brought death into the world, but Jesus has conquered death, offering eternal life to all who believe in Him. The chains of sin can be broken, and the death sentence overturned for those who surrender to the Savior.

TRANSFORMING THE JOURNEY WITH GOD

The journey with God is one of immense transformation, where believers move from the old life of sin and separation to a new life of righteousness and fellowship with God. This transformation, powered by grace and sustained by the Holy Spirit, is both immediate and ongoing. It begins with salvation and continues through sanctification, shaping believers into the image of Christ until the journey culminates. The journey begins with salvation, a free gift of God's grace received through faith. *Ephesians 2:8-9* states, "*For it is by grace you have been saved, through faith, and this is not from yourselves, it is the gift of God; not by works, so that no one can boast.*" This moment marks the believer's entry into God's family, where their sins are forgiven, and they are made righteous in Christ.

However, salvation is not the end; it is the beginning of a lifelong process of sanctification. Sanctification is the work of the Holy Spirit, who refines and purifies believers, conforming them to the likeness of Christ. *2 Corinthians 5:17* describes this transformation; "*Therefore, if anyone is in Christ, the new creation has come: The old has gone, the new is here!*" While salvation is instantaneous, sanctification is progressive, requiring ongoing surrender, obedience, and trust in God. Paul's life exemplifies this journey. In *1 Timothy 1:15*, he humbly calls himself the "*chief of sinners,*" acknowledging his past as a persecutor of the church. Yet, through God's grace, he was transformed into a powerful instrument for the gospel. His journey demonstrates that no one is beyond God's reach and that transformation is possible for all who submit to His will. Becoming a new creation in Christ means walking in spiritual freedom, liberated from the bondage of sin. The old self, characterized by sinful desires and behaviors, is replaced with a new self that seeks to glorify God in every aspect of life. **This freedom is not a license to sin but an invitation to live in the fullness of God's purpose.** As Paul declares in *2 Corinthians 5:17, "The old has passed away, the new has come."* This passing away signifies the believer's death to sin and the power it once held. Through Christ's victory on the cross, believers are empowered to resist temptation and walk in righteousness. Walking as a new creation involves daily dependence on the Holy Spirit. Spiritual disciplines like prayer, studying Scripture, and fellowship with other believers strengthen the believer's resolve to live according to God's will. This journey is not free from struggles, but each step is a testament to God's faithfulness and transformative power. The transformation from old to new is a lifelong journey, requiring endurance and perseverance. *Philippians 1:6* provides encouragement; "*Being confident of this, that He who began a good work in you will carry it on to completion until the day of Christ Jesus.*" God is actively working in every believer's life, ensuring that the process He started will reach its fulfillment. Believers are called to press on, even when the journey is difficult. Trials and challenges are opportunities for growth, refining faith and character. The assurance of God's presence and promise sustains believers, reminding them that they are never alone on this path.

THE WORD OF GOD: SOUL FOOD FOR VICTORY

The Word of God is essential for transformation, providing nourishment for the soul and guidance for the journey. *Hebrews 4:12* describes it as *"living and active, sharper than any double-edged sword,"* revealing truth, exposing sin, and equipping believers for every good work. Scripture renews the mind, aligning thoughts with God's truth and dismantling lies from the enemy. It equips believers to stand firm against spiritual attacks, offering wisdom and strength for daily living. Just as physical food sustains the body, God's Word sustains the spirit, ensuring victory over sin and temptation. The journey with God is a transformative process, taking believers from their old, sinful nature to a new life in Christ. It begins with grace, is sustained by sanctification, and culminates in eternal glory. Along the way, believers are empowered to live as new creations, walking in spiritual freedom and growing in Christlikeness. Endurance is essential, but God's Word and Spirit provide the strength needed to complete the journey. Transformation is not only possible, it is promised for all who trust in Yahweh.

God's Word is the ultimate sustenance for the believer's soul, offering nourishment, strength, and direction for life's journey. It stands in stark contrast to the temporary satisfaction offered by the world's **"comfort food,"** such as prosperity gospel messages and shallow motivational speaking. True soul food equips believers to face life's trials, overcome spiritual attacks, and grow in Christlikeness, providing eternal sustenance that transforms from the inside out.

The Bible consistently emphasizes God's Word as a source of light, life, and protection. *Psalm 119:105 declares, "Your word is a lamp to my feet and a light to my path,"* emphasizing its role in guiding believers through the darkness of a fallen world. Just as physical food sustains the body, God's Word sustains the spirit, directing believers toward righteousness and away from sin. Jesus Himself demonstrated the power of Scripture during His wilderness temptation. In *Matthew 4:4, 7*, and *10*, Jesus responded to each of Satan's temptations by saying, "*It is written,*" countering the enemy's lies with the truth of God's Word. This shows that Scripture is not only food for the soul but also a weapon for defense. Ephesians 6:17 reinforces this by describing the Word of God as the "sword of the Spirit," a vital piece of spiritual armor that enables believers to stand firm against the devil's schemes. God's Word doesn't just sustain—it equips. It sharpens discernment, builds faith, and fortifies believers to resist lies and temptations. Without it, the soul becomes malnourished, leaving believers vulnerable to spiritual attacks.

SOUL FOOD, NOT COMFORT FOOD

The difference between soul food and comfort food lies in their purpose and effect. God's Word, as soul food, nourishes the spirit, providing eternal sustenance and equipping believers to live victoriously in Christ. In contrast, comfort food, such as prosperity gospel teachings or motivational speeches, offers fleeting emotional highs without addressing deeper spiritual needs.

1. Soul Food

God's Word feeds the soul with truth, shaping the believer's character and aligning their life with God's will. It is challenging and refining, often calling believers to repentance, obedience, and sacrifice. *Hebrews 4:12* describes the Word as "*living and active, sharper than any double-edged sword.*" It penetrates the heart, exposing sin and transforming the believer into a new creation. Soul food sustains during trials, providing hope and strength when circumstances are difficult. It roots believers in the eternal promises of God, ensuring that their faith is anchored in His unchanging truth.

2. Comfort Food

The prosperity gospel and motivational speaking focus on temporary gratification, promising health, wealth, and success while neglecting the reality of suffering, sin, and the need for repentance. These messages appeal to emotions, offering feel-good platitudes rather than the enduring truth found in Scripture. They may momentarily encourage, but they lack the power to sustain believers through hardship or refine them for God's purpose. Like physical comfort food, they may taste good in the moment but ultimately leave the soul malnourished and unprepared for spiritual warfare.

God's Word challenges believers to pursue holiness, not just happiness. It equips them to endure trials with faith, recognizing that spiritual growth often comes through refining rather than ease. Ephesians 6:17 reminds us that the Word is a weapon for battle, not just a tool for self-help or personal comfort.

3. Call to Action

Believers are called to feast on God's Word daily, finding strength, guidance, and truth in its pages. Just as the body needs daily nourishment, the soul requires the consistent intake of Scripture to remain healthy, strong and on guard against the enemy. The writer of Hebrews emphasizes the power of the Word in Hebrews 4:12: "For the word of God is living and active. Sharper than any double-edged sword, it penetrates even to dividing soul and spirit, joints and marrow; it judges the thoughts and attitudes of the heart." Regular engagement with Scripture renews the mind, equips the believer for spiritual battle, and deepens their relationship with God. Believers must approach the Word with humility, allowing it to transform their hearts and minds. This involves meditating on its truths, applying its principles, and seeking God through prayer and study. The goal is not merely knowledge but transformation, a life shaped by the truth and empowered to reflect Christ.

The Word of God is the ultimate soul food, offering sustenance that leads to eternal life and spiritual victory. Unlike the fleeting comfort of worldly messages, Scripture provides enduring truth that equips believers to face trials, resist temptation, and grow in Christlikeness. Just as Jesus relied on the Word in His wilderness temptation, so too must believers feast on it daily, ensuring their souls are nourished and ready for the battles ahead. Choose soul food over comfort food and experience the transformative power of God's living Word.

JESUS CAME TO DESTROY THE WORKS OF THE DEVIL

The victory of Christ on the cross is the soul- foundation of the believer's ability to overcome the works of the devil. As Jesus approached His crucifixion, He declared, "Now is the time for judgment on this world; now the prince of this world will be driven out" (John 12:31). On the cross, Jesus accomplished two pivotal things; He bore the penalty of our sin, and He provided us with His righteousness. This means that Satan no longer has the power to condemn us or influence our eternal destiny. "There is now no condemnation for those who are in Christ Jesus" (Romans 8:1).

Beyond securing our salvation, Jesus' victory also ensures our personal sanctification. Through the indwelling of the Holy Spirit, believers are empowered to grow in holiness and resist the devil's schemes (Ephesians 4:30). The Spirit leads us into Christlikeness, helping us crucify our flesh and align our desires with God's will. Jesus' triumph over the devil means that believers no longer have to live under the dominion of sin; they are set free to pursue righteousness.

From the very beginning, the mission of Jesus Christ was to undo the damage caused by the stain of sin committed by Adam in the Garden of Eden. In *1 John 3:8,* the apostle declares, "*The reason the Son of God appeared was to destroy the works of the devil.*" The devil's works include sin, death, and separation from God, consequences of his rebellion

and his deceit of Adam and Eve. By taking on human flesh, Jesus entered the world as the promised Messiah, fulfilling God's plan of redemption foretold in Genesis 3:15, where the "seed of the woman" would crush the serpent's head. Through His sinless life, Jesus exposed the devil's lies, embodying truth and righteousness that overcame every temptation the enemy could devise (Matthew 4:1-11). His obedience revealed the path to reconcile humanity to God.

The ultimate destruction of the devil's works occurred through Jesus' death and resurrection. At the cross, Jesus bore the penalty of sin, disarming the enemy's greatest weapon, the power of sin to bring eternal death. As *Colossians 2:15* states, *"He disarmed the rulers and authorities and put them to open shame, by triumphing over them in Him."* In rising from the dead, Jesus defeated the sting of death itself, securing eternal life for those who believe in Him (1 Corinthians 15:55-57). The resurrection confirmed His authority over all creation, including Satan and his demonic forces, and inaugurated the promise of ultimate victory for all who are in Christ. By His work, Jesus ensured that the devil's grip on humanity would no longer have the final say for those who accept His salvation.

Jesus' mission to destroy the works of the devil extends to empowering His followers to resist the enemy's schemes. Through the gift of the Holy Spirit, believers are equipped to overcome sin and walk in the freedom Christ secured (Galatians 5:1). They are no longer slaves to the devil's lies but are transformed by the renewing power of God's truth (John 8:32). Moreover, Jesus' victory provides believers with spiritual armor to stand firm against the devil's schemes (Ephesians 6:10-18). The devil's works, though still active in the world, are ultimately futile in light of Christ's victory. Revelation 20:10 promises that Satan's final defeat is certain; he will be cast into the lake of fire, never to deceive or harm God's people again. Thus, Jesus' triumph not only ensures salvation but also empowers His people to live victoriously, reflecting His glory until the day of ultimate redemption.

HOLDING FAST TO OUR
CROWN OF SALVATION

The works of the devil are relentless, but Jesus has already secured victory on the cross. <u>As believers, our task is to walk in that victory by crucifying our flesh, resisting distractions, and staying vigilant in prayer.</u> The enemy's goal is to keep us from receiving our crown of salvation, whether through temptation, laziness, or distraction. But through the Holy Spirit, we are empowered to stand firm, pursue righteousness, and finish the race set before us.

The Bible exhorts us to *"hold fast what you have, that no one may take your crown" (Revelation 3:11).* This requires intentional effort, binding the spirit of distraction, crucifying sinful desires, and staying connected to God through prayer, fasting, and His Word. As we persevere, we fulfill our purpose as Ambassadors for Christ and secure the eternal reward that awaits us in heaven.

In this spiritual journey, our crown is worth the fight. Let nothing hinder your pursuit of Christ! Stay focused, stay armored, and keep chasing Yahweh! The enemy may try to deceive and distract, but through the power of Jesus, we can destroy the works of the devil and walk victoriously in the promise of eternal life.

JESUS CAME TO DESTROY THE
WORKS OF THE DEVIL

The victory of Christ on the cross is the soul- foundation of the believer's ability to overcome the works of the devil. As Jesus approached His crucifixion, He declared, *"Now is the time for judgment on this world; now the prince of this world will be driven out" (John 12:31).* On the cross, Jesus accomplished two pivotal things; He bore the penalty of our sin, and He provided us with the priceless gift of Salvation. This means that Satan no longer has the power to condemn us or influence our eternal destiny. *"There is now no condemnation for those who are in Christ Jesus" (Romans 8:1).* Beyond securing our salvation, Jesus'

victory also ensures our personal sanctification. Through the indwelling of the Holy Spirit, believers are empowered to grow in holiness and resist the devil's schemes (Ephesians 4:30). The Spirit leads us into Christlikeness, helping us crucify our flesh and align our desires with God's will. Jesus' triumph over the devil means that believers no longer have to live under the dominion of sin; they are set free to pursue righteousness.

From the very beginning, the mission of Jesus Christ was to undo the damage caused by the stain of sin committed by Adam in the Garden of Eden. In *1 John 3:8*, the apostle declares, "*The reason the Son of God appeared was to destroy the works of the devil.*" The devil's works include sin, death, and separation from God. It was the full consequences of his rebellion and his deceit of Adam and Eve. By taking on human flesh, Jesus entered the world as the Promised Messiah, fulfilling God's plan of redemption foretold in Genesis 3:15, where the "seed of the woman" would crush the serpent's head. Through His sinless life, Jesus exposed the devil's lies, embodying truth and righteousness that overcame every temptation the enemy could devise (Matthew 4:1-11). His obedience revealed the path to reconcile humanity to God.

The ultimate destruction of the devil's works occurred through Jesus' death and resurrection. At the cross, Jesus bore the penalty of sin, disarming the enemy's greatest weapon; the power of sin to bring eternal death. As *Colossians 2*:15 states, "*He disarmed the rulers and authorities and put them to open shame, by triumphing over them in Him.*" In rising from the dead, Jesus defeated the sting of death itself, securing eternal life for those who believe in Him (1 Corinthians 15:55-57). The resurrection confirmed His authority over all creation, including Satan and his demonic forces, and inaugurated the promise of ultimate victory for all who are in Christ. By His work, Jesus ensured that the devil's grip on humanity would no longer have the final say for those who accept His salvation.

Jesus' mission to destroy the works of the devil extends to empowering His followers to resist the enemy's schemes. Through the gift of the Holy Spirit, believers are equipped to overcome sin and walk in the freedom Christ secured (Galatians 5:1). They are no longer slaves to the devil's lies but are transformed by the renewing power of God's truth (John 8:32). Moreover, Jesus' victory provides believers with spiritual armor to stand firm against the devil's schemes (Ephesians 6:10-18). The devil's works, though still active in the world, are ultimately futile in light of Christ's victory. Revelation 20:10 promises that Satan's final defeat is certain; he will be cast into the lake of fire, never to deceive or harm God's people again. Thus, Jesus' triumph not only ensures salvation but also empowers His people to live victoriously, reflecting His glory until the day of ultimate redemption. Beware and know that Jesus Christ already destroyed the works of the devil and all of his demonic forces are part of the footstool of Christ the King. When he whispers lies don't be afraid to remind him of his bleak future.

Behold I'm Coming Quickly

Romans 13:12-14

Crowned for Purpose

Ephesians 1:13-14

IS YOUR LAMP FILLED WITH KINGDOM OIL

SPIRITUAL PREPAREDNESS OF CHRIST RETURN

Jesus' parable of the ten virgins (Matthew 25:1-13) offers an intense, yet fascinating illustration of spiritual readiness, drawing upon the rich symbolism embedded in traditional Jewish Galilean wedding traditions. Jesus Christ was not only Jewish, He was Galilean, closely insync with these Galilean traditions he spoke forth phrophetic parrables that intricately illistrate the "return of Christ as the Bride-Groom for His Church which is the Bride. These cultural practices are deeply interconnected to the Biblical applications intricately described in the book of Revelation, providing a tangible framework for understanding the Kingdom of Heaven. Today, exploring this historical context sheds light on the parable's, spiritual truths, emphasizing the urgency of preparation and the necessity of a genuine relationship with Jesus Christ. In the Galilean wedding tradition, the betrothal between the bridegroom and bride marked the beginning of their nuptial covenant relationship. During the betrothal ceremony, the groom would present a covenantal offer, symbolized by a shared cup of wine. If the bride accepted, it was her declaration of commitment, and she became set apart for him. This act parallels the covenant Christ offered to His Church through His sacrifice. During the Last Supper, Jesus shared the cup with His disciples, saying, "This is my blood of the covenant, which is poured

355

out for many for the forgiveness of sins" (Matthew 26:28). In accepting this covenant, believers become spiritually betrothed to Christ. After the betrothal, the bridegroom would leave to prepare a home for the bride, often an addition to his father's house. This preparation period could last up to a year, during which **the bride had to remain faithful, watchful, and ready to leave at a moment's notice.** Jesus mirrored this tradition when He told His disciples, "I go to prepare a place for you" (John 14:2). His ascension marked the beginning of this preparatory period, during which the Church, His bride, is called to readiness. The parable of the ten virgins emphasizes this waiting period, urging believers to maintain vigilance and keep their spiritual "lamps" filled.

While the bridegroom prepared the home, the bride was not idle. Her time was spent in active preparation, assembling her wedding garments, staying pure, and ensuring her lamp had enough oil for the journey to the bridegroom's home. This reflects the believer's call to *spiritual readiness*, characterized by a life of faith, obedience, and reliance on the Holy Spirit. Just as the bride did not know the exact day or hour of the groom's return, followers of Christ do not know when Christ will return. Jesus emphasized this in *Matthew 24:36, "But about that day or hour no one knows, not even the angels in heaven, nor the Son, but only the Father."* The lamp carried by the bride in the parable symbolizes faith, the outward profession of trust in Christ. However, the lamp alone is insufficient; it requires oil to produce light. The oil represents spiritual readiness, the indwelling of the Holy Spirit and the believer's spiritual vitality. This vital element cannot be bought, borrowed or substituted; it must be personally maintained through an abiding relationship with God. The wedding feast, a grand celebration following the bridegroom's return, foreshadows the Marriage Supper of the Lamb described in Revelation 19:7-9. Only those who are prepared will partake in this eternal celebration.

The Ten Virgins (Matthew 25:1-13)

In the parable of the ten virgins, Jesus outlined a detailed illustration of the Kingdom of Heaven, focusing on the ideas of readiness and preparation for His return. He compares the Kingdom to ten virgins awaiting the arrival of the bridegroom, symbolizing Christ. Each virgin has a lamp, representing their faith and spiritual life, yet their readiness is determined by one critical factor; the presence or absence of kingdom-oil. This oil, often interpreted as a metaphor for the Holy Spirit and active faith, becomes the defining difference between the wise and foolish virgins. The wise virgins bring extra oil, fully prepared for the possibility of the bridegroom's delay. Their actions reflect the foresight and diligence of true believers who live with an eternal perspective. These individuals understand the importance of maintaining a continual relationship with God, nurturing their faith through prayer, Scripture, and the guidance of the Holy Spirit. Their lamps remain lit, their readiness unwavering, no matter how long they must wait.

In contrast, the **foolish virgins** fail to bring extra oil. They carry lamps, outwardly appearing like the wise, but their lack of preparation reveals a deeper and broader complex issue; a *"hollow-superficial faith"*. Their lamps, devoid of oil, symbolize a life lacking the Holy Spirit's indwelling and the sustenance of genuine belief. When the bridegroom arrives at midnight, they are caught unprepared. In desperation, they plead with the wise to share their oil, but the wise decline, explaining there is only enough for their own lamps. This moment underscores the personal responsibility of each believer to cultivate and maintain their spiritual readiness. Faith and the Holy Spirit cannot be borrowed or transferred—they must be personally received and nurtured.

The **arrival of the bridegroom at midnight** is significant. It represents the unexpected nature of Christ's return, echoing His warning in Matthew 24:44 that no one knows the day or hour of His coming. The midnight timing also reflects life's darkest moments when faith must shine the brightest. Only the wise, with their lamps burning, can join the bridegroom in the wedding feast, a joyous celebration symbolizing eternal life and communion with Christ. The foolish virgins, on the other hand, find the door to the feast shut, and their cries of "Lord, Lord, open to us" are met with the chilling response: *"Truly, I say to you, I do not know you" (Matthew 25:12).*

This parable delivers a sobering message; outward appearances of faith are insufficient without the inward reality of readiness. The lamp alone symbolizing a profession of faith is not enough. It must be accompanied by oil, representing the sustaining presence of the Holy Spirit and an active, enduring relationship with God. Jesus concludes with a powerful exhortation; "Watch therefore, for you know neither the day nor the hour" (Matthew 25:13).

This call to vigilance and preparedness challenges every believer to reflect on their spiritual condition. Are our lamps filled with oil, and are we ready to meet the Bridegroom, or are we merely going through the motions of outward religiosity? The parable of the ten virgins serves as both an encouragement and a warning, urging us to live with intentionality and anticipation of Christ's return.

Illuminating Spiritual Realities

The Lamp:

> ➤ Represents faith, the visible aspect of a believer's relationship with Christ. A lamp without oil is like a profession of faith without spiritual substance empty and incapable of producing light.

The Oil:

> ➤ Symbolizes the Holy Spirit, who empowers and sustains believers.
> ➤ It also signifies spiritual preparedness and vitality, cultivated through prayer, worship, and obedience.

The Wedding Feast:

> ➤ Represents the joyous union of Christ and His Church at His return.
> ➤ It is the ultimate fulfillment of God's promise of eternal life and communion with Him.
>
> These scriptural imagery reinforces and emphasize the importance of readiness. Just as the bride needed oil to light her lamp and navigate the journey to the groom's home, believers need the Holy Spirit to guide and sustain them through life's trials and uncertainties.

READINESS BEGINS WITH SALVATION

Spiritual readiness begins with the foundational act of accepting Christ's covenant. Without this "yes" to His offer of salvation, there is no oil to sustain the lamp. Salvation is the starting point, but the parable makes it clear that readiness is not a one-time decision it is an ongoing process. The wise virgins demonstrate this through their foresight in bringing extra oil, signifying a continual reliance on the Holy Spirit and a commitment to living in alignment with God's will.

The foolish virgins, on the other hand, carried lamps but brought no oil, revealing a superficial faith. Their outward appearance of readiness masked an inward lack of preparation. When the bridegroom arrived, they were unprepared and ultimately excluded from the wedding feast. This stark contrast serves as a sobering reminder that mere external religiosity is insufficient and obsolete. Genuine faith requires an inward transformation, marked by the indwelling of the Holy Spirit, repentance, compassion and a life of obedience.

Jesus concludes the parable with the exhortation, *"Watch therefore, for you know neither the day nor the hour" (Matthew 25:13).* This warning underscores the unpredictable nature of His return and the necessity of living each day with intentionality. Believers are called to examine their spiritual lives regularly; Is their faith vibrant and alive, or are they merely carrying empty lamps? The Galilean wedding tradition, with its emphasis on preparation and expectation, provides a powerful blueprint for understanding this call to vigilance.

The imagery of the bridegroom's unexpected return challenges readers to evaluate their relationship with Christ. Are they living in joyful anticipation of His return, or have they become complacent? By exploring the cultural context of the Galilean wedding and its parallels to the believer's journey regarding Jesus Christ Return for His Bride (His-Church), this context from a biblical perspective lays a strong foundation for understanding the parable's spiritual implications. It reminds us that readiness is not about fear but about cultivating a deep, abiding love for the Bridegroom and a joyful anticipation of the eternal union that awaits.

THE TEN VIRGINS: CRUCIAL LESSONS ON PREPAREDNESS

The parable of the ten virgins (Matthew 25:1-13) is more than a story; it is a important call to every believer about the urgency of "living in spiritual readiness". By the examples of the wise and foolish virgins, Jesus illustrates the vital importance of faith ***that is not only professed but sustained***. This section dives into the characteristics of the wise virgins, who exemplify spiritual vigilance, and contrasts them with the foolish virgins, whose complacency leads to devastating consequences.

THE WISE VIRGINS LIVING IN READINESS

The five wise virgins in the parable represent believers who embody true spiritual readiness. They are prepared not just for the initial stages of faith but for the entire journey, even when delays or challenges arise. Their actions teach us four key principles for maintaining readiness. Walking in Righteousness (Philippians 1:11) Righteousness is living in alignment with God's will, a life marked by integrity, obedience, and fruitfulness. Just as oil sustains a lamp's flame, righteousness sustains the light of faith. The wise virgins

symbolize those who live daily in a manner that reflects God's character. Walking in righteousness is not passive but an intentional effort to grow in godliness, pursue holiness, and display the fruit of the Spirit. It is evidence of a faith that is active and alive.

FILLED WITH THE HOLY SPIRIT (EPHESIANS 5:18)

The oil in the parable represents the Holy Spirit, who empowers, fills, and sustains believers. Without the Holy Spirit, the "lamp" of faith is empty and unable to produce light. The wise virgins' extra oil signifies their continual reliance on the Holy Spirit. Believers must engage in daily practices prayer, worship, and surrender that invites' the Holy Spirit's presence into every aspect of their lives. Being filled with the Holy Spirit is not a one-time event but an ongoing relationship. Just as a lamp needs regular refueling, believers must continually seek the Spirit's guidance, strength, and renewal. Guarding the Heart (Proverbs 4:23) Proverbs 4:23 describes the heart as the wellspring of life, influencing every action and decision. Guarding it as essential for maintaining spiritual vigilance. The wise virgins' preparedness reflects their ability to stay focused on their purpose, avoiding distractions that could lead them astray. Believers must actively protect their hearts through Scripture, prayer, and accountability, ensuring they remain aligned with God's purposes.

Enduring Trials (James 1:2-4)

Refining Faith: Trials are an inevitable part of the believer's journey. Like the wise virgins who prepared for delays, believers must view trials as opportunities to strengthen their faith and develop perseverance. The delay of the bridegroom tests the virgins' readiness, mirroring how life's challenges test the endurance of our faith. Embrace trials as refining tools, trusting God to use them for His glory and your growth. Let perseverance deepen your readiness for the Bridegroom's arrival. The wise virgins exemplify the principle of "active waiting," living in a state of constant readiness and expectation. Their actions highlight the necessity of a faith that is not only professed but practiced, sustained by righteousness, the Holy Spirit, vigilance, and perseverance.

THE FOOLISH VIRGINS: A WARNING AGAINST COMPLACENCY

The five foolish virgins provide a stark contrast, representing those who may outwardly appear prepared but lack the inward substance necessary for readiness. Their story serves as a cautionary tale, warning believers of the dangers of superficial faith.

Superficial Faith

Empty Lamps: The foolish virgins' lamps symbolize a faith that is shallow and unprepared. Outwardly, they carry lamps, but without oil, their profession of faith is hollow. Their failure to bring oil reveals their neglect of an active relationship with God. They rely on appearances rather than substance, leaving them unprepared for the bridegroom's arrival. True readiness requires an inward transformation and continual dependence on the Holy Spirit. Superficial faith will not sustain in times of testing.

The Chilling Consequences

Eternal Exclusion from the Wedding Feast: When the bridegroom arrives, the foolish virgins' lack of preparation excludes them from the celebration. The closed door symbolizes the finality of judgment. These haunting words from the bridegroom in <u>Matthew 25:12 emphasize the tragedy of a life lived without true **relationship** or **readiness**</u>. It is not enough to appear ready; the bridegroom must know the bride personally on an intimate relationship to cultivate a meaningful spiritual relationship. This warning urges believers to examine their faith deeply, ensuring it is genuine and sustained. Salvation cannot be borrowed or postponed; it must be embraced and nurtured today.

LIVING LIFE AS A WISE VIRGIN

The parable of the ten virgins should compel every believer to thoughtfully examine their spiritual readiness and take intentional, proactive steps to remain vigilant for the Bridegroom's return. Let this be your call to action. The wise virgins bring extra oil, showing that they were prepared for the wait and the unknown timing of the bridegroom's arrival. This preparedness is likened to a believer who is Rapture-Ready for Christ return!

Self-Reflection with a Kingdom Purpose

Heart Check: Are you truly prepared to meet the Bridegroom, or is your faith merely a façade? Take inventory of your spiritual condition.

The Lamp of Faith: Is your lamp burning brightly with the oil of intimacy with Christ, or are you running dangerously low? Genuine readiness flows from a deep, personal relationship with Jesus.

- ✓ Are you truly prepared for the Bridegroom's return, or is your faith superficial?
- ✓ Is your lamp burning brightly, fueled by a genuine relationship with Christ, or is it running low on oil?

Act with Commitment

Daily Devotion: Make spiritual disciplines like prayer, Scripture meditation, worship, and fellowship a daily priority. These practices replenish your oil and keep your faith vibrant.

Spirit-Filled Living: Actively seek the infilling of the Holy Spirit each day, allowing Him to renew, empower, and guide your every step. Let Him illuminate your path and stoke the flame of devotion in your heart.

- ✓ Commit to daily spiritual disciplines that sustain your faith, such as prayer, Scripture reading, and worship.
- ✓ Seek the Holy Spirit's filling each day, allowing Him to empower and guide you.

Examine with Vigilance

Eliminate Obstacles: Identify anything, distractions, temptations, or unconfessed sin, that threatens to dim or extinguish your light. Be ruthless in removing these barriers.

Guard Your Focus: Protect your heart and mind by anchoring your gaze on Christ. Regularly remind yourself of His promises and the glory of His return. Let your hope in Him fuel your perseverance.

- ✓ Identify and remove distractions, temptations, or sin that threaten to extinguish your light.
- ✓ Guard your heart, ensuring that your focus remains on Christ and His promises.

A CALL TO READINESS

The wise and foolish virgins embody two distinct approaches to faith, resilience and wisdom. The wise show us the beauty and necessity of living in readiness, walking in righteousness, relying on the Spirit, guarding the heart, and persevering through trials. The foolish remind us of the dangers of complacency, where appearances mask a lack of true preparation, possessing a form of Godliness denying the power thereof.

This parable invites every believer to live with urgency and expectation, cultivating a bold confidence that endures and shines brightly until the Bridegroom comes. Will you be among the wise, ready and filled with oil, or among the foolish, left outside when the door closes? The choice is yours, but the time to act is now.

The wise virgins were prepared because they understood the value of readiness and the cost of neglect. Be vigilant, for the Bridegroom is coming at an hour no one expects. Let your light shine brightly, fully fueled by an unshakable faith and unwavering devotion to Christ. **Be ready. Be steadfast. Be wise.**

JESUS CHRIST THE BRIDEGROOM'S RETURN: THE MIDNIGHT RETURN

The bridegroom returning at midnight in the parable of the ten virgins is both astonishing and sobering. It captures the unexpected nature of Jesus Christ's second coming and the critical need for believers to remain spiritually awake and prepared. The midnight arrival challenges us to live with a constant heart of expectancy, ready to respond to the call of the Bridegroom whenever it comes. The Bridegroom's return at midnight in the parable of the ten virgins highlights the unexpected nature of Christ's second coming. It emphasizes the need for believers to maintain a constant state of spiritual readiness and be fully prepared for His arrival. It highlights unexpected nature of the anticipated second coming of Jesus Christ. It underscores the urgency for believers to live in a state of perpetual readiness, spiritually awake and fully prepared for His arrival. Jesus emphasizes the uncertainty of His return in *Matthew 24:36; "But about that day or hour no one knows, not even the angels in heaven, nor the Son, but only the Father."* The arrival of the bridegroom at midnight mirrors this unpredictability. The late hour also symbolizes life's darkest moments, times when faith is most tested, and the need for spiritual vigilance is at its peak.

Spiritual Watchfulness

Midnight represents the hour of deepest darkness when the world least expects His return. It is a symbolic wake-up call for the Church, urging us not to be lulled into spiritual slumber or complacency. Just as the cry rang out in the parable, "Here is the bridegroom! Come out to meet him!" (Matthew 25:6), so too will the announcement of Christ's return pierce through the stillness, separating the ready from the unprepared. Believers are called to remain spiritually awoke, alert to the signs of the times, and ready for Christ's return. This watchfulness is not passive but active, involving prayer, study of Scripture, and a daily walk with the Holy Spirit. The ten virgins all began with lamps, but only the wise, who carried extra oil, were prepared for the delay and the call at midnight. Their readiness highlights the importance of perseverance and spiritual diligence. The midnight arrival challenges every believer to embrace a heart of expectancy, living each day as though the Bridegroom could return at any moment. This anticipation isn't born of fear but of love, a longing to meet the One who has redeemed us, clothed us in righteousness, and promised us eternal union with Him. To be ready for the midnight call is to cultivate a life filled with the oil of the Holy Spirit, fueling our faith, illuminating our path, and keeping our lamps burning brightly. It requires vigilance, intentionality, and reliance on God's grace to endure. The bridegroom's arrival shall be heralded by a shout and a trumpet blast, a direct parallel to the rapture described in (*1 Thessalonians 4:16*); *"For the Lord himself will come down from heaven, with a loud command, with the voice of the archangel and with the trumpet call of God."* This moment signals the gathering of believers to the wedding feast of the Lamb (Revelation 19:7-9).

The Shout: The announcement of the bridegroom's arrival symbolizes Christ's call to His Church. It is an awakening moment for those who are ready and a startling reality for those who are not.

The Trumpet: In biblical tradition, the trumpet often signals momentous events, such as the gathering of God's people or the arrival of a king. Here, it serves as a divine summons, urging readiness and calling believers into eternal fellowship with Christ.

Illuminating the Light of Spiritual Realities

Bride Groom Midnight Arrival

➤ Symbolizes the darkest hour when faith must shine its brightest. It is a time when distractions and doubts could easily extinguish the light of faith, yet the wise virgins remain prepared, their lamps burning brightly with the oil of the Holy Spirit.

➤ In life's "midnights", times of hardship, uncertainty, and waiting, our spiritual readiness is tested most intensely. The wise virgins demonstrate the endurance and faith required to navigate these moments.

The Shout and Trumpet

➤ The shout represents the voice of Christ calling His Church to Himself, a moment of awakening for those ready to meet Him.

➤ The trumpet parallels the rapture call, reminding believers that readiness is non-negotiable. It is not a matter of if Christ will return **but when**, and only those prepared will hear and respond to this call.

Living in Expectancy

The parable and its midnight setting challenge us to evaluate our spiritual lives and live with an attitude of readiness. Jesus' return will come without warning, and the stakes are eternal. Here's how we can apply these truths:

CULTIVATE A FIXED HEART OF EXPECTANCY

Live Each Day as if Christ Could Return: Make every moment count. Expectancy is not fear-based but joy-filled, rooted in the anticipation of being united with the Bridegroom.

Stay Spiritually Awake: Avoid spiritual complacency by actively engaging with God through prayer, worship, and Scripture. Watchfulness is a posture of faith, not passivity.

Seek Intimacy with the Holy Spirit: The oil of the Holy Spirit is essential for navigating life's challenges and remaining steadfast in faith. Seek His presence daily, allowing Him to guide your thoughts, decisions, and actions.

Daily Renewal: Like a lamp needing regular refueling, your faith requires consistent renewal through spiritual disciplines. Intimacy with the Holy Spirit ensures your lamp burns brightly, even in the darkest hour.

Embrace Waiting as Refinement: Just as the virgins waited for the bridegroom, believers must endure periods of waiting and delays, trusting that God's timing is perfect.

Keep the Flame Alive: Trials and hardships can dim the flame of faith, but through perseverance and reliance on God, believers can remain steadfast.

THE ETERNAL JOY A BENEFIT OF READINESS

For the wise virgins, the midnight call was not a moment of fear but one of joy. Their preparation allowed them to follow the bridegroom to the wedding feast, symbolizing eternal union with Christ. This scene reflects the glorious promise of Revelation 19:7-9: "Let us rejoice and be glad and give him glory! For the wedding of the Lamb has come, and his bride has made herself ready." For believers today, this promise serves as a source of hope and motivation. The assurance of the wedding feast should inspire us to live in readiness, not as a burden but as a privilege. Our preparation is an act of love, a response to the Bridegroom's invitation.

The Bridegroom's midnight arrival serves as both a warning and an invitation. It reminds us of the unpredictable nature of Christ's return

and the necessity of being spiritually awake and prepared. Just as the wise virgins carried extra oil and kept their lamps burning, we must cultivate a vibrant, Spirit-filled faith that endures through delays and hardships. Let this parable ignite a renewed sense of urgency in your walk with Christ. **Live each day as if the shout and trumpet could sound at any moment.** Let your lamp burn brightly, filled with the oil of the Holy Spirit, so that when the Bridegroom comes, you are ready to follow Him into the joy of the eternal wedding feast. The question is not whether Christ will return, it is whether we **will be ready when He does**.

In the parable of the ten virgins (Matthew 25:1-13), oil holds a central and symbolic role, representing the spiritual readiness essential for entering the Kingdom of Heaven. Drawing from the Galilean wedding tradition, Jesus uses the imagery of lamps fueled by oil to emphasize the necessity of being prepared for His return. This oil, a metaphor for the Holy Spirit, becomes a defining factor in whether a believer is ready to meet the Bridegroom or left outside the wedding feast. Understanding the significance of oil in both cultural and spiritual contexts unveils a deeper appreciation for the indwelling and work of the Holy Spirit in the believer's life.

GALILEAN TRADITION:
THE PRACTICAL NEED FOR OIL

The Galilean tradition and the practical need for oil was of utmost importance. In Galilean weddings, the bride's procession to the groom's home often took place at night. Oil lamps were not just symbolic; they were practical, providing light to navigate the darkness and illuminating the bride's path. Without oil, the lamps would go out, leaving the bride and her party unable to follow the groom. The wise virgins in the parable understood this and brought extra oil, while the foolish virgins, lacking foresight, were unprepared when the groom arrived.

The need for oil in these ancient traditions parallels the believer's need for spiritual preparation. Just as the bride's lamp guided her through the night, the Holy Spirit illuminates the path of the believer, offering guidance, sustenance, and endurance until the return of Christ. Without the "oil" of the Spirit, faith falters, leaving the individual unprepared for the challenges and uncertainties of life and ultimately, for the Bridegroom's arrival. Oil in Scripture frequently symbolizes the Holy Spirit, whose indwelling empowers, sustains, and prepares believers for Christ's return. In the parable, the wise virgins' extra oil signifies their continual reliance on the Spirit. They understood that readiness is not a one-time act but a daily, ongoing relationship with God. The Holy Spirit plays a crucial role in this process. The extra oil carried by the wise virgins symbolizes their continual dependence on the Holy Spirit. They understood that spiritual readiness isn't a one-time decision but a daily, ongoing relationship with God. The Holy Spirit is central to this process, equipping believers to live faithfully as they await the Bridegroom's return.

Empowerment for Daily Victory

> The Holy Spirit empowers believers to live lives that align with God's will, enabling them to overcome sin, resist temptation, and persevere through trials.

> Without the Spirit's strength, the "lamp" of faith falters and dims, leaving the believer vulnerable to spiritual weariness. As *Zechariah 4:6 reminds us: "Not by might nor by power, but by My Spirit," says the Lord Almighty.*

Sustenance for Spiritual Vitality

> Just as oil keeps a lamp burning, the Holy Spirit sustains the believer's inner life, renewing and refreshing their heart daily.

> In seasons of waiting, difficulty, or spiritual dryness, the Spirit breathes new life into weary souls, ensuring that faith remains vibrant. *Isaiah 40:31 promises: "But those who hope in the Lord will renew their strength."*

Preparation for Christ's Return

> ➤ The Holy Spirit actively prepares believers for the Bridegroom's coming by convicting them of sin, guiding them into all truth, and shaping their character to reflect Christ.

> ➤ This process of sanctification ensures that they are ready and blameless when He appears. As Ephesians 5:27 declares, Christ will present His Church "without stain or wrinkle or any other blemish, but holy and blameless."

Carrying "extra oil" signifies a heart fully reliant on God, a heart that daily seeks the Spirit's guidance, strength, and renewal. It is a commitment to live intentionally, keeping the flame of faith alive through communion with the Spirit. Are you cultivating a reservoir of oil that will sustain your faith through life's uncertainties? Embrace the Holy Spirit's work in your life, allowing Him to empower, sustain, and prepare you for the glorious day when the Bridegroom returns.

Old Testament Symbolism: Oil As God's Presence and Blessing

> ➤ In the Old Testament, oil held deep symbolic significance as a representation of God's presence and favor. Anointing oil was used to consecrate individuals and objects for sacred purposes, marking them as set apart for God. This act signified divine approval, empowerment, and blessing, underscoring the spiritual connection between the anointed and the presence of God. The significance of oil in biblical tradition begins in the Old Testament, where anointing oil was used to consecrate people and objects for holy purposes, symbolizing God's presence and blessing.

Priestly Anointing (Exodus 30:25-29):

God commanded Moses to anoint the tabernacle and its furnishings with sacred oil, setting them apart as holy. This act signified that these items were dedicated to God's service, carrying His presence and blessing. Similarly, the anointing of priests, prophets, and kings with oil represented their divine calling and the empowerment of the Spirit for their roles.

Zechariah's Vision (Zechariah 4:6):

In a vision of a golden lampstand fed by a continuous flow of oil, God declares, "Not by might nor by power, but by my Spirit." This imagery reinforces that the oil represents the Spirit's power in accomplishing God's purposes, not human effort.

For believers, this Old Testament imagery of oil distinctively highlights that the Spirit's oil distinguishes us, empowers us for God's work, and guarantees His constant presence.

THE HOLY-SPIRIT- ADVOCATE , GUIDING BELIEVERS UNTO ETERNAL LIFE.

In the New Testament, the Holy Spirit is revealed as the divine seal and guarantee of salvation, a pledge of the believer's eternal inheritance. Through His indwelling, the Holy Spirit confirms God's ownership of His people and assures them of the fulfillment of His promises. *Ephesians 1:13-14 declares, "When you believed, you were marked in Him with a seal, the promised Holy Spirit, who is a deposit guaranteeing our inheritance until the redemption of those who are God's possession."* This guarantee is not merely a future hope but an active, present reality, empowering, sanctifying, and guiding believers as they live out their faith in anticipation of eternal life.

Seal of Belonging (Romans 8:9):

➤ Paul teaches that anyone without the Spirit of Christ "does not belong to Him." The Spirit's indwelling is the defining mark of a true believer, ensuring that their faith is genuine and alive.

Guarantee of Eternal Life (Ephesians 1:13-14):

> ➢ Paul describes the Spirit as the deposit guaranteeing our inheritance. This assurance of eternal life is likened to the wise virgins' extra oil, evidence of their preparation and readiness for the Bridegroom's return.

Without the Holy Spirit, there is no assurance of salvation or readiness for Christ's return. The foolish virgins, lacking oil, stand as a sobering warning against neglecting the essential relationship with the Holy Spirit, a relationship that sustains and fuels faith. The Holy Spirit's role is multifaceted. He seals believers as God's own, empowers them to live victoriously over sin, and prepares their hearts for the Bridegroom's coming. His presence is the divine source of spiritual vitality, ensuring that the flame of faith burns brightly even in seasons of waiting. Without Him, believers risk spiritual emptiness and unpreparedness, just as the foolish virgins were left outside when the Bridegroom arrived.

A Personal Relationship with the Holy Spirit

The parable of the ten virgins emphasizes the necessity of a **personal** and **active** relationship with the Holy Spirit. Just as oil was vital for keeping the lamps burning, the Holy Spirit is essential for illuminating the believer's journey, sustaining their faith, and ensuring their readiness for Christ's return.

Illuminating the Path

> ➢ The Holy Spirit provides wisdom, discernment, and guidance, enabling believers to navigate the spiritual darkness of the world.
> ➢ He reveals God's truth, leading them in righteousness and aligning their steps with God's will. As Psalm 119:105 declares, *"Your word is a lamp to my feet and a light to my path."*

Sustaining Faith

- ➢ In moments of trial, delay, or weariness, the Spirit strengthens and comforts believers, ensuring their "lamps" of faith remain lit.
- ➢ He is the source of perseverance and hope, empowering them to remain watchful and steadfast as they await the Bridegroom's arrival.

Ensuring Readiness

- ➢ The Holy Spirit sanctifies believers, transforming their hearts and conforming them to the image of Christ.
- ➢ This preparation demands intentionality, daily surrender through prayer, immersion in Scripture, and obedience to God's Word. Through this, the Spirit readies them to stand blameless before Christ at His coming.

A life fully reliant on the Holy Spirit is essential, especially in the perilous times of the last days. The Spirit's presence brings light to navigate the deepening spiritual darkness, strength to endure trials, and expectancy rooted in the hope of Christ's return. Without the Holy Spirit, there is no true readiness for the Bridegroom; faith falters, discernment declines, and hearts grow cold. With Him, however, believers are empowered to stand firm, their faith sustained, and their path illuminated by divine truth. The Spirit prepares, purifies, and positions God's people for eternal joy in the presence of the Lord, ensuring they are found faithful at His coming. The oil in the parable of the ten virgins represents far more than preparation, it represents the life-giving, empowering, and sustaining work of the Holy Spirit. Without the Spirit, faith is empty and incapable of enduring the trials and waiting periods that define the believer's journey. Just as the wise virgins carried extra oil, believers must cultivate an ongoing, Spirit-filled relationship with God, ensuring they are ready to meet the Bridegroom when He comes.

The question is not whether the Bridegroom will return but whether we will have oil in our lamps when He does. Are you walking in step with the Spirit, allowing Him to guide, sustain, and prepare you for Christ's return? The time to fill your lamp is now.

THE WEDDING FEAST: THE JOY OF BEING FOUND READY

The parable of the ten virgins (Matthew 25:1-13) accentuates the ultimate goal of the bride and groom's journey, the long-awaited wedding feast. This grand celebration is more than just an event; it embodies the culmination of their covenant relationship, marked by unparalleled joy, unity, and fulfillment. In the Galilean wedding tradition, the feast was the pinnacle of the entire process, a jubilant gathering where the bride and groom's union was not only celebrated but affirmed by the community. Spiritually, this wedding feast serves as a vital foreshadowing of the ultimate union between Christ and His Church at the Wedding Supper of the Lamb (Revelation 19:7-9). It represents the fulfillment of God's eternal plan, where the Bridegroom (Jesus Christ) rejoices over His Bride (The Faithful Church & Kingdom Believers), and the redeemed enter into everlasting communion with Him. This imagery emphasizes the beauty of divine intimacy, the shared joy of redemption, and the eternal satisfaction found in the presence of the Lord. For believers, it is a reminder to remain watchful and prepared, ensuring they are counted among those invited to this glorious celebration.

In Galilean weddings, the reunion of the bride and groom marked the beginning of the wedding feast. The groom, having prepared a place for his bride, returned to bring her to his father's house, where the celebration would take place. This feast was not a brief gathering; it was an extended celebration lasting several days, filled with joy, laughter, music, and fellowship. The bride's readiness was essential because only those who were prepared could enter the groom's house and partake in the feast. Once the doors were shut, no one else could enter.

➤ **The Bridegroom's Preparation:** The groom's return for his bride reflects Christ's promise to return for His Church after preparing a place for them (John 14:2-3).

➤ **The Bride's Readiness:** The bride's preparation mirrors the believer's call to live in readiness, ensuring they are spiritually prepared to join Christ when He comes.

For those invited to the Galilean wedding feast, it was a moment of overwhelming joy, a time of unity, fellowship, and celebration. This earthly tradition serves as a powerful image of the eternal joy awaiting believers who are prepared for Christ's return.

The wedding feast in the parable points to the heavenly celebration described in *Revelation 19:7-9: "Let us rejoice and be glad and give him glory! For the wedding of the Lamb has come, and his bride has made herself ready. Fine linen, bright and clean, was given her to wear."* This event, known as the Wedding Supper of the Lamb, represents the eternal union of Christ and His Church, a moment when all of God's promises are fulfilled, and the faithful enter into everlasting joy and communion with Him.

The Bridegroom's Return and Gathering of His Bride:

➤ Just as the Galilean groom gathered his bride, Christ will return to gather His Church. This moment, heralded by the shout and trumpet call, marks the beginning of eternal joy for those who are ready (1 Thessalonians 4:16-17).

➤ The bride's preparation, symbolized by fine linen, reflects the righteousness of the saints, those who have lived faithfully, keeping their "lamps" filled with the oil of the Holy Spirit.

The Joy of Eternal Communion:

➤ The Wedding Supper of the Lamb is the ultimate celebration of God's redemptive plan. It signifies the culmination of His covenant relationship with His people, a time of perfect unity and fellowship.

➤ This eternal feast contrasts sharply with the exclusion experienced by the foolish virgins, who are left outside the closed door. Their unpreparedness robs them of the joy and fellowship they could have shared.

Anticipating the Wedding Feast with Joy

The parable of the ten virgins carries a sobering call to readiness, but at its heart, it points to the joy of being found prepared for the Bridegroom's arrival. <u>Readiness is not driven by fear of exclusion but by the joyful anticipation of eternal communion with Christ.</u> This anticipation should permeate every aspect of a believer's life, shaping their priorities and actions.

Readiness as a Response to Love

➤ The bride's preparation was motivated by her love for the groom and her longing to be with him. Similarly, a believer's readiness should flow from a deep and abiding love for Christ, not from a sense of duty or fear.

➤ "We love because He first loved us" (1 John 4:19). This love inspires a life of holiness, obedience, and devotion, aligning the believer's heart with God's will. As Jesus said, "If you love me, keep my commands" (John 14:15).

Joyful Anticipation

➤ The promise of the Wedding Supper of the Lamb (Revelation 19:7-9) fills believers with hope and excitement, transforming the waiting period into a time of active growth and preparation.

➤ This future reality gives present trials meaning, encouraging perseverance and focus. *"But if we hope for what we do not yet have, we wait for it patiently" (Romans 8:25).* Joyful anticipation fuels a life of worship and gratitude, as believers look forward to eternal communion with their Savior.

The parable challenges believers to live with an eternal perspective, prioritizing the things of God over the fleeting distractions of this world. As Paul writes, *"Set your minds on things above, not on earthly things" (Colossians 3:2).* Readiness is about cultivating a relationship with Christ, allowing His Spirit to prepare the heart for His return. The temporary concerns of this life pale in comparison to the glory of eternity, making it vital to remain steadfast and watchful. *"Therefore, keep watch, because you do not know the day or the hour" (Matthew 25:13).*

Anticipating the Wedding Feast with joy transforms readiness into a response of love, a pursuit of holiness, and a declaration of trust in God's promises. This joyful expectancy encourages believers to embrace their waiting season as an opportunity to grow closer to Christ, reflecting His love and preparing for the day when they will enter into eternal joy with their Bridegroom.

While the wedding feast represents joy and fulfillment for the wise virgins, it also underscores the consequences of unpreparedness for the foolish virgins. The closed door and the groom's chilling words, *"I do not know you,"* serve as a stark reminder of the finality of judgment. For those who are found ready, the feast is a celebration of grace and reward; for those who are not, it is a moment of eternal loss. The account of the ten virgins reveals both the joy of inclusion and the devastating loss of exclusion. For the wise virgins, the wedding feast is the ultimate celebration of grace, reward, and eternal communion with the Bridegroom. Yet, for the foolish virgins, the closed door and the solemn words, *"I do not know you" (Matthew 25:12),* underscore the sobering reality of unpreparedness and the finality of divine judgment. This stark contrast is a powerful reminder: readiness is not optional, it is eternal.

LIVING FOR THE <u>INVITATION TO THE WEDDING FEAST</u>

➢ Readiness should not be viewed as a burdensome obligation but as a joyful privilege and an expression of love for the Bridegroom. Celebrate the opportunity to prepare for the greatest reunion in history. Let your anticipation of His return fill your heart with hope and your actions with purpose.

➢ *"Rejoice in the Lord always. I will say it again: Rejoice!" (Philippians 4:4).*

<u>Focus on Spiritual Preparation</u>

➢ Just as the bride diligently prepared her wedding garments and ensured her lamp remained lit, believers must cultivate a daily relationship with Christ. Through prayer, worship, and the study of God's Word, faith is sustained, and hearts are refined.

➢ *"Therefore, as God's chosen people, holy and dearly loved, clothe yourselves with compassion, kindness, humility, gentleness, and patience" (Colossians 3:12).*

<u>Live with Expectancy</u>

➢ The promise of the Wedding Supper of the Lamb (Revelation 19:7-9) is a source of unwavering hope, inspiring believers to live faithfully and persevere through trials and distractions. This expectancy transforms the waiting period into a time of active preparation and enduring joy.

➢ *"Let us hold unswervingly to the hope we profess, for He who promised is faithful" (Hebrews 10:23).*

THE ETERNAL CELEBRATION AWAITS

The wedding parable gives an intricate glimpse into the eternal joy and glory awaiting those who are found ready for the Bridegroom's arrival. The Wedding Supper of the Lamb (Revelation 19:7-9) is not merely a celebration; it is the culmination of God's redemptive plan, a moment of ultimate fulfillment, unity, and unbroken communion with Christ, the Bridegroom. To be invited to this feast signifies acceptance, belonging, and the reward of faithfulness. It is a declaration that the believer's journey of faith has led to the eternal presence of God, where sorrow, pain, and separation are no more. Being invited to the wedding feast is crucial because it confirms the believer's relationship with Christ. It is the eternal affirmation that they are part of His bride, the Church, and heirs to His kingdom. This invitation is not about human merit but about living in readiness, sustained by a genuine, ongoing relationship with the Holy Spirit. The oil-filled lamps symbolize this preparedness, a heart devoted to Christ and a life aligned with His will.

The importance of readiness lies in the reality that this feast is the gateway to eternal joy. Once the door is shut, there is no second invitation. The Bridegroom's arrival will be sudden, and only those prepared will enter into the eternal celebration. As Jesus warned in *Matthew 25:13, "Therefore keep watch, because you do not know the day or the hour."*

The question is not whether the feast will happen but whether you will be ready to enter when the Bridegroom comes.

Are your lamps filled with kingdom oil? Are you living with joyful anticipation, letting the promise of the wedding feast shape your priorities, decisions, and devotion? Let the certainty of this eternal celebration inspire you to live every day in readiness, fueled by love and hope, so that when the Bridegroom's call comes, you may enter with joy and join the celebration that will never end.

CONSEQUENCES OF BEING UNPREPARED: THE CLOSED DOOR AND THE FINALITY OF JUDGMENT

Matthew 25:10-12 expresses a sobering symbol of the irreversible nature of divine judgment. For the foolish virgins, their unpreparedness led to exclusion from the wedding feast, signifying eternal separation from God. The Bridegroom's chilling declaration, "I do not know you," highlights that readiness is not merely about external appearances or good intentions but about cultivating a genuine, ongoing relationship with Christ. **This moment underscores the finality of judgment, there are no second chances after the door is shut.** It is a call for every believer to live with vigilance and urgency, ensuring their hearts are aligned with God and their lamps are filled with the oil of faith and devotion. For those who neglect this readiness, the cost is eternal, and the opportunity to prepare is only available now.

The parable serves not only as a call to spiritual readiness but also as a sobering warning about the eternal consequences of unpreparedness. While the five wise virgins enter the wedding feast with the bridegroom, the five foolish virgins are met with devastating exclusion. Their failure to prepare reveals the dangers of superficial faith and complacency. This section unpacks the parable's warnings, highlighting the gravity of being unprepared for Christ's return and the finality of judgment.

Jesus describes the tragic moment when the foolish virgins, having gone to purchase oil, return to find the door to the wedding feast shut. This representation is rich with meaning, symbolizing the irreversible nature of God's judgment. The closed door emphasizes that the opportunity for salvation is now, in this life, and once Christ returns, that window will be sealed forever.

The parable underscores the urgency of readiness. The foolish virgins' lack of preparation cost them their place in the wedding feast, and their cries of "Lord, Lord, open to us" (Matthew 25:11) go unanswered. This mirrors other warnings in Scripture, such as Hebrews 2:3: "How shall we escape if we ignore so great a salvation?". The door's closure symbolizes the finality of Christ's judgment. Just as Noah's ark's door was shut before the flood, leaving those outside to face destruction (Genesis 7:16), the door to the wedding feast represents the point of no return. The foolish virgins' plight illustrates that readiness cannot be borrowed or achieved at the last moment. Their scramble for oil is futile because spiritual preparation requires consistent and intentional effort throughout one's life. Salvation cannot be postponed or presumed. Believers must act today to ensure their hearts and lives are aligned with God's will. The closed door also signifies eternal separation from God. Those outside the feast are not just excluded from the celebration but are cut off from the Bridegroom Himself. This is the ultimate consequence of unpreparedness; being forever separated from the joy and presence of Christ.

THE WORDS "I DO NOT KNOW YOU": THE CONSEQUENCES OF ARTIFICIAL FAITH

Perhaps the most chilling moment in the parable comes in *Matthew 25:12,* when the bridegroom responds to the foolish virgins' pleas with the words, *"Truly, I say to you, I do not know you."* This statement reveals the heart of the issue: the foolish virgins' lack of readiness was not just a logistical failure but a relational one. Their unpreparedness reflected a deeper issue, the absence of a genuine relationship with the bridegroom.

The Delusion of Artificial Faith

> ➤ The foolish virgins carried lamps, outwardly appearing like the wise virgins, but without oil, their lamps were useless. This symbolizes a faith that is external and superficial, lacking the sustaining presence of the Holy Spirit.

> ➤ Their plight serves as a warning to those who may profess faith in Christ but lack the inward transformation and ongoing relationship with Him that true faith requires.
> *Faith must be genuine and enduring, not just an outward display of religiosity. Believers must examine their hearts to ensure their faith is alive and rooted in Christ.*

The Danger of Complacency

> ➤ The foolish virgins' unpreparedness reflects a complacent attitude, one that assumes there is always more time to make things right. This complacency blinds them to the urgency of spiritual readiness.
> *Complacency can manifest as neglecting prayer, Scripture, and fellowship with God, leading to a faith that withers and dies.*

A Relationship Rooted in Sincere Love & Intimacy

The bridegroom's words, "I do not know you," reflect the absence of a personal, intimate relationship. In John 10:14, Jesus describes Himself as the Good Shepherd who knows His sheep, and His sheep know Him. The absence of this relationship is the ultimate tragedy of the foolish virgins' unpreparedness.

A personal relationship with Christ is the foundation of readiness. Without it, all outward appearances of faith are meaningless.

The parable concludes with a powerful exhortation in Matthew 25:13: "Watch therefore, for you know neither the day nor the hour in which the Son of Man is coming", This command emphasizes the unpredictability of Christ's return and the necessity of living in constant readiness.

Readiness Is a Daily Commitment

> ➤ Spiritual readiness requires ongoing effort, daily prayer, Scripture study, and seeking the guidance of the Holy Spirit.

It is a lifestyle of faith and obedience, not a last-minute decision.

Readiness is not about perfection but persistence. It is about living each day with the intention of being prepared for Christ's return.

The Opportunity Is Now

➤ The foolish virgins' greatest mistake was assuming they had more time. The closed door reminds us that the time for preparation is now. Procrastination in spiritual matters can have eternal consequences.

Believers must seize the opportunity to deepen their faith and relationship with Christ today, not tomorrow.

The Joy of Being Found Ready

➤ For the wise virgins, the Bridegroom's arrival is not a moment of fear but of joy and fulfillment. Their readiness allows them to enter the wedding feast and enjoy eternal communion with Christ. This joy is available to every believer who lives in readiness.

Readiness is not a burden but a privilege. It is an act of love and devotion to the Bridegroom, who has gone to prepare a place for us (John 14:2-3).

Living with Urgency

The consequences of being unprepared, as illustrated by the parable of the ten virgins, are eternal and irreversible. The closed door and the Bridegroom's chilling words, "I do not know you," serve as sobering reminders of the importance of spiritual readiness. However, these warnings are also invitations, calls to examine our faith, deepen our relationship with Christ, and live with urgency. Believers are not called to readiness out of fear but out of love for the Bridegroom and joyful anticipation of His return. The time to prepare is now. Let us live each day with lamps filled and burning brightly, eagerly awaiting the moment when the door to the wedding

feast is opened and we are welcomed into eternal communion with Christ.

ARE YOU READY FOR THE BRIDEGROOM?

The story of the ten virgins presents a simple yet thought-provoking question. *Are you ready for the Bridegroom?* This question is not rhetorical but deeply personal, urging every believer to reflect on their spiritual condition. Is your lamp filled with oil, or are you relying on outward appearances to sustain your faith? Readiness for Christ's return requires more than superficial preparation; it demands a heart continually filled with the Holy Spirit and a life shaped by devotion to Him.

The exact time of Christ's return remains a divine mystery, as Jesus reminds us in Mark 13:33-37, "Be on guard! Be alert! You do not know when that time will come." This unpredictability demands a life of watchfulness, prayer, and unwavering preparedness. Believers are not called to live in fear but with joyful expectancy, knowing that the Bridegroom's return is the fulfillment of God's promises, a moment of eternal communion and divine reward for those who remain faithful. The time of Christ's return is unknown, as Jesus reminds us in Mark 13:33-37, "Be on guard! Be alert! You do not know when that time will come." This unpredictability underscores the need for watchfulness, prayer, and a life of preparedness. Believers are called to live with expectancy and joy, not fear. The Bridegroom's return is a moment of fulfillment and eternal communion for those who are ready. It is the culmination of God's promises and the reward for a life lived in faithfulness. Commit to daily prayer, immerse yourself in Scripture, and cultivate a heart of worship. These practices sustain your faith, keeping your lamp filled with the oil of devotion and truth. The Holy Spirit is the source of spiritual vitality, guiding, renewing, and empowering believers. Seek His presence daily, allowing Him to refine your heart and align your life with God's will. Let the certainty of the Bridegroom's return shape your priorities and decisions. Pursue what matters eternally; faith, love, and obedience over the fleeting distractions of this world. The Bridegroom is coming. The question is, will you be ready to meet Him? Live each day as if the call could come at any moment, ensuring your lamp burns brightly with the oil of faith and love. Proverbs 4:18 reminds us, *"The path of the righteous is like the morning sun, shining ever brighter till the full light of day."* Even in the darkest moments, let your life radiate the light of Christ, that's shines like the stars over a thousand hills for readiness.

When the midnight call echoes, it will not catch the wise off guard. For them, it will be a moment of unparalleled joy, the culmination of a life lived in expectation. As 1 Thessalonians 5:6 exhorts us, *"So then, let us not be like others, who are asleep, but let us be awake and sober."*

Jesus Christ, the King of Kings, is coming. The only question is whether you will be ready to meet Him. Live today as if the call could come at any moment, ensuring your lamp burns brightly, filled with the oil of faith, love, and devotion. Jesus Christ will come suddenly, yet His coming will not be a surprise to those who are prepared. The midnight call will be a moment of joy for the wise, whose hearts are ready and whose lamps are full. *Proverbs 4:18* declares, *"The path of the righteous is like the morning sun, shining ever brighter till the full light of day."* Let your life radiate the light of Christ, even in the darkest hour, as you eagerly await His return. *1 Thessalonians 5:6 exhorts, "So then, let us not be like others, who are asleep, but let us be awake and sober."*

A SOUL-SEARCHING QUESTION

Will your light be shining when the Bridegroom comes? Will your lamp be filled, your heart prepared, and your soul eager to meet Him? Let today be the day you resolve to live expectantly, faithfully, and wisely, ready to welcome Him with joy. For those who are prepared, the Bridegroom's return will not be a surprise but the long-awaited fulfillment of their greatest hope. ***Will your light be shining when the Bridegroom comes? Live expectantly, faithfully, and wisely— ready to welcome Him with joy.***

Crowned for Purpose

Acts 13:46-47

SALTH OF THE EARTH

CHRIST'S AMBASSADORS, PILGRIMS IN A FOREIGN LAND

In 2 Corinthians 5:20, Paul reminds believers of their sacred calling: "We are therefore Christ's ambassadors, as though God were making His appeal through us." This astonishing statement encapsulates the role of <u>Christians as representatives of God's Kingdom on earth</u>. Ambassadors are not merely messengers; they are living representations of the One who sent them. Just as an ambassador represents the interests and character of their independence in a foreign land, believers represent Christ, charged with the ministry of reconciliation (2 Corinthians 5:18-19). This mission calls for proclaiming the message of salvation and living lives that reflect Christ's love, truth, and holiness. As *Philippians 3:20* declares, "*Our citizenship is in heaven.*" This identity shapes every aspect of a believer's life. Ambassadors of Christ are tasked with bridging the gap between a heavenly Kingdom and a broken, sinful world. Their lives are meant to serve as billboards, pointing others toward the hope and redemption found in Jesus. Unlike earthly ambassadors who represent nations with shifting policies and flawed leaders, Christ's ambassadors represent the eternal, unchanging, and holy nature of God. *Ephesians 6:20 "for which I am an ambassador in chains; that in it I may speak boldly, as I ought to speak"*, underscores the gravity of this role, as Paul describes himself as "an ambassador in chains," boldly proclaiming the Gospel despite persecution. His example demonstrates that being an ambassador often involves enduring

hardship, but it also brings unparalleled purpose and joy. Believers are called to embrace this role with courage and faithfulness, empowered by the Holy Spirit *(Acts 1:8) "But you shall receive power when the Holy Spirit has come upon you; and you shall be witnesses to Me in Jerusalem, and in all Judea and Samaria, and to the end of the earth"*, to testify about Christ in every corner of the earth. In Matthew 5:13, Jesus calls His followers "*the salt of the earth.*" This metaphor emphasizes the transformative and preservative role of believers in a decaying world. Salt has two primary functions; that is to preserve and to enhance flavor. Similarly, Christians are called to preserve God's truth and offer hope to a world marred by sin and corruption. Salt prevents decay by inhibiting the spread of rot, just as believers are to stand against moral and spiritual corruption.

This task requires living in stark contrast to the world's values. Where the world often embraces selfishness, deception, and compromise, ambassadors of Christ uphold truth, integrity, and selfless love. John 17:15-18 captures Jesus' prayer for His disciples: "*My prayer is not that You take them out of the world but that You protect them from the evil one.*" Believers are meant to remain in the world, engaging with its people and challenges, but not conforming to its sinful ways. They must model holiness, offering a glimpse of God's Kingdom to a world desperate for hope.

THE APOSTLE PAUL: A MODEL AMBASSADOR

Paul's life provides a powerful example of what it means to be a Christ-centered ambassador. In *Acts 13:46-47 "Then Paul and Barnabas grew bold and said, "It was necessary that the word of God should be spoken to you first; but since you reject it, and judge yourselves unworthy of everlasting life, behold, we turn to the Gentiles. For so the Lord has commanded us ' I have set you as a light to the Gentiles,"* That you should be for salvation to the ends of the earth., he boldly declares the Gospel to both Jews and Gentiles, unafraid of opposition or rejection. His letters reveal a heart consumed with love for God and for people, as well as a relentless commitment to spreading the message of reconciliation. Paul's message in 2 Corinthians 5:17 reinforces the transformative nature of the Gospel; *"Therefore, if anyone is in Christ, he is a new creation; old things have passed away; behold, all things have become new."* As ambassadors, believers are called not only to proclaim this message but also to live it out, demonstrating the reality of a changed life. In a world filled with moral compromise and spiritual decay, ambassadors of Christ serve as leaders of example and stability. Their role is not passive; it is one of active engagement. They must preserve God's truth by standing firm on Scripture, even when it is unpopular, nonconformist or unconventional. This includes upholding biblical values in conversations, workplaces, and community interactions, as well as modeling the compassion and grace of Christ in every relationship. Furthermore, ambassadors offer hope by pointing others to the life-transforming power of the Gospel. In a culture often characterized by hopelessness and despair, the message of reconciliation shines as a light in the darkness. Through their words and actions, ambassadors invite others to experience the peace, joy, and purpose that comes from being reconciled to God. The task of representing Christ in a fallen world may seem daunting, but believers are not left to accomplish it in their own strength. *Acts 1:8* promises, *"You will receive power when the Holy Spirit comes on you; and you will be My witnesses in Jerusalem, and in all Judea and Samaria, and to the ends of the earth."* This divine empowerment enables ambassadors to speak boldly, act courageously, and endure trials with grace. Modern believers can live out their ambassadorship by standing firm in their values, sharing their testimonies, and engaging their communities with love and humility. Whether in the workplace, at school, or among friends, Christians have countless opportunities to be salt and light. For example, maintaining integrity in a corrupt environment or extending forgiveness to someone undeserving demonstrates the transformative power of Jesus Christ.

Ultimately, the role of an ambassador is about glorifying God. By preserving His truth, proclaiming His message, and exemplifying His

character, believers fulfill their calling to reflect heaven's values on earth. As Paul reminds us in 2 Corinthians 5:20, God makes His appeal through His people. This is both a sacred privilege and a profound responsibility, one that demands faithfulness, courage, and reliance on the Holy Spirit. By embracing this calling, believers can bring glory to God and draw others into His Kingdom.

<u>Living as Pilgrims</u>
<u>Navigating Earth as a Temporary Home</u>

Believers are called to live as "strangers and pilgrims" in this world, seeking a heavenly home that far surpasses anything earth can offer (Hebrews 11:13-16), *"These all died in faith, not having received the promises, but having seen them afar off were assured of them, embraced them and confessed that they were strangers and pilgrims on the earth. For those who say such things declare plainly that they seek a homeland. And truly if they had called to mind that country from which they had come out, they would have had opportunity to return. But now they desire a better, that is, a heavenly country. Therefore God is not ashamed to be called their God, for He has prepared a city for them"*. This identity reminds Christians that their true citizenship lies in the eternal Kingdom of God, not in the fleeting pleasures and pursuits of this world. Just as Abraham left his homeland, trusting God's promises and living as a sojourner (Genesis 12:1-4), believers are called to navigate life with a mindset focused on eternal treasures rather than temporary gains. The pilgrim mindset demands detachment from worldly desires and unwavering faith in God's purposes. This perspective enables believers to stand firm amidst distractions in workplaces, schools, and communities, living with integrity and prioritizing their faith. It calls for daily decisions that glorify God, whether through acts of kindness, sharing the Gospel, or resisting temptations that compromise their witness.

Joseph provides a powerful example of this. Though he lived in a foreign land, sold into slavery and later elevated to a position of great power, Joseph remained faithful to God. His integrity and forgiveness glorified God, even in the face of betrayal and hardship *(Genesis 50:20) But as for you, you meant evil against me; but God meant it for good, in order to bring it about as it is this day, to save many people alive".* Similarly, modern pilgrims can glorify God by living out their faith, demonstrating trust in His promises, and offering hope to those around them. Ultimately, the pilgrim's journey is not just about enduring earthly trials but about achieving the ultimate goal, glorifying God through obedience and witness. The promise of the Crown of Life awaits those who faithfully navigate this temporary world, pointing others toward the eternal home that God has prepared for His people. As pilgrims, believers can joyfully press on, knowing their journey serves a greater purpose.

THE REWARDS (CROWNS) OF
FAITHFUL AMBASSADORSHIP

The Bible promises eternal rewards to those who live faithfully as Christ's ambassadors, steadfastly fulfilling their calling amidst trials. Among these rewards are the heavenly crowns, which symbolize the honor and recognition given to those who persevere in faith and service. In 2 Timothy 4:8, Paul describes one such reward, the "*crown of righteousness*," reserved for all who eagerly anticipate Christ's return and live lives of obedience to Him. This crown reflects not only a believer's steadfastness but also their love for God's Kingdom and their commitment to sharing His message with the world. Similarly, 1 Peter 5:4 speaks of "an *unfading crown of glory*" for those who shepherd God's flock willingly and faithfully. This promise serves as both encouragement and motivation for believers in leadership roles to care for others and remain steadfast in their duties. The crowns symbolize the eternal honor of fulfilling one's responsibilities as a representative of Christ. Far from being material rewards, these crowns signify the spiritual victory and eternal joy of a life lived in faithful service to God.

The assurance of such rewards should inspire believers to persevere through challenges. Serving as Christ's ambassadors often comes with significant trials, whether in the form of persecution, rejection, or the daily struggles of standing firm in faith. The promise of eternal crowns helps believers maintain an eternal perspective, recognizing that their labor for the Lord is not in vain. As Paul reminds us in *1 Corinthians 15:58, "Always give yourselves fully to the work of the Lord, because you know that your labor in the Lord is not in vain."* Importantly, the ability to fulfill this role as an ambassador is not through human effort alone but through God's grace and the empowerment of the Holy Spirit. *Acts 1:8* highlights the essential role of the Spirit; *"But you will receive power when the Holy Spirit comes on you; and you will be My witnesses in Jerusalem, and in all Judea and Samaria, and to the ends of the earth."* This divine empowerment equips believers with boldness, wisdom, and endurance to proclaim the Gospel and live as faithful witnesses for Christ. The Apostle Peter's encouragement to shepherd the flock of God willingly (1 Peter 5:2-4) is an example of how the promise of rewards motivates believers to live with purpose. While their work may go unnoticed or unappreciated by the world, God sees their faithfulness and promises eternal honor in His Kingdom. This assurance of heavenly recognition should fuel believers' commitment to their calling, even when their efforts feel insignificant or unfruitful. Moreover, the pursuit of heavenly rewards keeps believers focused on glorifying God, the ultimate goal of their ambassadorship. The crowns they will receive are not meant for self-exaltation but as an offering of worship to the One who enabled their victory. Revelation 4:10 describes the elders casting their crowns before God's throne, acknowledging that all glory and honor belong to Him.

In practical terms, kingdom believers can live for these eternal rewards by embracing the opportunities to witness for Christ, serve others, and persevere in righteousness. Whether it is sharing the Gospel, encouraging a fellow believer, or standing firm in faith under pressure, every act of obedience contributes to their eternal legacy. These seemingly small acts accumulate into a life that reflects God's love and truth, pointing others to the hope of salvation. Ultimately, the promise of crowns is not merely about personal reward but about the joy of hearing Christ's commendation: "Well done, good and faithful servant" (Matthew 25:23). The anticipation of such recognition encourages believers to endure hardships with faith and to live with unwavering dedication to their heavenly calling. Through the power of the Holy Spirit, they can fulfill their role as Christ's ambassadors, secure in the knowledge that their faithfulness will be eternally honored.

BEARING THE AMBASSADOR'S BADGE: SUFFERING FOR CHRIST SAKE

Suffering is an inherent part of the journey for ambassadors of Christ, who represent Him in a world that often rejects His truth. Scripture reminds believers that suffering is as common to the Christians it is to the soldier. In order to please the commanding officer both the soldier and the Christian will abandon the worldly conveniences of civilian life for the sake of a higher calling, those that are called to such and submit to Gods will, shall endure. Suffering for Christ is both an honor and a testimony, a reflection of their unwavering allegiance to God's Kingdom. *Philippians 1:29* states, "*For it has been granted to you on behalf of Christ not only to believe in Him but also to suffer for Him.*" This verse underscores the dual privilege of faith and suffering, positioning trials as a means of glorifying God and strengthening the believer's witness to the world. Stephen, the first Christian martyr, provides a powerful example of this principle. As he boldly proclaimed the Gospel, Stephen faced fierce opposition and ultimately death by stoning (Acts 7:54-60). Even in his final moments, his faith did not waver. Instead, he experienced a divine vision of heaven, seeing "*the glory of God, and Jesus standing at the right hand of God*" *(Acts 7:55)*. This vision not only sustained him but also served as a testimony to those who witnessed his death, highlighting the eternal hope that strengthens believers in the face of suffering. Stephen's story reminds modern ambassadors of Christ, that

suffering is not the end but a gateway to eternal glory. This perspective is reinforced in *Romans 8:18*, where Paul writes, " *For I consider that the sufferings of this present time are not worthy to be compared with the glory which shall be revealed in us.*" Suffering for Christ is never in vain; it is a refining process that shapes believers into the image of Christ and deepens their reliance on God. Such trials also serve as a powerful witness to the world, demonstrating the transformative power of faith and the hope that sustains believers even in the most challenging circumstances.

Joy in suffering may seem contradictory, but it becomes possible when believers adopt an eternal perspective. Knowing that their trials have a purpose and that they are participating in Christ's sufferings, enables them to endure with joy. In *Matthew 5:11-12*, Jesus Himself encourages this mindset: "*Blessed are you when people insult you, persecute you and falsely say all kinds of evil against you for my namesake. Rejoice and be exceedingly glad, because great is your reward in heaven.*" This promise of heavenly rewards provides believers with the strength to persevere, assuring them that their faithfulness will not go unnoticed by God. For kingdom believers, suffering may not always take the form of physical persecution, as it did for Stephen, but it can manifest in ridicule, rejection, or opposition for standing firm in their faith. Whether it is in the workplace, at school, or within relationships, remaining true to biblical values often requires courage and resilience. By enduring these trials with grace and integrity, believers glorify God and offer a testimony to His sustaining power.

The joy of suffering for Christ is anchored in the knowledge that such trials are temporary and purposeful. Each difficulty is an opportunity to draw closer to God, to reflect His character more clearly, and to inspire others to seek Him. As ambassadors of Christ, believers wear the badge of suffering not as a mark of defeat but as a symbol of victory and eternal hope. In the words of James 1:12, "Blessed is the one who perseveres under trial because, having stood the test, that person will receive the crown of life that the Lord has promised to those who love Him." Ultimately, suffering for Christ points to the greater reality of His Kingdom, where every trial will be redeemed, and every tear will be wiped away. Until then, believers can endure with joy, confident that their suffering is producing an eternal glory far beyond anything they can imagine.

ACTIVE ENGAGEMENT WITHOUT SPIRITUAL CONFORMITY

Believers are called to engage with the world while remaining distant from its sinful patterns, embodying the truth of *Romans 12:2*: "*Do not conform to the pattern of this world, but be transformed by the renewing of your mind.*" This verse highlights the believer's dual responsibility to participate in the world as Christ's representatives while resisting its corrupting influences. Such engagement requires spiritual steadfastness, an unwavering commitment to God's Word, and a daily renewal of the mind through prayer and fellowship.

The life of Daniel offers a compelling example of engagement without conformity. Taken captive to Babylon, Daniel served in a pagan court, surrounded by all types of pagan practices and beliefs contrary to his faith. Yet, he remained committed to God's standards, refusing to defile himself with the king's food (Daniel 1:8). Daniel's resolve was not an act of rebellion but an intentional choice to honor God above all else. His faithfulness earned him favor with both God and man, demonstrating how believers can positively influence their surroundings without compromising their principles. Kingdom believers, much like Daniel, live, work or attend school in environments where they are often pressured to conform to societal norms that conflict with biblical values. In workplaces, schools, and communities, they are called to be "*the light of the world*" *(Matthew 5:14),* shining Christ's truth through their actions and words. This requires courage and a firm foundation in faith, ensuring their engagement with the world remains purposeful and godly. Preparation is vital for navigating the tension between engagement and conformity.

Believers must be grounded in Scripture, as *1 Peter 3:15* advises: *"Always be prepared to give an answer to everyone who asks you to give the reason for the hope that you have."* This readiness comes through consistent prayer, study of God's Word, and fellowship with other believers. Such practices equip ambassadors of Christ with the wisdom and spiritual strength needed to face challenges while remaining true to their calling.

In addition to spiritual preparation, believers must cultivate a heavenly perspective. Colossians 3:2 encourages them to *"set your minds on things above, not on earthly things."* This focus on eternal treasures allows believers to engage with the world without becoming entangled in its fleeting concerns. By remembering that their ultimate citizenship is in heaven (Philippians 3:20), believers can approach worldly interactions with a clear purpose, to glorify God and draw others to Him.

Living as distinct yet engaged ambassadors also involves standing firm in values and offering hope to those around them. Whether it is refusing unethical practices at work, showing kindness to a homeless individual, or sharing the Gospel with a neighbor, believers demonstrate God's truth through the works of their actions. By doing so, they fulfill their role as agents of change, bringing light into dark places and hope into broken lives. Furthermore, believers are encouraged to keep their eyes fixed on Christ's return. This anticipation provides strength and joy, even amidst worldly pressures. As 1 Thessalonians 4:16-17 reminds us, the promise of being united with Christ motivates believers to persevere, knowing their current trials are temporary. Ultimately, engaging with the world without spiritual conformity is about embodying Christ's transformative power. Through faithful living, believers point others to the hope found in Him, serving as holy examples in an unholy world. By standing firm in faith and focusing on eternal treasures, they reflect God's love and truth, fulfilling their mission as ambassadors of His Kingdom.

THROUGH THE DARKNESS: WALKING
BY FAITH, NOT BY SIGHT

Walking by faith is a defining characteristic of the ambassadors journey, a pilgrimage through a world often shrouded in uncertainty. *2 Corinthians 5:7* encapsulates this principle: "*For we walk by faith, not by sight.*" Faith is the foundation that enables pilgrims to trust God's promises, even when they are not immediately visible or comprehensible. This reliance on God's Word and guidance is what sets believers apart, directing them to move forward with confidence in His sovereign plan.

Noah's story in the Bible exemplifies what it means to walk by faith. In a time of widespread rebellion against God and disbelief, Noah received a divine command to build an ark in preparation for a great flood, a phenomenon he had never experienced or seen. *Hebrews 11:7* captures his remarkable response; "*By faith Noah, when warned about things not yet seen, in holy fear built an ark to save his family.*" Noah's obedience, rooted in trust in God's Word, not only preserved life on earth but also demonstrated God's faithfulness and justice. His story reminds believers that faith often requires acting on unseen realities and trusting God's promises against the tide of worldly skepticism. Modern believers face similar challenges as they navigate their journey of faith. The world demands tangible evidence and immediate results, yet God often calls His people to trust Him in the unseen and the unknown. This can mean waiting patiently for answers to prayer, stepping out into unfamiliar territory, or clinging to God's promises amidst trials. Walking by faith involves fully surrendering control and embracing the truth of *Proverbs 3:5-6*, "*Trust in the Lord with all your heart and lean not on your own understanding; in all your ways submit to Him, and He will make your paths straight.*"

The pilgrim's path is marked by a reliance on God's Word. Scripture serves as a lamp to guide believers through life's uncertainties, offering, instruction, wisdom, encouragement, and assurance of God's faithfulness. Just as Noah trusted in God's instruction,

believers today are called to anchor their lives in His Word, allowing it to shape their decisions and sustain their hope. Faith is not blind optimism but a steadfast confidence in God's will and promises. This confidence equips believers to face challenges with courage, knowing that God is working all things for their good and His glory (Romans 8:28). Walking by faith often requires enduring periods of waiting, uncertainty, or even suffering, yet it is through these experiences that faith is refined and strengthened.

Noah's faith preserved life and fulfilled God's purposes, just as the faith of modern pilgrims can bring about God's plans in their lives and communities. By trusting in God's promises, believers become living testimonies of His grace and power. They point others to the hope and assurance found in Him, even when the path ahead seems unclear. Ultimately, the pilgrim's journey is one of perseverance, shaped by a vision of eternal promises. Faith enables believers to walk forward with assurance, knowing that their ultimate destination is a heavenly home prepared by God. As they journey, they glorify Him through their trust, obedience, and witness, embodying the truth that walking by faith is the heart of the believer's calling. As believers, Philippians 3:20 declares a profound truth; "Our citizenship is in heaven." This statement transforms the way Christians perceive and navigate their lives on earth. It is a reminder that this world is not their permanent home; rather, they belong to a heavenly kingdom where Christ reigns as King. This identity as heaven's citizens reshapes priorities, influences daily choices, and directs attention toward God's eternal kingdom, transcending earthly allegiances and temporary concerns.

The Church of Pentecost offers a powerful example of what it means to live as citizens of heaven. Acts 4:32-35 reveals a community that demonstrated their allegiance to God's Kingdom through selflessness and unity. They shared resources, cared for the needy, and boldly proclaimed Christ, even in the face of persecution. This radical commitment showcased their priorities: they valued spiritual treasures over material wealth and eternal truths over fleeting comforts. Their actions reflected their unwavering trust in God's provision and a steadfast hope in His promises.

For Christ Ambassadors, living as heavenly citizens involves a similar alignment of priorities. It means seeking first God's Kingdom (Matthew 6:33), standing firm in faith, and resisting the enticement of carnal worldly distractions. Earthly nations and allegiances may demand attention, but the believer's ultimate loyalty lies with Christ and His eternal reign. This perspective fuels a life of purpose, one marked by spiritual growth, service, and anticipation of the day when the fullness of God's Kingdom will be revealed. To embody heaven's citizenship effectively, believers must cultivate spiritual growth and readiness. This requires being grounded in God's Word, persistent in prayer, and committed to fellowship with other believers. Scripture emphasizes the importance of preparation, as seen in 1 Peter 3:15: "Always be prepared to give an answer to everyone who asks you to give the reason for the hope that you have." This readiness is not passive but active, a continuous pursuit of knowing God deeply and living out that knowledge boldly.

Spiritual growth equips believers to withstand challenges and live as Christ's ambassadors in a dark and broken world. It nurtures a heart of compassion, a spirit of discernment, and a resolve to persevere through trials. The believer's journey is marked by transformation, becoming more Christlike and reflecting His glory to a world in need. The concept of heavenly citizenship carries with it a profound anticipation, the return of Christ. Believers are pilgrims on a journey, awaiting the day when they will be united with their Savior in glory. This hope is beautifully captured in *1 Thessalonians 4:16-17*: *"For the Lord himself will come down from heaven, with a loud command, with the voice of the archangel and with the trumpet call of God, and the dead in Christ will rise first. After that, we who are still alive and are left will be caught up together with them in the clouds to meet the Lord in the air. And so, we will be with the Lord forever."*

This promise fuels the pilgrim's journey, providing hope amidst trials and a forward-looking perspective that keeps the eyes fixed on eternal realities. It encourages believers to live in readiness, not merely enduring the struggles of the present but rejoicing in the certainty of their future with Christ. Living as a citizen of heaven is not accomplished by human effort alone. It is through God's grace and the power of the Holy Spirit that believers are equipped to fulfill their roles as Christ's ambassadors. *Acts 1:8* reminds believers of this empowering truth, "*You will receive power when the Holy Spirit comes upon you; and you will be my witnesses in Jerusalem, and in all Judea and Samaria, and to the ends of the earth.*"

The Holy Spirit enables believers to live boldly, love sacrificially, and serve faithfully. Through His empowerment, they can overcome weaknesses, resist temptation, and proclaim the Gospel with confidence. Grace, too, plays a vital role, reminding believers that their citizenship in heaven is not earned but gifted through Christ's atoning sacrifice. This unmerited favor inspires humility, gratitude, and a commitment to extend grace to others. Heavenly citizenship is an amazing privilege and responsibility. It shapes a life that transcends earthly boundaries, prioritizing God's Kingdom over shallow allegiances. By grounding themselves in God's Word, cultivating spiritual growth, and relying on the grace and power of the Holy Spirit, believers can live as effective ambassadors for Christ. Their journey is marked by hope, anticipation of Christ's return, and a determination to reflect the glory of their heavenly King. As pilgrims on this earth, they press on with eyes fixed on eternity, faithfully representing their true home until the day they are called to their eternal inheritance.

> ➢ **Heaven's Citizenship Living Beyond Borders**
> ➢ **Living as Heavenly Citizens**
> ➢ **Spiritual Growth and Readiness**
> ➢ **Looking Forward to Christ's Return**
> ➢ **Empowered by Grace and the Holy Spirit**

Behold I'm Coming Quickly

1 Thessalonians 4:16-17

BEHOLD IM COMING QUICKLY

I'M BRINGING MY ETERNAL REWARD WITH ME

The return of Jesus Christ, the King of Kings, is the most anticipated, kingdom closing event of our Biblical history, prophesized in the scrolls and foretold in Scripture. This moment is a divine inevitability that shapes the faith, purpose, and circumstance of every believer. His return will be visible, undeniable, and filled with glory, bringing the culmination of God's redemptive plan to fruition. The heavens will reveal the One who has been awaited for a millennium. Riding on a white horse, crowned with many diadems, and bearing a name known only to Himself, the King of Kings and Lord of Lords will descend in unparalleled majesty. His return is not a passing promise but a divine certainty foretold in the Word of God. *"Behold, I am coming quickly, and My reward is with Me, to give to every one according to his work. I am the Alpha and the Omega, the Beginning and the End, the First and the Last." (Revelation 22:12-13).* These words of Christ echo through the ages, an urgent appeal to readiness. His return is not a passing promise <u>but a divine certainty foretold in the Word of God</u>. *"Behold, I am coming quickly, bringing my reward with me",* We can't get ready, it is imperative that we, be ready. His return is imminent, His timing perfect, and His reign eternal. His return will not be a Mear brief transitional promise but a heavenly certainty foretold in the Word of God.

"Behold, I am coming quickly, bringing my recompense with me, to repay each one for what he has done. I am the Alpha and the Omega, the first and the last, the beginning and the end" (Revelation 22:12-13). <u>His return is imminent, His timing perfect, and His reign eternal.</u>

Christ's Promise to Return

Jesus Christ, the Alpha and the Omega, has assured His believers of His return. He who spoke the world into existence and declared, "It is finished", on the cross will once again speak authoritatively, what's to come, but also fulfill the ultimate culmination of His kingdom. *"Behold, he is coming with the clouds, and every eye will see him, even those who pierced him"* (Revelation 1:7).

Unlike His first coming, marked by "meekness in a manger", His second coming will be an undeniable display of supreme power and glory. (Matthew 24:30-31) proclaims, *"Then will appear in heaven the sign of the Son of Man... and they will see the Son of Man coming on the clouds of heaven with power and great glory."* This will not be a quiet soft return. The trumpet will sound thunderously, the angels will brazenly gather His elect from every corner of the earth. It will be visible, audible, and utterly undeniable beholding to see His face, The Face of a King. No one will escape the reality of His presence. For the believer, it will be a moment of unparalleled joy. For the unrepentant, it will be a moment of reckoning and a harsh reality.

In Revelation 22:12, Jesus declares, *"Behold, I am coming quickly, and My reward is with Me, to give to every one according to his work."* This verse encapsulates His promise to return, bringing justice, reward, and the full manifestation of His kingdom. It highlights His sovereignty as the Alpha and Omega, the beginning and the end of all things (Revelation 1:8). From the dawn of creation to its consummation, Jesus Christ reigns supreme. His promise to return underscores His faithfulness to His Word, reminding us that He does not delay arbitrarily. The timing of His return is perfect, aligned with the eternal counsel of God's will. Though centuries have passed since these

words were spoken, 2 Peter 3:8-9 reminds us, *"With the Lord one day is as a thousand years, and a thousand years as one day."* The seeming delay is not a failure but an expression of His patience, giving humanity the opportunity to repent and prepare.

THE VISIBLE AND UNDENIABLE
NATURE OF HIS COMING

Revelation 1:7 emphasizes, "Behold, He is coming with clouds, and every eye will see Him, even they who pierced Him." This imagery is echoed in *Matthew 24:30-31: "Then the sign of the Son of Man will appear in heaven, and all the tribes of the earth will mourn, and they will see the Son of Man coming on the clouds of heaven with power and great glory."* Unlike His first coming as a humble servant, Jesus' second coming will be majestic, awe-inspiring, and universally visible. Every eye will see Him, not just those who believe, but also those who rejected Him. Even those who pierced Him, a reference to those who have opposed and mocked Him throughout history, will witness His glory. The King's arrival will leave no room for doubt or denial.

This global revelation is also marked by the sound of a trumpet, as the angels gather His elect from the four winds (Matthew 24:31). The trumpet is a symbol of divine proclamation, signaling the completion of God's redemptive work. It will be a moment of triumph for the faithful and a sobering reality for the unprepared. (Revelation 19:11-16) is a vivid portrayal of the King's return; *"Then I saw heaven opened, and behold, a white horse! The one sitting on it is called Faithful and True, and in righteousness he judges and makes war. His eyes are like a flame of fire, and on his head are many diadems... and the armies of heaven, arrayed in fine linen, white and pure, were following him on white horses."* This is not obsolete symbolic imagery, John in (Revelation 19:11-16) describes the return of Jesus with vivid imagery: *"Now I saw heaven opened, and behold, a white horse. And He who sat on him was called Faithful and True, and in righteousness He judges and makes war."* The white horse signifies victory and purity, while the rider, Jesus Christ embodies righteousness and truth. His eyes, blazing like fire, pierce through all pretense, and His name, *"King of Kings and Lord of Lords,"* is written on His robe and thigh, affirming His supreme authority.

This descension of Christ contrasts sharply with His first coming, where He arrived as the humble Lamb of God, meek and lowly. In His Second Coming, He returns as the Lion of Judah, the Righteous Judge who executes justice and establishes His eternal kingdom. The sword proceeding from His mouth symbolizes the power of His Word, by which He will vanquish His enemies. For believers, this vision is one of hope and triumph. Jesus comes not as a distant figure but as our Savior and King, fulfilling His promises to redeem and restore. It will inevitably be the culmination of Jesus Christ's our Promised Messiahs' role as <u>Judge</u>, <u>Redeemer</u>, and <u>King</u>. His robe dipped in blood signifies His victory over sin and death through His sacrifice, while the sharp sword from His mouth symbolizes His authority to execute divine judgment. He is Faithful and True, unchanging in His promises, and righteous in all His ways. The armies of heaven, those redeemed by His blood, will follow Him, arrayed in purity, reflecting the King's holiness. The return of Christ is not only the manifestation of His glory but the ultimate vindication of the faith of His people. (Revelation 1:7) assures us, *"Behold, He is coming with the clouds, and every eye will see Him, even they who did not believe nor accept Him as Lord. And all the tribes of the earth will mourn because of Him."* This vivid imagery emphasizes the public and kingdom nature of Christ's return. It will not be hidden or metaphorical; it will be a literal, awe-inspiring occasion that transcends all earthly comprehension. Matthew 24:30-31 further expands this truth; *"Then the sign of the Son of Man will appear in heaven, and then all the tribes of the earth will mourn, and they will see the Son of Man coming on the clouds of heaven with power and great glory. And He will send His angels with a great sound of a trumpet, and they will gather together His elect from the four winds, from one end of heaven to the other."* This passage illustrates a clear picture of Jesus Christ descending in all of His Glory and majesty, accompanied by heavenly hosts and the sound of a trumpet. His coming will signal

the end of the age, bringing salvation to the faithful and judgment to the unrepentant. This historic kingdom event will not be subject to human interpretation or debate; it will be a divine act of revelation for ALL to see. Every knee will bow, and every tongue will confess that Jesus Christ is Lord (Philippians 2:10-11).

THE KING'S PERFECT TIMING

Though centuries have passed since these prophetic-promises have been written in scripture, the Bible assures us that Jesus' return is neither delayed nor uncertain. (2 Peter 3:9) reminds us, "*The Lord is not slack concerning His promise, as some count slackness, but is longsuffering toward us, not willing that any should perish but that all should come to repentance.*" God's apparent delay is an act of mercy, providing time for repentance and salvation. The sovereignty of Jesus as the Alpha and Omega ensures that His timing is flawless. He operates beyond the constraints of human understanding, fulfilling His plan at the appointed moment. Revelation 19:11-21 speaks of the King's return; a Rider on a white horse, faithful and true, executing judgment and establishing His eternal reign. ***His timing, perfect and preordained, will usher in the end of this age and the dawn of His everlasting kingdom***.

While obscured <u>human understanding</u> and <u>impatience</u> might question the delay, Scripture assures us of God's perfect timing. Revelation 19:11-16 describes *Jesus as the victorious King who will return to wage righteous war against sin and establish His eternal rule.* He is riding a white horse, His eyes like flames of fire, and His robe dipped in blood, signifying His victory over sin and death. The Kingdom armies of heaven strategically follow Him, clothed in fine linen, white and clean, symbolizing the purity and righteousness of the saints. This triumphant imagery reminds believers that the King is never late. <u>His delay serves a purpose: to fulfill every prophecy, extend mercy, and demonstrate His long-suffering love toward humanity.</u>

JUDGMENT AND REWARD

When the Son of Man returns as King of Kings in His glory, He will not come alone. (Matthew 25:31-32) declares, *"**When the Son of Man comes in his glory, and all the angels with him, then he will sit on his glorious throne. Before him will be gathered all the nations, and he will separate people one from another as a shepherd separates the sheep from the goats**."*

This moment is sobering. The sheep, those who followed Christ and lived according to His commands, will inherit the kingdom prepared for them from the foundation of the world. The goats, those who rejected Him, will face eternal separation.

The criteria for this judgment are love in action. *"Then the King will say to those on His right hand, 'Come, you blessed of My Father, inherit the kingdom prepared for you from the foundation of the world: for I was hungry and you gave Me food; I was thirsty and you gave Me drink; I was a stranger and you took Me in; I was naked and you clothed Me; I was sick and you visited Me; I was in prison and you came to Me.' 'Then the righteous will answer Him, saying, 'Lord, when did we see You hungry and feed You, or thirsty and give You drink? When did we see You a stranger and take You in, or naked and clothe You? Or when did we see You sick, or in prison, and come to You?' And the King will answer and say to them, 'Assuredly, I say to you, inasmuch as you did it to one of the least of these My brethren, you did it to Me.' 'Then He will also say to those on the left hand, 'Depart from Me, you cursed, into the everlasting fire prepared for the devil and his angels: for I was hungry and you gave Me no food; I was thirsty and you gave Me no drink; I was a stranger and you did not take Me in, naked and you did not clothe Me, sick and in prison and you did not visit Me. 'Then they also will answer Him, saying, 'Lord, when did we see You hungry or thirsty or a stranger or naked or sick or in prison, and did not minister to You?' Then He will answer them, saying, 'Assuredly, I say to you, inasmuch as you did not do it to one of the least of these, you did not do it to Me.' And these will go away into everlasting punishment, but the righteous into eternal life".*

(Matthew 25:35). This is not salvation by works but the evidence of genuine faith. How we treat "the least of these" reflects our relationship with Christ.

The return of the King is not only a moment of glory but also a time of reckoning. Matthew 25:31-46 vividly portrays the judgment scene, where Christ separates the sheep from the goats. To the sheep, He says, *"Come, you blessed of My Father, inherit the kingdom prepared for you from the foundation of the world"* (Matthew 25:34). To the goats, He declares, *"Depart from Me, you cursed, into the everlasting fire prepared for the devil and his angels"* (Matthew 25:41). For (1 Corinthians 13:2-4) reminds us that the highest in the kingdom of God is "Bankrupt without Love" and [Compassion]. *"And though I have the gift of prophecy, and understand all mysteries and all knowledge, and though I have all faith, so that I could remove mountains, but have not love, I am nothing. And though I bestow all my goods to feed the poor, and though I give my body to be burned, but have not love, it profits me nothing.* For (Matthew 7:21) states *Not everyone who says to me, 'Lord, Lord,' will enter the kingdom of heaven, but only the one who does the will of my Father who is in heaven.*

These passages emphasize the importance of faithful stewardship and the call to live a life that reflects Christ's love and righteousness. The reward is eternal joy and fellowship with God, while the punishment is eternal separation from His presence.

The Eternal Urgent Necessity of Being Ready

Jesus Himself warned of the necessity of being ready. *"Therefore you also must be ready, for the Son of Man is coming at an hour you do not expect"* (Matthew 24:44). This urgency reflects the reality that no one knows the day or hour of Christ's return, but every day is an opportunity to respond to His call. Salvation is a gift, freely offered through Christ's sacrifice on the cross. *"For this is the will of my Father, that everyone who looks on the Son and believes in him should have eternal life, and I will raise him up on the last day"* (John 6:40). Yet this gift must be received in faith, and the decision to accept or reject it determines one's eternal destiny. To delay is to risk missing the greatest opportunity of all; reconciliation with God. The gospel invites everyone to come as they are, broken, burdened, and in need of grace. There is no sin too great, no past too dark, that the blood of Jesus cannot cover. But the window of opportunity will not remain open forever.

The mystery that echoes throughout the ages; *Will we be ready for the King's return?* Jesus warned of the dangers of complacency, urging believers to remain vigilant, awoke and faithful. In Matthew 24:42, He says, *"Watch therefore, for you do not know what hour your Lord is coming."* The return of Christ will be sudden, like a thief in the night, and only those who are prepared will enter into His eternal joy. Christ's return is not delayed, it is perfectly timed. While the world may scoff and grow complacent, Scripture reminds us, *"The Lord is not slow to fulfill his promise as some count slowness, but is patient toward you, not wishing that any should perish"* (2 Peter 3:9).

The question is not whether He will return but whether we are prepared to meet Him. Are our lamps filled with oil, as in the parable of the ten virgins (Matthew 25:1-13)? Are we living with eternity in view, actively pursuing righteousness, sharing the gospel, and serving others in His name? For those who are in Christ, the King's return is a moment of triumphant joy. His reward is not merely a crown of glory but eternal communion with Him. Revelation 22:14 declares, *"Blessed are those who wash their robes, so that they may have the right to the tree of life and that they may enter the city by the gates."* To be ready is to live a life of faith, obedience, and expectation. It is to align our hearts with His will, serving others in love and proclaiming the gospel until He comes. It will come suddenly, like a thief in the night, altering the course of eternity. For this reason, repentance and readiness are non-negotiable, forming the foundation of a life lived in anticipation of the King's return.

As the invitation of salvation is extended to all, it demands a response. Scripture presents a clear choice:

- ➢ **Accept the Invitation:** To believe in Jesus Christ and accept the invitation of salvation is to receive eternal life, forgiveness of sins, and reconciliation with God. It is the path of joy, hope, and peace.
- ➢ **Reject the Invitation:** To ignore or reject the invitation of salvation is to choose eternal separation from God, forfeiting the blessings of eternal life for the despair of eternal judgment.

This decision is not merely about avoiding punishment; it is about embracing the abundant life God offers through Christ. *"I am the way, and the truth, and the life. No one comes to the Father except through me"* (John 14:6). Joshua's challenge to the Israelites rings true for every generation; *"Choose this day whom you will serve"* (Joshua 24:15). The stakes are eternal, and the time to decide is now.

NO ONE KNOWS THE DAY OR THE HOUR OF ASSURANCE THROUGH CHRIST'S RETURN

The Grandeur and Awe of Christ Return, *"For as the lightning comes from the east and shines as far as the west, so will be the coming of the Son of Man"* (Matthew 24:27). The return of Christ will not be hidden or subtle. It will be as unmistakable as a flash of lightning illuminating the sky. This is a kingdom historic event, visible to every eye and undeniable to every heart. *The earth will groan under the weight of His glory, and every knee will bow before Him (Philippians 2:10).* For believers, this moment will be one of unspeakable joy. "For the Lord himself will descend from heaven with a cry of command, with the voice of an archangel, and with the sound of the trumpet of God. And the dead in Christ will rise first" (1 Thessalonians 4:16). The resurrection of the saints and their gathering to meet the Lord in the air signifies the ultimate fulfillment of His promise. **Yet for the unprepared**, this day will be a day of terror. Matthew 25:31-46 portrays the judgment that follows the separation of the sheep and the goats. Those who rejected Christ will face eternal separation, their rebellion against Him sealing their fate.

AN INVITATION OR A WARNING

The glory of Christ's Second Coming is both an invitation and a warning. For the faithful, it is the fulfillment of their greatest hope, a day when sorrow, pain, and death are no more. For the unrepentant, it is a day of reckoning, a reminder that every decision, every act, and every thought will be brought before the Righteous Judge.

Are you prepared for this day? Have you washed your robes in the blood of the Lamb (Revelation 22:14)? The King is coming quickly, and His reward is with Him. For those who are in Christ, this reward is eternal life, joy, and communion with God. For those outside of Christ, it is eternal separation from His presence. The grandeur of His coming cannot be overstated. It is the moment when time itself bows to eternity, when the kingdoms of this world give way to the everlasting Kingdom of God. Let the believer rejoice and the unrepentant tremble, for the glory of His return will leave no one untouched. The question remains; Will you be ready when the King returns in all His glory? The time to prepare is now. Behold, He is coming. One of the greatest assurances for believers is the promise of Christ's second coming. Jesus Himself declared, *"Let not your hearts be troubled. Believe in God; believe also in me. In my Father's house are many rooms... And if I go and prepare a place for you, I will come again and will take you to myself, that where I am you may be also"*, (John 14:1-3). This promise reassures us that Jesus is actively preparing an eternal home for His followers. The certainty of His return fills believers with a sense of anticipation and peace, knowing that our ultimate destination is with Him. Paul echoes this assurance in 1 Thessalonians 4:16-17; *"For the Lord himself will descend from heaven with a cry of command, with the voice of an archangel, and with the sound of the trumpet of God. And the dead in Christ*

will rise first. Then we who are alive, who are left, will be caught up together with them in the clouds to meet the Lord in the air, and so we will always be with the Lord."

<u>This vivid description of Christ's return reminds believers that death is not the end.</u> Those who have placed their faith in Him will be resurrected to eternal life and reunited with Christ forever. Jesus Himself declared in Matthew 24:42-44, *"Watch therefore, for you do not know what hour your Lord is coming. But know this, that if the master of the house had known what hour the thief would come, he would have watched and not allowed his house to be broken into. Therefore, you also be ready, for the Son of Man is coming at an hour you do not expect."* This imagery of a thief in the night captures the suddenness and unpredictability of Christ's return. Just as a homeowner prepares vigilantly to protect their possessions, so believers must guard their spiritual lives, ensuring they are ready for their Lord's arrival. This readiness is not passive but active, involving daily repentance, righteousness, and unwavering faith. 1 Thessalonians 5:2 reinforces this truth; *"For you yourselves know perfectly that the day of the Lord so comes as a thief in the night."* It is not a matter of "if" He will come but "when," and His timing will catch the unprepared off guard.

THE CALL TO REPENTANCE

"Repentance-Readiness" begins with repentance. It is through repentance that we restore our relationship with God. True Repentance begins with the act of turning away from sin and returning to God acknowledging His sovereignty, preparing our hearts for His purpose. Repentance stretches further than mere sorrow for wrongdoing; it is a transformative process that compels us to "turn from sin" and restores our relationship with Yahweh preparing our hearts for His kingdom purpose.

➤ **Restoration of Relationship with God**
Sin separates us from God, but repentance bridges the gap. Through repentance, we return to the Father's embrace, reestablishing the intimate relationship for which we were created.

> ➤ **Acknowledgment of God's Sovereignty**
> Repentance requires humility, an acknowledgment that God is holy, just, and sovereign. It is a recognition that we are utterly dependent on His grace and mercy.

> ➤ **Pathway to Forgiveness and Redemption**
> Scripture assures us that repentance leads to forgiveness. *"If we confess our sins, he is faithful and just to forgive us our sins and to cleanse us from all unrighteousness"* (1 John 1:9).

> ➤ **Transformation and Renewal**
> Genuine repentance brings transformation. It is not merely a change of behavior but a renewal of the heart and mind, aligning us with God's will.

> ➤ **Prepares the Way for God's Purpose**
> Repentance clears the obstacles that hinder us from fulfilling God's purpose. It opens the door for His plans to unfold in our lives.

> ➤ **An Expression of Godly Sorrow**
> True repentance stems from godly sorrow, a deep awareness of how our sin grieves the heart of God. This sorrow leads to lasting change.

> ➤ **Essential for Salvation**
> Jesus declared, *"Unless you repent, you will all likewise perish"* (Luke 13:3). Repentance is a non-negotiable step toward salvation.

> ➤ **Encourages Reconciliation and Healing**
> Repentance not only restores our relationship with God but also fosters reconciliation with others, bringing healing to broken relationships.

> ➤ **Demonstrates Love and Gratitude for God**
> By repenting, we show our love and gratitude for God's grace, recognizing that His mercy is undeserved yet freely given.

For those unprepared, this moment will be one of **terror** and **regret**. The sight of the King they rejected will be overwhelming, leaving them without excuse. In contrast, those who eagerly await Him will experience unspeakable joy. For them, the day of His return is the culmination of their faith and hope. They will hear the words, *"Well done, good and faithful servant; enter into the joy of your Lord"* (Matthew 25:23).

JESUS' PROMISE TO REWARD EVERY PERSON ACCORDING TO THEIR DEEDS

In Matthew 16:27, Jesus declares, *"For the Son of Man will come in the glory of His Father with His angels, and then He will reward each according to his works."* This statement emphasizes that no deed, whether good or evil, will escape the notice of the Righteous Judge. His rewards are not arbitrary but perfectly aligned with the lives we live, reflecting His justice and omniscience. Similarly, Hebrews 9:28 assures believers of the reward that awaits those who eagerly wait for Christ's return: *"So Christ was offered once to bear the sins of many. To those who eagerly wait for Him, He will appear a second time, apart from sin, for salvation."* For the faithful, His return is not a moment of fear but one of fulfillment, a time when their steadfast devotion will be crowned with eternal life and joy. This promise serves as both encouragement and challenge. While salvation is a gift of grace, the works we do in Christ's name demonstrate our allegiance to Him and our transformation by His Spirit. While the Second Coming is a moment of joy for believers, it is one of terror for those unprepared. Revelation 19:17-18 describes a chilling scene where the birds of the air are summoned to feast on the flesh of those who opposed God. This vivid imagery serves as a sobering reminder of the consequences of rejecting Christ. *__For the unrepentant, the Second Coming marks the end of grace and the beginning of eternal separation from God. It is a call to repentance, urging all to turn to Christ before it is too late.__*

The fairness of Jesus' judgment is evident throughout Scripture. In (John 5:28-29), Jesus says, *"Do not marvel at this; for the hour is coming in which all who are in the graves will hear His voice and come forth—those who have done good, to the resurrection of life, and those who have done evil, to the resurrection of condemnation."* His judgment is impartial, rooted in truth, and based on the evidence of our lives. (Jude 1:14-15) affirms this, stating that the Lord will execute judgment on all, convicting the ungodly of their deeds and words. This prophetic vision, delivered by Enoch, underscores the certainty of judgment and the righteousness of Christ's decisions. Every action, whether seen or hidden, will be brought to light, demonstrating the thoroughness of His justice. (Revelation 20:1-3) further highlights this fairness through the binding of Satan, ensuring that evil no longer deceives the nations during Christ's reign. This act of divine justice underscores God's commitment to restoring righteousness and eradicating sin.

The Scriptures speak of an urgency that cannot be ignored. Jesus' return is imminent, and the time for readiness is now. There is no room for complacency or delay. The thief will come in the night, but for those who are prepared, His coming will be a moment of joy and fulfillment. Will you be ready when the King returns? Will your lamp be filled with oil? Will you be found clothed in righteousness? Today is the day to repent, to return to God, and to prepare your heart for His glorious arrival. *"Blessed is the one who stays awake."* The time is now. Be ready. The King is coming

THE UNMISTAKABLE GLORY OF
HIS SECOND COMING

The Second Coming of Jesus Christ is the pinnacle of God's redemptive plan for both those who are His and Retribution for those who forsake His will along with the fulfillment of promises spanning the breadth of Scripture. This event will not only affirm Christ's sovereignty but also demonstrate His authority as the

Righteous Judge, Son of God and Lion of Judah. His power in triumph over evil, and His eternal rule. It will be a moment of breathtaking glory for believers and unmatched terror for those who rejected Him.

The Second Coming of Christ will ultimately be unparalleled in grandeur and awe. Matthew 24:27 describes it vividly; *"For as the lightning comes from the east and flashes to the west, so also will the coming of the Son of Man be."* This imagery of lightning conveys both the suddenness and the brilliance of His return. It will be a moment that cannot be ignored or mistaken, as the entire earth witnesses His glory. 1 Thessalonians 4:16-17 adds another layer to this historic breathtaking event: *"For the Lord Himself will descend from heaven with a shout, with the voice of an archangel, and with the trumpet of God. And the dead in Christ will rise first. Then we who are alive and remain shall be caught up together with them in the clouds to meet the Lord in the air. And thus, we shall always be with the Lord."* For believers, this is the moment of ultimate reunion and redemption. The dead in Christ are raised, the living are transformed, and all are united with their Savior forever. Matthew 25:31 emphasizes the magnificence of this event; *"When the Son of Man comes in His glory, and all the holy angels with Him, then He will sit on the throne of His glory."* This throne of glory symbolizes His authority and the finality of His judgment. The Kingdom of God is built on both grace and justice, offering hope to the faithful and solemn accountability to all. The return of Jesus Christ brings with it the promise of rewards for the righteous and judgment for the unrepentant. Scripture unveils this dual reality with clarity and authority, emphasizing the fairness of Christ's judgment and the eternal consequences of our mere mortal earthly lives.

The unmistakable glory of Christ's Second Coming will forever alter the course of kingdom history. It is the moment where justice is executed, evil is vanquished, and Christ establishes His eternal reign. For believers, it is the fulfillment of every promise and the dawn of unending joy. For the unprepared, it is a moment of terror and judgment. As we await this glorious event, let us live in readiness, with hearts fixed on our coming King. *"Even so, come, Lord Jesus!"* (Revelation 22:20).

THE SEPARATION OF SHEEP AND GOATS: AN ETERNAL DESTINY DETERMINED BY ALLEGIANCE TO CHRIST

Matthew 25:31-46 presents a vivid depiction of the final judgment. Jesus, seated on His glorious throne, gathers all nations before Him and separates them as a shepherd divides the sheep from the goats. To the sheep, those who lived lives marked by love, compassion, and obedience to Christ, He says, *"Come, you blessed of My Father, inherit the kingdom prepared for you from the foundation of the world"*, (Matthew 25:34). In contrast, the goats, those who rejected Christ through their indifference and self-centeredness, hear the chilling words, *"Depart from Me, you cursed, into the everlasting fire prepared for the devil and his angels"* (Matthew 25:41). Their eternal destiny is separation from God, a fate that underscores the seriousness of rejecting His call. This was also expressed in Matthew 13:24-30 (ESV), *"The kingdom of heaven may be compared to a man who sowed good seed in his field, but while his men were sleeping, his enemy came and sowed weeds among the wheat and went away. So when the plants came up and bore grain, then the weeds appeared also. And the servants of the master of the house came and said to him, 'Master, did you not sow good seed in your field? How then does it have weeds?' He said to them, 'An enemy has done this.' So the servants said to him, 'Then do you want us to go and gather them?' But he said, 'No, lest in gathering the weeds you root up the wheat along with them. Let both grow together until the harvest, and at harvest time I will tell the reapers, "Gather the weeds first and bind them in bundles to be burned, but gather the wheat into my barn."*

This passage highlights that allegiance to Christ is not merely a matter of words but of action. The sheep demonstrated their faith by feeding the hungry, clothing the naked, and visiting the sick, reflecting the heart of their Shepherd. The goats, though they may have claimed to

know Him, failed to live out reflecting His love, compassion, forgiveness and selflessness.

The parable of the ten virgins in Matthew 25:1-13 illustrates this point vividly. The wise virgins, who kept oil in their lamps, were prepared for the bridegroom's unexpected arrival and entered the wedding feast with him. The foolish virgins, however, neglected to prepare, and when the time came, they found themselves locked out. The oil represents a life filled with the Holy Spirit, fueled by repentance and readiness. This stark contrast reminds us that readiness is not optional; it is essential. To live in readiness is to live with purpose, knowing that every moment is an opportunity to glorify God and align our lives with His will. It is a call to vigilance, ensuring that we are not distracted by the cares of this world but focused on our eternal hope. The urgency of readiness cannot be overstated. Jesus is coming, and His arrival will be sudden and unmistakable. To be ready is to live a life of repentance, clothed in righteousness, and filled with the Spirit. Let us heed His warning, embrace His call, and prepare for the glorious day when He returns to take His faithful home. *"Even so, come, Lord Jesus!"* (Revelation 22:20).

TRIUMPH OVER EVIL: THE DEFEAT OF THE BEAST , THE FALSE PROPHET AND THE BINDING OF SATAN

The Second Coming will mark the ultimate triumph over evil. Revelation 19:19-21 declares that **the beast**, the **false prophet**, and **their armies** will gather to oppose Christ. Yet their resistance is futile. *"Then the beast was captured, and with him the false prophet... These two were cast alive into the lake of fire burning with brimstone."*

This decisive victory signals the end of earthly rebellion against God. The beast and the false prophet, who led multitudes astray with deception , temptation, spiritual manipulation and idolatry, are utterly defeated. The armies that followed them will be struck down by the Word and Kingdom Authority of Jesus Christ, demonstrating His unmatched kingdom power. This victory is not just a historical event but a historic-kingdom one. It heralds the end of sin, rebellion, and corruption. For the faithful, it is the beginning of eternal peace under the reign of their King. For the wicked, it is the final reckoning that confirms their doom. Revelation 20:1-3 reveals another significant event following Christ's return, the binding of Satan. An angel descends from heaven with a great chain and seizes the dragon, casting him into the abyss for a thousand years. During this time, Satan is unable to deceive the nations, and Christ reigns with His saints.

This period of Christ's rule, often referred to as ***The Millennial Reign***, will be a time of peace, righteousness, and restoration. It is the fulfillment of prophecies that speak of a world where justice prevails, and creation is renewed. For believers, this reign is the long-awaited reward for their faith and perseverance. They will reign with Christ, sharing in His glory and joy. For the world, it is the ultimate manifestation of God's kingdom on earth as it is in heaven. The binding of Satan demonstrates that evil does not have the final word. The adversary, who has wrought so much destruction and pain, will be rendered powerless before the authority of Christ.

The Word of God points to a glorious future, a time of unparalleled peace and righteousness when Jesus Christ will reign as King on earth. This period, known as the Millennial Reign, offers a glimpse of the divine peace and restoration that humanity has longed for since the fall of Adam from sin in the "Garden of Edon". It is a testament to God's faithfulness, a reward for the faithful, and a foretaste of the eternal glory that awaits in the new heaven and new earth. Following His triumphant return, Jesus will establish His kingdom on earth for a thousand years, fulfilling the prophecy of Revelation 20:1-6. During this time, Satan will be bound, his power to deceive the nations restrained. The reign of Christ will be characterized by justice, righteousness, and peace, a stark contrast to the turmoil of the preceding ages. *"Then I saw thrones, and seated on them were those to whom*

the authority to judge was committed... They came to life and reigned with Christ for a thousand years" (Revelation 20:4).

This reign will not only showcase Christ's sovereign authority but also fulfill humanity's deepest longing for harmony and restoration. The prophet Isaiah paints a vivid picture of this peace: *"The wolf shall dwell with the lamb, and the leopard shall lie down with the young goat... They shall not hurt or destroy in all my holy mountain; for the earth shall be full of the knowledge of the Lord as the waters cover the sea"* (Isaiah 11:6-9).

Nature itself will be transformed, reflecting the peace of Christ's rule. No longer will creation groan under the weight of sin (Romans 8:22). Instead, it will flourish in the presence of its Creator. The Millennial Reign provides a glimpse of the eternal reality that follows; the new Jerusalem, a radiant city where God will dwell with His people. Revelation 21:1-4 describes this breathtaking vision; *"And I saw the holy city, new Jerusalem, coming down out of heaven from God, prepared as a bride adorned for her husband. And I heard a loud voice from the throne saying, 'Behold, the dwelling place of God is with man. He will dwell with them, and they will be his people, and God himself will be with them as their God."* This city is not merely a physical location but a profound expression of God's desire to be with His people. It is adorned like a bride, signifying purity, beauty, and the intimate relationship between God and His church. In this place, sorrow, pain, and death will be no more. Every tear will be wiped away, and the joy of God's presence will fill every heart. The new Jerusalem is the culmination of the Millennial Reign, a tangible reminder that God's redemptive plan will ultimately restore all things.

The Millennial Reign of Christ transitions into the ultimate fulfillment of God's promises; the creation of a new heaven and a new earth. (Revelation 21):1 declares, *"Then I saw a new heaven and a new earth, for the first heaven and the first earth had passed away. "*This new creation will be free from the curse of sin. It will be a place where righteousness dwells, where humanity and creation are fully restored, and where God's glory shines without end. (Philippians 1:6) assures us that *"He who began a good work in you will bring it to completion at the day of Jesus Christ."* This completion is seen in the perfection of the new creation. In this renewed world, there will be no need for sun or moon, for the glory of God will be its light (Revelation 21:23). The nations will walk by this light, and the gates of the city will never be shut. This is the eternal home of the redeemed, a place of unending joy and communion with God.

The Millennial Reign is not only a promise of peace and restoration upon Jesus Christ return but also it is an invitation to hope. It summons us to place where our faith in the King who will make all things new. Revelation 3:11 reminds us, *"I am coming soon. Hold fast what you have, so that no one may seize your crown."* This reign serves as a foretaste of eternity, a glimpse of the reward awaiting those who remain faithful. It encourages believers to persevere through trials, knowing that their labor is not in vain. Revelation 16:15 echoes the urgency of readiness: *"Behold, I am coming like a thief! Blessed is the one who stays awake."* The Millennial Reign is both a reward for the faithful and a reminder to remain vigilant, steadfast in our walk with Christ to dwell in the kingdom of God for eternity.

CHRIST'S PROMISE TO TAKE BELIEVERS TO THE PLACE HE HAS PREPARED

Christ's Promise of an Eternal Home

"Let not your hearts be troubled. Believe in God; believe also in me. With these words, Jesus assured His disciples, and all who would follow Him, of His return and the eternal home awaiting them. This promise is deeply personal. Jesus is not sending angels to retrieve His people; He Himself will come to gather them. This underscores His intimate love and care for every believer.

The reality of this promise speaks directly to the heart of every Christian. It assures us that this life is not the end. Beyond the pain, the struggles, and the brokenness of the world lies an eternal dwelling

place prepared by the Savior. Jesus' words in John 14:1-3 are among the most comforting in all of Scripture;

"Let not your heart be troubled; you believe in God, believe also in Me. In My Father's house are many mansions; if it were not so, I would have told you. I go to prepare a place for you. And if I go and prepare a place for you, I will come again and receive you to Myself; that where I am, there you may be also."

These verses reveal Christ's deep love and care for His sheep as the good shepherd and Lord. He has gone ahead to prepare an eternal dwelling in the Father's house, a place of unimaginable beauty and peace. His promise to "come again" assures us that His return is not just a distant hope but a certainty. The King of Kings Himself will welcome His own into the place He has lovingly prepared. This blessed hope serves as a powerful persuader for believers to persevere through trials and tribulations. It reminds us that our current struggles are temporary and that a glorious future awaits. *"So Christ, having been offered once to bear the sins of many, will appear a second time, not to deal with sin but to save those who are eagerly waiting for him"* (Hebrews 9:28).This passage speaks to the duality of the Christian experience. While we face difficulties in this life, we also eagerly anticipate Christ's return. This anticipation transforms how we endure suffering, shifting our focus from present pain to eternal glory.

The Assurance of Salvation and Resurrection

Followers of Christ can rest in the promise that Jesus will not lose even one of those entrusted to Him by the Father. The resurrection is not just a future hope but a present guarantee, sealed by the Holy Spirit within every believer. Paul echoes this confidence in (Philippians 1:6) *"And I am sure of this, that he who began a good work in you will bring it to completion at the day of Jesus Christ."* The work of salvation, begun by Christ, will be completed in His perfect timing. We are not left to wonder about their eternal destiny. The assurance of salvation is firmly grounded in Jesus' words and work. In (John

6:39-40,) He declares; *"This is the will of the Father who sent Me, that of all He has given Me I should lose nothing, but should raise it up at the last day. And this is the will of Him who sent Me, that everyone who sees the Son and believes in Him may have everlasting life; and I will raise him up at the last day."* "These verses underscore the certainty of resurrection for all who trust in Christ. Not one person who belongs to Him will be lost. His promise is eternal security for the believer, sealed by His own sacrifice and resurrection. (Hebrews 9:28) echoes this assurance, *"So Christ was offered once to bear the sins of many. To those who eagerly wait for Him He will appear a second time, apart from sin, for salvation."* His return is the completion of the salvation He secured on the cross, a salvation that includes glorification and eternal fellowship with Him. For those who are in Christ, the promise of rewards is a source of hope and motivation. (Revelation 22:12) reiterates Christ's words; *"And behold, I am coming quickly, and My reward is with Me, to give to everyone according to his work."* This assurance reminds us that our labor in the Lord is not in vain. Every act of faith, every moment of perseverance, and every sacrifice made for His glory will be rewarded in eternity.

Such persons who have yet to believe, the opportunity remains to turn to Christ and receive the gift of salvation. The door of grace is open, but the time is short. The same Savior who offers eternal life will also judge the **living** and the **dead**. The Kingdom promise of rewards and judgment reveals the heart of God; a God of justice who rewards faithfulness and punishes rebellion, yet extends mercy to all who repent. Jesus will return to fulfill this promise, separating the sheep from the goats and establishing His eternal reign. Today is the day of salvation. Choose allegiance to the King of Kings and prepare for the eternal rewards that await the faithful. *"He who testifies to these*

things says, 'Surely I am coming quickly.' Amen. Even so, come, Lord Jesus!" (Revelation 22:20).

The Blessed Hope and Assurance for Believers

For believers in Christ, the promises of God serve as an eternal anchor against life's storms. This "blessed hope" is not just a vague wish for a better future but a confident assurance rooted in the unchanging Word of God. It is the promise of eternal life, the certainty of Christ's return, and the joy of being with Him forever. Let us explore and internalize the Scriptures that unveil this hope and the Blessed-Assurance it provides to those who trust in Him.

The certainty of Christ's return should inspire us to.

> **Live Faithfully:** Align our lives with God's Word, reflecting His love and grace in every area.

> **Persevere Boldly:** Face trials with courage, knowing that they are temporary and serve a greater purpose.

> **Witness Joyfully:** Share the gospel, inviting others to experience the same assurance of salvation.

Titus 2:13 calls this hope *"the blessed hope and glorious appearing of our great God and Savior Jesus Christ."* It is a hope that inspires believers to persevere through trials and tribulations, knowing that the struggles of this life are temporary compared to the eternal glory to come. The apostle Paul reinforces this in Philippians 1:6, *"Being confident of this very thing, that He who has begun a good work in you will complete it until the day of Jesus Christ."* This assurance motivates believers to remain steadfast, trusting that God is faithful to finish what He started. No trial, no hardship, no persecution can derail His plan for those who are His.

The hope of eternal life is not only a future reality but also a present strength. It reminds believers that their labor is not in vain, that their faithfulness will be rewarded, and that their Savior is worth every sacrifice. The blessed hope of Christ's return is deeply personal. It is not merely about escaping judgment but about being united with the One who loves us beyond measure. This hope calls us to live in expectation, eagerly awaiting His appearing.

> ➢ **In trials, it reminds us of the joy set before us.** The pain of this world will pale in comparison to the glory of eternity with Christ (Romans 8:18).
> ➢ **In temptation, it strengthens us to live holy lives.** Knowing that Christ could return at any moment compels us to walk in righteousness and purity (1 John 3:3).
> ➢ **In everyday life, it fills us with purpose.** We are not aimlessly wandering through life but pressing toward the upward call of God in Christ Jesus (Philippians 3:14).

Let us cling to this hope with unwavering faith, as the writer of Hebrews exhorts in Hebrews 10:23;
"Let us hold fast the confession of our hope without wavering, for He who promised is faithful." The blessed hope and assurance for believers are treasures that anchor our souls. Christ's promise to prepare a place for us, His guarantee of resurrection and eternal life, and the hope of His glorious appearing are truths that fill our hearts with joy and our lives with purpose.

As we wait for Him, let us fix our eyes on Jesus, the Author and Finisher of our faith. Let us live in readiness, perseverance, and anticipation, confident that the One who promised is faithful. With hearts full of hope, we can echo the words of Revelation 22:20 *"Even so, come, Lord Jesus!" The return of Jesus Christ, the King of Kings, is the blessed hope of every believer. It is a promise rooted in His sovereignty, fulfilled in His perfect timing, and marked by His unparalleled glory. His return will bring eternal reward for the faithful and divine judgment for the rebellious. As we wait for this glorious day, let us live in readiness, walking in His light and proclaiming His truth to a world in need. "Surely I am coming quickly." Amen. Even so, come, Lord Jesus! (Revelation 22:20).*

THE INVITATION OF SALVATION TO ALL

In the divine account of Holy Scripture, the invitation to salvation resounds as the ultimate call to the lost, sick and cast out, a call from a loving Creator who desires none to perish <u>but all to come to repentance.</u> From Genesis to Revelation, God's invitation is clear; come, receive life, and dwell eternally in His presence. As we reflect on the key Scriptures, this message of hope, urgency, and eternal joy unfolds with undeniable clarity. The final chapter of the Bible closes with an exclamation of Christ's promise: *"Yes, I am coming quickly"* (Revelation 22:20). These words serve as both a promise and a warning. Jesus assures His followers that His return is imminent, though the exact timing remains known only to the Father. For believers, this promise stirs joy and anticipation, but for those who have not yet embraced salvation, it underscores the urgency of making a decision before time runs out. The invitation of salvation is not casual or optional, it is imperative. In the same chapter, we hear the Spirit and the Bride saying: *"Come! Let the one who is thirsty come; and let the one who wishes take the free gift of the water of life"* (Revelation 22:17). This open invitation reminds us that salvation is a gift freely given through grace, accessible to all who will accept it.

THE URGENCY FOR NON-BELIEVERS TO RESPOND TO THE GOSPEL

A Call to Action for Non-Believers

For those who have not yet placed their trust in Christ, the promise of rewards and judgment serves as a wake-up call. Scripture makes it clear that repentance leads to life, while rejecting Christ leads to eternal separation from God. In Acts 3:19, Peter exhorts, *"Repent therefore and be converted, that your sins may be blotted out, so that times of refreshing may come from the presence of the Lord."* Rejecting this call is a decision with eternal consequences. Revelation 20:15 warns, *"And anyone not found written in the Book of Life was cast into the lake of fire."* This stark reality is not meant to terrify but to provoke sincere reflection and repentance. God's desire is that none should perish but that all should come to repentance (2 Peter 3:9).

The invitation to salvation comes with an urgent plea. Jesus Himself warned of the suddenness of His return in Matthew 24:44: *"Therefore you also be ready, for the Son of Man is coming at an hour you do not expect. "*This reminder compels every listener to prepare their hearts now. **_The coming of Christ will be swift, leaving no time for second chances._** Similarly, 2 Peter 3:10 describes the day of the Lord as coming *"like a thief,"* when the heavens will pass away and the earth's works will be laid bare. For those who delay, this day will be one of terror and regret. Yet God, in His mercy, extends this invitation to salvation, desiring that all come to Him. As 2 Peter 3:9 says, *"The Lord is not slack concerning His promise, as some count slackness, but is longsuffering toward us, not willing that any should perish but that all should come to repentance."* The gospel's urgency lies in either its ability to transform lives or its eternal consequences. Salvation is the dividing line between eternal life and eternal separation from God. To reject it is to forfeit the greatest gift ever offered, the gift of eternal life through Jesus Christ.

THE PROMISE OF NEW CREATION AND ETERNAL JOY FOR THOSE IN CHRIST

For those who respond to the invitation of salvation, the promise of a new creation and eternal joy is certain. Jesus assures us in (John 6:39-40) *"This is the will of the Father who sent Me, that of all He has given Me I should lose nothing, but should raise it up at the last day. And this is the will of Him who sent Me, that everyone who sees the Son and believes in Him may have everlasting life; and I will raise him up at the last day."* This assurance fills believers with hope. We know that through Christ's sacrifice, we are not only saved from eternal separation from God but also granted a future where every tear is wiped away, and all things are made new. The new heaven and new earth described in

Revelation are not mere concepts, they are a guaranteed reality for those who have placed their trust in Jesus. This promise motivates us to persevere, to endure trials, and to share this invitation with others. The joy of salvation is not just for the individual but a collective celebration among all who belong to Christ.

The invitation of salvation demands a response. Neutrality is not an option. To ignore the call is to reject it. Joshua's challenge to the Israelites echoes powerfully today; *"Choose for yourselves this day whom you will serve"* (Joshua 24:15). The decision to accept or reject Christ carries eternal significance. For those who choose Him, there is life, peace, and joy forevermore. For those who refuse, there remains only eternal separation from the presence of God.

In Revelation 22:20, the Apostle John responds to Christ's promise with the words, *"Amen. Even so, come, Lord Jesus!"* This is the heart cry of every believer, a longing for the day when faith becomes sight, and we dwell with our Savior forever. But for those who have yet to receive Him, the question remains; <u>will you respond to the invitation?</u> The door to salvation is open now, but it will not remain open forever. The choice is yours, and eternity hangs in the balance. The invitation of salvation is the most weighty and consequential offer ever made. Jesus, in His love and mercy, extends this call to all, regardless of race, status, or past mistakes. He stands at the door and knocks, waiting for you to open your heart to Him (Revelation 3:20). The invitation of salvation is universal, urgent, and life-changing. It is a call to turn from sin, trust in Christ, and embrace the hope of eternal life. For those who respond, the promise of eternal joy and communion with God awaits. For those who reject it, the consequences are eternal separation.

The choice is before you, life or death, hope or despair, Christ or the world. Hear His words, *"Yes, I am coming quickly."* Will you be ready? The time is now, accept His invitation and experience the joy of salvation. The urgency of His return, the certainty of His promises, and the joy of eternal life all compel us to respond without delay. Will you say yes to His invitation? Will you drink from the water of life and experience the fullness of joy in His presence? Today is the day of salvation. Do not wait. Choose life, and join the countless others who have said, *"Even so, come, Lord Jesus!"*

Closing Exhortation
Are You Prepared for the King's Return?

The focal core question is not "Rather if Jesus Christ will return?" but "Are you ready?" Matthew 25:31-46 provides a sobering parable of the final judgment, where the Son of Man separates the sheep from the goats. This passage reveals that preparation is not merely about belief but about action, **feeding the hungry, clothing the naked, visiting the sick,** and **living out the love of Christ**. When the King returns, He will reward the faithful, who have lived as true ambassadors of His kingdom. Revelation 22:12 affirms that His reward is with Him, given to each according to their deeds. For the righteous, this reward is eternal life in His presence. For the unfaithful, it is eternal separation from God. This stark contrast should stir every heart to examine its readiness. Are we living as faithful servants, eagerly anticipating our King's return? Are we sharing the gospel and walking in obedience? The time for preparation is now. Jesus' promise to return quickly is both a comfort and a challenge. The return of the King of Kings is the long-anticipated moment of history, that those who are in Christ have been anticipating. It is a day of glory, justice, and eternal reward. Revelation 22:12 reminds us of this urgency, while passages like Revelation 19:11-21 and Matthew 24:30-31, provide vivid illustrations of His majesty. Every eye will see Him; every heart will respond, either in joy or in sorrow. As we await this glorious day, let us remain steadfast in faith, fervent in good works, and vigilant in hope. The King is coming quickly. **May we be found ready, clothed in His righteousness, and eager to hear the words, "Well done, good and faithful servant."**

The hope of salvation is breathtakingly glorious, yet its urgency cannot be overstated. Jesus Himself declared in Revelation 22:12; *"Behold, I am coming quickly, and My reward is with Me, to give to every one according to his work."* This promise reminds us that His return is not far off. It is imminent, certain, and all-encompassing. For those who have accepted the invitation to salvation, it is a moment of unspeakable joy, a reunion with the Savior who has prepared a place for them. For others, it is a sobering reality, a day of reckoning where decisions made in this life carry eternal weight.

Imagine the splendor of all its beauty, the heavens split open, and the King of Kings appears in all His radiant glory. His eyes blaze like fire, His voice thunders like rushing waters, and on His head are many crowns. Every knee bowed; every tongue confesses that He is Lord. Believers rejoice, their faith fulfilled as they rise to meet Him in the air. But for those unprepared, the moment is filled with dread, a realization that the opportunity to accept Him has passed. The invitation of salvation is open now, but time is fleeting. The King is coming quickly. His return is not a matter of *if* but *when*. Hallelujah, glory to the King of Kings! May His return find us ready and steadfast, clothed in righteousness and filled with holy anticipation. Come, Lord Jesus, come! Jesus Christ, Life, Death and Resurrection are a reflection of the power and majesty of His promise. Let the Spirit stir in every heart, calling us to live prepared and to proclaim His truth boldly and walk in faith Fearlessly .

7 Apocalyptic Warnings of the Rapture in the last Days	
Apocalyptic Warning	Reference
The rise of false prophets and deception	Matthew 24:11, 24
Increasing lawlessness and many growing cold	Matthew 24:12
Wars, famines, earthquakes, and pestilences	Matthew 24:6-7, Luke 21:11
The great falling away (apostasy)	2 Thessalonians 2:3
Global preaching of the Gospel before the end	Matthew 24:14
The revealing of the Antichrist	2 Thessalonians 2:3-4
Signs in the heavens and the return of the Jesus Christ	Matthew 24:29-30, Revelation 6:12-17

JESUS' WARNINGS OF THE LAST DAYS

➤ _False Messiahs and Deception_ Jesus warned that many would come in His name claiming to be the Messiah, deceiving many. (Matthew 24:4-5)

➤ _Wars and Rumors of Wars_ Jesus stated that wars and rumors of wars would precede the end but were not yet the sign of the end.(Matthew 24:6)

➤ _Famines, Earthquakes, and Pestilences_ Jesus described natural disasters and plagues as signs of the beginning of sorrows. (Matthew 24:7)

➤ _Persecution of Believers_ Matthew 24:9 – Jesus foretold that His followers would be handed over to be persecuted and killed for His name's sake.

➤ _The Increase of Wickedness_ Jesus warned of growing lawlessness and the love of many growing cold. (Matthew 24:12)

➤ _The Gospel Preached to All Nations_ Jesus said that the Gospel would be proclaimed to all nations before the end would come. (Matthew 24:14)

➤ _The Abomination of Desolation_ Jesus referenced Daniel's prophecy, warning about the desecration of the holy place. (Matthew 24:15)

➤ _Signs in the Heavens_ Jesus described cosmic disturbances before His return, such as the sun being darkened and the stars falling. (Matthew 24:29)

Preparing for Jesus Christ Return!

Characteristic Of Preparedness	Explanation
Faithfulness to Christ	Remaining steadfast in faith and not swayed by worldly distractions (Matthew 24:13).
Spiritual Watchfulness	Living with constant awareness and anticipation of Christ's return (Matthew 24:42-44).
Obedience to God's Word	Following God's commandments and living a holy life (John 14:15; 1 Peter 1:16).
Love for Others	Showing love and compassion as evidence of a transformed heart (John 13:34-35).
Devotion to Prayer	Maintaining a strong relationship with God through prayer (1 Thessalonians 5:17).
Empowerment by the Holy Spirit	Being filled with the Spirit to live a fruitful life and resist sin (Galatians 5:22-25).

Crowned for Purpose

Acts 13:46-47

RAPTURE READY,
TRIALS TO TRIUMPH

ANOINTED WITH THE "OIL OF PROMISE"

L astly, we will examine the crucial signifgance of being *"Rapture Ready," in the last days* , a concept many call the "Beginning of Sorrows". As we contemplate the significant notion of being 'Rapture Ready,' it is critical to heed the stark-warnings Jesus Christ left to "His sheep" and the world, regarding the last days. These admonitions are not merely prophetic insights but also are meant to awaken and prepare believers to persevere through trials, walk in triumph, and be anointed with the spiritual oil of promise necessary for His return. In the Gospels, particularly in Matthew 24, Mark 13, and Luke 21, Jesus unfolds a vivid mystery of events and conditions that characterize the end times, calling His followers to remain steadfast, discerning, and spiritually vigilant. One of the clearest warnings Jesus gave is about the rise of <u>false prophets</u> and <u>false messiahs</u>. He said, "For many will come in My name, saying, 'I am the Christ,' and will deceive many" (Matthew 24:5). This spirit of deception, aimed at leading even the elect astray, is further emphasized by Paul in 2 Thessalonians 2:3, where he speaks of a "great falling away" before the man of lawlessness [Satan] is revealed. In a world saturated with counterfeit gospels and self-proclaimed saviors, believers must cling to the truth of God's Word, testing every spirit against the Scriptures.

Jesus described global turmoil as a hallmark of the end times. He said, "You will hear of wars and rumors of wars... For nation will rise against nation, and kingdom against kingdom. And there will be famines, pestilences, and earthquakes in various places. *All these are the beginning of sorrows*" (Matthew 24:6–8). The imagery of these events points to the groaning of creation under the weight of sin, as Paul echoes in Romans 8:22. These signs are not to evoke fear but to remind believers of God's sovereign control amid chaos. Christ, the promised Messiah also forewarned of increasing persecution, stating, "Then they will deliver you up to tribulation and kill you, and you will be hated by all nations for My name's sake" (Matthew 24:9). This persecution will not only come from governments and institutions but also from personal betrayals within families and communities. Paul affirms this in 2 Timothy 3:12, reminding us that "all who desire to live godly in Christ Jesus will suffer persecution." This trial by fire refines believers, preparing them to reign with Christ. With boldness Jesus also warned of a chilling reality: "Because lawlessness will abound, the love of many will grow cold" (Matthew 24:12). Coupled with Paul's warning in 1 Timothy 4:1 about some departing from the faith and following deceitful spirits, this highlights the moral and spiritual decay of the last days. Believers are called to stand firm, guarding their hearts against apathy and aligning their lives with the eternal hope found in Christ.

One of the most urgent calls in Jesus' warnings is to remain watchful and spiritually prepared. Through parables such as the ten virgins (Matthew 25:1–13) and the faithful servant (Matthew 24:45–51), Jesus underscores the importance of readiness. He compares His coming to a thief in the night, unexpected and sudden, urging His followers to live with unwavering faith and vigilance. In these warnings, Jesus outlines a roadmap for navigating the end times. They serve not as a source of fear but as a call to spiritual endurance, trust in God's sovereignty, and a life anointed with the oil of His Spirit. For the trials ahead, the promise remains; those who persevere to the end shall be saved (Matthew 24:13). Let this chapter ignite a fervent commitment to be ready in heart, mind, and spirit, for the glorious day of the Lord's return.

- ➤ False Prophets and Deception (Matthew 24:4–5; 2 Thessalonians 2:3)
- ➤ Wars, Famines, and Natural Disasters (Matthew 24:6–8; Luke 21:11)
- ➤ Persecution and Betrayal (Matthew 24:9–10; 2 Timothy 3:12)
- ➤ The Great Falling Away and Increase of Wickedness (Matthew 24:12; 1 Timothy 4:1)
- ➤ Watchfulness and Spiritual Readiness (Matthew 24:42–44; 25:1–13)

ENOCH, PROCLAIMING AND PROPHESYING THE COMING OF OUR LORD JESUS CHRIST

Enoch, the righteous author of the Book of Enoch, and also called the scribe of judgment, the noble ancestor of Noah , the oldest living sibling of Adams lineage, holds a unique place in sacred ancient biblical chronology. While much about him remains concealed in mystery, the Scriptures and historical writings attribute to him an extraordinary legacy of faith, righteousness, and prophetic insight. Enoch is distinguished in the biblical record for his intimate relationship with God, being one who "walked with God" and was taken up to heaven without experiencing death (Genesis 5:24; Hebrews 11:5). *Yet, his most profound contribution to the biblical worldview lies in his proclamation of the coming of the Lord Jesus Christ, as referenced in Jude 14–15,* echoing the apocalyptic themes found in the non-canonical Book of Enoch. Jude 14–15 explicitly attributes a prophecy to Enoch, stating, *"Enoch, the seventh from Adam, prophesied about them; 'See, the Lord is coming with thousands upon thousands of his holy ones to judge everyone, and to convict all of them of all the ungodly acts they have committed in their ungodliness, and of all the defiant words ungodly sinners have spoken against him."*

This prophecy illustrates a vivid picture of the Lord's return, surrounded by a host of holy ones, to execute judgment on the ungodly. The imagery is striking and resonates with other apocalyptic passages in Scripture, such as Matthew 25:31, where Jesus speaks of coming in His glory with all His angels to sit on His glorious throne for judgment. It also parallels the triumphant vision of Revelation 19:14, where Christ appears with the armies of heaven, clothed in white, as the righteous Judge and King.

The essence of Enoch's prophecy *lies in the accountability of humanity before a holy God*. His words serve as an urgent appeal to faithfulness and holiness, reminding every believer that every ungodly act and every defiant word will be brought to light. This is a sobering message of justice but also a testament to the righteousness and sovereignty of God, who will not allow sin to go unchecked. For believers, it underscores the urgency of repentance and the pursuit of holiness in anticipation of the Lord's return.

The Book of Enoch, particularly *1 Enoch 1:9*, is the source of the prophecy cited by Jude. While *1 Enoch* is not part of the official recognized Scripture or Synoptic-Gospels, it holds historical significance, especially in its influence on New Testament writers. The verse reads *"And behold! He cometh with ten thousand of His holy ones to execute judgment upon all, and to destroy all the ungodly: And to convict all flesh of all the works of their ungodliness which they have ungodly committed, and of all the hard things which ungodly sinners have spoken against Him."* This passage aligns closely with Jude's quotation, reflecting the apocalyptic worldview of the Second Temple period, where the expectation of divine judgment and the coming of the Messiah loomed large. The text emphasizes the Lord's majestic return, accompanied by a multitude of holy ones, to bring judgment and destruction upon the wicked. While *1 Enoch* is not considered inspired Scripture, it is reinforced as part of the inspired word of God in Jude with its thematic consistency, with canonical apocalyptic text, it lends a unique place in biblical studies.

The Relevance of Enoch's Prophecy

Enoch's prophetic declaration about the coming of the Lord is as relevant today as it was in ancient times. His message is consistent throughout the ages, pointing to the ultimate fulfillment in Jesus Christ's second coming. The prophecy highlights key aspects of the end times.

➤ **The Certainty of Judgment**: Just as Enoch proclaimed, judgment is inevitable. Jesus Himself affirmed this truth, teaching that every idle word and action will be accounted for on the day of judgment (Matthew 12:36; Revelation 20:11–15).

➤ **The Sovereignty of Christ**: Enoch's vision of the Lord surrounded by holy ones reflects the majesty and authority of Christ, who is both Savior and Judge. This vision invites believers to marvel at His glory and prepare their hearts for His return.

➤ **The Call to Holiness**: Knowing that Christ will return to judge the living and the dead (2 Timothy 4:1), Enoch's prophecy inspires believers to live lives marked by righteousness, faith, and perseverance, echoing the Apostle Peter's rebuke to be found spotless and blameless at His coming (2 Peter 3:14).

Enoch's prophetic proclamation of the Lord's coming is a powerful reminder of God's justice, sovereignty, and faithfulness. Though he lived in the earliest days of human history, his words reverberate through time, pointing to the glorious return of Jesus Christ. The citation of Enoch's prophecy in Jude serves as a bridge between the ancient and the eternal, urging every generation to live with watchful anticipation. May his legacy inspire us to walk faithfully with God, proclaim His truth boldly, and remain steadfast as we await the fulfillment of the Lord's promise; "Behold, I am coming soon!" (Revelation 22:12).

The Stern Prophetic Warnings of the Apostle Paul: End Times and the Second Coming of Christ

The Apostle Paul, an outspoken servant of Christ and advocate of the early Church, issued prophetic warnings about the second coming of Christ and the perilous times preceding it. He revealed deep spiritual insight into the sinful nature of people in the last days and the hope believers should cling to as they await the Lord's return. Today, his warnings resonate attentively as we observe real-world scenarios that mirror his prophetic words, reminding us of the urgency to remain steadfast in faith. Paul's warning in 2 Timothy 3:1–5 serves as a sobering description of the perpetual moral and spiritual decline of humanity in the last days; *"But know this, that in the last days perilous times will come: For men will be lovers of themselves, lovers of money, boasters, proud, blasphemers, disobedient to parents, unthankful, unholy, unloving, unforgiving, slanderers, without self-control, brutal, despisers of good, traitors, headstrong, haughty, lovers of pleasure rather than lovers of God, having a form of godliness but denying its power."*

In today's world, these traits are not hard to find. For instance, social media platforms often reflect a culture of self-obsession, where people seek validation through likes and followers, becoming "lovers of themselves." The pursuit of wealth at any cost, seen in corporate greed and exploitation, aligns with Paul's description of people as "lovers of money." Rising violence, lawlessness, and the rejection of biblical morality reveal humanity's trajectory toward being "despisers of good." In our modern era, the umbilical cord harnessing families to values face unprecedented attack, with generational curses and conflicts amplifying the breakdown of mutual respect and obedience. Paul's prophetic warning of children becoming "disobedient to parents" (2 Timothy 3:2) resounds louder than ever, as societal norms increasingly reject the God-ordained structure of family. This erosion extends beyond households, infiltrating every corner of society.

To elaborate: *The surge in brutal mass shootings serve as a stark reminder of societal, ethical, spiritual and moral decay, while the venomous nature of political* *corruption, strife, disdainful slander and manipulation, further highlights the collective mass departure from moral truth and spiritual integrity. Entertainment, once a mirror reflecting the glorification of God and his kingdom, along with fun-healthy cultural ideals, now often, encourages, entices and glorifies sin, numbing, pacifying and justifying consciences to what God abhors. These troubling trends underscore a world hurtling further from the Creator's standards. It is a sobering call to the faithful to stand firm, shining as lights of hope amid the darkness.*

Amidst these perilous times, Paul offers hope to believers with the promise of the Rapture. In *1 Thessalonians 4:16–17*, he writes, *"For the Lord Himself will descend from heaven with a shout, with the voice of an archangel, and with the trumpet of God. And the dead in Christ will rise first. Then we who are alive and remain shall be caught up together with them in the clouds to meet the Lord in the air. And thus we shall always be with the Lord."*

Paul urges believers to find comfort in this promise, reminding them that death is not the end, but a transition into eternal life with Christ. This hope becomes even more critical as we face an uncertain and chaotic world. The global pandemic swept across nations, leaving a trail of fear, sorrow, and grief as millions mourned the loss of loved ones. Yet, for Christians, a fervent hope shines through the darkness; **_the promise of the Rapture._** This divine assurance declares that those who have died in Christ will rise first, and believers who remain alive at His coming will be caught up together with them in a glorious reunion (1 Thessalonians 4:16-17). This hope is not merely wishful thinking but a steadfast anchor for the soul, reminding believers that present suffering is momentary and insignificant when compared to the eternal glory that awaits (Romans 8:18). It compels us to persevere, not as those without hope but as heirs of a kingdom unshaken by the trials of this world. Even amidst the pain of loss, this promise stirs our hearts with anticipation of the day when every tear will be wiped away, and sorrow will be swallowed up in victory (Revelation 21:4, 1 Corinthians 15:54).

In 1 Corinthians 15:51–52, Paul describes the mystery of the Rapture; *"We shall not all sleep, but we shall all be changed, in a moment, in the twinkling*

of an eye, at the last trumpet. For the trumpet will sound, and the dead will be raised incorruptible, and we shall be changed. "This moment signifies the instantaneous transformation of believers into their glorified bodies. It underscores the urgency to be spiritually prepared, as Christ's return will be sudden and unexpected. The suddenness of natural disasters and the volatility of geopolitical crises serve as sobering reminders of life's fragility and briefness. These unpredictable events underscore a deeper truth: the imminent return of Christ, which will unfold "in the twinkling of an eye" (1 Corinthians 15:52). Just as no one can foresee the exact moment of a storm or turmoil, so too will the Rapture come without warning, catching the unprepared off guard. Believers are thus called to live with unwavering vigilance, heeding the parable of the ten virgins (Matthew 25:1–13). Their spiritual lamps must remain filled with the oil of faith, obedience, and righteousness, lest they find themselves outside, locked-out, when the Bridegroom arrives. This call to readiness is not one of fear but of eager expectation, urging the faithful to redeem the time, walk in holiness, and shine as lights in a dark and unpredictable world (Ephesians 5:15-16; Philippians 2:15).

Biblical Prophecy in Today's Context

Paul's prophetic warnings are not abstract predictions but vivid realities unfolding before our eyes. The rise of false teachings, moral decay, and widespread apostasy confirms his insights. For instance, the embrace of "a form of godliness but denying its power" is evident in the proliferation of prosperity gospels and secularized "Motivational-Christianity", where people profess faith but lack the transformative power of the Holy Spirit.

On the other hand, Paul's words also provide immense hope. The promise of the Rapture reminds us that God's plan for His people transcends the trials of this world. As believers witness the fulfillment of these prophecies, they are called to stand firm, proclaim the

Gospel boldly, and encourage one another with the hope of Christ's return.

Paul's stern warnings are a wake-up call to every generation, urging believers to discern the times and prepare for the Lord's return. As perilous times grow increasingly evident, the Church must cling to the promises of God, finding comfort in the assurance of the Rapture and the hope of eternal life. Let us heed Paul's warnings, reject the distractions of this world, and live in anticipation of the day when we will meet our Savior face to face, forever transformed in His presence.

> ➤ **Perilous Times and Perilous Men** (2 Timothy 3:1–5)
> ➤ **The Comfort of Christ's Coming** (1 Thessalonians 4:13–18)
> ➤ **The Twinkling of an Eye** (1 Corinthians 15:51–52)

THE GREAT FALLING AWAY: A PROPHETIC REALITY OF THE LAST DAYS

The "Great Falling Away," also known as the "Great Apostasy," is one of the most sobering prophecies concerning the last days. Foretold in 2 Thessalonians 2:3, it describes a widespread rebellion against God, characterized by a mass departure from the Christian faith as well as the Church. This apostasy serves as an indication of the ultimate unveiling of the "man of lawlessness," commonly interpreted as the Antichrist, who will rise in opposition to all that is holy and true.

The signs of this prophecy are unmistakably manifest in our world today. A tidal wave of deceptive teachings, moral decline, frustration with hypocrisy, compromise, worldly conformity, biblical ignorance and demonic influence, prioritizing self over God, coupled with spiritual apathy and widespread deception, is eroding faith and causing many to forsake the Church and even God Himself. The allure of moral relativism, hypocrisy and the normalization of sin

have further hardened hearts, fulfilling Paul's warning that some would abandon sound doctrine in favor of teachings that cater to their desires (2 Timothy 4:3-4).

Yet even amidst this growing darkness, the faithful are called to stand firm, holding fast to the truth of God's Word. This prophecy serves as both a warning and a call to vigilance, reminding believers to remain rooted in Christ, for the day of the Lord draws near (Hebrews 10:23-25).

What is the Great Falling Away?

The "Great Falling Away," also known as the "Great Apostasy," represents a monumental and deliberate departure from the truth of God's Word and the faith entrusted to the saints (Jude 1:3). This rebellion is not a mere drifting or wavering in belief but a profound, widespread renunciation of biblical doctrine, certain preachers of the gospel and even the church itself, fueled by deception and spiritual defection. In 2 Thessalonians 2:3, Paul warns, *"Let no one deceive you in any way. For that day will not come, unless the rebellion comes first, and the man of lawlessness is revealed, the son of destruction."* This prophecy reveals that before the return of Christ, there will be an unprecedented abandonment of faith, preparing the way for the Antichrist, the embodiment of rebellion against God. This apostasy is orchestrated by deceitful spirits and doctrines of demons, as Paul cautions in 1 Timothy 4:1: *"Now the Spirit expressly says that in later times some will depart from the faith by devoting themselves to deceitful spirits and teachings of demons."* It is marked by a turning away from the gospel of Christ to embrace ideologies that exalts itself against the true knowledge of God, worldly pleasures, and human reasoning over divine truth.

In this falling away, the love for God grows cold (Matthew 24:12), and people substitute the eternal gospel for messages that gratify their desires, rejecting sound doctrine in favor of teachings that tickle their ears (2 Timothy 4:3-4) "For the time will come when people will not put up with sound doctrine. Instead, to suit their own desires, they will gather around a great number of empty false teachers to say what their itching ears want to hear. Further, they will turn their ears away from the truth and turn aside to myth's, Churches may compromise, prioritizing cultural relevance over spiritual fidelity, and individuals may abandon the faith altogether under the influence of seductive lies that blur the line between truth and error. The "Great Falling Away" is a sobering fulfillment of prophecy, calling believers to vigilance. It reminds us that spiritual complacency is dangerous, and the <u>cost of forsaking the truth is eternal</u>. Yet for those who remain steadfast, it is also a call to perseverance and a renewed commitment to contend for the faith, standing firm in the unshakable foundation of God's Word as the day of the Lord approaches (Hebrews 10:23-25).

The Modern Reality of Apostasy

Today, the signs of the Great Falling Away are undeniable. Churches once filled with worshipers are now empty, while others prioritize entertainment and self-help motivational messages over the uncompromising truth of Scripture. Here are key factors contributing to this apostasy.

These factors highlight the dangers and vulnerabilities that contribute to the Great Apostasy, urging believers to remain steadfast in their faith, grounded in Scripture, and watchful for Christ's return.

- ➤ Deception by False Teachers and Prophets
- ➤ Increase in Lawlessness and Love Growing Cold
- ➤ Persecution of True Believers
- ➤ Worldly Conformity and Compromise
- ➤ Lack of Biblical Knowledge and Discernment
- ➤ Deliberate Rejection of the Truth
- ➤ Overemphasis on Prosperity and Worldly Success
- ➤ Spiritual Apathy and Lukewarm Faith
- ➤ Seducing Spirits and Doctrines of Demons
- ➤ Denial of Christ's Second Coming

Deception Through False Teachers

Peter warns in 2 Peter 2:1, *"But false prophets also arose among the people, just as there will be false teachers among you, who will secretly bring in destructive heresies, even denying the Master who bought them, bringing upon themselves swift destruction."* These false teachers infiltrate the Church, subtly introducing doctrines that distort the gospel and undermine Christ's authority. They offer enticing messages, fun or emotional stories along with scripture-baseless motivational speaking that prioritize personal comfort, self-will and self-reliance over sound biblical doctrine, divine conviction, and Holy-Spirit filled worship; replacing the call to repentance and holiness with promises of prosperity, self-empowerment, and a universal salvation void of sin, repentance or following Gods law or commands. Such teachings appeal to the flesh, drawing many believers away from the truth and leaving them vulnerable to spiritual drift. The gospel, meant to transform hearts and lead sinners to Christ, is diluted into a message that excuses sin, sidesteps the necessity of repentance, and disregards the holiness of God.

Movements embracing hyper-grace theology exemplify this deception, minimizing sin and portraying repentance as unnecessary. While grace is central to the gospel, false teachings twist it into a license for spiritual complacency and a VIP-Pass for sin (Jude 1:4). Similarly, the rise of progressive Christianity and prosperity gospel often reinterprets Scripture to align with secular ideologies, abandoning foundational doctrines such as the authority of the Bible, the exclusivity of Christ, and the reality of eternal judgment. Paul forewarned of this trend in 2 Timothy 4:3–4: *"For the time is coming when people will not endure sound teaching, but having itching ears they will accumulate for themselves teachers to suit their own passions, and will turn away from listening to the truth and wander off into myths."* Such teachings lead many to reject absolute truth, trading the unchanging Word of God for subjective interpretations that cater to worldly desires. In this age of deception, believers are ***called to be discerning, testing every spirit*** (1 John 4:1) and clinging to the full counsel of God's Word.

The faithful must stand firm in the gospel, recognizing that any teaching that diminishes Christ's lordship or denies His truth is a destructive heresy.

Moral and Spiritual Decline

Paul's portrayal of humanity in the last days, as outlined in 2 Timothy 3:1–5, is a chilling reflection of the world today: *"But understand this, that in the last days there will come times of difficulty. For people will be lovers of self, lovers of money, proud, arrogant, abusive, ungrateful, unholy, heartless, unappeasable..."* This moral and spiritual decay is not limited to the secular world, it has infiltrated the Church itself. Many who once upheld biblical truth now compromise, conforming to cultural norms rather than standing firm in faith. The love of self has replaced the love of God, and the pursuit of wealth has overshadowed the call to righteousness. Gratitude and holiness are discarded, leaving a void filled with pride, selfishness, and hostility. Such compromises dilute the gospel, leading believers astray and tarnishing the witness of the Church.

In recent years, some churches that once boldly proclaimed the Word of God and sound doctrines of the gospel have surrendered to societal pressures and trivial traditions. Practices once deemed sinful by biblical standards are now openly embraced or tolerated under the guise of inclusivity and progress. The redefinition of marriage according to fleshly carnal standards, opposed to Gods law and the normalization of behaviors contrary to Scripture serve as glaring examples of this decline. Isaiah's warning echoes through these times, *"Woe to those who call evil good and good evil, who put darkness for light and light for darkness"* (Isaiah 5:20). This moral inversion not only distorts God's design but also deceives many into believing that cultural acceptance equates to spiritual truth. This decline calls for boldness among the faithful, a refusal to conform to the patterns of this world (Romans 12:2). Believers must reclaim the driving force of Gods truth, standing as unwavering guiding lights of Gods Truth in

a world where darkness masquerades as enlightenment. The Church must resist the temptation to conform with modern day norms and peer pressure attempting to blend in with a satanic-fueled-culture. Instead, it ought to take pride in being set apart, reflecting God's holiness and truth.

Disillusionment and Discouragement

In these challenging times, many Christians grapple with heavy discouragement. Scandals within the Church, the hypocrisy of leaders, and the apparent lack of spiritual power in modern Christianity have left countless believers disheartened and ready to walk away. Paul's warning in 2 Timothy 3:5 speaks directly to this phenomenon; "having a form of godliness but denying the power thereof." This verse encapsulates the tragedy of bootleg, artificial faith, an outward appearance of virtue that lacks the transformative power of the Holy Spirit.

This disconnects between professing faith and living it; authentically, it creates fertile ground for disillusionment. When the Church, meant to be a virtuous example of hope and truth, becomes grossly tainted by compromise or corruption and blatant disregard for Sound-Biblical Doctrine, it shakes the confidence of the faithful. Believers long for a vibrant, Spirit-filled Church but often encounter hollow rituals and baseless traditions, as well as some leadership that falls short of the gospel's high calling.

High-profile scandals involving church leaders, whether moral failures, sexual abuse or harassment disgrace, financial misconduct, or abuse of power, have inflicted deep wounds on the body of Christ. Such betrayals erode trust and stunts spiritual growth, leading many to question the authenticity of the faith they once cherished. The fallout from these failures extends beyond individuals; it damages the Church's witness to the world, causing skeptics to scoff and believers to withdraw in disillusionment. Inevitably the adverse mission is accomplished; instead of drawing souls to Jesus Christ many are thrusted into the lap of the devil.

Compounding this discouragement is the erosion of genuine community within many churches. <u>A lack of spiritual accountability, meaningful discipleship, and deep fellowship leaves believers feeling isolated in their struggles.</u> Instead of finding refuge and restoration in the Church, many withdraw entirely, their hearts burdened by hurt, confusion and unmet spiritual needs.

The Urgent Call to Persevere

Yet, even in the face of such discouragement, Scripture reminds us that our eternal, heavenly hope does not rest in human institutions nor the construct of stone buildings rather, in Christ Himself, the unshakable cornerstone of our faith (Ephesians 2:20). While leaders may falter and institutions may fail, the power of God remains unchanging. Believers are called to write the word of God on their hearts and fix their eyes on Jesus, who *"is able to do immeasurably more than all we ask or imagine, according to His power that is at work within us"* (Ephesians 3:20).

This season of discouragement is also a call to action, a challenge to return to the purity and power of the gospel. It is a reminder to uphold leaders in prayer, seek accountability, and build authentic relationships within the body of Christ. For the faithful who persevere, God's promise stands firm; *"Those who hope in the Lord will renew their strength"* (Isaiah 40:31).

Scoffers and Doubters

The Apostle Peter forewarned of a troubling phenomenon in the last days, *"Scoffers will come in the last days with scoffing, following their own sinful desires. They will say, 'Where is the promise of His coming?'"* (2 Peter 3:3–4). These words speak prophetically to our time, where skepticism abounds, and the promise of Christ's return is met with

disparagement. Such scoffing is not merely intellectual resistance; it is a willful rejection rooted in sinful desires and a refusal to submit to God's authority.

This spirit of doubt has taken deep root in a world increasingly dominated by carnal-secularism and atheism. Cultural narratives now exalt human reason and progress while dismissing the timeless truth of Scripture as outdated or irrelevant. This skepticism erodes faith, leading many to view Christianity as incompatible with modern thought.

To elaborate: Some Modern-Day Academic institutions, often hailed as strongholds of enlightenment, frequently treat biblical truth with contempt, portraying it as myth rather than divine revelation. Young minds shaped in such environments, are faintly and overtly encouraged, tough and even brain washed into abandoning the faith of their lineages. Similarly, mainstream social media dismissals of biblical principles, offering instead a motivational message and common carnal worldview that celebrates relativism and self-determination over submission to God's will.

Social media compounds this problem, amplifying the voices of scoffers. Platforms teeming with influencers and commentators mock biblical beliefs, reducing sacred truths to the punchlines of jokes. This ridicule fosters an environment where believers, particularly younger generations, are tempted to question their faith or remain silent about it. Yet, even as scoffers multiply, Scripture calls believers to hold fast to their hope in Christ. Peter reminds us of God's unchanging faithfulness, *"The Lord is not slow to fulfill His promise as some count slowness, but is patient toward you, not wishing that any should perish, but that all should reach repentance"* (2 Peter 3:9). The mockery of the world does not negate the certainty of Christ's return, it underscores the urgency of sharing the gospel.

Believers must stand firm, ready to defend the faith with gentleness and respect (1 Peter 3:15). They are called to be salt and light in a world darkened by doubt, proclaiming the truth with boldness while reflecting the love and patience of Christ. For though scoffers may mock, God's Word endures forever, and His promises remain unshakable.

WHY ARE BELIEVERS FALLING AWAY?

Some obvious reasons for this modern-day mass exodus!

> **Spiritual Deception:** Many are led astray by teachings that appeal to their desires but lack biblical truth.
> **Cultural Pressures:** Peer Pressure and the demand for conformity to secular ideologies causes believers to compromise their faith.
> **Discouragement:** Disillusionment with church leadership, hypocrisy, and a perceived lack of relevance in traditional church settings lead to disengagement.
> **Lack of Discipleship:** Without strong discipleship, many believers lack the foundation to withstand trials and temptations.

A CALL TO SPIRITUAL-WATCHFULNESS IN THE LAST DAYS

The Great Falling Away is not the end of the story for the Church. Jesus promised that He would build His Church and that "the gates of Hell shall not prevail against it" (Matthew 16:18). While apostasy is inevitable, so is the triumph of the faithful. Believers must remain vigilant, discerning, and deeply rooted in God's Word. Paul calls us to avoid those who promote a hollow form of godliness (2 Timothy 3:5) and instead to stand firm, encouraging one another as the Day of the Lord approaches (Hebrews 10:25).

This is a time for believers to rise up, proclaim the truth boldly, and shine as lights in the darkness. The falling away is a call to action, to live authentic, Spirit-filled lives that glorify Christ and draw others

back to Him. Let us heed the warnings and remain faithful, knowing that the Lord's return is near.

The One World Government and the False Church

The Antichrist's Empire in the Last Days

The prophetic visions of a One World Government and a One World False Church serve as chilling warnings throughout the Book of Revelation and other apocalyptic literature. These two entities, crafted and orchestrated by the Antichrist, will dominate the political, economic, and religious spheres during the end times. Together, they represent the pinnacle of humanity's rebellion against God, a rebellion destined to meet divine judgment. This examination delves into the establishment of these entities, their defining characteristics, and their ultimate demise, drawing upon biblical evidence and reflecting on their relevance in today's world.

The establishment of a One World Government in the "last days" is central to the Antichrist's reign, as foretold in Revelation 13:1–10. The "beast," described as emerging from the sea, symbolizes a political figure of unparalleled power who will unite the world under his authority. This regime will implement a centralized political and economic system, imposing its satanic-will on nations and individuals alike. The Antichrist's rule will be marked by oppressive control, enforced worship, and the denial of basic freedoms for those who refuse allegiance to its twisted agenda. The Antichrist will ascend to power by promising <u>peace and stability</u> (2 Thessalonians 2:9–10). However, his reign will be marked by oppression, blasphemy, and persecution of God's people. The False Prophet, acting as a deceptive mouthpiece for the Antichrist, will play a pivotal role in pushing this global agenda. Through a mirage of deceptive signs, wonders, and persuasive rhetoric, he will publicly deceive and manipulate the masses, directing their loyalty toward the Antichrist and away from Yahweh (Revelation 13:11–18). The False Prophet's motives are rooted in the ultimate deception; to divert humanity from Yahweh and entangle them in a counterfeit kingdom built on lies. By promoting the One World Government, he seeks to replicate God's sovereign reign, but his efforts serve only to glorify rebellion and destruction.

Simultaneously, the False Prophet will champion the rise of a One World False Church, a religious system designed to consolidate faiths under a counterfeit spirituality. This unification will appeal to the desire for peace and inclusivity but will mask a sinister agenda; to replace true worship of Yahweh with idolatry and allegiance to the Antichrist. Revelation 17 paints a vivid picture of this entity as the "Mother of Prostitutes," symbolizing spiritual corruption and apostasy. This false religious system will intoxicate nations with her influence, drawing them further from the truth of Gods Word.

The False Prophet's push for this false church stems from his role as the ultimate deceiver. His aim is to erode the foundation of true faith, promoting a religion that glorifies humanism and scientology rather than God. By doing so, he mirrors Satan's ancient desire to undermine God's authority and exalt himself under false pretenses. This False Church will serve as a vessel for the Antichrist's agenda, binding worship, economics, and politics into a single spiritually poisoning diabolical structure. It will exalt self-reliance, tolerance of sin, and moral relativism, in stark opposition to the holiness and sovereignty of Yahweh.

Why This Push?

The False Prophet's drive to establish these systems is deep rooted in an evolving spiritual war. Satan, working through the Antichrist and the False Prophet, will seek to counterfeit every aspect of God's divine order. The One World Government and False Church represent the ultimate perversions of God's design for society and worship. By consolidating power and faith under the Antichrist, the enemy seeks to replicate God's kingdom while corrupting its

purpose. These systems aim to enthrone humanity's pride and rebellion, offering a fleeting illusion of unity and progress while leading multitudes to eternal destruction and permanent separation from God.

This push also serves to test the hearts of humanity. As Paul warns in 2 Thessalonians 2:9–12, those who refuse to love the truth will be given over to strong delusion. The False Prophet's signs and wonders will be so convincing that even the elect would be deceived, were it not for God's grace (Matthew 24:24). This period of deception underscores the importance of unwavering faith and discernment, as believers are called to stand firm in the truth of God's Word. Despite their apparent dominance, the One World Government and False Church are destined for destruction. Revelation 19:20 declares that the beast and the False Prophet will be thrown into the lake of fire, their rebellion utterly defeated by the Lamb of God, Jesus Christ. Babylon, the symbolic representation of this false system, will fall in one hour, a testament to God's swift and decisive judgment (Revelation 18:10). This victory affirms the sovereignty of Yahweh and the triumph of His eternal kingdom.

The One World Government and False Church stand as sobering reminders of the dangers of rebellion and deception. Their rise serves God's purpose, separating those who follow Him from those who reject His truth. For believers, this prophetic vision is both a warning and a call to action; to remain steadfast, rooted in Scripture, and vigilant against the schemes of the enemy. As the end times approach, may we cling to the promise of Christ's return and the ultimate restoration of His kingdom, where righteousness and truth will reign forever.

A Time of Global Chaos

The emergence of the Antichrist will unfold amidst a world gripped by unprecedented turmoil. Wars will rage, pandemics will claim countless lives, economies will crumble, and natural disasters will ravage the earth. In this crucible of global instability, humanity's collective yearning for peace and order will intensify, opening the door for the Antichrist's deceitful ascendancy. As foretold in Scripture, *"Through his cunning, he shall cause deceit to prosper under his rule; and he shall exalt himself in his heart. He shall destroy many in their prosperity. He shall even rise against the Prince of princes; but he shall be broken without human means"* (Daniel 8:25, NKJV). This prophetic vision resonates profoundly in our interconnected age. Recent crises, such as the COVID-19 pandemic and escalating geopolitical conflicts, underscore how global challenges amplify calls for centralized leadership. People seek stability and security, often at the cost of discernment, making them susceptible to promises of false peace. These present realities serve as a shadow of what is to come; a world not fully aware of the rise of one who will wield power through deception and coercion, fulfilling the ancient prophecies of a dark yet divinely permitted chapter in human history.

Global Political Authority

The Antichrist will usher in an unprecedented era of centralized political dominion, exerting authority over every tribe, language, people, and nation. As Revelation declares, *"It was given power to wage war against God's holy people and to conquer them. And it was given authority over every tribe, people, language, and nation"* (Revelation 13:7, NIV). This verse unveils a chilling vision of a world devoid of national sovereignty, where all facets of life are subsumed under a singular, oppressive regime.

In today's world, the rise of international organizations, treaties, and movements championing global governance mirrors this prophetic

warning. Initiatives advocating for one-world ideologies, often presented as solutions to global crises, subtly erode the autonomy of nations. These efforts, though often masked in the language of unity and peace, serve as a precursor to the complete centralization of power foretold in Scripture.

The foundation is being laid for a system where allegiance to the Antichrist will be demanded, and resistance will come at great cost and freedoms. Yet, even amidst this foreboding narrative, believers can find solace in God's sovereignty. This era, dark as it may seem, is under His divine orchestration, fulfilling what has been foretold from the beginning.

Economic Control through the Mark of the Beast

A defining characteristic of the Antichrist's One World Government is its control over the global economy, epitomized by the infamous "mark of the beast." As Revelation 13:16–17 prophesies, *"It also forced all people, great and small, rich and poor, free and slave, to receive a mark on their right hands or on their foreheads, so that they could not buy or sell unless they had the mark"* (NIV). This mark will serve as a means of total economic enslavement, binding individuals to a system where their very survival is contingent upon allegiance to the beast's regime.

In our contemporary world, the rise of digital currencies, biometric technologies, and surveillance systems, while not inherently evil, illustrates how economic mechanisms will eventually be harnessed then dispensed upon the nations for global domination. These advancements, though often presented as advancements for convenience and security, carry the potential to monitor, track, and control every financial transaction. The threat of economic exclusion, denying access to goods, services, and even basic necessities for those who resist the system, echoes the chilling realities foretold in Scripture.

As we witness these technologies take root, it becomes increasingly apparent how they could evolve into instruments of oppression, fulfilling the prophecy of Revelation. In this future, those who refuse the mark will face isolation and persecution, but those who endure are promised the eternal rewards of faithfulness to the Lamb.

The One World False Church

Alongside the rise of the One World Government, Scripture warns of the emergence of a False Church, vividly symbolized as the harlot in Revelation 17. This corrupt and apostate religious system will align itself with the Antichrist, serving as a tool of spiritual seduction and deception. As Revelation 17:2 states, *"With her the kings of the earth committed adultery, and the inhabitants of the earth were intoxicated with the wine of her adulteries"* (NIV). This unholy alliance will lead many astray, enticing the nations into spiritual infidelity, while offering a counterfeit peace that denies the truth of Christ. In this dark age, the False Church will flourish through compromise and deceit, promoting a gospel that is diluted and powerless. It will be a system of empty rituals and false promises, designed to unite the masses under the banner of the Antichrist, all while persecuting and silencing those who remain steadfast in the faith of Jesus Christ. True believers will be marked for their refusal to bow to this idolatrous system, and yet, they will find refuge in the promise of God's protection and deliverance. The harlot's influence will spread like a cancer, deceiving multitudes with a false sense of security, but ultimately, her judgment is sealed. As Revelation 17:16 warns, *"The beast and the ten horns you saw will hate the prostitute. They will bring her to ruin and leave her naked; they will eat her flesh and burn her with fire"* (NIV). The False Church, though seemingly powerful, is destined for destruction, and in the end, the true Bride of Christ will stand triumphant in purity and righteousness.

Spiritual Adultery and Compromise

In Revelation 17:1–2, the harlot is seen *"sitting on many waters,"* symbolizing her far-reaching influence over the peoples, multitudes, nations, and tongues. Her position reveals a seductive power, drawing the nations into spiritual adultery. The harlot's illicit alliances with the kings of the earth epitomize the betrayal of God's covenant, as she compromises her purity for the sake of worldly gain. This unholy union serves as a mirror of spiritual infidelity, where the love of God is exchanged for the temporary pleasures of this world.

The harlot's actions find their ancient counterpart in Babylon, the epitome of rebellion and defiance against God. As Revelation 17:5 describes, *"The name written on her forehead was a mystery: Babylon the Great, the mother of prostitutes and of the abominations of the earth."* Babylon, in its original form, blended false worship with political ambition, establishing a kingdom that sought to rival God's sovereignty. Likewise, the harlot in Revelation engages in a similar mixture, where political power and religious compromise are intertwined, leading to an apostasy that rejects the true God Yahweh.

In the age of the Anti-Christ, the spirit of the harlot will continue to manifest through global movements that seek unity at the expense of doctrinal truth. These efforts, often presented as pathways to peace and harmony, encourage the merging of world religions under a banner of false unity. Such movements, while seemingly benevolent, set the stage for the rise of a counterfeit faith that will ultimately align with the Antichrist's global system. These compromises dilute the purity of the gospel and invite spiritual seduction, paving the way for a future where truth is sacrificed on the altar of political and religious conformity.

Deceptive Teachings

The False Church will be marked by the propagation of doctrines that distort, dilute, or outright deny the unchanging truths of Scripture. As the Apostle Paul warns in 2 Timothy 4:3–4, *"For the time will come when people will not put up with sound doctrine. Instead, to suit their own desires, they will gather around them a great number of teachers to say what their itching ears want to hear."* This prophetic warning speaks to an age when the desire for convenience, comfort, and self-interest will conceal or make difficult the pursuit of truth. The church will become a marketplace of ideas, with teachers peddling doctrine that aligns with worldly desires, leading many away from the narrow path of righteousness.

In this era of spiritual apostasy, we see modern parallels through movements like prosperity theology, universalism, and moral relativism. **Prosperity theology, with its promise of material wealth as a sign of divine favor, distorts the gospel by prioritizing earthly blessings over spiritual truths.** Universalism, the belief that all paths lead to God, denies the exclusive truth of Christ as the only way to salvation. Moral relativism, which teaches that truth is subjective and ever-changing, undermines the authority of Scripture and leads people into a lawless, self-centered existence.

These deceptive teachings, though popular and alluring, leave many unprepared for the return of Christ. Instead of preparing hearts for holiness, they cultivate a generation of believers whose faith is shallow and whose expectations are misaligned with God's eternal kingdom. The time will come when these doctrines will be exposed for what they are, empty promises that fail to deliver true salvation, and a counterfeit gospel that leads to destruction.

Alliance with Political Power

In Revelation 17:3, we see the harlot riding the beast, a striking image that symbolizes her reliance on and complicity with the Antichrist's political system. This unholy alliance grants her temporary influence and power, but as Scripture reveals, her dependence on the beast ultimately leads to her downfall. *"The beast you saw... was, and is not, and yet is about to come up out of the Abyss and go to its destruction"* (Revelation 17:8, NIV). The harlot's political entanglement is both her means of temporary ascendancy and her certain demise, as she becomes a tool of the beast's tyranny while also being consumed by it in the end.

Throughout history, we have witnessed the manipulation of religion to legitimize and support political regimes. Empires and dictatorships have often cloaked themselves in religious rhetoric to justify their authority, co-opting faith for control. However, the False Church will take this manipulation to an unprecedented scale. She will align herself with the Antichrist, offering religious sanction to his global rule, blending false worship with political power in an unparalleled display of deceit. The False Church's embrace of political power will not only tarnish the purity of the gospel but will also serve as a tool of oppression for those who remain faithful to Christ. In the end, the harlot's political collusions will crumble, revealing that her partnership with the beast was nothing more than a passing moment of power, leading her to the same judgment that awaits the Antichrist's kingdom, complete and irreversible destruction.

Persecution of the Faithful in the End Times

Revelation 17:6 portrays the harlot as being *"drunk with the blood of the saints,"* a chilling image that underscores the ruthless nature of her opposition to true followers of Christ. The False Church, in her apostasy, will not tolerate dissent. Those who remain faithful to the gospel will be marked as enemies and will endure intense persecution.

The harlot's bloodlust represents her insatiable desire to silence the righteous, her greed for power and conformity driving her to violently eradicate any opposition to her unholy system. Throughout Scripture, we see that the faithful are often persecuted for their devotion to God's truth. This pattern will reach its pinnacle in the age of the Antichrist, when the False Church, in alliance with the powers of the world, will unleash unparalleled persecution against the saints. Those who refuse to bow to the beast will be targeted, their lives threatened, and their voices silenced in an attempt to crush the testimony of Christ.

Modern parallels already echo this looming reality. In various regions of the world, religious and political alliances have begun to suppress biblical Christianity, ostracizing and inflicting harsh punishment upon believers and restricting their freedom to worship according to the truth of Scripture. During the rise of the second Roman Empire, under the False Church, this suppression will escalate to a global scale, as the Antichrist's system seeks to extinguish all who remain loyal to the true gospel of Jesus Christ. Yet, even in the face of persecution, the faithful are promised victory, for as Revelation 12:11 declares, *"They triumphed over him by the blood of the Lamb and by the word of their testimony; they did not love their lives so much as to shrink from death."*

End-Time Doctrines

A UNIFIED REBELLION AGAINST GOD

The One World Government and the False Church represent the pinnacle of societies rebellion against the sovereignty of God. This final act of defiance echoes the spirit of the Tower of Babel (Genesis 11:1–9), where humanity, in its pride and self-sufficiency, sought to build a united kingdom apart from God's authority. The people's desire for unity, rooted in independence from the Creator, led to confusion and division as God upset their plans. Similarly, in the end times, the Antichrist and the harlot (otherwise known as the mother-son-cult) will bring this age-old rebellion to its climax. Through

deception and manipulation, they will lead the nations into a false unity, worshiping the beast in place of the true Christ, rejecting the Lordship of God in favor of a counterfeit peace.

This rebellion is not merely political or religious but anti-theistic at its core. It is an outright rejection of God's eternal truth, an attempt to displace and up-root His authority with human-made systems of control. The ultimate aim is to dethrone the Creator and establish a false kingdom that denies His sovereignty. The unity sought by the Antichrist and his followers is one founded on deceit, rebellion, and the false promise of peace, a false peace that can only lead to spiritual apathy, self-compromise and self-destruction .

DANIEL'S PROPHECIES FULFILLED

The prophecies of Daniel offer a sobering glimpse into the rise of the Antichrist and the oppression of the saints. In Daniel 7:23–25, the prophet describes the kingdom of the Antichrist as one that *"will devour the whole earth, trampling it down and crushing it."* This kingdom will not only consume the nations but will also oppress the people of God, *"wearing down the saints of the Most High."* These words resonate powerfully with the visions of Revelation, where the Antichrist is depicted as waging war against the saints, attempting to destroy the faithful by every means at his disposal. The consistency between Daniel's visions and the Revelation given to John underscores the certainty of God's warnings concerning the last days. Both prophets reveal a world in which God's people will face intense persecution, but also a world where God's justice will ultimately prevail. The reign of the Antichrist may be brief and brutal, but the triumph of the Lamb of God will be eternal and unshakable.

THE ULTIMATE FATE OF THE ANTICHRIST
AND THE FALSE CHURCH

Despite their power, the One World Government and False Church will face divine judgment. Revelation 17:16–17 reveals that the Antichrist's political system will turn against the harlot, destroying her and fulfilling God's purposes. The Antichrist himself will be defeated at Christ's return; *"But the beast was captured, and with it the false prophet... The two of them were thrown alive into the fiery lake of burning sulfur"* (Revelation 19:20).

Implications for Believers

> ➢ **Discernment** Believers must exercise discernment, rejecting false teachings and remaining faithful to biblical truth (1 John 4:1).
> ➢ **Vigilance** Jesus warned, *"Watch out that no one deceives you"* (Matthew 24:4). The Church must stay alert to the signs of the times and resist compromise.
> ➢ **Faithfulness Under Persecution** Revelation 13:10 encourages perseverance: *"This calls for patient endurance and faithfulness on the part of God's people."*
> ➢ **Hope in Christ's Victory** Though the last days will be perilous, Revelation 21:1–4 assures believers of the ultimate triumph of God's kingdom, where there will be no more death, mourning, or pain.

The rise of the One World Government and the False Church is not just a distant possibility but a sobering reality foreordained in Scripture. These demonic systems will come to dominate the end times, leading the masses into a great deception and a united rebellion against the holy and sovereign God. Their seductive promises of peace, unity, and security will be irresistible to the undiscerning, but for those who remain awake and watchful, these warnings serve as a distress signal to vigilance, discernment, and unwavering faithfulness.

In the face of these dark forces, believers are not left defenseless. The call is clear; **stay prayerful, discerning, and spiritually awakened.** We are to be watchful, clothed in the full armor of God, fully equipped to stand against the schemes of the devil. In this perilous hour, we must be *rooted in the Word of God*, standing firm on the rock of truth so that we are not swayed by the false doctrines of the One World False Church or seduced by the lies of the Antichrist.

The urgency of this moment cannot be overstated. It is a call to be suited up in spiritual armor, the belt of truth, the breastplate of righteousness, the shoes of peace, the shield of faith, the helmet of salvation, and the sword of the Spirit (Ephesians 6:10–18). These weapons are not merely symbolic but vital in this war for our souls. We must be **worded-up**, with Scripture written upon our hearts and minds, ready to discern the times and the counterfeit messages of a world lured by darkness.

We are called to stand firm in faith, not in our own strength, but in the power of Christ, who has already secured the victory at the cross. *"Greater is He who is in you than he who is in the world"* (1 John 4:4). The victory is already won in Christ, and though we may face persecution, deception, and trials, we are more than conquerors through Him who loved us. The glorious return of our Savior will mark the ultimate fulfillment of God's kingdom, where every tear will be wiped away, and we will reign with Christ in eternal glory.

So, let us be steadfast, immovable, and ever abounding in the work of the Lord. Let us proclaim the Gospel with boldness and prepare for the day when our Redeemer comes to set all things straight. With hearts anchored in hope, let us remain watchful, for *the night is far spent, the day is at hand* (Romans 13:12), and soon we will see our Savior face to face. May we be found faithful, ready, and armed for His return.

THE SATANIC TRINITY, OR "THE EVIL COUNTERFEIT TRIO, DECEPTION AND SPIRITUAL MANIPULATION IN THE LATTER DAYS

The Book of Revelation unveils the dark and insidious workings of the satanic trinity, the dragon (Satan), the beast (the Antichrist), and the false prophet. This unholy trio stands in direct opposition to the divine Trinity of God the Father, Son, and Holy Spirit, seeking to pervert and counterfeit God's eternal reign. Through deceit, manipulation, and sheer power, the satanic trinity will endeavor to lead humanity astray, crafting a counterfeit kingdom in stark contrast to the glorious kingdom of God. In their diabolical scheme, Satan, as the dragon, seeks to assume the position of God the Father, striving for supremacy and ultimate control. The Antichrist, the beast, will serve as the false Christ, a counterfeit savior who deceives the world with promises of peace and unity while leading them into rebellion. The false prophet, a twisted mockery of the Holy Spirit, will perform signs and wonders to deceive the nations, drawing them into worship of the Antichrist and away from the one true God.

Through this false unity, fueled by deception and miraculous signs, the satanic trinity will seduce the world into worshiping the Antichrist, establishing a global system that rejects God's sovereignty. Their ultimate goal is not merely to deceive, but to destroy, ensuring the destruction of all who reject their false kingdom, while leading multitudes to eternal separation from God.

Let us examine this deception in detail, exploring the roles of each member of the satanic trinity, with special emphasis on the false prophet's role as the enforcer of this unholy alliance.

Satan: The Counterfeit Father

Satan – The Great Imitator, the False Father:

➤ **Role**: Satan seeks to be the supreme ruler, attempting to assume the role of God the Father. He is the ultimate deceiver, attempting to assume God's Holy Throne and lead humanity into rebellion.

➤ **Scriptural Foundation**: In Isaiah 14:12–14, Satan's fall is described as his desire to exalt himself above God; *"I will ascend above the tops of the clouds; I will make myself like the Most High."*

Satan's ultimate desire is to usurp the worship and authority that belong to God alone. His rebellion against God, described in Isaiah 14:12–14, reveals his ambition to exalt himself above the heavens *"I will ascend above the heights of the clouds; I will make myself like the Most High."*

As the counterfeit Father, Satan mimics God in the following ways.

Desire for Worship and Authority: Satan desires to be the object of worship. In Matthew 4:8–9, during the temptation of Jesus, he offered dominion over all the kingdoms of the world in exchange for worship. In the last days, he will achieve this through the Antichrist, who compels the world to worship Satan through his rule (Revelation 13:4).

Spreading Lies and Deception: John 8:44 identifies Satan as the "father of lies." Unlike God, who is the embodiment of truth (John 14:6), Satan's kingdom is founded on deceit. His lies twist the Word of God, leading people away from salvation. This deception will intensify in the last days as he empowers the Antichrist and false prophet to spread false doctrines.

Counterfeit Signs and Miracles: Satan performs counterfeit miracles to mimic God's power, as seen in 2 Thessalonians 2:9–10:

"The coming of the lawless one is by the activity of Satan, with all power and false signs and wonders, and with all wicked deception." These false signs will deceive those who reject the truth, drawing them into idolatry and rebellion.

Persecution of the Saints: Satan's hatred for God extends to God's people. In 1 Peter 5:8, Peter warns believers to be vigilant, as Satan seeks to devour them. During the tribulation, persecution will escalate to unprecedented levels, as Satan uses the Antichrist to wage war against the saints (Revelation 13:7).

The Antichrist: The Counterfeit Son

The Antichrist – The False Christ, the Imitation Son:

➤ **Role**: The Antichrist mirrors Christ in a deceptive way. Just as Jesus came as the Messiah to save the world, the Antichrist will present himself as a world savior, offering false peace and unity. His appearance and actions will mimic the true Christ, but he will be a tool of Satan, leading the world into ultimate rebellion.

➤ **Scriptural Foundation**: 1 John 2:18 refers to the Antichrist as *"the last hour"*, emphasizing his role in the end times. Revelation 13 describes him as a leader who deceives the nations and blasphemes against God.

The Antichrist copies the role of Jesus Christ, the true Son of God, in Satan's counterfeit system. Empowered by Satan, the Antichrist seeks to establish a false kingdom through deception, false miracles, and coercive worship.

Desire for Worship and Authority Satan desires to be the object of worship. In Matthew 4:8–9, during the temptation of Jesus, he offered dominion over all the kingdoms of the world in

exchange for worship. In the last days, he will achieve this through the Antichrist, who compels the world to worship Satan through his rule (Revelation 13:4).

Spreading Lies and Deception John 8:44 identifies Satan as the "father of lies." Unlike God, who is the embodiment of truth (John 14:6), Satan's kingdom is founded on deceit. His lies twist the Word of God, leading people away from salvation. This deception will intensify in the last days as he empowers the Antichrist and false prophet to spread false doctrines.

Counterfeit Signs and Miracles Satan performs counterfeit miracles to mimic God's power, as seen in 2 Thessalonians 2:9–10: "The coming of the lawless one is by the activity of Satan, with all power and false signs and wonders, and with all wicked deception." These false signs will deceive those who reject the truth, drawing them into idolatry and rebellion.

Persecution of the Saints Satan's hatred for God extends to God's people. In 1 Peter 5:8, Peter warns believers to be vigilant, as Satan seeks to devour them. During the tribulation, persecution will escalate to unprecedented levels, as Satan uses the Antichrist to wage war against the saints (Revelation 13:7).

The False Prophet: The Counterfeit Holy Spirit

The False Prophet – The Imitation Holy Spirit, the Deceiver:

> ➤ **Role**: The False Prophet serves as a deceptive religious leader, promoting the worship of the Antichrist and performing signs and wonders to convince the world of the Antichrist's divinity. His role is to point people to the Antichrist, just as the Holy Spirit testifies to Christ.
> ➤ **Scriptural Foundation**: Revelation 13:11–15 describes the False Prophet as one who performs great signs, even causing fire to come down from heaven to deceive the people.

The false prophet, the third member of the satanic trinity, serves as the enforcer of the Antichrist's agenda. Just as the Holy Spirit glorifies Christ and draws people to God (John 16:14), the false prophet glorifies the Antichrist and leads humanity into idolatry.

Deception through Signs and Wonders Revelation 13:13–14 describes the false prophet performing great signs, such as calling fire from heaven, to deceive the world: *"It performs great signs, even making fire come down from heaven to earth in front of people, and by the signs it is allowed to work in the presence of the beast, it deceives those who dwell on earth."* These counterfeit miracles mirror God's true power, like Elijah's fire from heaven (1 Kings 18:38), lending false credibility to the Antichrist's reign.

Creation of the Image of the Beast The false prophet directs the creation of the image of the beast, which becomes the centerpiece of idolatrous worship (Revelation 13:14–15). This image is empowered by demonic forces, allowing it to "speak" and demand worship under the threat of death.

Enforcement of the Mark of the Beast Revelation 13:16–17 details the false prophet's role in implementing the "mark of the beast," a symbol of allegiance to the Antichrist. Without this mark, individuals will be unable to buy or sell, establishing an oppressive system of economic control that excludes those who remain faithful to Christ.

Persecution of True Believers The false prophet, in collaboration with the Antichrist, will persecute and martyr those who refuse to worship the beast or take his mark. This global persecution will test the faith of believers, many of whom will pay the ultimate price for their unwavering loyalty to Christ (Revelation 13:7).

The Deception of the Satanic Trinity at End of Times

Together, these three, Satan, the Antichrist, and the False Prophet, **form a demonic counterfeit trio of the divine Trinity**, seeking to deceive and draw humanity away from the one true God, Yahweh.

Their malevolent mission is to lead the world into a false worship that mirrors the glory and power of God, yet is steeped in lies, deception, and destruction. This unholy trio will relentlessly strive to undermine the kingdom of God, vying for the allegiance of the nations. The satanic trinity operates as a perverse parody of God's sovereign reign, imitating the holy Trinity in order to deceive and ensnare the hearts of mankind. Their deception is specifically designed to obscure the truth of Christ's eternal kingdom, steering humanity into rebellion against the Almighty.

- ➤ **A False Kingdom:** Satan's counterfeit kingdom is built on lies, coercion, and idolatry, standing in stark contrast to God's kingdom of truth, love, and justice. The Antichrist's reign will be defined by oppression, deception, and the ultimate betrayal of those who trust in him.

- ➤ **A Counterfeit Gospel:** The satanic trinity spreads a false gospel, offering counterfeit hope and salvation through allegiance to the beast. This gospel denies the atonement of Christ, replacing it with a works-based system of idolatry.

- ➤ **Global Deception:** Revelation 12:9 identifies Satan as the deceiver of the whole world. In the final days, this deception will reach its peak through the Antichrist and the false prophet, leading nations to worship the beast and reject the true God.

- ➤ **Inevitable Judgment:** Despite their apparent success, the reign of the satanic trinity is temporary. Revelation 19:20 declares their ultimate fate: *"And the beast was captured, and with it the false prophet who in its presence had done the signs by which he deceived those who had received the mark of the beast and those who worshiped its image. These two were thrown alive into the lake of fire that burns with sulfur."* Satan will be bound and ultimately cast into the lake of fire, ensuring the final defeat of evil (Revelation 20:10).

Implications for Believers

__Discernment__ Believers must be vigilant, testing every spirit and holding fast to God's truth (1 John 4:1). Deception will be rampant, and only those grounded in Scripture will be able to recognize the lies of the satanic trinity.

__Faithfulness__ Enduring persecution requires unwavering faith. Revelation 14:12 encourages believers to remain steadfast: *"Here is a call for the endurance of the saints, those who keep the commandments of God and their faith in Jesus."*

Hope in Christ's Victory While the reign of the satanic trinity is temporary, Christ's victory is eternal. Believers can take heart in the promise of Christ's return, which will bring justice, restoration, and eternal peace.

An Urgent Appeal for Watchfulness not Slothfulness

The satanic trinity and the false prophet represent the ultimate manifestation of evil, seeking to deceive and destroy humanity along with Gods Sheep. Their counterfeit system mimics the holy Trinity to redirect worship from God to Satan. However, their reign is destined to fail, for the Lamb of God will ultimately triumph over them. As believers, we must remain vigilant, discerning, and faithful, trusting in the promise of Christ's return and the establishment of His eternal kingdom. Let us stand firm in truth, rejecting the lies of the satanic trinity and proclaiming the Gospel until the very end.

God's Judgment in the Last Days.
The 21 Prophetic Judgments and
the Binding of Satan

The Book of Revelation unveils a series of divine judgments that will descend upon the earth during the last days, culminating the ultimate defeat of Satan and the establishment of Christ's millennial reign. These judgments, the Seven Seals, Seven Trumpets, and Seven Bowls, manifest the righteous wrath of God against sin and rebellion. They stand as both warnings to a rebellious world and fulfillments of divine justice, emphasizing God's sovereignty over history. The binding of Satan for 1,000 years heralds the triumph of Christ's authority, ushering in a period of peace and righteousness under His reign.

The Seal Judgments mark the beginning of the Tribulation, unveiling the initial stages of God's wrath. Each seal, opened by the Lamb of God, reveals escalating events tied to humanity's rebellion. The first seal introduces a rider on a white horse, symbolizing deception and the rise of false peace, aligning with Jesus' warnings in Matthew 24:4–5. Subsequent seals depict war, famine, death, martyrdom, and cosmic disturbances, culminating in the sixth seal, which unleashes terror and devastation that shake the heavens and the earth (Revelation 6:12–17). These events echo Daniel's visions of the Antichrist (Daniel 7:23–25) and the Old Testament prophets' warnings of divine judgment.

The seventh seal is a profound moment of silence in heaven, lasting about half an hour, as described in Revelation 8:1. This silence underscores the gravity of the impending Trumpet Judgments, signaling a transition to even greater expressions of God's righteous anger.

A rider on a white horse emerges, symbolizing conquest. Many interpret this as the rise of the Antichrist, a charismatic leader promising peace but intent on global domination. Know this, Jesus doesn't come entering on a white horse until the **end of the Tribulation** not the beginning.

First Seal: The White Horse (Revelation 6:1–2)

A rider on a white horse appears, symbolizing conquest. This is widely interpreted as the rise of the Antichrist, a charismatic figure who promises peace but pursues global domination.

Second Seal: The Red Horse (Revelation 6:3–4)

The red horse represents war and widespread bloodshed. Peace is removed from the earth, plunging humanity into violent global conflict.

Third Seal: The Black Horse (Revelation 6:5–6)

This seal signifies famine and economic collapse. The rider carries scales, highlighting scarcity and exorbitant food prices, reflecting widespread suffering.

Fourth Seal: The Pale Horse (Revelation 6:7–8)

The pale horse brings death through war, famine, plague, and wild beasts. A quarter of the earth's population perishes, revealing the severity of God's judgment.

Fifth Seal: Martyrs Under the Altar (Revelation 6:9–11)

The souls of martyrs cry out for divine justice. They are given white robes and assured that their sacrifice will not be in vain, though others must still join them in martyrdom.

Sixth Seal: Cosmic Disturbances (Revelation 6:12–17)

A great earthquake, darkened skies, and celestial disturbances incite terror. Humanity hides in fear, recognizing the wrath of the Lamb, yet many will still refuse to repent.

Seventh Seal: Silence and Preparation (Revelation 8:1–5)

A solemn half-hour of silence in heaven precedes the trumpet judgments. This pause reflects the gravity of God's impending wrath.

The **Seven Seal Judgments** illustrate God's justice, retribution, and the ultimate triumph of His kingdom. As these judgments unfold, they expose humanity's sin, call for repentance, and prepare the way for the eternal reign of Christ. The Seven Seal Judgments underscore the core concepts of the ultimate triumph of God's kingdom. As these judgments unfold, they reshape humanity by purging evil, calling for repentance, and preparing the way for the eternal reign of Christ.

The Seven Trumpet Judgments, described in Revelation 8:6–13 and 9:1–21, represent a pivotal phase in God's plan for the end times. These judgments escalate the outpouring of divine wrath upon a rebellious world, serving as both a demonstration of God's sovereignty and a call to repentance. The first four trumpets bring catastrophic devastation to the earth, seas, rivers, and heavenly bodies, mirroring the plagues of Egypt and disrupting the natural order upon which humanity relies. These calamities emphasize that creation itself is subject to God's authority and judgment.

The fifth and sixth trumpets, also known as the first and second woes, intensify the severity of God's judgment. The fifth trumpet unleashes demonic locusts from the Abyss to torment those who do not bear the seal of God, highlighting the spiritual dimensions of the Tribulation. The sixth trumpet releases four bound angels who command a vast army, resulting in the death of a third of humanity. Despite these severe judgments, many remain unrepentant, refusing to turn from idolatry and wickedness, revealing the depth of humanity's defiance against God.

The seventh trumpet marks the climactic moment of God's redemptive plan, proclaiming the establishment of Christ's eternal kingdom. **"The kingdom of the world has become the kingdom of our Lord and of His Christ, and He shall reign forever and ever"** (Revelation 11:15). This final trumpet heralds the return of Christ, the resurrection and transformation of believers, and the final judgment of all people. It is a moment of ultimate triumph for believers, signifying the fulfillment of God's promises, the defeat of sin and death, and the inauguration of His eternal reign.

For Christians, the seventh trumpet represents hope and victory, while for non-believers, it serves as a sobering warning of the impending judgment. As both a declaration of God's sovereignty and a call to repentance, the final trumpet underscores the dual realities of redemption and judgment, urging all to prepare for the culmination of God's divine plan.

The Seven Trumpet Judgments

The trumpet judgments intensify God's righteous wrath, targeting both the natural world and humanity, each trumpet revealing escalating consequences for sin and rebellion.

First Trumpet: Hail, Fire, and Blood (Revelation 8:7)

Hail and fire mixed with blood are hurled to the earth, burning up a third of the land, trees, and green grass. This catastrophic event symbolizes severe ecological devastation, demonstrating God's power over creation and His judgment upon human idolatry and misuse of the earth.

Second Trumpet: The Burning Mountain (Revelation 8:8–9)

A fiery mountain is cast into the sea, turning a third of the waters to blood. This judgment leads to the destruction of marine life and ships, disrupting global trade and food supplies. It arouses the imagery of the harsh plagues of Egypt and serves as a notice of God's ultimate authority over the nations.

Third Trumpet: Wormwood (Revelation 8:10–11)

A great star, named Wormwood, falls from heaven, poisoning a third of the fresh water. This causes widespread suffering and death as humanity faces the consequences of its rebellion. Wormwood's bitterness signifies the spiritual and physical corruption that comes from rejecting God's provision.

Fourth Trumpet: Darkness (Revelation 8:12)

A third of the sun, moon, and stars are darkened, casting the earth into partial darkness. This judgment disrupts the natural order, symbolizing the spiritual blindness of humanity and the ominous nature of God's impending final wrath.

Fifth Trumpet: Locusts from the Abyss (Revelation 9:1–11)

Demonic locusts, released from the Abyss, torment humanity for five months. Led by demon Abaddon (Apollyon), their stings cause intense suffering but do not result in death. This judgment highlights the torment awaiting those who reject God's seal and serves as a call to repentance before it is too late.

Sixth Trumpet: Four Angels and the Army (Revelation 9:13–21)

Four bound angels at the Euphrates River are released, leading a massive army that kills a third of humanity. Despite the unimaginable horror of this judgment, many persist in their sins, refusing to repent of idolatry, murder, sorcery, immorality, and theft. This reveals the hardness of the human heart in the face of divine judgment.

Seventh Trumpet: Proclamation of Christ's Reign (Revelation 11:15–19)

The seventh trumpet heralds the establishment of Christ's eternal kingdom. Loud voices in heaven proclaim, **"The kingdom of the world has become the kingdom of our Lord and of His Christ, and He shall reign forever and ever."** The heavenly temple is opened, revealing the ark of His covenant amidst lightning, thunder, and an earthquake. This Biblically-Historic climactic moment underscores the victory of God's justice and the fulfillment of His redemptive plan. The Seven Trumpet Judgments not only intensify the consequences of humanity's rebellion but also declare the sovereignty of God and the certainty of His coming kingdom. These judgments call for repentance and point to the ultimate triumph of Christ over sin, death, and evil.

The Seven Bowl Judgments

(Referenced in Revelation 16:1–21) **The Bowl Judgments,** poured out during the latter half of the Tribulation, represent the apex of divine wrath. These judgments are swift, devastating, and unparalleled in intensity. They include plagues such as grievous sores upon those bearing the mark of the beast, the turning of the seas and rivers into blood, scorching heat, and utter darkness over the beast's kingdom. These catastrophic events vividly display God's justice against a rebellious and idolatrous world.

The seventh bowl concludes with thunder, lightning, and the greatest earthquake in human history, resulting in the complete collapse of Babylon the Great, the symbolic center of humanity's rebellion against God (Revelation 16:17–21). This final act of judgment prepares the earth for the return of Christ and the establishment of His kingdom.(Referenced in Revelation 16:1–21) These **vial judgments** represent the final and most severe outpouring of God's wrath during the end times. The vial/bowl judgments are the **last of the three series of judgments** (seals, trumpets, and bowls) unleashed during the Great Tribulation. These judgments represent the final and most severe outpouring of God's wrath upon the earth, signaling the culmination of the end times. These judgments are described in **Revelation 16** and signal the climax of God's wrath against the sinful and rebellious world, just before the return of Christ. Each bowl judgment is poured out by an angel, bringing catastrophic consequences to the earth, mankind, and the cosmic order. The bowl judgments represent the final outpouring of God's wrath, targeting the Antichrist's kingdom and the unrepentant.

The Seven Bowl/Vial Judgments, described in Revelation 16, represent the culmination of God's wrath poured out on a rebellious and unrepentant world. These judgments are swift, comprehensive, and final, demonstrating the justice of God and preparing the way for the establishment of His eternal kingdom.

First Bowl: Painful Sores (Revelation 16:2)

The first bowl judgment targets those who have worshiped the beast and received his mark. Painful and festering sores afflict them, serving as a visible manifestation of their rebellion against God. This plague mirrors the boils of Egypt, emphasizing the inescapable nature of divine judgment upon the unrepentant.

Second Bowl: The Sea Becomes Blood (Revelation 16:3)

The second bowl turns the entire sea into blood, killing every living creature within it. This catastrophic event completes the devastation of the oceans, rendering them lifeless and further disrupting the world's systems. It recalls the first plague of Egypt while magnifying its scope and intensity.

Third Bowl: Rivers Turn to Blood (Revelation 16:4–7)

The third bowl strikes the freshwater sources, turning them into blood. An angel proclaims the righteousness of this judgment, declaring it as retribution for the blood of the saints and prophets shed by the wicked. This judgment underscores the principle of divine justice (Revelation 16:6), as God vindicates His people.

Fourth Bowl: Scorching Heat (Revelation 16:8–9)

The fourth bowl intensifies the sun's heat, scorching people with its blazing rays. Rather than repenting, humanity curses the name of God, demonstrating their hardened hearts and unwillingness to acknowledge His sovereignty, even in the face of overwhelming evidence of His power.

Fifth Bowl: Darkness Over the Beast's Kingdom (Revelation 16:10–11)

The fifth bowl plunges the kingdom of the beast into utter darkness, mirroring the plague of darkness in Egypt. This tangible gloom is accompanied by intense pain, causing people to gnaw their tongues in agony. Yet, even in their despair, they continue to blaspheme God, refusing to repent of their deeds.

Sixth Bowl: Preparation for Armageddon (Revelation 16:12–16)

The sixth bowl dries up the Euphrates River, removing a natural barrier and enabling the kings of the East to advance. Demonic spirits, performing signs, deceive the nations into gathering for the ultimate confrontation against God at Armageddon. This judgment sets the stage for the final battle, symbolizing humanity's collective defiance and the futility of opposing the Almighty.

Seventh Bowl: Final Judgment (Revelation 16:17–21)

The seventh bowl unleashes a devastating earthquake, the greatest the world has ever known, reshaping the earth and toppling cities. Islands vanish, mountains crumble, and massive hailstones rain down upon the earth. Despite the unparalleled destruction, people persist in cursing God, showcasing the depth of their rebellion and the inevitability of divine judgment.

The Seven Bowl Judgments encapsulate the full measure of God's wrath against sin and rebellion, bringing His righteous justice to its ultimate conclusion. They prepare the earth for the fulfillment of God's promises: the establishment of **"a new heaven and a new earth"** (Revelation 21:1), where sin and suffering will be no more. These judgments not only vindicate God's holiness but also herald the triumph of His eternal kingdom and the redemption of creation.

The 21 judgments, **seals, trumpets,** and **bowls,** depict the severity of God's wrath against sin during the tribulation. They are not merely acts of destruction but part of God's redemptive plan to cleanse creation and establish His eternal kingdom. The binding of Satan and Christ's millennial reign offer a glimpse of the peace and righteousness that await those who remain faithful. As these prophetic events draw nearer, believers are called to live with urgency, faith, and hope, proclaiming the Gospel and preparing for the glorious return of the King of Kings Jesus Christ.

The Binding of Satan for 1,000 Years

The binding of Satan, described in Revelation 20:1–3, marks a monumental turning point in God's redemptive plan. Following the return of Christ in glory and the climactic defeat of the Antichrist at Armageddon, an angel descends from heaven, seizing Satan and binding him with an unbreakable chain. Cast into the Abyss, which is sealed to prevent him from deceiving the nations, Satan's imprisonment signifies the ultimate triumph of God's sovereignty over evil and the cessation of his dominion on earth.

This pivotal moment transitions the world from the horrors of the tribulation into Christ's millennial reign, a time of unparalleled peace, righteousness, and restoration. During this thousand-year period, the absence of Satan's influence allows humanity to experience the fullness of God's kingdom, as foretold in the prophetic visions of Isaiah 11:6–9, where the wolf dwells with the lamb, and Zechariah 14:9, proclaiming the Lord as King over all the earth.

Key Aspects of the Binding of Satan

✓ **Satan's Capture (Revelation 20:1–3)**
An angel, armed with divine authority, descends from heaven to subdue Satan. Bound with a great chain, he is cast into the Abyss, which is securely sealed to prevent his influence over the nations. This act vividly illustrates God's ultimate power over evil and the futility of Satan's rebellion.

✓ **Significance of the Millennium**
The millennial reign of Christ brings the fulfillment of God's promises of justice and restoration. It is a time when Christ's righteous governance will bring global peace, prosperity, and the restoration of creation. Freed from the influence of Satan, humanity will witness a foretaste of the new heaven and new earth, experiencing the harmony and order God intended from the beginning.

✓ **The End of the Millennium (Revelation 20:7–10)**

At the conclusion of the 1,000 years, Satan is released from the Abyss for a brief period. In his final act of defiance, he deceives the nations once more, inciting them to rebel against God. This uprising is swiftly and decisively crushed as fire from heaven consumes the rebels. Satan is then cast into the lake of fire, where he will remain in eternal torment, sealing his fate and the ultimate victory of Christ.

Implications of God's Judgments

God's Sovereignty

The judgments throughout Revelation, culminating in the binding of Satan, emphasize God's supreme authority over all creation. They affirm His power to execute justice and His control over the course of Biblical history.

The Consequences of Sin

The catastrophic judgments serve as a stark reminder of the destructive nature of sin and humanity's rebellion against God. They reveal the devastating results of rejecting God's sovereignty.

Call to Repentance

Even in the midst of judgment, God extends opportunities for repentance. However, Revelation portrays the tragic reality of human stubbornness, as many persist in their rebellion despite witnessing the consequences of sin and the display of God's power.

Victory of Jesus Christ

The binding of Satan and the establishment of Christ's millennial reign signify the ultimate triumph of Christ's kingdom. This victory fulfills God's promises, bringing justice to the oppressed, restoration to creation, and eternal hope to His people.

The binding of Satan and the subsequent millennial reign are not merely prophetic events but declarations of God's unshakable plan to restore His creation and establish His eternal kingdom. These events underscore the themes of justice, redemption, and the unstoppable victory of Christ, offering hope to believers while calling all to repentance before the final judgment.

The Rapture and the Second Coming of Christ: A Biblical Distinction

The Rapture and the Second Coming of Christ stand as two pivotal, yet, distinct events in the landscape of end-time prophecy. While both are vital to the hope of believers and the consummation of God's redemptive plan, they differ in their timing, audience, and global impact. Understanding these differences through the lens of Scripture offers clarity and encouragement for believers as they await the fulfillment of God's promises.

The Rapture: Christ Comes for His Church

The Rapture signifies the sudden and unannounced gathering of Christ's Bride, the Church. In this event, both the living and the dead in Christ will be "caught up" to meet the Lord in the air, marking the Church's deliverance from the wrath of the tribulation.

Key Scriptures

> ➤ **1 Thessalonians 4:16–17**
> "For the Lord Himself will descend from heaven with a shout, with the voice of an archangel, and with the trumpet of God. And the dead in Christ will rise first. Then we who are alive and remain shall be caught up together with them in the clouds to meet the Lord in the air. And thus we shall always be with the Lord."
> This passage vividly portrays the Rapture, emphasizing the Lord's direct involvement and the reunion of believers with Him.

> ➢ **1 Corinthians 15:51–52**
>
> *"Behold, I tell you a mystery; We shall not all sleep, but we shall all be changed, in a moment, in the twinkling of an eye, at the last trumpet. For the trumpet will sound, and the dead will be raised incorruptible, and we shall be changed."*
>
> Paul unveils the "mystery" of the Rapture, highlighting the instantaneous transformation of believers into their glorified bodies.

Characteristics of the Rapture

Sudden and Unexpected: The Rapture will occur like "a thief in the night" (1 Thessalonians 5:2), emphasizing its imminence and unpredictability.

Exclusive to the Faithful Church: This event is reserved for those who have placed their faith in Christ, His redeemed Bride. It spares believers from the wrath to come during the tribulation (1 Thessalonians 5:9).

A Heavenly Gathering: Unlike the Second Coming, where Christ physically descends to the earth, believers are caught up to meet Him in the air.

Purpose of the Rapture

The Rapture reflects God's profound love for His Church and serves as a fulfillment of Jesus' promise in John 14:2–3: *"In My Father's house are many mansions... I go to prepare a place for you. And if I go and prepare a place for you, I will come again and receive you to Myself; that where I am, there you may be also."*

This divine gathering not only spares the Church from the judgments of the tribulation but also ushers in the marriage of the Lamb in heaven (Revelation 19:7–9). It marks the beginning of a new phase in God's plan, paving the way for the tribulation on earth, a period of judgment and redemption for the unrepentant.

The Rapture is a glorious event of hope, assurance, and anticipation, reminding believers of the unfailing promises of Christ and the joy of eternal union with Him.

The Second Coming: Christ Comes with His Church

The Second Coming, often referred to as the Revelation of Christ, marks the triumphant, visible return of Jesus to the earth. This event differs profoundly from the Rapture. While the Rapture is a private gathering of the Church to meet Christ in the air, the Second Coming is a global and unmistakable manifestation of His glory, power, and sovereignty as He establishes His millennial kingdom.

Key Scriptures

> ### Revelation 19:11–16
> *"Now I saw heaven opened, and behold, a white horse. And He who sat on him was called Faithful and True... And the armies in heaven, clothed in fine linen, white and clean, followed Him on white horses."* In this vision, Christ is revealed as the conquering King, riding in victory and accompanied by His redeemed saints, the Church, arrayed in heavenly splendor.

> ### Matthew 24:30
> *"Then the sign of the Son of Man will appear in heaven, and then all the tribes of the earth will mourn, and they will see the Son of Man coming on the clouds of heaven with power and great glory."* This passage emphasizes the global visibility and awe-inspiring majesty of Christ's return, which will be undeniable to all of humanity.

Characteristics of the Second Coming

Visible and Glorious: Unlike the Rapture, which occurs in secrecy, the Second Coming is a dramatic event witnessed by the entire world. Jesus will descend from heaven, radiating divine glory and fulfilling every prophecy of His return.

Accompanied by His Saints: Christ's return is not solitary. He is accompanied by the armies of heaven, His redeemed Church, arrayed in fine, white linen, symbolic of righteousness (Revelation 19:14; Jude 14).

Judgment on the Wicked: The Second Coming brings final judgment upon the rebellious nations and the forces of the Antichrist. Revelation 19:19–21 describes the decisive defeat of these enemies as Christ establishes His dominion.

Purpose of the Second Coming

The Second Coming is the culmination of God's redemptive plan and the consummation of His kingdom on earth.

Judgment of Evil: Christ will execute righteous judgment upon the unrepentant, bringing an end to the reign of sin, rebellion, and wickedness. The Antichrist and the false prophet will be cast into the lake of fire, and Satan's influence will be restrained (Revelation 19:20; 20:1–3).

Redemption of Israel: This event fulfills the promises of God to the nation of Israel, as they recognize Jesus as their Messiah and are restored to covenant relationship with Him (Zechariah 12:10; Romans 11:26–27).

Establishment of the Millennial Kingdom: The Second Coming inaugurates the reign of Christ on earth, a thousand-year period of peace, justice, and restoration, where the promises of Isaiah 11:1–10 and Revelation 20:4–6 are fulfilled.

The Second Coming is a moment of ultimate triumph, as Christ, the King of kings and Lord of lords, returns in majesty to claim His rightful rule. It is a declaration of God's sovereignty, the vindication of His justice, and the glorious hope for all who belong to Him.

Key Differences Between the Rapture and the Second Coming

Aspect	The Rapture	The Second Coming
Timing	Before the tribulation	At the end of the tribulation
Nature	Sudden, private event	Public, visible to all
Participants	Christ comes *for* His Church	Christ comes *with* His Church
Location	Meeting in the air	Christ descends to the Mount of Olives (Zechariah 14:4)
Purpose	Deliverance of believers	Judgment and establishment of Christ's kingdom

The Judgment at the Great White Throne

The Great White Throne Judgment stands as the final and most solemn event in God's redemptive plan. Occurring after Christ's millennial reign, it is distinct from the Rapture and the Second Coming, serving as the ultimate reckoning for all whose names are not found in the Book of Life.

"Then I saw a great white throne and Him who sat on it, from whose face the earth and the heaven fled away. And there was found no place for them... And anyone not found written in the Book of Life was cast into the lake of fire."
—Revelation 20:11–15

Features of the Great White Throne Judgment

he Throne and the Judge

The "great white throne" symbolizes the purity, holiness, and ultimate authority of God. The One seated upon it is none other than Jesus Christ Himself, as confirmed in John 5:22: *"The Father judges no one but has committed all judgment to the Son."* This throne is not one of mercy but of justice, where eternal destinies are determined.

The Resurrection of the Dead

All the unsaved, "great and small," will be resurrected to stand before the throne. This resurrection is distinct from the first resurrection of the righteous, which occurs before the millennial reign (Revelation 20:5–6).

The Books Are Opened

> ➢ **The Book of Life**: The absence of one's name in this book seals their eternal separation from God.
> ➢ **The Books of Works**: These record every deed, revealing the undeniable evidence of human rebellion and sin. Judgment is rendered according to these works, demonstrating the justice of God (Romans 2:6).

The Lake of Fire: Those whose names are not found in the Book of Life are cast into the lake of fire, a place of eternal separation from God, described as the "second death" (Revelation 20:14). This judgment emphasizes the gravity of rejecting God's salvation.

Living in Light of These Events

The weight of eternal judgment and the hope of Christ's return compel believers to live lives marked by vigilance, faithfulness, and urgency in proclaiming the gospel.

Be Watchful

Jesus calls His followers to remain spiritually alert;
"Watch therefore, for you do not know what hour your Lord is coming" (Matthew 24:42).The imminent nature of the Rapture demands readiness and devotion to Christ.

> ➢ **Proclaim the Gospel**
> The certainty of eternal judgment should motivate believers to share the good news of salvation. As Paul writes in 2 Corinthians 5:11;
> *"Knowing, therefore, the terror of the Lord, we persuade men."*

> ➤ **Endure with Hope**
> The promise of Christ's Second Coming strengthens believers to endure trials and tribulations with steadfast hope, knowing that ultimate victory belongs to the Lord: *"Be faithful until death, and I will give you the crown of life"* (Revelation 2:10).

The Rapture and the Second Coming, though distinct, form a cohesive narrative of God's redemptive plan. The Rapture serves as the Church's deliverance, bringing believers into eternal fellowship with Christ. The Second Coming, however, is a glorious display of divine justice and authority, establishing Christ's reign on earth.

In contrast, the Great White Throne Judgment stands as the ultimate reminder of God's holiness and justice, underscoring the eternal consequences of rejecting His grace.

FAITHFUL OVERCOMERS: CROWNS FOR THOSE WHO ENDURE

The journey of the faithful is not without trials, yet it is crowned with divine reward. The crowns described in Scripture are tangible expressions of God's recognition of faithfulness, endurance, and love for Him.

1. **The Crown of Life** (James 1:12; Revelation 2:10)
   Bestowed upon those who persevere under trials, this crown signifies victory over tribulation and steadfastness in faith.
2. **The Incorruptible Crown** (1 Corinthians 9:25)
   Given to those who exercise self-discipline and run the race of faith with endurance, it reflects a life lived in devotion to God's purpose.
3. **The Crown of Righteousness** (2 Timothy 4:8)
   Reserved for those who eagerly await Christ's return, this crown is a celebration of lives lived in the hope of His appearing.

4. **The Crown of Glory** (1 Peter 5:4)
   Awarded to faithful shepherds and leaders in the Church, it honors those who serve with humility and dedication.

5. **The Crown of Rejoicing** (1 Thessalonians 2:19)
   Known as the soul-winner's crown, it is given to those who lead others to Christ, celebrating the eternal impact of evangelism.

These crowns are not merely rewards but reflections of a life lived for the glory of God. They testify to His faithfulness and affirm His promises to those who overcome by His grace. Let us, therefore, run with endurance the race set before us, keeping our eyes fixed on Jesus, the author and the finisher of our faith (Hebrews 12:1–2).

God's Essential "Crown of Purpose": <u>Every Life Matters</u>

Beyond the crowns explicitly mentioned in Scripture, there is an underlying truth woven throughout God's Word: ***every life has purpose***. God has uniquely designed each individual with gifts, talents, and anointing to fulfill His divine plan.

Jeremiah 29:11: A Plan and a Purpose

God's promise in Jeremiah 29:11 reminds us," *For I know the plans I have for you," declares the Lord, "plans to prosper you and not to harm you, plans to give you hope and a future."*

<u>Each believer is anointed for a specific purpose, whether raising a godly family, sharing the Gospel, or serving in the community. This purpose is not diminished by trials but refined through them.</u>

ANOINTED FOR PROMISES: LIVING FOR AN INTENDED PURPOSE

From the beginning of Scripture, God's anointing has been the divine empowerment for His servants to fulfill His promises. David, anointed as king, faced immense trials, yet through each hardship, he was refined for his destiny. Esther, chosen for "such a time as this" (Esther 4:14), was anointed to deliver her people from destruction. Similarly, believers today are anointed to walk in the promises of God, overcoming obstacles to fulfill their God-given purpose and destiny. God's purposes often unfold through seasons of pain and suffering, yet these trials are not in vain. They serve to refine, strengthen, and purify faith. James 1:2-4 calls believers to rejoice in their trials, knowing that through perseverance, spiritual maturity and completeness are forged. The journey of faith is not one of ease but of sanctification, where pain transforms into purpose. In fulfilling God's purpose, believers are never alone. The Holy Spirit empowers and equips them, providing strength far beyond their own. Acts 1:8 promises, "But you shall receive power when the Holy Spirit has come upon you; and you shall be witnesses to Me..." Through the Spirit, God's people are enabled to accomplish what is impossible in human strength, walking in His will with divine enablement and courage. Revelation 3:11 admonishes, "Hold fast what you have, that no one may take your crown." The crown of victory is not easily won and can be forfeited through complacency, compromise, or neglect. But for those who endure, remain faithful, and live with purpose, the eternal rewards are unmatched. These crowns represent the fruit of steadfast faith, purified through fire and trial. The crowns given to overcomers are more than just symbols of reward; they are the testimony of a life fully devoted to Christ. In the end, these crowns will be cast at His feet in worship (Revelation 4:10-11), acknowledging that every victory, every triumph, is through Him. The final victory is not about personal achievement but about glorifying the King of kings, whose strength and grace have enabled every faithful step.

491

Pressing Toward the Crown: Running the Race of Life with Endurance – "Redeemed from the "Death Sentence" of sin, We Ain't Going Back"

Faithful overcomers are those who, in the face of trials and adversity, remain unwavering in their faith, pressing forward toward the high calling of God. These individuals are marked by their steadfastness, their determination to fulfill God's divine purpose, and their refusal to turn back, no matter the cost. The crowns of life, righteousness, glory, and imperishable victory stand as eternal testimonies to God's faithfulness and the immeasurable worth of a life wholly devoted to Him. Let us, therefore, run this race with endurance, fixing our eyes on the prize of God's promises and the eternal rewards that await those who persevere. Let us live as those anointed for His purposes, driven by the certainty that every step we take in faith is part of His sovereign plan. May we hold fast to our faith, declaring His glory in all things, until that glorious day when we receive our crowns and hear our Savior's words, "Well done, good and faithful servant" (Matthew 25:21). We will not turn back, for the race is set before us, and the reward is eternal.

RESTORATION HAS FINALLY COME THROUGH THE PROMISE OF JESUS CHRIST, THE KING!

The pinnacle of God's redemptive plan is the ultimate restoration of all things through the reign of Jesus Christ, the King of kings and Lord of lords. What began with humanity's fall in the Garden of Eden will be completed in the full restoration of creation, the healing of fellowship with God, and the fulfillment of every promise made to His faithful. Through Christ, the curse of sin is forever broken, and the redeemed will rejoice in the eternal joy of God's perfect kingdom.

RESTORATION FOR THE FAITHFUL
AND REDEEMED

For those who remain faithful, the promise of restoration is both a present reality and a future hope. The psalmist David prayed, *"Restore to me the joy of Your salvation, and uphold me with a willing spirit" (Psalm 51:12)*. This cry for restoration is echoed in God's promise to His people: *"I will restore the years that the swarming locust has eaten" (Joel 2:25-26)*.

The eternal state will be the full realization of this restoration. In the final renewal, God declares, "For I will restore health to you, and your wounds I will heal" (Jeremiah 30:17) . Psalm 126:5-6 states " *Those who sow in tears shall reap with shouts of joy! He who goes out weeping bearing the seed for sowing, shall come home with shouts of joy, bringing his sheaves with him.* The redeemed will experience perfect health, everlasting peace, and boundless joy in the presence of their Savior, free from the effects of sin and suffering.

THE CURSE OF SIN IS BROKEN

Since the fall of Adam and Eve, humanity has borne the weight of sin's curse, as described in Genesis 3:14–17. Yet through Christ's atonement, that curse is lifted. *Revelation 22:3* declares, "*No longer will there be anything accursed, but the throne of God and of the Lamb will be in it, and His servants will worship Him.*"

This victory marks the end of suffering, toil, and separation from God. The earth, once marred by the fall, will be renewed, reflecting the perfect harmony and beauty of God's original creation. Every aspect of life will be restored to its intended glory, as God reigns supreme.

NO MORE DEATH

The entrance of death into the world was a devastating consequence of Adam's sin (Genesis 3:19). However, Christ's victory over the grave ensures that death will be no more. Revelation 21:4 proclaims,

"He will wipe away every tear from their eyes, and death shall be no more, neither shall there be mourning, nor crying, nor pain anymore, for the former things have passed away." In this eternal reality, the redeemed will no longer fear death. Instead, they will experience everlasting life in the presence of their Creator Yahweh, free from the shadow of sorrow, suffering, and loss.

RESTORED FELLOWSHIP WITH GOD

When Adam and Eve were expelled from the Garden of Eden (Genesis 3:24), humanity's intimate fellowship with God was severed. Yet through Christ, that fellowship is restored. *Revelation 22:14* promises, *"Blessed are those who wash their robes, so that they may have the right to the tree of life and that they may enter the city by the gates."* The imagery of the tree of life and the holy city reflects the return of humanity to a perfect relationship with God, once enjoyed in Eden. In this restored state, the redeemed walk with God in perfect harmony, never again to be separated by sin.

THE END OF PAIN AND SORROW
RESTORATION HAS FINALLY COME

Genesis 3:17 describes the pain and sorrow that entered the world through sin, but Revelation 21:4 assures us that these will be no more. Every burden, heartache, and affliction will be removed. The faithful will bask in the glory of God's love, where perfect peace reigns forever. The eternal state will be one of unbroken joy, where all things are made new, and the faithful find rest in the presence of God. Restoration has finally come through the promise of Jesus Christ, the King. The curse of sin is eradicated, death is vanquished, and humanity is restored to perfect fellowship with God. Every tear is wiped away, and the faithful dwell in a renewed creation, experiencing eternal joy and peace. This is the ultimate fulfillment of God's redemptive plan, a testament to His faithfulness and love. Through Christ, the promise of restoration is not merely a distant

hope but an everlasting reality. Let us rejoice and worship the King who has made all things new! As Revelation 21:5 declares, "Behold, I am making all things new." We have been made new, and in Christ, we are restored for eternity.

THE BRIDEGROOM RECEIVES HIS BRIDE: THE ETERNAL UNION OF CHRIST AND HIS FAITHFUL CHURCH

The divine-narrative of Scripture culminates in a wedding, the eternal union of the Bridegroom, Jesus Christ, with His Bride, the Church. This divine culmination is not only the fulfillment of God's promises but also the restoration of all creation to its intended glory. It is a celebration of faithfulness, refinement, purpose, triumph, and ultimate restoration, as foretold in Revelation 19:7–9: *"Let us rejoice and exult and give Him the glory, for the marriage of the Lamb has come, and His Bride has made herself ready; it was granted her to clothe herself with fine linen, bright and pure, for the fine linen is the righteous deeds of the saints."* This eternal union marks the completion of God's redemptive work. The Church, purified and prepared, will be presented to Christ, the Lamb of God, in perfect holiness, ready to dwell with Him forever in the glory of His presence.

The journey of the Bride has been one of unwavering faith and divine refinement. Through countless trials and tribulations, she has remained steadfast, holding fast to the promises of her Bridegroom. Each test, each hardship, has served as a refining fire, purging her of every imperfection and preparing her for this sacred moment. The Apostle Paul eloquently describes this sanctifying process in Ephesians 5:25–27:*"Christ loved the Church and gave Himself up for her, that He might sanctify her, having cleansed her by the washing of water with the word, so that He might present the Church to Himself in splendor, without spot or wrinkle or any such thing, that she might be holy and without blemish. "*This sacred refinement has been a labor of love, forged through the crucible of life's trials. The pain and suffering the Bride endured were not in vain but were purpose-driven. Each sorrow, each moment of testing, was designed to shape her into a radiant, holy companion for the Bridegroom.

The Bride's journey has been marked by purpose-driven pain, a reality underscored by the apostle Paul in Romans 8:18: *"For I consider that the sufferings of this present time are not worth comparing with the glory that is to be revealed to us. "*Every tear shed, every trial endured, every act of faith walked out was a step closer to the Bride's ultimate triumph. Like gold refined in fire, the Church has emerged from her trials purified and radiant, ready to stand beside the King in glory. Jesus Himself reassures the faithful in Revelation 3:10: **"Because you have kept my word about patient endurance, I will keep you from the hour of trial that is coming on the whole world."** This victory, however, is not of her own strength but is the gift of the Bridegroom, who has sustained her with His grace and love, ensuring her perseverance through every season. The moment of union between the Bride and the Bridegroom will be marked by incomparable joy and heavenly celebration. The marriage of the Lamb will finally be consummated, and the saints will be gathered in eternal fellowship. Revelation 19:9 proclaims: *"Blessed are those who are invited to the marriage supper of the Lamb. "*This feast represents the end of all separation, the fulfillment of every promise, and the inauguration of eternal fellowship with the Bridegroom. The Bride, clothed in fine linen, pure and radiant, will stand before the Lamb, her beauty a reflection of His righteousness, wrought through His Spirit.

As the Bridegroom receives His Bride, the restoration of all things will be completed. Revelation 21:2 offers a vivid portrayal of this moment, **"And I saw the holy city, new Jerusalem, coming down out of heaven from God, prepared as a bride adorned for her husband."** The curse that began in Eden will be fully reversed. Fellowship with God, broken by sin, will be perfectly restored. **Revelation 21:3–4 declares "Behold, the dwelling place of God is with man. He will dwell with them, and they will be His**

people, and God Himself will be with them as their God. He will wipe away every tear from their eyes, and death shall be no more, neither shall there be mourning, nor crying, nor pain anymore, for the former things have passed away."

In this restored creation, the faithful will dwell in perfect peace, with God Himself as their everlasting joy. The Bride's journey culminates in eternal triumph, a living testimony of God's unfailing love, grace, and faithfulness. From brokenness to glory, her story reflects the redemptive power of the Gospel. She is no longer defined by her struggles but by her union with the Bridegroom, who has crowned her with eternal purpose and unending joy. This union fulfills the deepest longing of the human heart and the promise of Revelation 22:17: *"The Spirit and the Bride say, 'Come.' And let the one who hears say, 'Come.' And let the one who is thirsty come; let the one who desires take the water of life without price."* In the eternal kingdom, the Bride's triumph will be complete, her union with Christ marking the culmination of God's glorious plan for redemption. As the Bride eagerly awaits her Bridegroom, the call is clear; remain faithful, endure the trials, and walk in holiness. The promise of the wedding feast urges believers to press on, knowing that every moment of obedience and every act of faithfulness draws them nearer to this glorious union. The words of the Bridegroom in Revelation 22:12–13 echo through the ages. *"Behold, I am coming quickly, bringing my reward with me, to repay each one for what he has done. I am the Alpha and the Omega, the first and the last, the beginning and the end."*

A GLORIOUS ETERNITY FOR THE FAITHFUL

Restoration has finally come through the promise of Jesus Christ, the King. The Bridegroom has received His Bride, and all creation rejoices in the eternal union of Christ and His Faithful Church. This moment of divine celebration is beyond words, as every tear is wiped away and every sorrow is replaced with perfect, unending peace. The culmination of God's redemptive plan has arrived, the fulfillment of His eternal love and the beginning of an everlasting reign. Let us live in anticipation, preparing our hearts for the day when we, as the Bride, will behold the face of our Bridegroom and enter into the joy of His eternal kingdom. As Matthew 6:19–21 reminds us, *"Do not lay up for yourselves treasures on earth, where moth and rust destroy and where thieves break in and steal; but lay up for yourselves treasures in heaven, where neither moth nor rust destroys and where thieves do not break in and steal. For where your treasure is, there your heart will be also."* In the light of this eternal reality, we press forward with hope, knowing that as we fight the good fight, we too will receive the crown of righteousness, as promised in 2 **Timothy** 4:7–8: *"I have fought the good fight, I have finished the race, I have kept the faith. Finally, there is laid up for me the crown of righteousness, which the Lord, the righteous Judge, will give to me on that Day, and not to me only but also to all who have loved His appearing."* And in the moment of victory, we will echo the truth found in 2 **Corinthians** 4:17: *"For our light affliction, which is but for a moment, is working for us a far more exceeding and eternal weight of glory."* This is the hope that sustains us, the promise that propels us forward, toward the eternal glory of the Bridegroom and His radiant Bride.

GOD IS INVITING YOU INTO A RELATIONSHIP WITH HIM TODAY!

The Prayer of Salvation!

Father, it is written in Your Word that if I confess with my mouth that Jesus is Lord and believe in my heart that You have raised Him from the dead, I shall be saved.

Father, I confess that Jesus is my Lord. I make Him my Lord and Savior right now. I believe in my heart and confess with my mouth that You raised Jesus from the dead. I renounce my past life with satan and close the door to any of his devices. I thank You for forgiving all my sins through the cost of shed blood. Jesus is my Lord, and through Him, I am a new creation. Old things have passed away; now all things become new in Jesus' name. Amen.

" Therefore, if anyone is in Christ, he is a new creation; old things have passed away; behold, all things have become new"**2 Corinthians 5:17**

For God so loved the world that He gave His only begotten Son, that whoever believes in Him should not perish but have everlasting life. **John 3.16**

Beatitudes in the Book of Revelation

Beatitude	Emphasis	Reference
The blessedness of those reading, hearing, and keeping this prophecy.	The importance of the Word of God.	Rev. 1:3
The happiness of the dead who die in the Lord.	The blessings of eternal life.	Rev. 14:13
The respect of those watching and keeping their garments.	The anticipation of the Lord's return.	Rev. 16:15
The delight of those invited to the marriage supper of the Lamb.	The joy of God's presence.	Rev. 19:9
The blessedness of those who participate in the first resurrection.	The freedom of deliverance from death.	Rev. 20:6
The joy of keeping the words of this prophecy.	The necessity of obedience to the Word.	Rev. 22:7
The happy result of washing one's robe and accessing the Tree of Life.	The guarantee of eternal sustenance.	Rev. 22:14

Behold I'm Coming Quickly

Revelation 13:11–18).

PRAYER FOR STEADFAST ENDURANCE

I SHALL WEAR A CROWN!

Father God, to whom we cry ABBA, the "Author and the Finisher" of our faith! We bow in complete and total surrender to you. Though the enemy has slayed me, Yet will I TRUST in your steadfast, enduring love! I'm running back to you , the alter is where I lay every burden, every weight, every mystery beyond my understanding into your all-powerful hands. Omnipotent, Omniscient, Omnipresent, Sovereign, Only Wise God, Jehovah Shamah, the one who is always "Right-there", Today you are exalted and the devil is defeated. I honor you with my mouth and surrender my heart to you, completely and unreservedly. The one who is able to keep me from falling and present me faultless and blameless before your majesty. Because of who you are; I give you all the honor and all the praise. Adonai, O Lord, our God, how majestic is your name in all the earth. "For You so loved the world, that You gave your only begotten Son, that whoever believes in him should not perish but have ever lasting life. You did not send your Son into the world to condemn the world, but in order that the world might be saved through the washing and the regeneration of sin by him. When the kindness and the love of Yahweh, our God, our Savior toward man appeared, not by works of righteousness which I have done, but according to His mercy, He saved me, through the washing and

regeneration and renewing of the Holy Spirit, whom He poured out abundantly through Jesus Christ our Savior, Hallelujah! In Jesus name, let me continue to complete good works while I'm waiting on my Saviors return. For if while we were enemies ,let me be reconciled to you oh God by the death of your dear Son Jesus Christ, who paid it all. A debt I could never afford to repay. For you have given to us the Ministry of reconciliation. That while we were still sinners, Christ died for us. Therefore, we are ambassadors for Christ, God is making his appeal through us. For our sake He made Him to be sin, knew no sin, so that in him we might become the righteousness of God. As good soldiers in Christ Jesus let us reconcile a dark and broken world back to El Shaddai in love , the same love that ransomed us from the penalty of sin through love. Though I speak with the tongues of men and of angels, but have not love, I have become sounding brass or a clanging cymbal. And though I have *the gift of* prophecy, and understand all mysteries and all knowledge, and though I have all faith, so that I could remove mountains, but have not love, I am nothing. And though I bestow all my goods to feed *the poor,* and though I give my body to be burned, but have not love, it profits me nothing because I am bankrupt without love. In the beginning the was God and God was Love, let Christ steadfast love shine through me. Refine me with Holy Ghost Fire from heaven, that when I come fourth . I am coming fourth as pure gold and not fool's gold. in Thy presence is fullness of joy; at Thy right hand there are pleasures for evermore. I will Bless the Lord, O my soul; And all that is within me, *bless* His holy name! He who healeth my iniquity and forgave my sins.

Let me run this race with endurance, that I say , I have fought the good fight, I have finished the race, I have kept the faith. Finally, there is laid up for me the crown of righteousness, which the Lord, the righteous Judge, will give to me on that Day, and not to me only but also to all who have loved His appearing. I shall wear a robe and I shall; wear a crown. For the Son of man shall come in the glory of his Father with his angels; he shall reward every man according to his works. **The Incorruptible Crown, A Soldier's Crown, The Crown**

of Life, The Crown of Glory, A Crown of Righteousness, The Crown of Rejoicing, Finally A Martyr's Crown. In Christ I have been made alive." I have been crucified with Christ. It is no longer I who live, but Christ who lives in me. And the life I now live in the flesh I live by faith through the Son of God, who loved me and gave himself for me. For to me to live is Christ, and to die is gain. He wipes away every tear from mine eyes, and death shall be no more, neither shall there be mourning, nor crying, nor pain anymore, for the former things have passed away." Blessed are the dead who die in the Lord. To live is Christ and to Die is Eternal Gain.

I don't mind waiting for King Jesus, for it is written , he who waits upon the Lord shall renew their strength; they shall mount up with wings like eagles, they shall run and not be weary, they shall walk and not faint. Surely, I would have fainted, lest I believed to see, the goodness of the Lord in the land of the living. I'm looking unto Jesus, the author and the finisher of my faith, who for the joy that was set before Him endured the cross, despising the shame, and has sat down at the right hand of the throne of God. Through the Holy Spirit Christ be magnified. Jehovah-Nissi, the banner over me is steadfast love, that love keeps me anchored to the umbilical cord of faith. I will take a stand against the devils' scams until He makes every enemy my foot-stool. Although the devil came in one way , Yahweh scatters him seven different ways, I am not moved by what I see, God is my stronghold and peace that enters my storm. I am walking in the full authority of the Holy Spirit who dwells in me, the crucifixion, the resurrection of Jesus Christ and the sovereign power of His Blood. I will run this race with endurance , I run this race for the prize. I will not stop running until heaven is mines! I can, and will do, all things through Jesus Christ who strengthens me. Forgetting those things which are behind and pressing forward to those things which are ahead, I press forward, to the upward call of God in Christ Jesus. I do not account my life of any value nor as precious to myself, it all belongs to God, who equips me to finish my course and the ministry that I received from the Lord Jesus, to testify to the gospel of the

grace of God. Increase my faith , that my faith lies in the eternal unseen things of God. Faith is the substance of things hoped for, the evidence of things not seen. By faith we understand that the world was framed by the word of God, so that the things which are seen were not made of things which are visible. By faith the walls of Jericho fell down after they were encircled for seven days. By faith the harlot Rahab did not perish with those who did not believe, when she had received the spies with peace. By faith we overcome every fear, every obstacle and every evil assignment which seeks to keep us from our heavenly reward. By your will and not my own I will Fight the good fight of faith. Take hold of the eternal life to which I have been called a in the presence of many witnesses. I Fear not, for you are with me; I shall be not dismayed, for you are my God; You will strengthen me, lead me, help me and guide me, You uphold me with your righteous right hand. Holding fast to the word of life, so that in the day of Christ I may be proud that I did not run in vain nor my labor be in vain, In Jesus Name! We rejoice in our sufferings, knowing that suffering produces endurance, and endurance produces character, and character produces hope, and the Hope of our Lord Jesus Christ never disappoints. For the suffering of this present time is not worthy to be compared to the glory that shall be revealed in us.

Blessed is the man who remains steadfast under trial, for when he has stood the test he will receive the crown of life, which God has promised to those who love him. Thank You God for being a shield all around me. You have established me and guarded me against every evil attack of the evil one. For this light momentary affliction is preparing for us an eternal weight of glory beyond all comparison. With endurance I will seek the Lord and his strength; seek his presence continually! For the Lord himself will descend from heaven with a cry of command, with the voice of an archangel, and with the sound of the trumpet of God. And the dead in Christ will rise first. Then we who are alive, who are left, will be caught up together with them in the clouds to meet the Lord in the air, and so we will always be with the Lord. While I wait on Jesus ,I will not be conformed to this world, but be transformed by the renewing of my mind, that I may prove what *is* that good , acceptable and perfect will of God. He restores my soul; and leads me in the paths of righteousness for His name's sake. "Behold, I am coming quickly, and My reward *is* with Me, to give to every one according to his work. I am the Alpha and the Omega, *the* Beginning and *the* End, the First and the Last." Blessed *are* those who do His commandments, that they may have the right to the tree of life, and may enter through the gates into the city. You God have testified to everyone who hears the words of your prophecies. Amen. Even so, come, Lord Jesus!

The grace of our Lord Jesus Christ *be* with us all, until kingdom come. In Jesus Name, Amen.

The seven crowns of Heaven represent divine rewards bestowed upon the faithful, each embodying a distinct aspect of our spiritual journey and victorious life in Christ. The **Incorruptible Crown** *(1 Corinthians 9:25) celebrates a disciplined life, awarded to those who conquer fleshly desires and pursue holiness. The* **Soldier's Crown** *(2 Timothy 2:3-5) honors spiritual warriors who endure hardship and contend for the faith with steadfast courage. The* **Crown of Life** *(James 1:12; Revelation 2:10) is bestowed upon those who endure trials and persecution, remaining faithful unto death. The* **Crown of Glory** *(1 Peter 5:4) is reserved for shepherds and leaders who serve God's people with humility and love. The* **Crown of Righteousness** *(2 Timothy 4:8) awaits those who long for Christ's appearing, living in expectation of His return. The* **Crown of Rejoicing** *(1 Thessalonians 2:19) is the reward for soul-winners, rejoicing in the salvation of others through their labor. Finally, the* **Martyr's Crown** *is granted to those who lay down their lives for Christ, bearing witness to their unwavering faith and love for the Savior (Revelation 20:4). Together, these seven crowns affirm God's recognition of faithfulness, endurance, and sacrificial devotion, crowning the redeemed with eternal glory.*

- ➤ **The Incorruptible Crown**
- ➤ **The Soldier's Crown**
- ➤ **The Crown of Life**
- ➤ **The Crown of Glory**
- ➤ **The Crown of Righteousness**
- ➤ **The Crown of Rejoicing**
- ➤ **The Martyr's Crown**

Blessed is the man who remains steadfast under trial, for when he has stood the test, he will receive the crown of life, which God has promised to those who love him.

James 1:12

Crowned for Purpose

1 Thessalonians 2:19

Behold I'm Coming Quickly

1 Corinthians 9:25

A LIFE DESIGNED BY GOD

"7 Pillars to Living a Life "Designed By God".

- ❖ Holiness
- ❖ Righteousness
- ❖ A Repentant Heart
- ❖ Willingness to Forgive
- ❖ Armored up "Ready to Battle"
- ❖ Vigilance / Watchfulness/Preparedness
- ❖ Wisdom and Knowledge of Gods' Holy Word
- ❖ Love For God &Neighbor/ Compassion/ & Fruits of The Spirit

Built for this! Designed for this! Delivered for This! Priceless Purpose in the Pain that did not define you

The 7 Pillars of Living a Life Designed by God

Holiness

Holiness is being set apart for God's purpose, reflecting His purity in thought, word, and deed. It requires consecration and intentional separation from sin, embracing a life that aligns with His divine character. To live a life designed by God, holiness must be pursued daily as an act of worship and obedience, empowered by the Holy Spirit.

> ➤ **1 Peter 1:15-16**: "But as He who called you is holy, you also be holy in all your conduct, because it is written, 'Be holy, for I am holy.'"
> ➤ **Hebrews 12:14**: "Pursue peace with all people, and holiness, without which no one will see the Lord."
> ➤ **Leviticus 20:26**: "And you shall be holy to Me, for I the Lord am holy, and have separated you from the peoples, that you should be Mine."

Righteousness

Righteousness is the state of being made right with God through faith in Jesus Christ. It is not earned but imputed by grace and maintained by walking in alignment with His Word. A life designed by God is one that continuously seeks His righteousness, allowing His truth to guide decisions and actions.

> ➤ **Matthew 6:33**: "But seek first the kingdom of God and His righteousness, and all these things shall be added to you."
> ➤ **Philippians 3:9**: "And be found in Him, not having my own righteousness, which is from the law, but that which is through faith in Christ, the righteousness which is from God by faith."

> ➢ **Romans 3:22**: "Even the righteousness of God, through faith in Jesus Christ, to all and on all who believe."

A Repentant Heart

A repentant heart acknowledges sin, seeks God's forgiveness, and turns away from wrongdoing. It is the foundation of a restored relationship with God. True repentance is not merely remorse but a transformation of mind and behavior, aligning one's life with His will.

> ➢ **Acts 3:19**: "Repent therefore and be converted, that your sins may be blotted out, so that times of refreshing may come from the presence of the Lord."
> ➢ **Psalm 51:17**: "The sacrifices of God are a broken spirit, a broken and contrite heart—These, O God, You will not despise."
> ➢ **1 John 1:9**: "If we confess our sins, He is faithful and just to forgive us our sins and to cleanse us from all unrighteousness."

Willingness to Forgive

Forgiveness mirrors God's grace and is essential for living in harmony with others. It frees the forgiver from bitterness and aligns with Christ's example of unconditional love. A life designed by God embraces forgiveness as a demonstration of His mercy working through us.

> ➢ **Matthew 6:14-15**: "For if you forgive men their trespasses, your heavenly Father will also forgive you. But if you do not forgive men their trespasses, neither will your Father forgive your trespasses."

- ➤ **Colossians 3:13**: "Bearing with one another, and forgiving one another, if anyone has a complaint against another; even as Christ forgave you, so you also must do."
- ➤ **Ephesians 4:32**: "And be kind to one another, tenderhearted, forgiving one another, even as God in Christ forgave you."

Armored Up (Ready to Battle)

Spiritual warfare is inevitable in a life designed by God. The believer must be armored with truth, righteousness, faith, salvation, the gospel, and the Word of God, all fortified by prayer. This readiness ensures victory over the enemy's schemes and steadfastness in trials.

Key Scriptures:

- ➤ **Ephesians 6:11**: "Put on the whole armor of God, that you may be able to stand against the wiles of the devil."
- ➤ **2 Corinthians 10:4-5**: "For the weapons of our warfare are not carnal but mighty in God for pulling down strongholds."
- ➤ **Psalm 18:39**: "For You have armed me with strength for the battle; You have subdued under me those who rose up against me."

Vigilance/Watchfulness/Preparedness

Living a God-designed life requires constant spiritual alertness and preparedness for Christ's return. This vigilance involves guarding one's heart, standing firm in faith, and remaining ready for the fulfillment of God's promises.

- ➤ **1 Peter 5:8**: "Be sober, be vigilant; because your adversary the devil walks about like a roaring lion, seeking whom he may devour."

- ➢ **Matthew 25:13**: "Watch therefore, for you know neither the day nor the hour in which the Son of Man is coming."
- ➢ **Luke 12:35-36**: "Let your waist be girded and your lamps burning; and you yourselves be like men who wait for their master."

Wisdom and Knowledge of God's Word

God's Word equips believers with wisdom for righteous living and discernment in all circumstances. A life designed by God prioritizes studying, meditating on, and applying His Word as the ultimate source of truth and guidance.

- ➢ **Proverbs 9:10**: "The fear of the Lord is the beginning of wisdom, and the knowledge of the Holy One is understanding."
- ➢ **2 Timothy 2:15**: "Be diligent to present yourself approved to God, a worker who does not need to be ashamed, rightly dividing the word of truth."
- ➢ **Psalm 119:105**: "Your word is a lamp to my feet and a light to my path."

Love for God & Neighbor / Compassion / Fruits of the Spirit

Love is the cornerstone of a life designed by God. It reflects His character and fulfills His law. This love is expressed through compassion, selflessness, and the fruits of the Spirit, demonstrating His presence and work in a believer's life.

- ➢ **Matthew 22:37-39**: "Jesus said to him, 'You shall love the Lord your God with all your heart, with all your soul, and with all your mind. This is the first and great commandment. And the second is like it: You shall love your neighbor as yourself.'"

> **Galatians 5:22-23**: "But the fruit of the Spirit is love, joy, peace, longsuffering, kindness, goodness, faithfulness, gentleness, self-control."

> **1 John 4:7-8**: "Beloved, let us love one another, for love is of God; and everyone who loves is born of God and knows God. He who does not love does not know God, for God is love."

These seven elements are the spiritual pillars of a life built for purpose, refined through trials, and secured in God's ultimate sovereign design. <u>The pain that shaped you, was not meant to define you but to refine you for His glory and a priceless calling that no one else can fulfill. The Pain that you endured was not to destroy, yet, rather to cultivate you into a divine place of purpose and to fortify your character and position in the Kingdon of God.</u>

Mary's Alabaster Box

Do You Know the Cost of the Kingdom-Oil?
Matthew 26:6-13, Mark 14:3-9, John 12:1-8 (NKJV)

These seven elements embody the spiritual pillars of a life consecrated for purpose, refined through trials, and secured within God's sovereign design. The pain that shaped you was never meant to define you but to refine you for His glory, a priceless calling uniquely crafted for you to fulfill. The trials you endured were not to destroy you but to cultivate you, forging your character and positioning you for, unstoppable kingdom impact.

Mary's selfless act of devotion of anointing Jesus' feet in Matthew 26:6-13, exemplifies the refining process of a true believer's heart. She boldly demonstrated complete surrender, humility, selflessness, devotion, and spiritual discernment, qualities likely birthed from bearing life's heavy burdens and enduring wounds unseen by others. Through her actions, she revealed a life transformed by grace and fortified by faith. Her willingness to give her very best to Jesus, without concern for consequences or fear of criticism, embodies the spiritual growth, refinement, and perseverance that sprung fourth from unwavering devotion.

The spikenard oil Mary used to anoint Jesus was extravagantly costly, valued at nearly a year's wages. Yet, without hesitation, she broke her precious alabaster box, pouring out its contents freely and with heartfelt sincerity. Mary's act demonstrated that nothing was too valuable to give to her King. She held nothing back, offering not the leftovers but the very best of her substance, worship, and love.

In this ageless, historical moment, Mary's worship went beyond words; it became an extravagant act of sacrifice, devotion, and prophetic insight. Her anointing prepared Jesus for His burial, aligning with God's redemptive plan. The fragrance of the oil filled the room, symbolizing how worship in spirit and truth should permeate our lives, influencing all who encounter us with the essence of Christ.

As Mary wept at Jesus' feet, washing them with her tears and drying them with her hair, she epitomized divine purpose birthed from pain. Her tears were not wasted; they bore witness to her journey with God, every hurt, every trial, and every triumph that led her to this sacred moment. Despite the harsh judgment of others, including Judas and some disciples, Mary pressed on with fearless boldness and an unshakable focus on Jesus.

Jesus Himself rebuked her critics, declaring that Mary's act of love and worship would be remembered wherever the gospel is preached. Her devotion was immortalized as a testament to true, sacrificial love, a love that esteems Christ above all else.

Through Mary's story, we learn:

- **Endurance through trials:** Her pain became the fuel for her purpose.
- **Giving the best to Jesus:** Nothing was withheld; her offering reflected her heart.
- **Overcoming criticism and judgment:** Mary's devotion outweighed the scoffers' contempt.
- **Understanding divine purpose:** She discerned the significance of Christ's redemptive mission.
- **Authentic worship:** Her actions reflected true, heartfelt surrender.
- **Prophetic insight:** She perceived what others could not, aligning her act with God's greater plan.
- **Total surrender:** Without hesitation or regret, Mary gave her all to the Savior.

Mary's alabaster box represents more than an offering of oil; it symbolizes a life wholly surrendered to Christ. Her story teaches us that our trials and sacrifices, when poured out for the Lord, carry eternal value. No one may ever fully understand the cost of the oil in your alabaster box, the pain, the tears, the unseen battles, but God does.

Like Mary, you were **built for this, designed for this, delivered for this.** Your pain has a purpose, and your worship has the power to glorify King Jesus. Break your alabaster box, pour out your love, and let the fragrance of your devotion fill the atmosphere with His glory.

You were built for this. Designed for this. Delivered for this. You Got This! Will you pour out your best for the King before He comes....

"And it shall come to pass in the last days, says God, That I will pour out of My Spirit on all flesh; Your sons and your daughters shall prophesy, Your young men shall see visions, Your old men shall dream dreams. And on My menservants and on My maidservants I will pour out My Spirit in those days; And they shall prophesy. **Acts 2:17-18...** *Father and of Christ, in whom are hidden all the treasures of* <u>wisdom</u> *and* <u>knowledge</u>*. Now this I say lest anyone should deceive you with persuasive words. For though I am absent in the flesh, yet I am with you in spirit, rejoicing ,to see your good order and the steadfastness of your faith in Christ.* **Colossians 2 3-5** <u>I have no greater joy than to hear that my children walk in truth</u> **3 John 4.**

<<< To listen, to hear, be discerned, to obey >>>

Crowned for Purpose

3 John 4

SCRIPTURES TO GROW ON

Romans 8:15 *"For you did not receive the spirit of bondage again to fear, but you received the Spirit of adoption by whom we cry out, 'Abba, Father.'"*

Hebrews 12:2 *"Looking unto Jesus, the author and finisher of our faith, who for the joy that was set before Him endured the cross, despising the shame, and has sat down at the right hand of the throne of God."*

Job 13:15 *"Though He slay me, yet will I trust Him. Even so, I will defend my own ways before Him."*

1 Peter 5:7 *"Casting all your care upon Him, for He cares for you."*

Jude 1:24-25 *"Now to Him who is able to keep you from stumbling, and to present you faultless before the presence of His glory with exceeding joy, to God our Savior, who alone is wise, be glory and majesty, dominion and power, both now and forever. Amen."*

Psalm 8:1 *"O Lord, our Lord, how excellent is Your name in all the earth, who have set Your glory above the heavens!"*

John 3:16-17 *"For God so loved the world that He gave His only begotten Son, that whoever believes in Him should not perish but have everlasting life. For God did not send His Son into the world to condemn the world, but that the world through Him might be saved."*

Titus 3:4-6 *"But when the kindness and the love of God our Savior toward man appeared, not by works of righteousness which we have done, but according to His mercy He saved us, through the washing of regeneration and renewing of the Holy Spirit, whom He poured out on us abundantly through Jesus Christ our Savior."*

2 Corinthians 5:18 *"Now all things are of God, who has reconciled us to Himself through Jesus Christ, and has given us the ministry of reconciliation."*

Romans 5:8-10 *"But God demonstrates His own love toward us, in that while we were still sinners, Christ died for us. Much more then, having now been justified by His blood, we shall be saved from wrath through Him. For if when we were enemies we were reconciled to God through the death of His Son, much more, having been reconciled, we shall be saved by His life."*

2 Corinthians 5:20 *"Now then, we are ambassadors for Christ, as though God were pleading through us: we implore you on Christ's behalf, be reconciled to God."*

1 Corinthians 13:1-3 *"Though I speak with the tongues of men and of angels, but have not love, I have become sounding brass or a clanging cymbal. And though I have the gift of prophecy, and understand all mysteries and all knowledge, and though I have all faith, so that I could remove mountains, but have not love, I am nothing. And though I bestow all my goods to feed the poor, and though I give my body to be burned, but have not love, it profits me nothing."*

Psalm 16:11 *"You will show me the path of life; in Your presence is fullness of joy; at Your right hand are pleasures forevermore."*

Psalm 103:1-3 *"Bless the Lord, O my soul; and all that is within me, bless His holy name! Bless the Lord, O my soul, and forget not all His benefits: who forgives all your iniquities, who heals all your diseases."*

2 Timothy 4:7-8 *"I have fought the good fight, I have finished the race, I have kept the faith. Finally, there is laid up for me the crown of righteousness, which the Lord, the righteous Judge, will give to me on that Day, and not to me only but also to all who have loved His appearing."*

Matthew 16:27 *"For the Son of Man will come in the glory of His Father with His angels, and then He will reward each according to his works."*

1 Corinthians 9:25 *"And everyone who competes for the prize is temperate in all things. Now they do it to obtain a perishable crown, but we for an imperishable crown."*

Galatians 2:20 *"I have been crucified with Christ; it is no longer I who live, but Christ lives in me; and the life which I now live in the flesh I live by faith in the Son of God, who loved me and gave Himself for me."*

Philippians 1:21 *"For to me, to live is Christ, and to die is gain."*

Revelation 21:4 *"And God will wipe away every tear from their eyes; there shall be no more death, nor sorrow, nor crying. There shall be no more pain, for the former things have passed away."*

Isaiah 40:31 *"But those who wait on the Lord shall renew their strength; they shall mount up with wings like eagles, they shall run and not be weary, they shall walk and not faint."*

Psalm 27:13 *"I would have lost heart, unless I had believed that I would see the goodness of the Lord in the land of the living."*

Philippians 4:13 *"I can do all things through Christ who strengthens me."*

Philippians 3:13-14 *"Brethren, I do not count myself to have apprehended; but one thing I do, forgetting those things which are behind and reaching forward to those things which are ahead, I press toward the goal for the prize of the upward call of God in Christ Jesus."*

Acts 20:24 *"But none of these things move me; nor do I count my life dear to myself, so that I may finish my race with joy, and the ministry which I received from the Lord Jesus, to testify to the gospel of the grace of God."*

Hebrews 11:1-31 *"Now faith is the substance of things hoped for, the evidence of things not seen. For by it the elders obtained a good testimony. By faith we understand that the worlds were framed by the word of God, so that the things which are seen were not made of things which are visible. ... By faith the walls of Jericho fell down after they were encircled for seven days."*

1 Timothy 6:12 *"Fight the good fight of faith, lay hold on eternal life, to which you were also called and have confessed the good confession in the presence of many witnesses."*

Isaiah 41:10 *"Fear not, for I am with you; be not dismayed, for I am your God. I will strengthen you, yes, I will help you, I will uphold you with My righteous right hand."*

Philippians 2:16 *"Holding fast the word of life, so that I may rejoice in the day of Christ that I have not run in vain or labored in vain."*

Romans 5:3-5 *"And not only that, but we also glory in tribulations, knowing that tribulation produces perseverance; and perseverance, character; and character, hope. Now hope does not disappoint, because the love of God has been poured out in our hearts by the Holy Spirit who was given to us."*

Romans 8:18 *"For I consider that the sufferings of this present time are not worthy to be compared with the glory which shall be revealed in us."*

James 1:12 *"Blessed is the man who endures temptation; for when he has been approved, he will receive the crown of life which the Lord has promised to those who love Him."*

2 Thessalonians 3:3 *"But the Lord is faithful, who will establish you and guard you from the evil one."*

2 Corinthians 4:17 *"For our light affliction, which is but for a moment, is working for us a far more exceeding and eternal weight of glory."*

1 Chronicles 16:11 *"Seek the Lord and His strength; seek His face evermore!"*

1 Thessalonians 4:16-17 *"For the Lord Himself will descend from heaven with a shout, with the voice of an archangel, and with the trumpet of God. And the dead in Christ will rise first. Then we who are alive and remain shall be caught up together with them in the clouds to meet the Lord in the air. And thus we shall always be with the Lord."*

Romans 12:2 *"And do not be conformed to this world, but be transformed by the renewing of your mind, that you may prove what is that good and acceptable and perfect will of God."*

Psalm 23:3 *"He restores my soul; He leads me in the paths of righteousness for His name's sake."*

Revelation 22:12-14 *"And behold, I am coming quickly, and My reward is with Me, to give to every one according to his work. I am the Alpha and the Omega, the Beginning and the End, the First and the Last. Blessed are those who do His commandments, that they may have the right to the tree of life, and may enter through the gates into the city."*

Revelation 22:20-21 *"He who testifies to these things says, 'Surely I am coming quickly.' Amen. Even so, come, Lord Jesus! The grace of our Lord Jesus Christ be with you all. Amen."*

1 Corinthians 9:25 *"And everyone who competes for the prize is temperate in all things. Now they do it to obtain a perishable crown, but we for an imperishable crown."*

2 Timothy 2:3-5 *"You therefore must endure hardship as a good soldier of Jesus Christ. No one engaged in warfare entangles himself with the affairs of this life, that he may please him who enlisted him as a soldier. And also if anyone competes in athletics, he is not crowned unless he competes according to the rules."*

James 1:12; Revelation 2:10 *"Blessed is the man who endures temptation; for when he has been approved, he will receive the crown of life which the Lord has promised to those who love Him. ... Be faithful until death, and I will give you the crown of life."*

1 Peter 5:4 *"And when the Chief Shepherd appears, you will receive the crown of glory that does not fade away."*

2 Timothy 4:8 *"Finally, there is laid up for me the crown of righteousness, which the Lord, the righteous Judge, will give to me on that Day, and not to me only but also to all who have loved His appearing."*

1 Thessalonians 2:19 *"For what is our hope, or joy, or crown of rejoicing? Is it not even you in the presence of our Lord Jesus Christ at His coming?"*

Revelation 20:4 *"And I saw thrones, and they sat on them, and judgment was committed to them. Then I saw the souls of those who had been beheaded for their witness to Jesus and for the word of God, who had not worshiped the beast or his image, and had not received his mark on their foreheads or on their hands. And they lived and reigned with Christ for a thousand years."*

Revelation 22:12-14 - *"Behold, I am coming quickly, and My reward is with Me..."*

Behold I'm Coming Quickly

Crown of Life

Revelation 22:12-14

WORKS CITED

Radmacher, E. D. (1978). **NKJV Study Bible**, Full Color Edition: A Complete and Reliable Guide to Studying God's Word (3rd ed.). Thomas Nelson. https://www.thomasnelsonbibles.com/product/nkjv-study-bible-full-color/.

Hudson, C. D. (Ed.). (2011). **The KJV Study Bible**: Red Letter Edition. Barbour Publishing. https://www.barbourbooks.com/bibles/king-james-version.

Nelson, Thomas. "**The Woman's Study Bible, NKJV**: Receiving Gods truth for Balance, Hope and Transformation." Thomas Nelson, n.d., https://www.thomasnelsonbibles.com/product/nkjv-womans-study-bible/. Accessed 4 February 2023.

Bible Study Tools. "**New King James Version NKJV:** About the New King James Version." Bible Study Tools, n.d., https://www.biblestudytools.com/nkjv/. Accessed 4 February 2023.

OpenBible.info. "Topical Bible: Bible Verses about Last Days." OpenBible.info, n.d., "'And in the last days it shall be, God declares, that I will pour out my Spirit on all flesh, and your sons and your daughters shall prophesy, and your young men shall see visions, and your old men shall dream dreams; https://www.openbible.info/topics/last_days. Accessed 2 May 2024.

King James Bible. "Verse of the Day." KJV Bible Online, n.d., "For which I am an ambassador in bonds: that therein I may speak boldly, as I ought to speak. Ephesians 6:20 " https://www.kingjamesbibleonline.org/Ephesians-6-20/. Accessed 1 January 2022.

Nelson, Thomas. (n.d.). Don't Give the Enemy a Seat at Your Table. (2021). Louie Giglio. It's Time to Win the Battle of Your Mind. https://louiegiglio.com/book/dont-give-the-enemy-a-seat-at-your-table/Accessed 20 July 2024.

Nelson, Thomas (n.d.). <u>Wisdom for Each Day</u>(2008). Billy Graham
https://bookstore.billygraham.org/wisdom-for-each-day.html /Thomas
Nelson/ Accessed February 20 2023

Chavis, Mya A. (n.d.). <u>Victorious Jesus: Supreme Teacher and Non-Violent
Rebel Without a Cause</u> (2024). Mya Chavis Enterprise Publishing
https://myachavis.com/ Accessed July 31 2025

Dr. Jimmy DeYoung (n.d.). <u>Daniel: Prophet to the Gentiles</u>. (2002) Shofar
Ministries. Author Dr. Jimmy DeYoung
https://archive.org/details/danielprophettog0000drji /Accessed July 31
2025

Dr. Jimmy DeYoung (n.d.). <u>Sound the Trumpets</u> (2002): The Four Major
Trends of Bible Prophecy. Shofar Ministries.
https://archive.org/details/soundtrumpets00deyo /Accessed February 12
2025

John Ankerberg & Dr. Jimmy DeYoung (n.d.). <u>Step by Step through the Book
of Revelation Study Guide</u>(2002). ATRI Publishing.
https://jashow.org/resources/product/step-by-step-through-the-book-of-
revelation /Accessed April 7 2024

Dr. Jimmy DeYoung (n.d.). <u>Revelation: A Chronology</u>. (2002) ATRI Publishing.
https://jashow.org/podcast_episode/through-the-book-of-revelation-
with-dr-jimmy-deyoung-part-1-program-1/Accessed July 30 2023

Dr. Jimmy DeYoung (n.d.). <u>Israel Under Fire: The Prophetic Chain of Events
That Threatens the Middle East</u>(2002). ATRI Publishing.
https://prophecywatchers.com/product/israel-fire-dvd-prophetic-chain-
events-threatens-middle-east/ Accessed February 5 2025

Mifflin, Houghton (n.d.). <u>Constantine's Sword: The Church and the Jews – A
History</u> (2001). James Carroll.
https://archive.org/details/constantinesswor0000carr Accessed April 20
2025

Wilken, Robert L. (n.d.). <u>The First Thousand Years: A Global History of
Christianity.</u> (2012) Robert Louis Wilken.
https://yalebooks.yale.edu/book/9780300198386/the-first-thousand-
years/ Accessed April 11 2024

Oxford University Press. (n.d.). <u>Constantine the Emperor Robert Louis Wilken.</u>
(2012) David Potter
https://archive.org/details/constantineemper0000pott_q2e2/ Accessed
April 27 2025

Harper One (n.d.). <u>The Triumph of Christianity: How the Jesus Movement
Became the World's Largest Religion.</u> (2011) Rodney Stark

https://archive.org/details/triumphofchristi0000star / Accessed April 30 2025

King James Bible Online. Scripture Text : Revelation-22-7 "Behold, I come quickly: blessed is he that keepeth the sayings of the prophecy of this book."(Revelation-22-7) King James version, n.d., https://www.kingjamesbibleonline.org/Revelation-22-7/. Accessed 23 June 2024.

King James Bible Online. Scripture Text: Isaiah 25:8 "He will swallow up death in victory; and the Lord GOD will wipe away tears from off all faces." (Isaiah 25:8) King James version, n.d., https://www.kingjamesbibleonline.org/Isaiah-25-8/. Accessed 4 February 2024.

King James Bible Online. Scripture Text: "Hebrews 12:2." Looking unto Jesus the author and finisher of *our* faith; who for the joy that was set before him endured the cross, King James version, n.d., https://www.kingjamesbibleonline.org/Hebrews-12-2/Accessed 12 March 2024.

King James Bible Online. Scripture: Text Isaiah-25-8 "Though he slay me, yet will I trust in him: but I will maintain mine own ways before him." (Job 13:15) King James version, n.d., https://www.kingjamesbibleonline.org/Isaiah-25-8/. Accessed 4 February 2024

Bible Gateway. (n.d.). Scripture Text: Psalm 8:1. "O Lord, our Lord, how excellent is Your name in all the earth, who have set Your glory above the heavens!" (Psalm 8:1). Retrieved February 4, 2023, from https://www.biblegateway.com/

King James Bible Online. Scripture Text: "Jude 1:24 - 1:25: Now viewing scripture range from the book of John chapter 12:31 through chapter 12:33." King James version, n.d., https://www.kingjamesbibleonline.org/Jude-1-24_1-25/ Accessed 27 July 2024.

King James Bible Online. Scripture Text: Titus-3-4_3-6 "But when the kindness and the love of God our Savior toward man appeared, not by works of righteousness which we have done, but according to His mercy He saved us," (Titus 3:4) King James version, n.d., https://www.kingjamesbibleonline.org/Titus-3-4_3-6/Accessed 5 March 2025

King James Bible Online. Scripture Text: "1 Corinthians 13:1-3: Now viewing scripture range from the book of 1 Corinthians chapter 13:1 through chapter 13:3. King James Bible Online, n.d.,

https://www.kingjamesbibleonline.org/Matthew-8-2_8-3/. Accessed 4 February 2023.

King James Bible Online. Scripture Text: "2 Corinthians 5:20 "And Jesus came and spake unto them, saying, All power is given unto me in heaven and in earth"." King James Version, n.d., https://www.kingjamesbibleonline.org/2-Corinthians-5-20/Accessed 2 August 2024.

King James Bible Online. Scripture Text: "Mark 4:35 - 4:41: Now viewing scripture range from the book of Mark chapter 4:35 through chapter 4:41." King James Bible Online, n.d., https://www.kingjamesbibleonline.org/Mark-4-35_4-41/. Accessed 4 February 2023.

King James Bible Online. Scripture Text: "John 11:1 - 11:44: Now viewing scripture range from the book of John chapter 11:1 through chapter 11:44." King James Bible Online, n.d., https://www.kingjamesbibleonline.org/John-11-1_11-44/. Accessed 4 February 2023.

King James Bible Online. Scripture Text: "Romans 5:8-10: Now viewing scripture range from the book of Romans chapter 5:8 through chapter 5:10." King James Bible Online, n.d., https://www.kingjamesbibleonline.org/Romans-5-8_5-10/ Accessed 24 April 2024.

King James Bible Online. Scripture Text: "Psalm 16:11: ""You will show me the path of life; in Your presence is fullness of joy; at Your right hand are pleasures forevermore." King James Bible Online, n.d., Psalm 16:11. Accessed 18 January 2025.

King James Bible Online. Scripture Text: "Matthew 16:27: ""For the Son of man shall come in the glory of his Father with his angels; and then he shall reward every man according to his works." King James Bible Online, n.d., https://www.kingjamesbibleonline.org/Matthew-16-27/ Accessed 21 March 2024.

King James Bible Online. Scripture Text: "Ephesians 4:9: "Now that he ascended, what is it but that he also descended first into the lower parts of the earth?"." King James Bible Online, n.d., https://www.kingjamesbibleonline.org/Ephesians-4-9/. Accessed 4 February 2023.

King James Bible Online. Scripture Text: "Hebrews 2:18: "For in that he himself hath suffered being tempted, he is able to succour them that are tempted"." King James Bible Online, n.d., https://www.kingjamesbibleonline.org/Hebrews-2-18/. Accessed 4 February 2023.

King James Bible Online. Scripture Text: "Matthew 9:2 - 9:8: Now viewing scripture range from the book of Matthew chapter 9:2 through chapter 9:8." King James Bible Online, n.d., https://www.kingjamesbibleonline.org/Matthew-9-2_9-8/. Accessed 4 February 2023.

King James Bible Online. Scripture Text: "Matthew 28:5 - 28:7: Now viewing scripture range from the book of Matthew chapter 28:5 through chapter 28:7." King James Bible Online, n.d., https://www.kingjamesbibleonline.org/Matthew-28-5_28-7/. Accessed 4 February 2023.

King James Bible Online. Scripture Text: "Ephesians 4:9: "Now that he ascended, what is it but that he also descended first into the lower parts of the earth?." King James Bible Online, n.d., https://www.kingjamesbibleonline.org/Ephesians-4-9/. Accessed 4 February 2023.

King James Bible Online. Scripture Text : "1 Corinthians 15:55: "O death, where is thy sting? O grave, where is thy victory?"." King James Bible Online, n.d., https://www.kingjamesbibleonline.org/1-Corinthians-15-55/. Accessed 7 October 2024.

King James Bible Online. Scripture Text: "Galatians 2-20": "I am crucified with Christ: nevertheless I live; yet not I, but Christ liveth in me: and the life which I now live in the flesh I live by the faith of the Son of God, who loved me, and gave himself for me." King James Bible Online, n.d., https://www.kingjamesbibleonline.org/Galatians-2-20/. Accessed 18 February 2024.

King James Bible Online. Scripture Text: "Philippians 1:21": "For to me to live is Christ, and to die is gain." King James Bible Online, n.d., https://www.kingjamesbibleonline.org/Philippians-1-21/ Accessed 18 February 2024.

King James Bible Online. Scripture Text: "Revelation 21:4": "And God shall wipe away all tears from their eyes; and there shall be no more death, neither sorrow, nor crying, neither shall there be any more pain: for the former things are passed away." King James Bible Online, n.d., https://www.kingjamesbibleonline.org/Revelation-21-4/Accessed 26 May 2024.

King James Bible Online. Scripture Text: "Psalm 27:13": "I had fainted, unless I had believed to see the goodness of the LORD in the land of the living." King James Bible Online, n.d.,

https://www.kingjamesbibleonline.org/Psalms-27-13/ Accessed 14 February 2024.

King James Bible Online. Scripture Text: "Galatians 2:20": "I am crucified with Christ: nevertheless I live; yet not I, but Christ liveth in me: and the life which I now live in the flesh I live by the faith of the Son of God, who loved me, and gave himself for me." King James Bible Online, n.d., https://www.kingjamesbibleonline.org/Galatians-2-20/. Accessed 18 February 20234.

King James Bible Online. Scripture Text: "Philippians 4:13": I can do all things through Christ who strengthens me." King James Bible Online, n.d., https://www.kingjamesbibleonline.org/Philippians-4-13/ Accessed 18 February 2025.

King James Bible Online. Scripture Text: "Isaiah 41:10": "Fear thou not; for I am with thee: be not dismayed; for I am thy God: I will strengthen thee; yea, I will help thee; yea, I will uphold thee with the right hand of my righteousness." King James Bible Online, n.d., https://www.kingjamesbibleonline.org/Isaiah-41-10/ Accessed 19 February 2024.

King James Bible Online. Scripture Text: "Galatians 2:20": "I am crucified with Christ: nevertheless I live; yet not I, but Christ liveth in me: and the life which I now live in the flesh I live by the faith of the Son of God, who loved me, and gave himself for me." King James Bible Online, n.d., https://www.kingjamesbibleonline.org/Galatians-2-20/. Accessed 18 February 20234.

King James Bible Online. Scripture Text : "Philippians 2:16": "Holding forth the word of life; that I may rejoice in the day of Christ, that I have not run in vain, neither laboured in vain." https://www.kingjamesbibleonline.org/Philippians-2-16/. Accessed 10 February 2025.

King James Bible Online. Scripture Text: "Galatians 2:20": "I am crucified with Christ: nevertheless I live; yet not I, but Christ liveth in me: and the life which I now live in the flesh I live by the faith of the Son of God, who loved me, and gave himself for me." King James Bible Online, n.d., https://www.kingjamesbibleonline.org/Galatians-2-20/. Accessed 4 February 2025.

King James Bible Online. Scripture Text: "Romans 8:18": "For I reckon that the sufferings of this present time are not worthy to be compared with the glory which shall be revealed in us." King James Bible Online, n.d., https://www.kingjamesbibleonline.org/Romans-8-18/. Accessed 12 March 2025.

King James Bible Online. Scripture Text: "James 1:12": "Blessed is the man that endureth temptation: for when he is tried, he shall receive the crown of life, which the Lord hath promised to them that love him." King James Bible Online, n.d., https://www.kingjamesbibleonline.org/Galatians-2-20/. Accessed 7 February 2025.

King James Bible Online. Scripture Text: 2 Thessalonians 3:3 "But the Lord is faithful, who will establish you and guard you from the evil one." King James Bible Online, n.d., https://www.kingjamesbibleonline.org/2-Thessalonians-3-3/Accessed 18 January 2025.

King James Bible Online. Scripture Text: "Galatians 2:20": "I am crucified with Christ: nevertheless I live; yet not I, but Christ liveth in me: and the life which I now live in the flesh I live by the faith of the Son of God, who loved me, and gave himself for me." King James Bible Online, n.d., https://www.kingjamesbibleonline.org/Galatians-2-20/. Accessed 18 February 20234.

King James Bible Online. Scripture Text: "2 Corinthians 4:17": "For our light affliction, which is but for a moment, worketh for us a far more exceeding and eternal weight of glory;" King James Bible Online, n.d., https://www.kingjamesbibleonline.org/2-Corinthians-4-17/ Accessed 21 February 2025.

King James Bible Online. Scripture Text: "1 Peter 5:4": ""And when the chief Shepherd shall appear, ye shall receive a crown of glory that fadeth not away." King James Bible Online, n.d., https://www.kingjamesbibleonline.org/1-Peter-5-4/ Accessed 21 February 2025.

King James Bible Online. Scripture Text: "2 Timothy 4:8": "Henceforth there is laid up for me a crown of righteousness, which the Lord, the righteous judge, shall give me at that day: and not to me only, but unto all them also that love his appearing." King James Bible Online, n.d., https://www.kingjamesbibleonline.org/2-Timothy-4-8/ Accessed 16 April 2025.

King James Bible Online. Scripture Text: "1 Thessalonians 2:19": "For what is our hope, or joy, or crown of rejoicing? Are not even ye in the presence of our Lord Jesus Christ at his coming?" King James Bible Online, n.d., https://www.kingjamesbibleonline.org/1-Thessalonians-2-19/Accessed 26 April 2025.

King James Bible Online. Scripture Text: "Revelation 20:4": "And I saw thrones, and they sat upon them, and judgment was given unto them: and I saw the souls of them that were beheaded for the witness of Jesus, and for the word of God, and which had not worshipped the beast, neither his image, neither had received his mark upon their foreheads, or in their

Crowned for Purpose: Anointed for Promise!

hands; and they lived and reigned with Christ a thousand years." King James Bible Online, n.d., https://www.kingjamesbibleonline.org/Revelation-20-4/19/Accessed 29 April 2025.

King James Bible Online. Scripture Text: "1 Thessalonians 2:19": "For what is our hope, or joy, or crown of rejoicing? Are not even ye in the presence of our Lord Jesus Christ at his coming?" King James Bible Online, n.d., https://www.kingjamesbibleonline.org/1-Thessalonians-2-19/Accessed 26 April 2025..

King James Bible Online. Scripture Text "Revelation 20:1 - 20:3: Now viewing scripture range from the book of Revelation chapter 20:1 through chapter 20:3." King James Bible Online, n.d., https://www.kingjamesbibleonline.org/Revelation-20-1_20-3/. Accessed 4 February 2023.

King James Bible Online. Scripture Text: "2 Corinthians 5:18": "And all things are of God, who hath reconciled us to himself by Jesus Christ, and hath given to us the ministry of reconciliation;" King James Bible Online, n.d., https://www.kingjamesbibleonline.org/1-Thessalonians-2-19/ Accessed 2 Febuary 2025.

King James Bible Online. Scripture Text: "1 Corinthians 9:25": "And every man that striveth for the mastery is temperate in all things. Now they do it to obtain a corruptible crown; but we an incorruptible." King James Bible Online, n.d., https://www.kingjamesbibleonline.org/1-Corinthians-9-25/Accessed 26 April 2025.

King James Bible Online. Scripture Text: "Revelation 20:4": "And I saw thrones, and they sat upon them, and judgment was given unto them: and I saw the souls of them that were beheaded for the witness of Jesus, and for the word of God, and which had not worshipped the beast, neither his image, neither had received his mark upon their foreheads, or in their hands; and they lived and reigned with Christ a thousand years." King James Bible Online, n.d., https://www.kingjamesbibleonline.org/Revelation-20-4/Accessed 7 May 2025.

King James Bible Online. Scripture Text "Psalms 103:1-3: Now viewing scripture range from the book of Psalms chapter 103:1 through chapter 3." King James Bible Online, n.d., https://www.kingjamesbibleonline.org/Psalms-103-1_103-3/ Accessed 4 February 2024.

King James Bible Online. Scripture Text "2 Timothy 4:7-8: Now viewing scripture range from the book of 2 Timothy chapter 4:7 through chapter 4: 8." King James Bible Online, n.d.,

533

https://www.kingjamesbibleonline.org/2-Timothy-4-7/. Accessed 17 May 2025.

King James Bible Online. Scripture Text "Romans 5:3-5: Now viewing scripture range from the book of Romans chapter 3 through chapter 5 King James Bible Online, n.d., https://www.kingjamesbibleonline.org/Romans-5-3_5-5/ 9/. Accessed 4 February 2023.

King James Bible Online. Scripture Text "1 Thessalonians 4:16-17": Now viewing scripture range from the book of 1 Thessalonians 4 chapter 16 through chapter 17." King James Bible Online, n.d., https://www.kingjamesbibleonline.org/1-Thessalonians-4-16_4-17/ Accessed 4 February 2023.

King James Bible Online. Scripture Text "Revelation 22:12-14": Now viewing scripture range from the book of Revelation 22 chapter 12 through chapter 14." James Bible Online, n.d., https://www.kingjamesbibleonline.org/2-Timothy-4-3_4-4/. Accessed 29 April 2023.

King James Bible Online. Scripture Text: "2 Timothy 2:3-5": Now viewing scripture range from the book of 2 Timothy chapter 3 through chapter 5." James Bible Online, n.d., https://www.kingjamesbibleonline.org/2-Timothy-2-3_2-5/. Accessed 4 March 2023.

King James Bible Online. Scripture Text: "James 1:12": "Blessed is the man that endureth temptation: for when he is tried, he shall receive the crown of life, which the Lord hath promised to them that love him." King James Bible Online, n.d., https://www.kingjamesbibleonline.org/James-1-12. Accessed 24 April 2025.

"Seeing God as Our Father - First15 Devotional, October 17, 2018." Bible Study Tools, Salem Web Network, https://www.biblestudytools.com/bible-study/today-s-devotionals/seeing-god-as-our-father-first15-october-17-2018.html. Accessed 17 Oct. 2024.

GotQuestions.org. (n.d.). What is the definition of grace?. Retrieved from https://www.gotquestions.org/definition-of-grace.html

GotQuestions.org. (n.d.). What is the ministry of reconciliation?. Retrieved from https://www.gotquestions.org/ministry-of-reconciliation.html

GotQuestions.org. (n.d.). What does it mean to be an ambassador for Christ?. Retrieved from https://www.gotquestions.org/ambassador-for-Christ.html

GotQuestions.org. (n.d.). What does it mean to have fought the good fight?. Retrieved from https://www.gotquestions.org/fought-the-good-fight.html

www.ingramcontent.com/pod-product-comp iance
Lightning Source LLC
Chambersburg PA
CBHW071657120626
46550CB00001B/17